Lecture Notes in Computer Science 4608

Commenced Publication in 1973
Founding and Former Series Editors:
Gerhard Goos, Juris Hartmanis, and Jan van Leeuwen

Heinz W. Schmidt   Ivica Crnkovic
George T. Heineman   Judith A. Stafford (Eds.)

Component-Based Software Engineering

10th International Symposium, CBSE 2007
Medford, MA, USA, July 9-11, 2007
Proceedings

 Springer

Volume Editors

Heinz W. Schmidt
RMIT University, Computer Science
124 La Trobe Street, Melbourne, VIC, 3001 Australia
E-mail: Heinz.Schmidt@rmit.edu.au

Ivica Crnkovic
Mälardalen University, Software Engineering Lab
721 23 Västerås, Sweden
E-mail: ivica.crnkovic@mdh.se

George T. Heineman
Worcester Polytechnic Institute, Department of Computer Science
100 Institute Road, Worcester, MA 01609, USA
E-mail: heineman@cs.wpi.edu

Judith A. Stafford
Tufts University, Computer Science
Boston, 161 College Avenue, Medford, MA 02155, USA
E-mail: jas@cs.tufts.edu

Library of Congress Control Number: 2007930208

CR Subject Classification (1998): D.2, D.1.5, D.3, F.3.1

LNCS Sublibrary: SL 2 – Programming and Software Engineering

ISSN   0302-9743
ISBN-10   3-540-73550-X Springer Berlin Heidelberg New York
ISBN-13   978-3-540-73550-2 Springer Berlin Heidelberg New York

Springer is a part of Springer Science+Business Media

springer.com

© Springer-Verlag Berlin Heidelberg 2007

Typesetting: Camera-ready by author, data conversion by Scientific Publishing Services, Chennai, India
Printed on acid-free paper   SPIN: 12088713   06/3180   5 4 3 2 1 0

Preface

CBSE 2007, the Tenth International ACM SIGSOFT Symposium on Component-Based Software Engineering was dedicated to the theme of "Global Software Services and Architectures."

Component-based software engineering (CBSE) has emerged as a key technology for developing and maintaining large-scale software-intensive systems, such as global networked information systems and services, distributed real-time automation systems, grids and sensor networks. CBSE combines elements of object-oriented technologies, software architecture, software verification, modular software design, configuration and deployment. CBSE has made major inroads into mainstream networked software-intensive systems. If you are taking a train, accessing your bank account or health insurance over the Internet, searching and ordering a book or tracking its delivery, very likely CBSE is at work in the distributed software enabling such everyday activities in transport, commerce, health, automation, environment and defense.

The CBSE Symposium has a track record of bringing together researchers and practitioners from a variety of disciplines to promote a better understanding of CBSE from a diversity of perspectives and to engage in active discussion and debate. CBSE has been open to all participants interested broadly in component software engineering. The symposium addresses participants from both universities and industry and combines formal refereed paper presentations, industrial experience presentations, invited keynotes and expert working sessions on key challenges that the field faces.

Scope

The theoretical foundations of component specification, composition, analysis and verification continue to pose research challenges. While the engineering models and methods for component software development are slowly maturing, new trends in global services and distributed systems architectures push the limits of established and tested component-based methods, tools and platforms:

- Model-driven development and grid technologies with their high-performance demands in massive data storage, computational complexity and global co-scheduling of scientific models in flagship science, technology and medicine research
- Global software development with its lowering of the cost of software capabilities and production, through automation, off-shoring and outsourcing of key components and subsystems
- Networked enterprise information systems and services architectures crossing enterprise, national, legal and discipline boundaries

– Shift from (globally distributed) software products to pervasive and ubiquitous services supported by deep software-intensive infrastructures and middleware and by increasingly flexible, adaptive and autonomous client and application server software

History

A decade ago, CBSE started off as a workshop of the International Software Engineering Conference (ICSE), the flagship conference in software engineering. While the CBSE community grew rapidly and demonstrated sufficient momentum of its own and a focus on the special issues in theory and practice surrounding components, CBSE matured quickly into a standalone conference attracting over 100 participants. In 2007, as in 2006, CBSE was co-located with software architecture workshops and shared an industrial experience day across these events.

Papers

Similar to previous years, the themes in the call for papers were broad:

– Software quality and extra-functional properties for components and component-based systems
– Component-based Web services and service-oriented architectures
– Component software architectures and product lines
– Global generation, adaptation and deployment of component-based systems and services
– Grid component software, services, workflows, co-ordination and choreography
– Components and model-driven development
– Specification, verification, testing and checking of component systems
– Compositional reasoning techniques for component models
  Global measurement, prediction and monitoring of distributed and service components
– Patterns and frameworks for component-based systems and services
– Integrated tool chains and methods for building component-based services
– Components for networked real-time information systems and sensor networks

In total, the call attracted some 89 papers of which 19 were selected for publication and presentation after a rigorous review and selection process. Each paper had at least three independent reviewers, papers of Program Committee members, four.

The papers in this volume represent a snapshot of current work at the forefront of CBSE. They are grouped into four broad themes:

- Component-Based Architectures and Change
- Quality of Service, Runtime Verification and Monitoring
- Challenges in Architectural Dynamics
- Extra-functional Properties and Compositional Reasoning

July 2007   Heinz W. Schmidt

Organization

Organization Chair

Judith A. Stafford, Tufts University, Medford, USA

Program Chair

Heinz W. Schmidt, RMIT University, Melbourne, Australia

Steering Committee

Ivica Crnkovic, Mälardalen University, Västerås, Sweden
Ian Gorton, Pacific North West National Laboratory, Richland WA, USA
George Heineman, Worcester Polytechnic Institute, Worcester MA, USA
Heinz W. Schmidt, RMIT University, Melbourne, Australia
Judith A. Stafford, Tufts University, Medford, USA
Clemens Szyperski, Microsoft, Redmond, USA

Program Committee

Uwe Assmann, Dresden University of Technology, Dresden, Germany
Mike Barnett, Microsoft Research, Redmond WA, USA
Antonia Bertolino, CNR Research, Pisa, Italy
Judith Bishop, University of Pretoria, Pretoria, South Africa
Michel Chaudron, University Eindhoven, Eindhoven, The Netherlands
Shiping Chen, CSIRO, Sydney, Australia
Thierry Coupaye, France Telecom R&D, Grenoble, France
Susan Eisenbach, Imperial College London, London, UK
Dimitra Giannakopoulou, RIACS/NASA Ames, Moffet Field CA, USA
Ian Gorton, Pacific North West National Laboratory, Richland WA, USA
Lars Grunske, University of Queensland, Brisbane, Australia
Richard Hall, LSR-IMAG, Grenoble, France
Dick Hamlet, Portland State University, Portland OR, USA
George Heineman, Worcester Polytechnic Institute, Worcester MA, USA
Paola Inverardi, University of L'Aquila, L'Aquila, Italy
Jean-Marc Jezequel, IRISA (INRIA and Univ. Rennes 1), Rennes, France
Bengt Jonsson, Uppsala University, Uppsala, Sweden
Gerald Kotonya, Lancaster University, Lancaster, UK

Table of Contents

Web Services, Late Composition and Verification

Data Encapsulation in Software Components

Kung-Kiu Lau and Faris M. Taweel

School of Computer Science, The University of Manchester
Manchester M13 9PL, United Kingdom
{Kung-Kiu,Faris.Taweel}@cs.manchester.ac.uk

Abstract. Data encapsulation is a familiar property in object-oriented programming. It is not only useful for modelling things in the real world, but it also facilitates reuse by enabling the creation of multiple instances of the same class, each with its own identity and private data. For CBSE, this kind of reuse is clearly also one of the key desiderata. However, it must be achieved in conjunction with composition, which is central to CBSE. In this paper we show how data encapsulation can be combined with composition, by extending a component model we have defined previously.

1 Introduction

Data encapsulation is a familiar property of objects, as in object-oriented programming. It is not only useful for modelling things in the real world, but it also facilitates reuse by enabling the creation of multiple instances of the same class, each with its own identity and private data. For CBSE, this kind of reuse is clearly also one of the key desiderata, since components are considered to be reusable templates for multiple component instances. However, since composition is central to CBSE, the question is how to design composition mechanisms or operators that make data encapsulation possible at every level of composition, that is, how to make sure that every *composite* component created by composition encapsulates its own data. In this paper, we argue that this combination of data encapsulation and composition is not possible in current component models; and then show that it can be achieved by extending a component model that we have defined previously.

Current component models can largely be divided into two categories [9,5]: (i) models where components are *objects*, as in object-oriented programming; (ii) models where components are *architectural units*, as in software architectures [14,1]. Exemplars of these categories are Enterprise JavaBeans (EJB) [3,12] and architecture description languages (ADLs) [2,10] respectively. In models where components are objects, components are assembled by method calls. However, this is not (algebraic) composition, since an object O_1 assembled with an object O_2 by calling a method in O_2 will result in two objects, not one (composite) object. Therefore, even though data encapsulation is possible in O_1 and O_2 separately, there is no composition mechanism that can compose O_1 and O_2 properly, let alone preserve data encapsulation.

H.W. Schmidt et al. (Eds.): CBSE 2007, LNCS 4608, pp. 1–16, 2007.

In component models where components are architectural units, port connections provide a composition mechanism, and composites can be defined. However, data encapsulation is not always defined or possible. In fact, the role of data is very unclear in architectural units. These units can represent both computation and data, or just data, and data encapsulation is not considered as part of composition in general. Where architectural units have data ports, it could be argued that these ports represent data encapsulation. Even in this case, however, it is not clear whether data encapsulation is possible at every level of composition.

In this paper, we describe an approach to composition that allows data encapsulation at every level of composition. Our approach is based on a component model [6] where composition operators are first-class citizens, and they also enable every component instance, in particular a composite component instance, to encapsulate its own data.

2   Composition with Data Encapsulation

Components are intended for composition, and so they should be compositional, i. e. if C_1 and C_2 are components, then a composition C_3 of C_1 and C_2 must be a component too. Furthermore, the composition should be defined as a composition operator that composes components into new (composite) components. In other words, in a component model, components and composition operators should be first-class citizens. Any component model should have this property.

A good component model should also allow components to encapsulate data, but to be really useful it should do so at every level of composition. We have proposed a component model in [6] and in this paper we describe how we can extend this model and use it to achieve this kind of data encapsulation.

For illustrative purposes, we shall consider a simple banking example.

Example 1. Consider a banking system with two bank consortia BC1 and BC2, consisting of the sets of banks {B11, B12} and {B21, B22} respectively. Each bank, in turn, consists of a set of branches, e.g. bank B21 has branches {BB211, BB212}, and so on.

In our component model we would build up the system by composing components using composition operators (see Fig. 2).

In our model, we have two kinds of components: *atomic* and *composite* components. Composite components are built from atomic (and other composite) components, but *all* components are templates, with no data except constants,

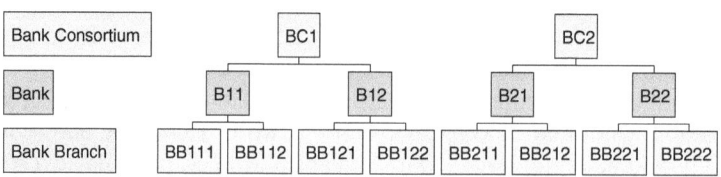

Fig. 1. A banking example

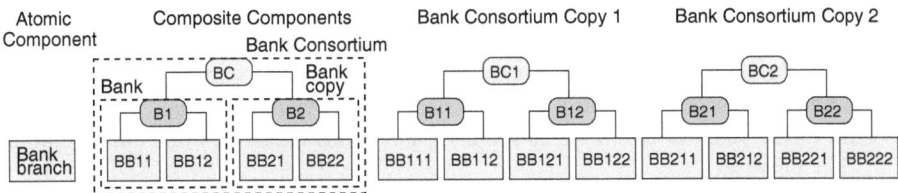

Fig. 2. A component-based implementation of the banking system

but with code for the services they provide. Since components are templates, it is meaningful and possible to make *copies* of components. For the bank system, for a particular bank consortium, a bank branch can be an atomic component with code for the usual operations like *withdrawal*, *deposit* and *check balance*. This provides a template for all bank branches, and so we can construct many bank branches (all the BB's) as copies of this component.

Furthermore, in our model, it is possible to create *instances* from different component copies. For example, bank branches BB111 and BB211, which are different copies of BB11 (which is in turn a copy of the bank branch atomic component), and which belong to different consortia, can be each instantiated with their own address, sort code and customer accounts.

In our model, composite components, just like atomic components, can also be copied (and the copies instantiated later). For example, two bank branches, say BB11 and BB12, can be composed by a suitable composition operator to produce a bank composite component B11. The latter is a template that contains all the operations its sub-components provide. Therefore, it would make sense to construct other bank components from this component by copying. The original component as well as its copies contain, in addition to operations, some place holders for private data that can be initialised when the complete (composite) components are instantiated.

Similarly, a bank consortium component can be constructed by composing bank components. In Fig.2, using a suitable composition operator, a bank component composed with a copy of a bank component yields a bank consortium component. This new component can be further composed with a copy of itself to build the bank system.

It is worth noting that in the bank example, only one atomic component (bank branch) and one composition operator are necessary to build the entire bank system. Each composition in our implementation results in a properly defined composite. Clearly our model provides proper composition mechanisms. The question is whether we can also make it encapsulate data.

3   Our Component Model

Before we discuss how we extend our component model to enable data encapsulation, in this section we briefly outline the model that we presented in [6].

In our model, we have two kinds of basic entities: (i) *computation units*, and (ii) *connectors*. A computation unit U encapsulates computation. It provides a set of methods (or services). *Encapsulation* means that U's methods do not call methods in other computation units; rather, when invoked, all their computation occurs in U. Thus U could be thought of as a class that does not call methods in other classes.

There are two kinds of connectors: (i) *invocation*, and (ii) *composition*. An invocation connector is connected to a computation unit U so as to provide access to the methods of U.

A composition connector encapsulates *control*. It is used to define and coordinate the control for a set of components (atomic or composite). For example, a *sequencer* connector that composes components $C_1, \ldots, C_n$ can call methods in $C_1, \ldots, C_n$ in that order. Another example is a *selector* connector, which selects (according to some specified condition) one of the components it composes, and calls its methods.

Components are defined in terms of computation units and connectors. There are two kinds of components: (i) *atomic*, and (ii) *composite* (see Fig. 3). An

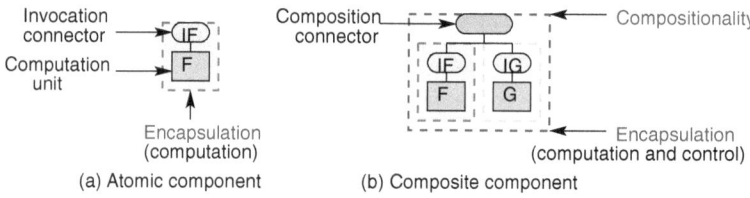

Fig. 3. Atomic and composite components: encapsulation and compositionality

atomic component consists of a computation unit with an invocation connector that provides an interface to the component. A composite component consists of a set of components (atomic or composite) composed by a composition connector. The composition connector provides an interface to the composite.

For example, in the bank system (Fig. 2) in Example 1, the atomic component BB11, a bank branch, may be defined as shown in Fig. 4(a), with an invocation connector IBB11, and a computation unit with the methods *deposit, withdraw, balance*. The composite component B1, a bank, may be defined as shown in

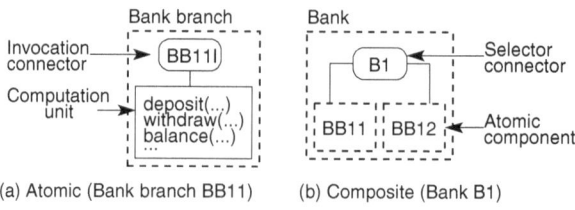

Fig. 4. Sample atomic and composite components in the bank example

Fig. 4(b), as a composition of the atomic components BB11 and BB12 using a selector connector (denoted here by B1 too, for convenience). The bank consortium composite component in Fig. 2 may also be composed (from banks) using a selector connector, since the consortium has to choose the bank with the branch to which the customer's account belongs.

In our model, invocation and composition connectors form a hierarchy [8]. This means that composition is done in a hierarchical manner. Furthermore, each composition *preserves* encapsulation. This kind of compositionality is the distinguishing feature of our component model. An atomic component encapsulates *computation* (Fig. 3(a)), namely the computation encapsulated by its computation unit. A composite component encapsulates *computation* and *control* (Fig. 3(b)). The computation it encapsulates is that encapsulated in its sub-components; the control it encapsulates is that encapsulated by its composition connector. In a composite, the encapsulation in the sub-components is preserved. Indeed, the hierarchical nature of the connectors means that composite components are *self-similar* to their sub-components; this property provides a basis for hierarchical composition.

In the next section, we will show how to extend our model to include data encapsulation.

4   Data Encapsulation

Our approach to data encapsulation is illustrated by Fig. 5. Basically, we want to extend our model (Fig. 3) to allow each component (atomic or composite) to define place-holders for its own data at *design* time. These place-holders are indicated by patterned squares in Fig. 5. Thus, whereas in our current model, a composite encapsulates computation and control (Fig. 3(b)), in the extended model, a composite additionally encapsulates data (Fig. 5(b)).

Our extension is centred on the constructor of a component. We want to be able to make copies of a component at design time, so that they all have the same types of data place-holders. Copies of a component will also have the same constructor as the of the original component. At run-time, we want to be able to create an instance of a component or a copy by using the component's constructor, and we want to be able to initialise its data place-holders with

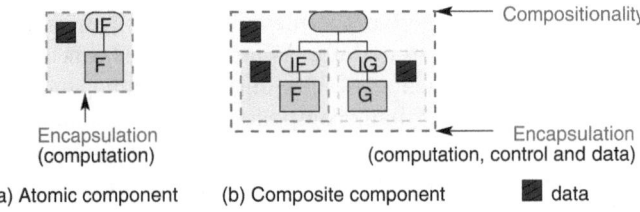

Fig. 5. Data encapsulation

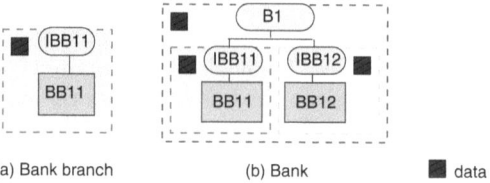

(a) Bank branch   (b) Bank   ■ data

Fig. 6. Data encapsulation in the bank example

actual data. This way, instances of different copies (atomic or composite) can encapsulate their own private data.

For the bank example, this is illustrated by Fig. 6. In Fig. 6(a), a branch component BB11 encapsulates its customers' data. Using a suitable composition connector, a bank component can be constructed from branch components BB11 and BB12, where both components are actually copies of the bank branch component. As shown in Fig. 6(b), the bank (composite) component encapsulates its own data which is separate from its sub-components' data. The encapsulation of the latter in each branch sub-component is preserved in the bank composite.

The process of instantiating a component (or a copy) often requires initialisation of encapsulated data. Such data can either be constants defined in the component's design phase; or data created at instantiation time. A component therefore must have a constructor which enables data initialisation to be performed. In our model, we use *data constructors* in the component constructor for this purpose. Data constructors may require to read data from external resources during the data initialisation process. Therefore, connectors must have data I/O semantics to carry out their tasks. In our model, connectors are capable of performing data I/O operations.

Initialisation of encapsulated data in the bank example is illustrated in Fig. 7. A bank branch component must be initialised with the branch name which is a constant string. It must also read and persist data about the process that owns the branch component instance. The latter data may include date, process account and network information, etc. For simplicity, we assume that the component only logs its instantiation date. The invocation connector of a branch component accesses these data values during component construction at runtime. A bank component composed from two branches also has its own separate constructor which performs its data initialisation operations. These operations include, for example, setting the bank name as well as logging a record on the instantiation date and other system data. As far as data is concerned, the bank component and its sub-components set their initial data independently, each using its own constructor. In Fig. 7, bank component B1 reads bank name (*B1*) and date (*sysdate*). Its sub-components perform similar data initialisation operations when their instances are created. Initialisation performed by each connector of B1 is indicated by arrows bearing data names.

Data encapsulation is a valuable notion for reuse by copying. A component that encapsulates its data (in addition to computation and control) and has

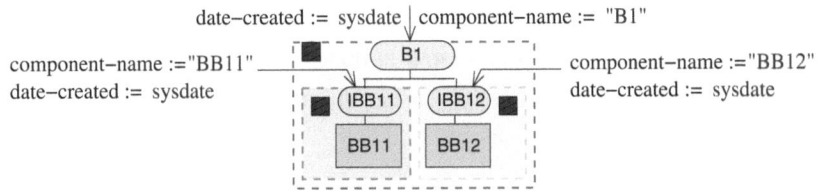

date−created := sysdate | component−name := "B1"

component−name :="BB11"   component−name :="BB12"
date−created := sysdate   date−created := sysdate

Fig. 7. Initialisation of encapsulated data

its own data constructor is a suitable unit for copying. A component in design phase specifies its local data as place holders. Copying a component creates a new component that encapsulates its own data (specifications). Data constructors of copies perform data initialisation of each copy. Therefore, data encapsulation enables copying of our components.

Furthermore, in a component-based system, it is often desirable to create multiple instances of a component or to create instances of different copies of a component. In the bank system, all branches are copies of a branch component. Instantiating all these branches must be possible. In fact, without each branch encapsulating its data together with a data constructor, it would be impossible to have different instances from different copies. In our model, it is even possible to make many copies of the same component, since instances maintain their own data.

5   Implementation

In this section we show how we implement data encapsulation in our extended component model, by using the bank example to show how a bank system can be constructed from two connectors and one computation unit. First, we outline our implementation of the extended component model using Oracle Database 10g Enterprise Edition, release 10.1.0.4.0. The choice of a database language is natural, since we are concerned with data here.

5.1   Connectors and Components

We have implemented our extended component model as a repository that stores computation units as well as templates for connectors and components (both atomic and composite), at both design time and run-time. While the repository depends on metadata that Oracle maintains on computation units, connectors and component templates are stored as records in database tables, e.g. CONNECTORS, COMPONENTS, ENC_DATA, ENC_DATA_INST, etc. The repository provides services such as creating and copying components, searching, browsing, and component instantiation. Components, connectors and computational units are coded in the *PL/SQL* programming language [13]. PL/SQL is a 4GL programming language that is used by Oracle to specify its programs' interfaces, so it is the obvious choice for us. However, PL/SQL lacks support

```
--- Specification (interface)
PACKAGE "BB" AS
      FUNCTION balance (p_accnt_no CHAR) RETURN INTEGER;
      FUNCTION withdraw (p_accnt_no CHAR, amnt NUMBER) RETURN CHAR;
      FUNCTION deposit (p_accnt_no CHAR, amnt NUMBER) RETURN CHAR;
END BB;
--- Implementation
PACKAGE BODY "BB" AS
      ...
      FUNCTION withdraw (p_accnt_no CHAR, amnt NUMBER) RETURN CHAR;
         IS BEGIN
         ...
         RETURN bal;
      END balance;
      ...
   END BB;
```

Fig. 8. PL/SQL specification and implementation of bank branch package

for reflection, which is necessary for implementing our component model. So our implementation of the repository has to compensate for this.

In our implementation, computation units are Oracle *packages* and connectors are Oracle *object types*. A package is a database construct that groups logically related PL/SQL types, variables, and subprograms (functions and procedures). It can implement a computation unit in our component model provided its subprograms do not call subprograms in other packages. A package has two parts, a specification and a body. The specification is the interface to the package. It publishes the types, variables, constants, exceptions, cursors (record sets) and subprograms. The body implements cursors and the subprograms. Fig. 8 shows an example of a PL/SQL package. It is an outline of a package for a bank branch in the bank example.

An object type is a user-defined composite data type representing a data structure and subprograms to manipulate the data. It is like an object in an object-oriented programming language. Like packages, object types are specified in two parts, a specification (interface) and a body (implementation). Fig. 9 shows an example of an object type. It is an outline of the invocation connector type, Invoker (see below).

We use object types to implement our connectors hierarchically. The root of the hierarchy is the supertype CConnector, with three sub-types Invoker, Selector and Sequencer, for invocation connectors, selector connectors and sequencer connectors respectively. For example, in Fig. 9, the Invoker type inherits from CConnector (indicated by the keyword *UNDER*).

The super-type CConnector provides the implementation of the most important procedure for data, the *data_constructor*. This procedure creates and initialises data instances from data specifications in components. Constructors of all sub-types of CConnector invoke the *data_constructor* procedure to create and initialise their components' data instances. In a sub-type, the constructor starts by creating and initialising its internal data. Then, it calls the *data_constructor* procedure which reads its component data specifications from the repository; and creates and initialises the required data instances. This is illustrated in Fig. 9 for the constructor of Invoker. The call to *data_constructor* is highlighted.

```
---- Specification (interface)
CREATE OR REPLACE TYPE "INVOKER" UNDER  CCONNECTOR  (
  CONSTRUCTOR FUNCTION invoker(p_cname VARCHAR2, p_cuname VARCHAR2)
    RETURN SELF AS RESULT,
END; — Invoker specifications.
---- Implementation
CREATE OR REPLACE TYPE BODY "INVOKER" IS
  CONSTRUCTOR FUNCTION invoker(p_cname VARCHAR2, p_cuname VARCHAR2)
   RETURN SELF AS RESULT IS
  l_data_value raw(16);
  BEGIN
  ... — other initialization operations.
  SELF.cuname := p_cuname;
  ...
    self.data_constructor(p_cuname); — CREATE COMPONENT LOCAL DATA
  END;
END; ---- Invoker.
```

Fig. 9. PL/SQL specification of an invocation connector

An atomic component is constructed from a package for a computational unit and an object type for an invocation connector. The invocation connector keeps a reference to the computation unit's name. For example, in Fig. 9, the variable *cuname* is assigned the user-provided computation unit name *p_cuname*. The component is created in the repository by executing a procedure which generates a specification and stores it as records in the relevant repository database tables. These records contain data on the component, its invocation connector, interface, services and their return types and parameters, etc. At this point, the component is in the design phase. Copying the component is equivalent to retrieving all the component specification (records) and storing it back under a new component name. The new name can be a unique user- or system-provided string. The computation unit must exist in the repository for this operation to complete successfully.

A composite component is constructed from existing components. The procedure concerned takes three parameters: a string name for the new component, a list containing the sub-components' names and a connector type. The number of components that can be composed depends on the semantics of the composition connector. This procedure generates and stores the specification of the constructed component in a similar manner to the the procedure for constructing atomic components. In our repository, a composite component is always constructed from copies of other components. That is, if F and G are components in the repository, then in a composite H of F and G, the sub-components must be copies of F and G, each renamed by the repository. Thus the repository is implemented in such a way that any composition operation leaves unchanged the original components involved in the composition process.

5.2   Data Encapsulation

Once a component is constructed and stored in the repository, a set of operations are available to support the specification of data intended for encapsulation in the component. Data specification for a component include information on the properties of component's encapsulated data elements such as their names, types, state (persistent or transient), initial values, initial actions, etc. The specification is used by the repository to create and manage data instances at run-time.

At design time, repository operations generate, update and store components' data specifications in a repository database table named *ENC_DATA*. The operation to encapsulate a data element in a component takes a parameter (a positive integer value) for specifying the order for data instantiation. Names for data elements must be unique in the scope of the component that owns them. Data properties of a data element entry are set using either a generic procedure that is used to define arbitrary data elements, or a compatible type-specific procedure, e.g. for integer and string data elements. Copying a component in the repository results in copying its data specification too. Accordingly, for a component to be reusable, data initialisation must be delayed to the run-time phase, except when data is not application specific.

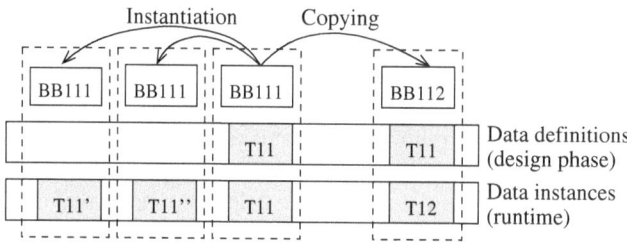

Fig. 10. Encapsulated data in component copies and instances

At run-time, a component constructor is used to create an instance of the component. This instance is uniquely identified in our run-time system by a CID (component ID). During the construction process, the *data_constructor* procedure is invoked. It retrieves the component's data specification stored in the *ENC_DATA* table; creates and initialises data instances; and stores these instances in a global temporary data space. The initialisation of a data element can either be achieved by a simple assignment of a constant or a computed value. Computed values are specified as scripts (anonymous PL/SQL blocks) and are executed by the run-time system during component construction. Data instances stored in the data space are made available to their components by reference. The repository identifies them via their CIDs. The global data space is implemented as an Oracle global temporary table. Entries in this kind of tables pertaining to a particular component are automatically garbage collected when the parent process of the component terminates. Further instantiations of a component create new, different and independent data instances for each component instance. Different instances of a component maintain their own data instances at run-time. Fig. 10 shows encapsulated data in component copies and instances in the bank example. Branch BB111 owns its data definition T11. A copy BB112 has its own copy T11 of the data definition. Two instances of BB111 own two different instances of data: T11' and T11". The two instances start with the same data, but their data becomes different over time.

Component constructors must be capable of performing data I/O operations required for data initialisation, among others. These operations (read, write) are implemented as *data connectors* used to input and output data from various data sources including the global temporary data space. The repository automatically creates a data connector for each encapsulated data element, method parameter and return value. For standard data sources such as relational databases, a complete set of data connectors is available and ready for use. For non-standard or unknown data sources, data connectors are created as stubs that must be manually replaced before running the system. Data connectors for non-standard data sources can be added to the repository and reused in building new systems. Few of the current component models support relational data sources, and only .NET supports additionally XML data sources [11].

5.3   The Bank System

Now, we can work out the implementation of a bank system based on the bank example in Example 1 (Fig. 1) in detail. In particular, we demonstrate data encapsulation and how our component model enables copying and multiple instantiation of its components. We also show that the composition scheme in our model preserves and propagates data encapsulation at every level of composition.

Consider a bank system consisting of the 2 consortia BC1 and BC2, as shown in Fig. 1, with a simplified entity-relationship (ER) diagram as shown in Fig. 11.

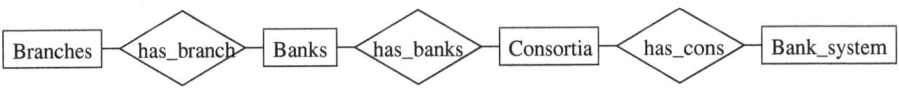

Fig. 11. A simple ER diagram for the bank system

For simplicity, we choose to encapsulate only three data elements in each component, namely, a component name, date of instantiation and data details. A bank branch encapsulates separately its name (BRANCH_NAME), date and customers' data (CUSTOMERS). A bank component encapsulates data on its branches (BRANCH) as well as the bank's name (BANK_NAME) and date. A consortium holds local data on its member banks (BANK), the name of the consortium (CONST_NAME) and a date. The bank system holds local data on all the consortia it has (CONST), its name (BNET) and a date. The date (named SYS_DATE in each) is a place holder that stores the component's instantiation date. The date holds an initialisation script (PL/SQL anonymous block) that can be executed by the run-time system to return the instantiation date. In Fig. 11, the relationships *has-cons*, *has-banks* and *has-branch* are data encapsulated in the components bank system, consortia and banks respectively.

To build the system, we start with one computational unit BB (an Oracle package), one invocation connector and one selector composition connector.

```
EXEC REPOSITORY.CREATE_ATOMIC_COMPONENT('BB111', 'BB');
EXEC REPOSITORY.ENCAPSULATE('BB111', 'BRANCH_NAME', 0);
EXEC REPOSITORY.ENCAPSULATE('BB111', 'SYS_DATE', 0);
...
EXEC REPOSITORY.SET_ENC_DATA_PROPERTIES(132, 'VARCHAR2', 'T');
EXEC REPOSITORY.SET_ENC_DATA_VALUES
  (133, NULL, 'BEGIN :A:=ANYDATA.CONVERTDATE(SYSDATE);END;',NULL);
```

Fig. 12. The construction of atomic component BB111

```
L_LIST(1) := 'BB111';
L_LIST(2) := 'BB111';
L_REF_CONN := REPOSITORY.CREATE_COMPOSITE_COMPONENT('B11', 'SELECTOR', L_LIST);
EXEC REPOSITORY.ENCAPSULATE('B11', 'BANK_NAME', 0);
...
EXEC REPOSITORY.SET_ENC_DATA_VALUES
  (145, NULL, 'BEGIN :A:=ANYDATA.CONVERTDATE(SYSDATE);END;',NULL);
```

Fig. 13. The construction of composite component B11

These three elements are sufficient to build the entire bank system outlined above. Our first component is an atomic component for a bank branch (BB111). It is constructed from BB and an invocation connector (Fig. 12). In Fig. 12, the first command creates the component, and the third defines one of its encapsulated data elements, SYS_DATE. This variable is stored in the repository with a unique ID (integer) which is used at run-time in initialising the data element. The last command assigns SYS_DATE a script ('BEGIN...END;') that returns the system date when executed. This script is required in every branch component, therefore it has been assigned to SYS_DATE in the design phase. The rest of BB111's encapsulated data is not initialised until the final system has been constructed.

We assume that the business logic for all bank branches is the same. Therefore, bank components are constructed from copies of BB111. In Fig. 13 we construct a bank component B11 using a selector connector to compose two copies of BB111. The resulting composite component encapsulates its own data. Its SYS_DATE is also initialised with the same script used for BB111. Data encapsulated in B11 is independent of its sub-components' data. Fig. 14 shows a listing of B11 specification where data encapsulated in its sub-components has not been influenced by the composition. The composition process has preserved the sub-components' encapsulated data and propagated data encapsulation to the next level.

Similarly, a bank consortium component BC1 can be created in the same way. We also define its encapsulated data. Finally, we create the bank system component (BS) from two copies of BC1 and a definition of its local date. With this step, the system is complete and it is possible to proceed with data initialisation. Data initialisation is based on knowledge provided by the repository on the components' encapsulated data. Many steps similar to those for initialising SYS_DATE are performed to make BS ready to run.

```
SQL> EXEC GET_DATA_SPECS('BS');        — Listing of B11 component architecture & its data
............
    Data Name              Q  S  Type        Initial Value
─ B11 renamed by the repository
  .    BANK_NAME          1  T  VARCHAR2  B11
  .    SYS_DATE           2  T  DATE         BEGIN :A := ANYDATA.CONVERTDATE(SYSDATE)....
  .    BRANCH             3  P  TABLE
─ BB112 renamed by the repository
  .    BRANCH_NAME        1  T  VARCHAR2  BB112
  .    SYS_DATE           2  T  DATE         BEGIN :A := ANYDATA.CONVERTDATE(SYSDATE)...
  .    CUSTOMERS          3  P  TABLE
─ BB111 renamed by the repository
  .    BRANCH_NAME        1  T  VARCHAR2  BB111
  .    SYS_DATE           2  T  DATE         BEGIN :A := ANYDATA.CONVERTDATE(SYSDATE)...
  .    CUSTOMERS          3  P  TABLE
```

Fig. 14. Data encapsulation in composite component B11

It is clear from the design phase process outlined above, how data encapsulation is supported by the composition scheme in our model. Composition preserves data encapsulation and propagates it. Furthermore, reuse by copying has been demonstrated in the creation of BS; all branches are copies of BB111, banks are copies of B11 and consortia are copies of BC1.

At run-time, BS and its sub-components must first be initialised with data, before BS can be instantiated. After this, creating a BS component results in creating instances for all its sub-components. Each component constructor creates its independent data instances and stores them in a data space identified by a CID. A data trace extracted from the run-time system for two instances of B11 and B11' shows different data instances for each component (Fig. 15).

The system can now receive client requests such as withdraw, deposit, balance, etc. This is illustrated by Fig. 16. By getting its account information via an ATM, the top-level connector reads the client's consortium code (BCC) to decide which consortium to direct control to. The consortium's top-level connector (BC2) reads the bank code (BC) to choose the bank. The bank then reads the client sort code (SC) to determine the client's bank branch. The bank branch reads the service requested, account number and amount, processes the client's request and returns a report. In this process, each component's top-level connector performs the necessary I/O operations it needs to coordinate control flow to the right bank branch. Fig. 16 shows a client request for (*withdraw*) to branch BB212.

DATA_NAME	COMP. NAME	CID	References to data in data space
BANK_NAME	B11	229	29AF4BB598B860ABE0440003BA3A89CB
SYS_DATE		229	29AF4BB598B960ABE0440003BA3A89CB
BRANCH_NAME	BB111	230	29AF4BB598BB60ABE0440003BA3A89CB
SYS_DATE		230	29AF4BB598BC60ABE0440003BA3A89CB
BRANCH_NAME	BB112	231	29AF4BB598BF60ABE0440003BA3A89CB
SYS_DATE		231	29AF4BB598C060ABE0440003BA3A89CB
BANK_NAME	B11'	232	29C6EA036AF801A1E0440003BA3A89CB
SYS_DATE		232	29C6EA036AF901A1E0440003BA3A89CB

Fig. 15. Data trace at run-time for two instances of B11

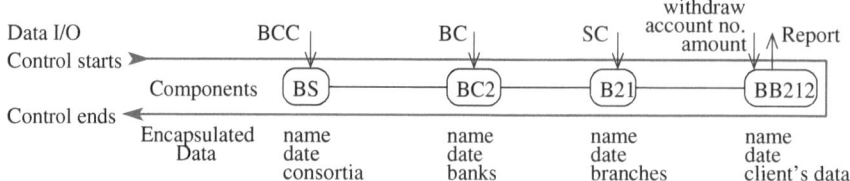

Fig. 16. Processing a withdraw request for a BB212 client

6   Discussion and Related Work

In current component models, a component is either an object or an architectural unit [9,5]. Components that are objects in these models are not compositional and so data encapsulation in composites is not meaningful. However, data encapsulation does occur at the level of atomic components. In component models where components are architectural units, composites are defined and can be (new) entities in their own right. Therefore, in these models, data encapsulation is potentially meaningful for both atomic and composite components. Of these models, only Koala [15] and PECOS [4] address data encapsulation.

In Koala, data is specified as attributes and data components. The latter are modules (non-interface components). Initialisation of attributes is expressed as either provides interfaces or requires interfaces. In a composition, both kinds of interfaces must either be exposed via the interface of the composite, or satisfied internally by a data component. Such a data component is encapsulated inside the composite, which compromises reuse if the data encapsulated is application specific. For example, to implement the bank system in Koala, encapsulated data must be initialised at the composite level, thus breaching information privacy of customers of each branch. An alternative is to initialise data at the level of each branch component. However, this compromises reuse. Therefore, in Koala, composition and reuse are conflicting concerns. Furthermore, copying and multiple instantiation are not supported because their components are C modules.

PECOS models data as *ports*, *attributes* (properties) and *connectors*. A port is a type containing a data type, range and direction. Attributes are constant data that can be specified for any PECOS component. A connector is a data type shared between two or more ports. Connections between components in a composite can not cross the composite's boundary. A connector between two composites represents an independent variable which must be synchronised with data variables held at the connected ports [4].

With respect to data, PECOS components can be classified as controllers (with their own thread of control) or passive components. The first category includes active and event components. Composites in PECOS are hierarchical. In a composite, the root must be a controller component. A controller holds data and shares it with all the passive components it controls (its sub-components). This leads us to conclude that the general notion of data encapsulation is achieved only at the level of composite components. Components' ports are points for passing, but not holding, data. Because of the need for data synchronisation among components, data initialisation in PECOS is not recommended to be performed in constructors, but rather in a special method provided by the model. Copying is not possible in PECOS, but multiple instantiation is possible because a component defines its encapsulated data and has its own data constructor method to create its data instances.

In contrast to these models, our model provides a constructor which is the only method needed for instantiating the component and its data. Data initialisation occurs at the level of each component's top-level connector, and not recursively, as in Koala. Copying and multiple instantiation is supported because of our approach to data in the model.

Our notion of data encapsulation is defined at the level of component models, not at the level of programming languages. In particular, it should not be confused with encapsulation in object-oriented languages, where objects can encapsulate private data. Our notion of data encapsulation comes with composition, whereas data encapsulation in objects does not. No object-oriented language provides a single programmatic operator for composition that preserves data encapsulation in the way that our composition connectors do.

Furthermore, our notion of data encapsulation with composition leads to more reuse, via copies and instances. In the bank example, we only need one atomic component and one connector to build the whole system. This kind of increased reusability is not found in other component models. For instance, in Koala, copies and instances are not possible, and in PECOS, copies are not possible.

Finally, in [7] we defined data encapsulation in a different way. We defined it as a way to handle data operations separately from all other operations in component-based systems. This is unrelated to our definition here. Previously, separating dataflow and control flow was our focus. In that context, our goal was achieved by storing data in a global space, but only at the expense of encapsulation. In the present work, we have achieved separation and encapsulation at the same time.

7   Conclusion

In this work, we have encapsulated data in components. Our goals have been achieved by extending the semantics of the composition connectors and, accordingly, the composition scheme, in the component model we proposed in [6]. As a result, data encapsulation has not only become an invariant property of the scheme but it is also propagated in composition to newly constructed components (components are self-similar). Furthermore, data encapsulation has enabled component copying at design time, and multiple instantiation at run-time. Data encapsulation and reuse are not conflicting concerns in our model, in contrast to other models. Therefore, our model provides truly reusable software building blocks.

References

1. Bass, L., Clements, P., Kazman, R.: Software Architecture in Practice, 2nd edn. Addison-Wesley, Reading (2003)
2. Clements, P.C.: A survey of architecture description languages. In: 8th Int. Workshop on Software Specification and Design, pp. 16–25. ACM Press, New York (1996)
3. DeMichiel, L., Keith, M.: Enterprise JavaBeans, Version 3.0. Sun Microsystems (2006)
4. Genssler, T., Christoph, A., Schulz, B., Winter, M., Stich, C.M., Zeidler, C., Müller, P., Stelter, A., Nierstrasz, O., Ducasse, S., Arévalo, G., Wuyts, R., Liang, P., Schönhage, B., van den Born, R.: PECOS in a Nutshell (September 2002), http://www.pecos-project.org/
5. Lau, K.-K.: Software component models. In: Proc. ICSE06, pp. 1081–1082. ACM Press, New York (2006)
6. Lau, K.-K., Ornaghi, M., Wang, Z.: A software component model and its preliminary formalisation. In: de Boer, F.S., Bonsangue, M.M., Graf, S., de Roever, W.-P. (eds.) FMCO 2005. LNCS, vol. 4111, pp. 1–21. Springer, Heidelberg (2006)
7. Lau, K.-K., Taweel, F.: Towards encapsulating data in component-based software systems. In: Gorton, I., Heineman, G.T., Crnkovic, I., Schmidt, H.W., Stafford, J.A., Szyperski, C.A., Wallnau, K. (eds.) CBSE 2006. LNCS, vol. 4063, pp. 376–384. Springer, Heidelberg (2006)
8. Lau, K.-K., Velasco Elizondo, P., Wang, Z.: Exogenous connectors for software components. In: Heineman, G.T., Crnković, I., Schmidt, H.W., Stafford, J.A., Szyperski, C.A., Wallnau, K. (eds.) CBSE 2005. LNCS, vol. 3489, pp. 90–106. Springer, Heidelberg (2005)
9. Lau, K.-K., Wang, Z.: A survey of software component models. 2nd edn., Pre-print CSPP-38, School of Computer Science, The University of Manchester (May 2006), http://www.cs.man.ac.uk/cspreprints/PrePrints/cspp38.pdf
10. Medvidovic, N., Taylor, R.N.: A classification and comparison framework for software architecture description languages. IEEE Transactions on Software Engineering 26(1), 70–93 (2000)
11. Microsoft. Data access development overview: within the Microsoft Enterprise Development Platform. Microsoft Enterprise Development Strategy Series. Microsoft (March 2005), http://msdn.microsoft.com/netframework/technologyinfo/entstrategy/default.as px
12. Monson-Haefel, R.: Enterprise JavaBeans 3.0, 5th edn. O'Reilly & Associates (2006)
13. Russell, J.: PL/SQL User's Guide and Reference, 10g Release 1 (10.1). Oracle (2003)
14. Shaw, M., Garlan, D.: Software Architecture: Perspectives on an Emerging Discipline. Prentice-Hall, Englewood Cliffs (1996)
15. van Ommering, R., van der Linden, F., Kramer, J., Magee, J.: The Koala component model for consumer electronics software. IEEE Computer 33(3), 78–85 (2000)

Binary Change Set Composition

Tijs van der Storm

Centrum voor Wiskunde en Informatica
P.O. Box 94079, 1090 GB
Amsterdam, The Netherlands
storm@cwi.nl

Abstract. Binary component-based software updates that are lightweight, efficient, safe and generic still remain a challenge. Most existing deployment systems that achieve this goal have to control the complete software environment of the user which is a barrier to adoption for both software consumers and producers. Binary change set composition is a technique to deliver incremental, binary updates for component-based software systems in an efficient and non-intrusive way. This way application updates can be delivered more frequently, with minimal additional overhead for users and without sacrificing the benefits of component-based software development.

Keywords: deployment, update management, component-based software engineering, software configuration management.

1 Introduction

An important goal in software engineering is to deliver quality to users frequently and efficiently. Allowing users of your software to easily take advantage of new functionality or quality improvements can be a serious competitive advantage. This insight seems to be widely accepted [9]. Software vendors are enhancing their software products with an automatic update feature to allow customers to upgrade their installation with a single push of a button. This prevents customers from having to engage in the error-prone and time consuming task of deploying new versions of a software product. However, such functionality is often proprietary and specific to a certain vendor or product, thereby limiting understanding and broader adoption of this important part of the software process.

The aim of this paper is to maximize the agility of software delivery without sacrificing the requirement that applications are developed as part of a component-based product line. While it may not be beneficial to force the user environment to be component-based, it certainly can be for the development environment. One would like to develop software in a component-based fashion, and at the same time allow users to transparently deploy an application as a whole.

If certain actions are tedious, error-prone or just too expensive, they tend to be performed less frequently. If the effort to package a software product in such a way that it is ready for deployment is too high, releases will be put out less

---

H.W. Schmidt et al. (Eds.): CBSE 2007, LNCS 4608, pp. 17–32, 2007.

frequently. Similarly, if deploying a new release is a time consuming activity with a high risk of failure, the user probably will not upgrade every day. Therefore, if we want to optimize software delivery this can be achieved by, on the one hand, reducing the cost of release, and on the other hand, by reducing the cost of deployment.

How would one optimize both release and deployment in a platform and programming language independent way, when many products composed of multiple shared components have to be released and deployed efficiently? In this paper I present a technique, called *binary change set composition*, which provides an answer to this question. Using this technique, applications are updated by transferring *binary* change sets (patches). These change sets are computed from the compositional structure of application releases. It can be used to implement lightweight incremental application upgrade in a fully generic and platform independent way. The resulting binary upgrades are incremental, making the upgrade process highly efficient.

Contributions. The contributions of this paper are summarized as follows:

1. A formal analysis of automatic component-based release and delivery.
2. The design of a lightweight, efficient, safe and platform independent method for application upgrade.
3. The implementation of this method on top of Subversion.

Organization. This paper is organized as follows. Section 2 provides some background to the problem of application upgrade by identifying the requirements and discussing related work. Section 3 forms the technical heart of this paper. I describe how to automatically produce releases and deliver updates in an incremental fashion. The implementation of the resulting concepts is then discussed in Section 4. Then, in Section 5, I evaluate the approach by setting it out against the requirements identified in Section 2. Finally, I present a conclusion and list opportunities for future work.

2   Background

2.1   Requirements for Application Upgrade

Application upgrade consists of replacing a piece of software that has previously been installed by a user. The aim of an upgrade for the user is to be able to take advantage of repaired defects, increased quality or new functionality. The business motivation for this is that customer satisfaction is increased. To achieve this goal, the primary requirement is that upgrades *succeed*. Nevertheless, there are additional requirements for application upgrade. In the paragraphs below I discuss four requirements: *lightweightness, efficiency, genericity* and *safety*.

For an software deployment method to be lightweight, means that (future) users of a software product should not be required to change their environment to accomodate the method of deployment of the product. Reasoning along the same lines, the method of creating deployable release should not force a development organization to completely change their development processes. Furthermore, the effort to create a release on the one hand, and the effort to apply an upgrade on the other hand, should require minimum effort.

Efficiency is the second requirement. If the aim is to optimize software delivery, both release and upgrade should be implemented efficiently. If deploying an upgrade takes too much time or consumes too much bandwidth, users will tend to postpone the possibly crucial update. Again, also the development side gains by efficiency: the storage requirements for maintaining releases may soon become unwieldy, if they are put out frequently.

To ease the adoption of a release and deployment method, it should not be constrained by choice of programming language, operating system or any other platform dependency. In other words, the third requirements is *genericity*. It mostly serves the development side, but obviously has consequences for users: if they are on the wrong platform they cannot deploy the application they might desire.

The final and fourth requirement serves primarily users: safety of upgrades. Deployment is hard. If it should occur that an upgrade fails, the user must be able to undo the consequences quickly and safely. Or at least the consequences of failure should be local.

2.2   Related Work

Related work exists in two areas: update management and release management,— both areas belong to the wide ranging field of software deployment. In this field, update management has a more user oriented perspective and concerns itself with the question how new releases are correctly and efficiently consumed by users. Release management, on the other hand, takes a more development-oriented viewpoint. It addresses the question of how to prepare software that is to be delivered to the user.

In the following I will discuss how existing update and release tools for component-based software deployment live up to the requirements identified in Section 2.1.

Research on software deployment has mostly focused on combining both the user and development perspectives. One example is the Software Dock [10], which is a distributed architecture that supports the full software deployment life cycle. Field docks provide an interface to the user's site. These docks connect to release docks at producer sites using a wide area event service. While the software dock can be used to deploy any kind of software system, and thus satisfies the genericity requirement, the description of each release in the Deployable Software Description (DSD) language presents significant overhead. Moreover, the Software Dock is particularly good at deploying components from different, possibly distributed origins, which is outside the scope of this paper. The same can be said of the Software Release Manager (SRM) [17].

Deployment tools that primarily address the user perspective fall in the category of software product updaters [11]. This category can be further subdivided into monolithic product updaters and component-based product updaters. Whereas product updaters in general do not make assumptions on the structure of the software product they are updating, component (or package) deployment tools are explicitly component-based.

JPloy [12] is a tool that gives users more control over which components are deployed. The question is, however, whether users are actually interested in how applications are composed. In that sense, JPloy may not be a good match for application deployment in the strict sense.

Package deployment tools can be further categorized as based on source packages or binary packages. A typical example of source-based package deployment tools is the FreeBSD ports system [13]. Such systems require users to download source archives that are subsequently built on the user's machine. Source tree composition [5] is another approach that works by composing component source distributions into a so-called *bundle*. The tool performing this task, called AutoBundle, constructs a composite build interface that allows users to transparently build the composition. Source-based deployment, however, is relatively time-consuming and thus fails to satisfy the efficiency requirement.

Binary package deployment tools do, however, satisfy the efficiency requirement. They include Debian's Advanced Package Tool (APT) [14], the Redhat Package Manager (RPM) [3], and more recently AutoPackage [2]. These tools download binary packages that are precompiled for the user's platform. Both APT and RPM are tied to specific Linux distributions (Debian/Ubuntu and Redhat/SuSe respectively) whereas autopackage can be used across distributions. Nevertheless AutoPackage only works under Linux. Although these deployment tools are independent of programming language, they are not generic with respect to the operating system.

The deployment system Nix [6] supports both source and binary deployment of packages in such a way that it is transparent to the user. If no binary package is found it falls back to source deployment. It features a store for non-destructively installing packages that are identified by unique hashes. This allows side-by-side installation of different versions of the same package. Nix is the only deployment tool that is completely safe because its non-destructive deployment model guarantees that existing dependencies are never broken because of an update. Furthermore, it is portable across different flavors of Unix and does not require root access (which is the case for all package deployment tools except AutoPackage).

One problem in general with package deployment tools is that they are invasive with respect to the environment of the user. For instance, the value of these tools is maximum when *all* software is managed by it. This explains why most such tools are so intertwined with operating system distributions, but it is a clear violation of the lightweightness requirement.

While some systems, such as Nix, AutoPackage and JPloy, can be used next to the 'native' deployment system, they still have to be able to manage all dependencies in addition to the component that the user actually wants to install. In the worst case this means that a complete dependency tree of packages is duplicated, because the user deployed her application with a deployment tool different from the standard one. Note that this is actually unavoidable if the user has no root access. Note also that the user is at least required to install the deployment system itself, which in turn may not be an easy task.

2.3 Overview of the Approach

The motivations for component-based development are manyfold and well-known. Factoring the functionality of an application in separate components, creates opportunities for reuse,—both within a single product or across multiple products [15]. A distinguising feature of component-based development is the fact that components have their own life-cylce, both within a product and across products. This means that components are evolved, released, acquired and deployed independently, by different parties and at different moments in time.

In this paper components are interpreted as groupings of files that can be versioned as a whole. Components, however, often are not stand-alone applications. This means that a component may require the presence of other components to function correctly. Such dependencies may be bound either at build-time or at runtime. Applications are then derived by binding these dependencies to implementation components, either at build-time, load-time or even runtime.

In the following I assume a very liberal notion of dependency, and consequently of composition. When one component requires another component it is left unspecified what the concrete relation between the two components amounts to. Abstract dependencies thus cover both build-time and runtime dependencies. Under this interpretation, composition is loosely defined as merging all files of all related components into a single directory or archive.

When a component has been built, some of the resulting object files will contribute to the composed application. This set of files is called the (component) distribution. To distribute an application to users, the relevant component distributions are composed before release, resulting in a single application distribution. Thus, an application is identified with a certain root node in the component dependency graph and its distribution consists of the transitive-reflexive closure of the dependencies below the root.

In the next section I will present a technique to efficiently create and deliver such application releases, called *binary change set composition*. We will see that continuous integration of component-based software extends naturally to a process of automatic continuous release. A component will only be built if it has changed or if one of its dependencies has changed. If a component has been built it is released automatically. The results of a build are stored persistently so that components higher up in the dependency graph may reuse previous builds from components lower in the dependency graph.

Apart from the files belonging to a single component, the composition of these sets of files is also stored. The space requirements for this can quickly become unwieldy, therefore these application distributions are stored differentially. Differential storage works by saving the changes between files. Instead of composing sets of files, one can now compose sets of change sets. In addition to storing many releases efficiently, binary change set composition yields an efficient way of updating user installations.

3   Binary Change Set Composition

3.1   Incremental Integration

Tools like *make* optimize software builds because it only updates targets when they are out of date. It is possible to lift this paradigm from the level of files to the level of components. Hence, a component is only built if it is out of date with respect to some saved state, or when one of its dependencies is out of date. If built artifacts are stored persistently they can be reused. Sharing of builds is particularly valuable when a software product is continuously integrated [8]. Traditionally continuous integration is defined as a process where developers continuously integrate small changes to main development branch in the source control system. Then, after every change, the complete application is automatically built from scratch and automated tests are run. A naive apporach to building large systems from scratch, however, may not scale.

Consider an example that derives from three real-world components, *toolbus*, *toolbuslib* and *aterm*. The Toolbus is a middleware component that allows components ("tools") to communicate using a centralized software bus. Tools implemented in C use the *toolbuslib* component for this. Using the Toolbus, tools exchange data in a tree-like exchange format called Annotated Terms (ATerms) this datastructure is implemented by the *aterm* component. Obviously, *toolbus* requires both the connection and the exchange format libraries, whereas the connection library only requires the exchange format. All three components are used with the ASF+SDF Meta-Environment, a component-based application for language development [16].

Figure 1 shows four build iterations. The dashed boxes indicate changes in that particular component. In the first iteration every component has been built. At the time of the second iteration, however, only the top-level toolbus component has changed, so it is built again but this time reusing the previous builds of *toolbuslib* and *aterm*. Similarly, in the third iteration there has been a change in the *toolbuslib* component. Since *toolbus* depends on *toolbuslib* a new build is

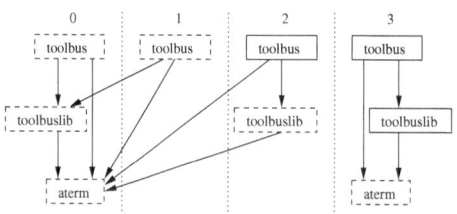

Fig. 1. Incremental integration

triggered for both *toolbuslib* and *toolbus*. Finally, in the last iteration changes have been committed to the *aterm* component and as a result all components are rebuilt.

An implementation of incremental continuous integration, called Sisyphus, has been described in [18]. This system works as follows. Every time a commit to the source control system occurs, Sisyphus checks out all components. It does this by starting with a root component, and reading a special file contained in the source tree that describes the dependencies of this component. This process is repeated for each of the dependencies. Meanwhile, if the current version of a component has not been built before, or one of its dependencies has been built in the current iteration, a build is triggered. Results are stored in a database that serves as saved state.

3.2 Build and Release Model

The build and release model presented in this section can be seen as the data model of a database for tracing change, build and release processes. Additional details can be found in [18]. The state of a component at a certain moment in time is identified with its version obtained from the source control system. Each version may have been built multiple times. The model records for every build of a component version which builds were used as dependencies. A set of built artifacts is associated to each build. Finally, a release is simply the labeling of a certain build; the set of releases is a subset of the set of builds.

In the context of this paper two sets are important: *Build*, the set that represents component builds, and *Use* defined as a binary relation between builds (i.e. $Use \subseteq Build \times Build$). This dependency relation derives from explicitly specified requires interface *within* the source tree of each component. At build-time the required components are bound the source trees of those components, *at that moment in time*. Thus, the integration process takes the *latest* revision of each component. Building a component then results in a set of built artifacts (libraries, executables etc), given by the function files($aBuild$).

The extent of a build is defined as the set of builds that have participated in a build. It is computed by taking right image of a build b in the transitive-reflexive closure of the *Use* relation: extent(b) = $Use^*[b]$. The extent of a build thus contains all builds that will make up an application release. The set of files that will be part of a release is derived from the set of files that each component in the extent contributes. This is discussed in the next section.

3.3 Prefix Composition

When a component has been built some of the resulting object files will contribute to the composed application. The set of files that is distributed to the user is called the application distribution, and it is composed of component distributions.

Figure 2 shows how the files contributed by each component to the toolbus application are taken together to form a single application distribution. On the

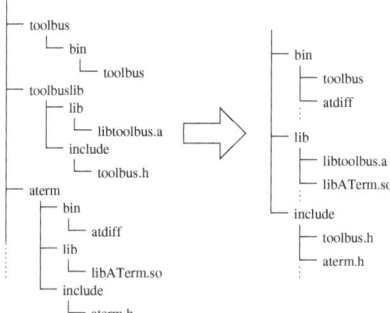

Fig. 2. Prefix composition

left is shown that all installable files of each component first end up in a component specific directory,—in the example this could have been the result of issuing *make install*. To release the *toolbus* as an application, these sets of files and directories are merged, resulting in a single application distribution, as shown on the right.

I call this way of composing components "installation prefix composition" since the component directories on the left correspond to directory prefixes passed to ./*configure* using the command line option --*prefix*. Such configuration scripts are generated by AutoConf [1], a tool to configure build processes that is widely used in open source projects. Among other things, it instructs *make install* to install files to a Unix directory hierarchy below the prefix. Prefix composition thus constitutes merging directories containing built artifacts.

Since components are composed by merging sets of files and directories we must ensure that no component overwrites files of another component. Formally, this reads:

$$\forall b \in Builds : \bigcap_{b' \in \text{extent}(b)} \text{files}(b') = \emptyset$$

In other words, this ensures that making a distribution is compositional. Instead of explicitly creating a global application distribution one can compose individual component distributions to achieve the same effect. What the property effectively states is that building a component, viewed as a function, distributes over composition.

There is one technicality which has to be taken care of: the distributed files should be relocatable. Because builds happen at the developer's site one must ensure that no (implicit) dependencies on the build environment are bound at build time. For instance, if a Unix executable is linked to a dynamic library that happens to be present at build time, then this library should also be present on the user's machine,—even on the same location. Since we do not want to require that users should reproduce the complete build environment, care must be taken to avoid such "imported" dependencies. I elaborate on this problem in Section 4.3.

3.4 Change Set Delivery

If the compositionality property holds the composition is defined by collecting all files that are in the extent of a build:

$$\text{files}^*(b) = \bigcup_{b' \in \text{extent}(b)} \text{files}(b')$$

The function files* computes the set of files that eventually has to be distributed to users. An update tool could transfer these files for every build that is released to the users of the application. If a user already has installed a certain release, the tool could just transfer the difference between the installed release and the new release. Let $F_{1,2} = \text{files}^*(b_{1,2})$. Then, the change set between two releases b_1 and b_2 is defined as:

$$\{\Delta(F_1 \cap F_2), +(F_2 \backslash F_1), -(F_1 \backslash F_2)\}$$

Change sets have three parts. The first part, indicated by Δ contains binary patches to update files that are in both releases. The second and third part add and remove the files that are absent in the first or second release respectively.

Table 1. Change set delivery

Upgrade	Change set delivered to user
$0 \rightarrow 1$	$\{\Delta_1^0 \text{bin/toolbus}\}$
$1 \rightarrow 2$	$\{\Delta_2^1 \text{bin/toolbus}, \Delta_2^0 \text{lib/libtoolbus.a}\}$
$2 \rightarrow 3$	$\{-\text{bin/atdiff}\}$

If we turn our attention once again to Figure 2, we see on the right the composed prefix for the *toolbus* application. Let's assume that this is the initial release that a typical user has installed. In the meantime, development continues and the system goes through three more release cycles, as displayed in Figure 1. The sequence of change sets transferred to our user, assuming she upgrades to every release, is listed in Table 1.

The second iteration only contains changes to the *toolbus* component itself. Since the only installable file in this component is *bin/toolbus*, a patch is sent over updating this file at the user's site. In the next iteration there is a change in *toolbuslib* and as a consequence *toolbus* has been rebuilt. Updating to this release involves transferring patches for both *bin/toolbus* and *lib/libtoolbus.a*. There must have been a change in the *bin/toolbus* since *libtoolbus.a* is statically linked. In the final iteration the changes were in the *aterm* component. However, this time neither *toolbuslib* nor *toolbus* are affected by it—even though they have been rebuilt—because the change involved the removal of a target: the *bin/atdiff* program appears to be no longer needed. Neither *toolbus*, nor *toolbuslib* referenced this executable, hence there was no change in any of the built files with respect to the previous release. As a result, the change set only contains the delete action for *bin/atdiff*. Note that these change sets can be easily reverted in order to support downgrades.

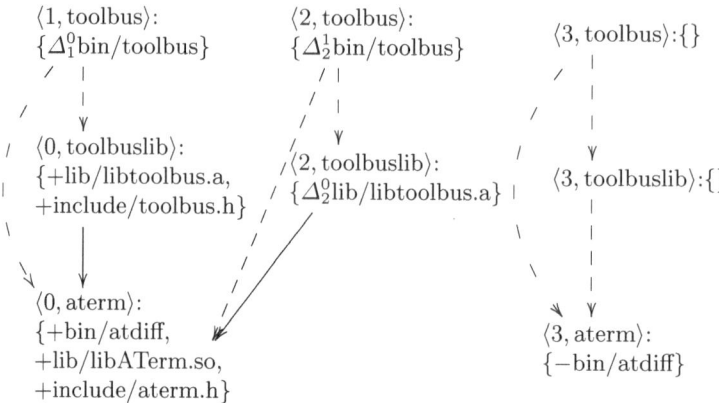

Fig. 3. Change set composition

3.5   Change Set Composition

Until now we have assumed that every application release was completely available and the change sets were only used to optimize the update process. From the use of change sets to update user installations, naturally follows the use of change sets for storing releases. Figure 3 shows how this can be accomplished.

Once again, the three integration iterations are shown. In the first iteration, only the *toolbus* had changed and had to be rebuilt. This resulted in an updated file *bin/toolbus*. The figure shows that we only have to store the difference between the updated file and the file of the previous iteration. Note that initial builds of *aterm* and *toolbuslib* (from iteration 0) are stored as change sets that just add files.

The second iteration involves a change in *toolbuslib*; again, patches for *toolbus* and *toolbuslib* are stored. However, in the third iteration, the change in the *aterm* component did not affect any files in *toolbus* or *toolbuslib*, so no change sets need to be stored for these components. But if users should be able to update their installation of the toolbus application, still the toolbus should be released. So there really are four toolbus releases in total, but the last one only contains changes originating from *aterm*.

I will now describe how this scheme of binary change set composition can be implemented on top of Subversion.

4   Implementation Using Subversion

4.1   Composition by Shallow Copying

Subversion [4] is a source control system that is gaining popularity over the widely used Concurrent Version System (CVS). Subversion adds many features that were missing in CVS, such as versioning of directories and a unified approach

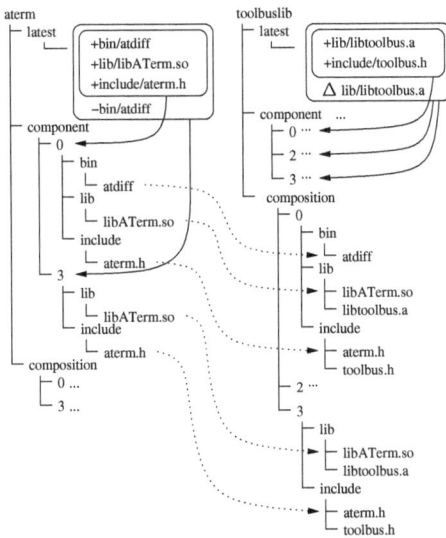

Fig. 4. Composition by shallow copying

to branching and tagging. Precisely these features prove to be crucial in the implementation of binary change set composition on top of Subversion.

Next, I will describe how Subversion repositories can be used as release repositories that allow the incremental delivery of updates to users. The release process consists of committing the component distributions to a Subversion repository, and then use branching to identify component releases. Such component-release branches are the unit of composition, which is also implemented by branching.

The crucial feature of Subversion that makes this work efficiently, is that branching is implemented by shallow copying. So, for instance a branch is created for some repository location—file or directory—by copying the tree to another location. At the new location, Subversion records a *reference* to the source of the copy operation. The copy operation is a constant-space operation and therefore a very efficient way to implement sharing.

Figure 4 shows a snapshot of a Subversion repository containing *aterm* and *toolbuslib* releases based on the change set graph displayed in Figure 3. For the sake of presentation releases of the *toolbus* have been omitted. On the left we see the Subversion tree for *aterm*, and on the left the tree for *toolbuslib*. The trees have subtrees indicated *latest*, *component* and *composition*. The *latest* tree is where component distributions are stored. The rounded boxes contain the change sets from Figure 3. The *component* tree and the *composition* tree contain shallow copies of versions of the latest tree; these are the releases proper. Solid arrows indicate copy relations the context of a single component,—dotted arrows indicate cross component copying (i.e. composition relations).

After every build the changes in the distributions are commited to the *latest* tree. The state of the *latest* tree at that time is then copied to a branch identifying this particular build; such branches are created by copying the files from latest to a separate directory under *component*. Note that since the change set for *toolbuslib* in iteration 3 was empty, *toolbuslib* release 3 is created from the state of the latest tree at iteration 2.

The tree below *composition* contains releases for compositions. This works by, instead of just copying the files belonging to a single build, copying the files in the extent of the build. In the example, this means that, next to the files contained in *toolbuslib* releases also the files in *aterm* releases are copied. If we compare *toolbuslib* composition 0 and 3, one can see in the figure that composition 0 is composed with release 0 of *aterm*, whereas composition 3 is composed with release 3 of *aterm*, exactly as in Figure 3.

4.2   Upgrade Is Workspace Switch

Assuming the proper access rights are in place, the Subversion repository can be made publicly accessible for users. A user can now *check out* the desired subtree of *compositions*; this can easily be performed by a bootstrap script if it is the initial installation. She then obtains the composed prefix of the application.

Now that the user has installed the application by checking out a repository location, it is equally easy to down- or upgrade to a different version. Since the subtrees of the *composition* tree contain all subsequent releases of the application, and the user has checked out one of them, up- and downgrading is achieved by updating the user's local copy of the composed prefix to another release branch. Subversion provides the command *svn switch* for this. Subversion will take care of adding, removing or patching where necessary.

Note that the sharing achieved in the repository also has an effect on how local checkouts are updated. For instance, recall that the third release of *toolbus* in the example involved the removal of *bin/atdiff*. If we assume that the user has installed the second release, and decides to upgrade, the only action that takes place at the user site is the removal of *bin/atdiff*, since the third release of both *toolbus* and *toolbuslib* contain the same change sets as second release of both these components.

4.3   Techniques for Relocatability

Installed application releases are ready to use with the exception of one technicality that was mentioned before, which is: relocation. Since the released files may contain references to locations on the build server at the side of development, these references become stale as soon as the users installed them. We therefore require that applications distributed this way should be binary relocatable. There are a number of ways to ensure that distributions are relocatable. Some of these are briefly discussed below.

There are ways to discover dynamically what the locations are of libraries and/or executables that are required at runtime. For instance, AutoPackage [2] provides a (Linux-only) library that can be queried at runtime to obtain 'your' location at runtime. Since the files contributed by each component are composed into a single directory hierarchy, dependencies can be found relative to the obtained location.

Another approach is to use wrapper scripts. As part of the deployment of an application a script could be generated that invokes the deployed application. This script would then set appropriate environment variables (e.g. PATH or LD_LIBRARY_PATH on Unix) or pass the location of the composed prefix on the commandline.

Finally, we could use string rewriting to effectively relocate unrelocatable files just after deployment. This amounts to replacing build time paths with their runtime counter-parts in every file. Special care must be taken in the case of binary files, since it is very easy to destroy their integrity. This technique, however, has been applied successfully.

5   Evaluation

5.1   Experimental Validation

A prototype implementation has been developed as part of the Sisyphus integration framework [19]. It has been used to deliver updates for a semi-large component-based system, consisting of around 30 components: the ASF+SDF Meta-Environment [16]. All built artifacts were put under Subversion, as described in the previous section. As expected, the repository did not grow exponentially, although all 40 component compositions were stored multiple times.

The ASF+SDF Meta-Environment is released and delivered using source tree composition [5]. This entails that every component has an abstract build interface based on AutConf. The prefixes passed using --*prefix* during build are known at the time of deployment so could be substituted quite safely. In order to keep binary files consistent, the prefixes passed to the build interface were supplanted with superfluous '/' characters to ensure enough space for the subtituted (user) path. This trick has not posed any problem as of yet, probably because package-based development requires that every dependency is always passed explicitly to the AutoConf generated ./*configure* script.

A small Ruby script served as update tool. It queries the repository, listing all available releases. If you select one, the tree is checked out to a certain directory. After relocation the Meta-Environment is ready to use. Before any upgrade or downgrade however, the tool undoes the relocation to prevent Subversion from seeing them as "local modifications".

5.2   Release Management Requirements

The subject of lightweight application upgrade belongs to the field of software release management. In [17], the authors list a number of requirements for effective release management in the context of component-based software. I discuss each of them briefly here and show that our approach satisfies them appropriately.

Dependencies should be explicit and easily recorded. Incremental continuous integration of components presumes that dependencies are declared as meta data within the source tree of the component. Thus, this requirement is satisfied.

Releases should be kept consistent. This requirement entails that releases are immutable. The incremental continuous integration approach discussed in this paper guarantees this.

The scope of the release should be controllable. Scope determines who is allowed to obtain a software release. The release repository presented in this paper enables the use of any access control mechanism that is provided by Subversion.

A history of retrievals should be kept. Although I do not address this requirement directly, if the Subversion release repository is served over HTTP using Apache, it is easily implemented by consulting Apache's access logs.

With respect to release management the implementation of change set composition using Subversion has one apparent weakness. Since Subversion does not allow cross-repository branching it would be hard to compose application releases using third-party components. However, this can be circumvented by using the Subversion dump utility that exports sections of a repository on file. Such a file can then be transferred to a different repository.

5.3   Update Management Requirements

In Section 1 I listed the requirements for application upgrade from the user perspective. Let's discuss each of them in turn to evaluate whether application upgrade using Subversion satsifies them.

Lightweightness. No invasive software deployment tool has to be installed to receive updates: only a Subversion client is required. Since, many language bindings exist for Subversion, self-updating functionality can be easily integrated within the application itself.

Genericity. Change set composition works with files of any kind; there is no programming language dependency. Moreover, Subversion is portable across many platforms, thereby imposing no constraints on the development or user environment.

Safety. The Subversion *switch* command is used for both upgrade and downgrade. A failed upgrade can thus be quickly rolled back. Another contribution to safety is the fact that Subversion repository modifications are atomic, meaning that the application user is shielded from inconsistent intermediate states, and that releases put out in parallel do not interfere.

Efficiency. Efficiency is achieved on two accounts. First the use of Subversion as delivery protocol ensures that an upgrade involves the transfer of just the differences between the old version and the new version. Secondly, while the unit of delivery is a full application, only the files per component are effectively stored, and even these are stored differentially.

Although all requirements are fulfilled satisfactory, the primary weakness of binary change set composition remains the fact that distributed files have to be relocatable. Solving this problem is left as future work.

6 Conclusion and Future Work

In this paper I have discussed the requirements that have to be fulfilled so that application upgrade is a burden neither for the development side, nor for the user side. Related work in the area of software release management did not live up to these requirements. The binary change set composition technique does live up to these requirements, and can be used to deliver new application releases accurately, frequently and quickly. The implementation on top of Subversion shows that the approach is feasible and may serve as a low impact adoption path.

However, ample opportunities for future work remain. First of all, the relocatability requirement of distributed files should be investigated. For instance, so-called application bundles on Mac OS X are always relocatable and would be perfect candidates for being updated using the techniques of this paper. Further research will have to point out if the notion of relocatable application bundles can be ported to other platforms. On the other had, I would like to investigate whether it is possible to make the binding of dependencies a first-class citizen in the model. For instance, one could envision a kind of service where components register themselves in order for them to be found by other components. This subject is closely related to the notion of dependency injection [7].

Another direction of future work concerns the integration of deployment functionality with the released application itself. Nowadays, many applications contain functionality to check for new updates. If they are available they are installed and the application is restarted. It would be interesting if using the approach of this paper one could design such "update buttons" in a reusable and generic way. Similarly, it should be investigated how such self-updating applications could be enhanced with functionality for reporting bugs or other kinds of feedback.

References

1. AutoConf. Online: http://www.gnu.org/software/autoconf
2. AutoPackage. Online: http://www.autopackage.org
3. Bailey, E.C.: Maximum RPM. Taking the Red Hat Package Manager to the Limit. Red Hat, Inc. (2000), Online: http://www.rpm.org/max-rpm
4. Collins-Sussman, B., Fitzpatrick, B.W., Pilato, C.M.: Version Control with Subversion. O'Reilly Media (2004), Online: http://svnbook.red-bean.com/
5. de Jonge, M.: Source tree composition. In: Gacek, C. (ed.) Software Reuse: Methods, Techniques, and Tools. LNCS, vol. 2319, pp. 17–32. Springer, Heidelberg (2002)
6. Dolstra, E., de Jonge, M., Visser, E.: Nix: A safe and policy-free system for software deployment. In: Damon, L. (ed.) LISA '04. 18th Large Installation System Administration Conference, pp. 79–92 (2004)

7. Fowler, M.: Inversion of control containers and the dependency injection pattern (April 2007), Online: http://martinfowler.com/articles/injection.html
8. Fowler, M., Foemmel, M.: Continuous integration (April 2007), Online: http://martinfowler.com/articles/continuousIntegration.html
9. Grossman, E.: An update on software updates. ACM Queue (March 2005)
10. Hall, R.S., Heimbigner, D., Wolf, A.L.: A cooperative approach to support software deployment using the software dock. In: ICSE'99. Proceedings of the 1999 International Conf. on Software Engineering, pp. 174–183 (1999)
11. Jansen, S., Ballintijn, G., Brinkkemper, S.: A process framework and typology for software product updaters. In: CSMR 2005. 9th European Conference on Software Maintenance and Reengineering (2005)
12. Lüer, C., van der Hoek, A.: JPloy: User-centric deployment support in a component platform. In: Second International Working Conference on Component Deployment, May 2004, pp. 190–204 (2004)
13. FreeBSD Ports. Online: http://www.freebsd.org/ports
14. Silva, G.N.: APT HOWTO. Debian (2004)
Online: http://www.debian.org/doc/manuals/apt-howto/index.en.html
15. Szyperski, C., Gruntz, D., Murer, S.: Component Software: Beyond Object-Oriented Programming, 2nd edn. ACM Press and Addison-Wesley, New York (2002)
16. van den Brand, M., Bruntink, M., Economopoulos, G., de Jong, H., Klint, P., Kooiker, T., van der Storm, T., Vinju, J.: Using The Meta-environment for Maintenance and Renovation. In: CSMR'07. Proceedings of the Conference on Software Maintenance and Reengineering, IEEE Computer Society Press, Los Alamitos (2007)
17. van der Hoek, A., Wolf, A.L.: Software release management for component-based software. Software—Practice and Experience 33(1), 77–98 (2003)
18. van der Storm, T.: Continuous release and upgrade of component-based software. In: Whitehead, J., Dahlqvist, A.P. (eds.) SCM-12. Proceedings of the 12th International Workshop on Software Configuration Management (2005)
19. van der Storm, T.: The Sisyphus continuous integration system. In: CSMR'07. Proceedings of the Conference on Software Maintenance and Reengineering, IEEE Computer Society Press, Los Alamitos (2007)

Automated and Unanticipated Flexible Component Substitution

Nicolas Desnos[1], Marianne Huchard[2], Christelle Urtado[1], Sylvain Vauttier[1], and Guy Tremblay[3]

[1] LGI2P - Ecole des Mines d'Alès, Nîmes, France
[2] LIRMM - UMR 5506 - CNRS and Univ. Montpellier 2, Montpellier, France
[3] Département informatique, UQAM, Montréal, QC, Canada

{Nicolas.Desnos, Christelle.Urtado, Sylvain.Vauttier}@site-eerie.ema.fr,
huchard@lirmm.fr, tremblay.guy@uqam.ca

Abstract. In this paper, we present an automatic and flexible approach for software component substitution. When a component is removed from an assembly, most existing approaches perform component-to-component substitution, relying on the fact that such a candidate component is available, which is hardly to happen because the constraints on its interfaces are too strong. When such a component does not exist, it would be more flexible to allow a single component to be replaced by a whole component assembly. We propose such an automatic substitution mechanism which does not need the changes to be anticipated and preserves the quality of the assembly.

1 Introduction

Today, software systems are becoming voluminous and complex like never before. Component-based software engineering [1] is a good solution to optimize the time and cost of software design while still guaranteeing the quality of the software. Moreover, the modularity it enables allows to tame the complexity of large systems. Typically, a component is seen as a black box which provides and requires services through its interfaces. An architecture is built to fulfill a set of functional objectives (its functional requirements)[1] and is described as a static interconnection of software component classes. A component assembly is a run-time instantiation of an architecture composed of linked component instances.

In this paper, we present an automatic and flexible approach for dynamic software component substitution. Anticipating component substitution, to overcome component obsolescence, failure or unavailability, is not always (cognitively) possible. Repairing a component assembly after a component has been removed while preserving its whole set of functionalities is difficult. When a component is removed from an assembly, most existing approaches perform component-to-component substitution [2,3,4,5]. However, these approaches rely on the fact that

---

[1] Our work does not yet handle non-functional requirements.

H.W. Schmidt et al. (Eds.): CBSE 2007, LNCS 4608, pp. 33–48, 2007.

such an appropriate component, candidate for substitution, is available. This situation is hardly to happen because it is difficult to find a component that has the same capabilities than the removed one.

When such a component does not exist, allowing a single component to be replaced by a whole component assembly would permit more flexibility. In this paper, we propose such an automatic substitution mechanism which does not need the changes to be anticipated. Our approach relies on primitive and composite ports for replacing a component by a whole assembly of components while preserving the quality of the assembly.

The rest of this paper proceeds as follows. Section 2 introduces component-based software engineering, presents existing work on component substitution and shows their limits. Section 3 describes our proposition for dynamically replacing a component. We first shortly present how ports allow us to automatically build valid assemblies [6]. We then show how this process can be used as part of a flexible component substitution process. We also present how it is possible to simplify the assembly by removing all the components that have become useless. Finally, Section 4 concludes and proposes perspectives to this work.

2   Context and Related Work

2.1   Software Architecture Correctness and Completeness in CBSE

Component-Based Software Engineering [7] makes it possible to build large systems by assembling reusable components. The life cycle of a component-based architecture can be divided into three phases: design-time, deployment-time and runtime.

At *design-time*, the system is analyzed, designed and the validity of the design is checked. An architecture is built to fulfill a set of functional objectives (its functional requirements) [8,9]. Functional objectives are defined as a set of functionalities to be executed on selected components. Selecting the functional objectives is typically a task performed during the analysis step. The structure of the architecture is described, during the design step, as a static interconnection of software component classes through their interfaces. It requires both selecting and connecting[2] the software components to be reused. This description, typically written in an architecture description language [10], expresses both the functional and non-functional capabilities of the architecture, as well as both the structural and the behavioral dependencies between components. Once the architecture is described, its validity is statically checked. Most systems verify the correctness of the architecture; some also guarantee its completeness.

Correctness. Verifying the correctness of an architecture amounts to verifying the connections between components and checking whether they correspond to a possible collaboration [9]. These verifications use various kinds of meta-information (types, protocols, assertions, etc.) associated with various structures

---

[2] We assume that the selected components need no adaptation (or have already been adapted).

(interfaces, contracts, ports, etc.). The finest checks are done by protocol comparisons, which is a combinatorial problem [11,12,13].

Completeness. The architecture must also guarantee that all its functional objectives are going to be supported. In other words, the connections of an architecture must be sufficient to allow the execution of collaborations that reach (include) all the functional objectives. We call this **completeness** of the architecture [6]. Indeed, the use of a component functionality (modeled by the connection of an interface) can necessitate the use of other functionalities which, in turn, entail new interface connections. Such functionalities (or interfaces) are said to be **dependent**. This information is captured in the description of component behavior and depends on the context in which the functionality is called (execution scenario). There are various ways to ensure completeness:

- For a first class of systems [14], completeness of an architecture is guaranteed by verifying that all the interfaces of all its components are connected. This view makes checking completeness very simple but over-constrains the assembly thus diminishing both the capability of individual components to be reused in various contexts and the possibilities of building a complete architecture, given a set of predefined components.
- To overcome the defects of the first class of systems, a second class of systems [3] defines two categories of interfaces (mandatory and optional). These systems allow complete architectures to be built while still leaving pending interfaces (the optional ones). This view does not complicate the checking of completeness and increases the opportunities of building a complete architecture, given a set of predefined components. However, associating the mandatory / optional property to an interface regardless of the assembly context does not increase the capability of individual components to be reused in various contexts.
- The third strategy requires connecting only the interfaces which are strictly necessary to reach completeness [12,15,16] by exploiting the description of the component behavior. This is typically done by analyzing protocols which makes completeness checking less immediate.

Example. Figure 1 illustrates that it is possible to ensure completeness of an assembly while connecting only the strictly necessary interfaces. The *Dialogue* interface from the *Client* component represents a functional objective and must therefore be connected. As deducted by analyzing the execution scenario that has to be supported, all the dependent interfaces (grayed on Figure 1) must also be connected in order to reach completeness. For example, the *Control* interface from the *MemberBank* component must be connected whereas the *Question* interface from the *Client* component does not need to be connected.

Once the validity of the architecture is checked, it can be deployed (*deployment-time*). Deployment requires instantiating the architecture, configuring its physical execution context and dispatching the components in this physical context. One of the results of deployment is a component assembly: a set of linked component instances that conforms to the architectural description.

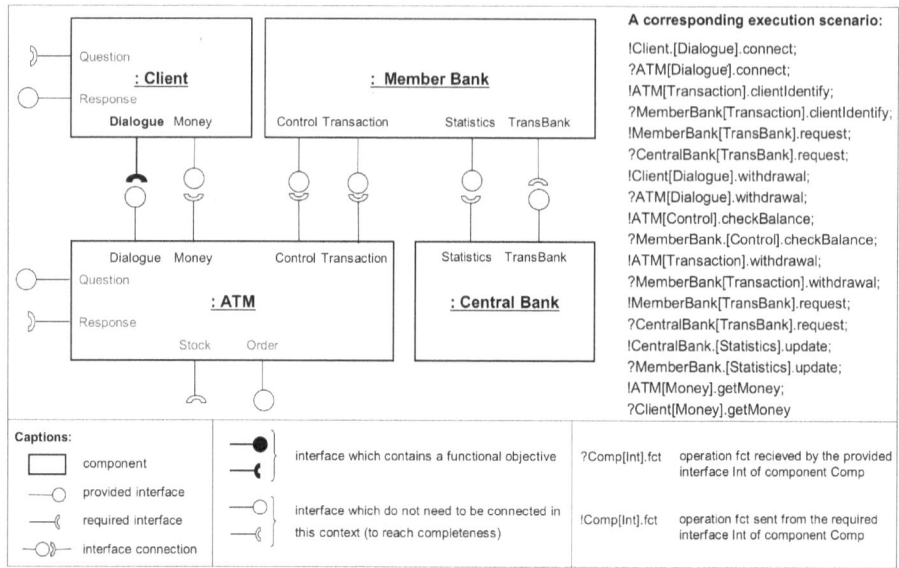

A corresponding execution scenario:

!Client.[Dialogue].connect;
?ATM[Dialogue].connect;
!ATM[Transaction].clientIdentify;
?MemberBank[Transaction].clientIdentify;
!MemberBank[TransBank].request;
?CentralBank[TransBank].request;
!Client[Dialogue].withdrawal;
?ATM[Dialogue].withdrawal;
!ATM[Control].checkBalance;
?MemberBank.[Control].checkBalance;
!ATM[Transaction].withdrawal;
?MemberBank[Transaction].withdrawal;
!MemberBank[TransBank].request;
?CentralBank[TransBank].request;
!CentralBank.[Statistics].update;
?MemberBank.[Statistics].update;
!ATM[Money].getMoney;
?Client[Money].getMoney

Fig. 1. A complete assembly and a possible corresponding execution scenario

At *runtime*, the component assembly executes. The evolution of this assembly is an important issue for the application to adapt to its environment in such situations, as maintenance, evolution of the requirements, fault-tolerance, component unavailability in mobile applications, etc. In this context, an important question is: What are the possible dynamic evolutions that can be supported by the component assembly and by the architecture itself? The remaining of this paper is a tentative answer to this question.

2.2   Dynamic Architecture Reconfiguration

To ensure that a component assembly will remain valid at runtime, all systems try to control how the assembly evolves. Different evolution policies exist:

- The simplest and most restrictive is to forbid dynamic reconfigurations: assemblies cannot evolve at runtime. This policy is not satisfactory.
- Some systems [17,3] allow the structure defined in the architecture to be violated when modifying component assemblies at runtime. They authorize component and connection modifications (addition, suppression) based on local interface type comparisons. The result is a lack of control on the assembly: its validity is not guaranteed anymore.
- The third category of systems ensures that component assemblies always conform to the structure defined in the architecture. All the possible evolutions must therefore be anticipated at design-time and described in the architecture itself [10]. Different techniques are used. ArchJava [18] and Sofa 2.0 [5] use patterns to know which interfaces can be connected or disconnected and

which components can be added or removed. Others [19,20] use logical rules that are a more powerful means to describe the possible evolutions. These solutions complicate the design process and make anticipation necessary while it is not always (cognitively) possible [5,21].

Dynamic Component Removal. Among the situations to handle to enable component assembly evolution is dynamic component removal. When removing a component from an assembly, the main issue is to ensure that there will not be any functional regression. The third category of systems typically allow a removed component to be replaced by a component which provides compatible services in order for the asssembly to still conform to the architecture. The anticipation of the possible evolutions allow these systems to ensure that the new component assembly will still satisfy the validity property that has been checked statically on the architecture at design-time. There are two major interpretations of component compatibility. In most of the systems [22,2,5,3], the components must strictly be compatible: the new component must provide at least all the provided interfaces the removed component did and it cannot require more required interfaces. In [23], compatibility is less restrictive and context-dependent. If a provided interface from the removed component is not used by another component in the assembly (not used in this context), the new component is not required to provide this interface (as it is not necesssary in this context). On the other hand, the new component can have extra required interfaces as soon as those interfaces find a compatible provided interface among the components of the assembly. This context-dependent definition of component compatibility allows better adaptability of the component assemblies.

Discussion. There are two main restrictions to the state of the art solutions to complete a component assembly after a component has been dynamically removed:

1. Anticipating all possible evolutions to include their description in the initial description of the architecture at design-time is not always possible because it requires to know all the situations that may occur in the future of the system. Ideally, it should be better to try and manage the evolution of software assemblies in an unanticipated way.
2. Replacing the removed software component by a single component is not always possible because it is quite unlikely that a component having compatible interfaces exist among the potential candidates for substitution. In the more general case when such an adequate component does not exist, it might be interesting to replace the removed component by a set of linked components that together can provide the required services.

Proposing a solution to replace a removed component by an assembly of components in an unanticipated way while trying as much as possible to guarantee the quality (executability) of the assembly is the initial motivation for the work presented in this paper.

3   Automated and Unanticipated Flexible Component Substitution

In previous work, we proposed [24] and optimized [6] a solution to automatically build component assemblies from components, given a set of functional objectives. The building process uses ports, which are extra information we suggest to add to components, and guarantees that the suggested assemblies are complete.

The idea we develop in this paper is to use this building process in order to re-build an assembly after a component has been removed, thus replacing a single component by a whole sub-assembly which is a more flexible solution. This can be done in four steps: (1) removing the target component, (2) removing all the (consequently) dead components, (3) re-build the assembly by adding new components and new bindings until the assembly is complete and (4) checking the validity of the suggested assembly.

In the remaining of this section, we first briefly present how primitive and composite ports are abstract concepts that embody the information needed to automatically build complete assemblies and describe the automatic building process. We then try to formalize the building process and rely on this formalization to describe how it can be used for component substitution (steps 2 and 3 listed above).

3.1   Building Valid Component Assemblies from Port Enhanced Components

This section briefly describes how adding ports to components provides a means to automatically build complete component assemblies [24,6]. Existing approaches usually statically describe architectures in a top-down manner. Once the architecture is defined, they verify its validity using costly validity checking algorithms [11,12,13]. Our building of assemblies from components obeys an iterative (bottom-up) process. This makes the combinatorial cost of these algorithms critical and prevents us from using them repeatedly, as a naive approach would have suggested to. To reduce the complexity, we chose to simplify the information contained in protocols and to represent it in a more abstract and usable manner through primitive and composite ports. Ports allow us to build a set of interesting complete assemblies from which it is possible to choose and check the ones that are best adapted to the architect's needs.

Primitive and Composite Ports. The idea for building a complete component assembly is to start from the functional objectives and to select the suitable components and make necessary links between them. Completeness is a global property that we are going to guarantee locally, in an incremental way all along the building process. The local issue is to determine which interfaces to connect and where (to which component) to connect them. This information is hidden into behavior protocols where it is difficult to exploit in an incremental assembly process. We are going to enhance the component model with the notion of port, in order to model the information that is strictly necessary to guarantee completeness in an abstract way. Primitive and composite ports will therefore represent two kinds of connection constraints on interfaces, so that the necessary connections can be correctly determined. In some way, ports express the different usage contexts of a component, making it possible to connect only the interfaces which are useful for completeness. As in UML 2.0 [25], one can also consider that the functional objectives of an architecture are represented by use cases, that collaborations concretely realize use cases and contain several entities that each play a precise role in the collaboration. Primitive and composite ports can be considered as the part of the component that enables the component to play a precise role to realize a given use case.

Primitive ports are composed of interfaces, as in many other component models [25,26]. Ports are introduced as a kind of structural meta-information, complementary to interfaces, that group together the interfaces of a component corresponding to a given usage context. More precisely, a primitive port can be considered as the expression of a constraint to connect a set of interfaces both at the same time and to a unique component.

In Figure 2, the *Money_Dialogue* primitive port gathers the *Dialogue* and the *Money* interfaces from the *Client* component. It expresses a particular usage context for this component. The connection between two primitive ports is an atomic operation that connects their interfaces: two primitive ports are connected together when all the interfaces of the first port are connected to interfaces of the second port (and reciprocally). Thus, port connections make the building process more abstract (port-to-port connections) and more efficient (no useless connections). In this example, the *Money_Dialogue* primitive port from the *Client* component is connected to the *Money_Dialogue* primitive port from the *ATM* component.

Composite ports are composed of other ports. A composite port expresses a constraint to connect a set of interfaces at the same time but possibly to different components. In Figure 2, the *ATM* component has a composite port which is composed of the two *Money_Dialogue* and *Money_Transaction* primitive ports.

Like a designer has to do with protocols, ports have to be manually added to document the design of components; however, we are currently working on their automatic generation from behavior protocols.

Completeness of an Assembly as Local Coherence of its Components. Calculating the completeness of an already built component assembly is of no interest in an incremental building approach. Our idea is to better consider a local property of components. We call this property **coherence** and have shown [24] that it is a necessary condition for validity. Intuitively, we can see that when all components of an assembly are coherent, the assembly is complete. A component is said to be coherent if all its composite ports are and a composite port is coherent if its primitive ports are connected in a coherent way (see below).

More formally, completeness can be described after setting some preliminary definitions.

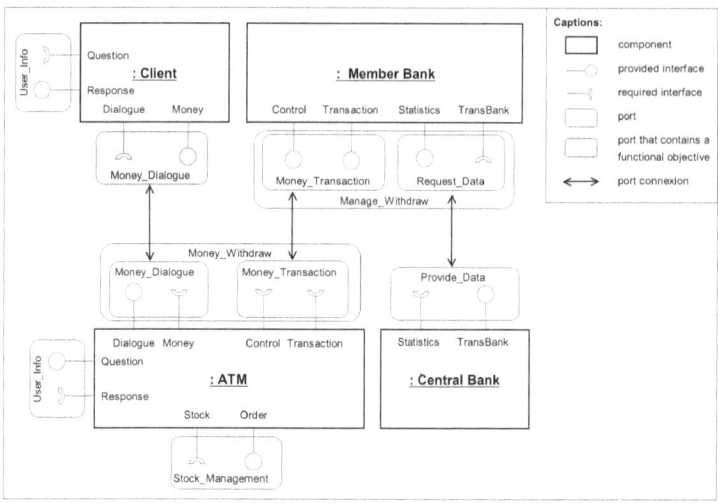

Fig. 2. Example of components with primitive and composite ports

- An **interface** is characterized by *a set of operations.*
- We define a **component** C as a quadruple:

$$C = (Prv_C, Req_C, Prim_C, Comp_C)$$

  Prv_C is the set of C's provided interfaces and Req_C its set of required interfaces. $Prim_C$ is the set of C's primitives ports and $Comp_C$ its set of composite ports.
- We denote by $Int_C = Prv_C \cup Req_C$ the whole set of C's interfaces, and $Ports_C = Prim_C \cup Comp_C$ the whole set of C's ports.
- A **primitive port** ρ is a set of interfaces. For any primitive port ρ of C, $\rho \subseteq Int_C$. We denote by $\widehat{\rho}$ the fact that, with respect to a set of components, ρ is *connected*—i.e., any required (resp. provided) interface of ρ is correctly linked with a provided (resp. required) interface of another (primitive) port.
- A **composite port** γ of C is a set of ports, primitives or composites, from C.
- Let $\gamma \in Comp_C$ be a composite port of C. We define $PrimPorts^*(\gamma)$, resp. $CompPorts^*(\gamma)$, as the set of primitive, resp. composite, ports that are directly or indirectly contained in γ:

$$PrimPorts^*(\gamma) = \{\rho \in \gamma \cap Prim_C\} \cup \bigcup_{\gamma' \in \gamma \cap Comp_C} PrimPorts^*(\gamma')$$

$$CompPorts^*(\gamma) = \{\gamma' \in \gamma \cap Comp_C\} \cup \bigcup_{\gamma' \in \gamma \cap Comp_C} CompPorts^*(\gamma')$$

- We denote $\widehat{\gamma}$ when all primitive ports contained in γ are connected[3]:

$$\widehat{\gamma} = \forall \rho \in PrimPorts^*(\gamma) \cdot \widehat{\rho}$$

---

[3] As in VDM [27] and B [28], "·" is used to separate the (typed) variable introduced by the quantifier and the associated predicate.

– We define a relation *Unrelated* between two different composite ports γ and γ' of $Comp_C$, denoting that neither port is directly or indirectly composed of the other:

$$Unrelated(\gamma, \gamma') = \gamma \neq \gamma' \wedge \gamma \notin CompPorts^*(\gamma') \wedge \gamma' \notin CompPorts^*(\gamma)$$

– Let $\gamma \in Comp_C$ be a composite port. $Shared(\gamma)$ is the set of primitive ports shared by γ and by another unrelated composite port of C:

$$Shared(\gamma) = \{\rho \in PrimPorts^*(\gamma) \mid$$
$$\exists \gamma' \in Comp_C \cdot Unrelated(\gamma', \gamma) \wedge \rho \in PrimPorts^*(\gamma')\}$$

To determine the completeness of an assembly, we need to know if the interfaces that must be connected are indeed connected. The main idea is to check the coherence of each composite port. Two cases must be checked: when the composite port does not share any primitive ports with another unrelated composite port and when it does share some primitive ports.

Let us now define the coherence of a composite port. Given a composite port γ, three mutually exclusive cases are possible for γ to be coherent:

1. All its primitive ports are connected.
2. None of its primitive ports is connected.
3. Some, but not all, of its primitive ports are connected. In this case, γ can still be coherent if it shares some port with another unrelated composite port (of the same component) which is itself entirely connected. Indeed, sharing of primitive ports represents alternative connection possibilities [6]. A partially connected composite port can represent a role which is useless for the assembly as soon as its shared primitive ports are connected in the context of another (significant) composite port.

– Port γ is **coherent** if the following holds, where ρ is restricted to primitive ports of γ:

$$\oplus \begin{cases} \forall \rho \in PrimPorts^*(\gamma) \cdot \widehat{\rho} & \text{(which is equivalent to } \widehat{\gamma}) \\ \forall \rho \in PrimPorts^*(\gamma) \cdot \neg\widehat{\rho} \\ \wedge \begin{cases} \forall \rho \in Shared(\gamma) \cdot \\ \quad \widehat{\rho} \Rightarrow \exists \gamma' \in Comp_C \cdot Unrelated(\gamma, \gamma') \wedge \rho \in PrimPorts^*(\gamma') \wedge \widehat{\gamma'} \\ \forall \rho \in PrimPorts^*(\gamma) \setminus Shared(\gamma) \cdot \neg\widehat{\rho} \end{cases} \end{cases}$$

– A component C is said to be **coherent** if all its composite ports are coherent:

$$\forall \gamma \in Comp_C \cdot \gamma \text{ is coherent}$$

– An assembly of components is said to be **complete** if $i)$ all the primitive ports which represent functional objectives are connected; $ii)$ all its components are coherent.

Building Complete Component Assemblies. This coherence property allows us to concentrate on a local property of composite ports which is easier to include in an iterative assembly process. The principle of the automatic assembly process (detailed in [6]) is to try and connect all the ports representing a functional objective and iteratively discover and try to fulfill new connection needs. This process has been implemented as the searching of a construction tree using a depth-first policy. Backtracking is used to explore all the alternate construction paths (alternative possible components or alternative connection choices due to composite port intersections). This complete exploration of the construction tree is used to guarantee that any possible solution is always found. Furthermore, optimization strategies and heuristics have been added for the traversal of the construction space. The use of ports, and particularly of composite ports, is prominent in our approach: as they express the local dependencies that exist between interfaces, ports provide a simple means to evaluate the completeness of an architecture. As a result, the building algorithm provides a set of interesting complete architectures. Since architecture completeness is a necessary condition for architecture validity, the resulting set of complete architectures thus provides a reduced search space on which classical correctness checkers such as [5] are finally used on few selected assemblies.

3.2 Flexible Component Substitution Using the Automatic Building Process

To react to the dynamic removal of a software component, we propose a two step process that allows a flexible replacement of the missing component:

1. analyze the assembly from which the component has been removed and re-move the now useless (dead) components,
2. consider the incomplete component assembly as an intermediate result of our iterative building algorithm and therefore run the building algorithm on this incomplete assembly to re-build a complete assembly.

Removing the Dead Components. When a component has been removed from a complete assembly, there are parts of the assembly that become useless. Indeed, some of the components and connections in the original assembly might have been there to fulfill needs of the removed component. To determine which parts of the assembly have become useless, let us define a graph which provides an abstract view of the assembly.

An assembly can be represented as a graph where each node represents a component and each edge represents a connection between two (primitive) ports of two of its components. We also distinguish two kinds of components: those which fulfill a functional objective—i.e., the components which contain a port which contains an interface which contains a functional objective—and those which do not (cf. Figure 3).

An **assembly** A can then be seen as a graph along with a set of functional objectives:

$$A = (G_A, FO_A)$$

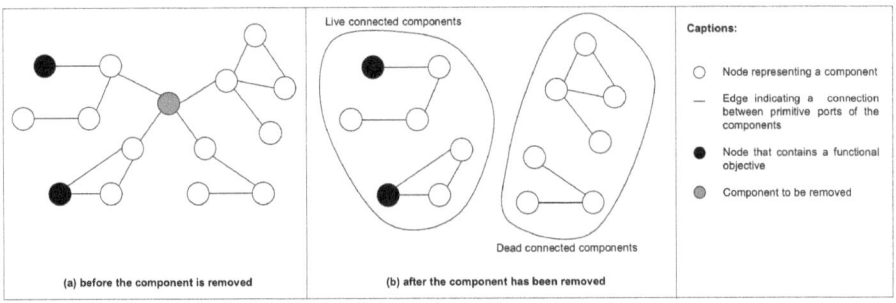

Fig. 3. An assembly can be seen as an abstract graph (a) and divided in two sets of connected components when a component has been removed (b)

Here, $G_A = (Cmps_A, Conns_A)$ is a graph, with $Cmps_A$ the set of nodes—each node being a component, $Conns_A$ the set of edges—each edge indicating the existence of some primitive port connection between the components, and $FO_A \subseteq \bigcup_{C \in Cmps_A} Prim_C$ the set of primitive ports that contain some functional objectives[4].

If we consider the graph that results from the removal of the node representing the removed component, it is possible to partition it in two parts: the connected components[5] that have at least a node which contains a functional objective and the connected components that have no node that contains a functional objective. The second part of the graph is no longer useful because the components of this part of the graph were not in the assembly to fulfill functional objectives but to fulfill the needs of the removed component. Removing this part of the graph amounts to removing now useless parts of the assembly before trying to re-build the missing part with new components and connections.

Let $A = (G_A, FO_A)$ be an assembly and let $C \in Cmps_A$ be the component to remove. We define $H_{A,C}$ as the graph G_A from which we removed component C and all the edges (denoted by $Conns_C$) corresponding to primitive port connections between C and another component of G_A:

$$H_{A,C} = (Cmps_A \setminus \{C\}, Conns_A \setminus Conns_C)$$

We define $\mathcal{L}_{A,C}$ the live connected components of $H_{A,C}$ as the graph composed of all the connected components of $H_{A,C}$ that have at least a node which contains a functional objective.

We also define $\mathcal{D}_{A,C}$ the dead connected components of $H_{A,C}$ as the graph composed of all the connected components of $H_{A,C}$ that have no node which contains a functional objective.

---

[4] Recall that a functional objective is simply an operation defined in one of the provided interfaces.

[5] In this subsection of the paper, connected component refers to a subgraph that is connected, meaning that there exists a path between any of its two nodes.

Let us just notice that:

$$H_{A,C} = \mathcal{L}_{A,C} \cup \mathcal{D}_{A,C}$$

Figure 3 illustrates the definitions of $\mathcal{L}_{A,C}$ and $\mathcal{D}_{A,C}$. When a component is removed from the assembly, it is possible to remove all the components which do not participate any more to the completeness. Components from the dead connected components $\mathcal{D}_{A,C}$ can be removed from the assembly because they only participated to the coherence of the removed component.

Removing the dead components is a necessary step because keeping useless components add useless dependencies that make the resulting assembly considerably bigger thus complicating the building process, making the validity checks more difficult and making the assembly more subject to failures, less open for extensions, etc. Let us just also note that the components in $\mathcal{D}_{A,C}$ are dead components but that there still might be useless components in $\mathcal{L}_{A,C}$ (those we keep). We are thinking of future improvements on the detection of dead components that would better exploit the protocols.

3.3   Re-building the Removed Part from the Architecture

Once the dead components have been removed from the component assembly, the assembly contains all the components necessary to ensure completeness but one (the removed component) and its dependent components. Some of the dependencies of the remaining components are not yet satisfied. The issue is to find a component (like other systems do) or a series of assembled components that can fulfill the unsatisfied dependencies as the removed component did. We assume that it is quite unlikely that there exists a component that exactly matches the role the removed component had in the assembly. It is more likely (more flexible) that we have the possibility of replacing the removed component by a set of assembled components that, together, can replace the removed component.

In order to do so, we use the automatic building process presented in Section 3.1. The partial assembly in $\mathcal{L}_{A,C}$ is the starting point. It is considered as an intermediate result of the global building process. It is not complete yet: there still exist unsatisfied dependencies that were fulfilled by the removed component. The building process we described above is used to complete the architecture.

Evolution Scenario. On our *ATM* example, Figure 4 (a) represents the graph corresponding to the example of Figure 2. The *Client* node represents the *Client* component which contains a functional objective. The other nodes (*MemberBank*, *ATM* and *CentralBank*) represent components which do not contain any functional objective. Figure 4 (b) shows that the partial component assembly from $\mathcal{L}_{ATMexample,MemberBank}$ is not complete because the *ATM* component has become incoherent after the *MemberBank* component and the consequently dead components ($\mathcal{D}_{ATMexample,MemberBank} = \{CentralBank\}$) have been removed. To complete the assembly, new components must be added. Figure 4 (c) illustrates the result of this re-building process: The *IndependentBank* component

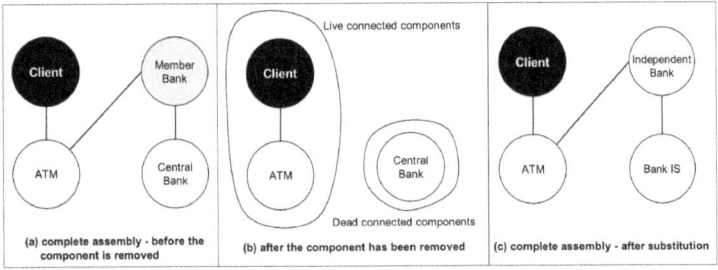

Fig. 4. Evolution scenario on the ATM example

is connected to the *BankIS* component and they both replace the components that had been removed to complete the *ATM* example assembly.

Figure 5 details the resulting architecture. In this example, the component to remove is the *MemberBank* component. When the *MemberBank* component is removed, completeness of the architecture is lost. Indeed, the *ATM* component is not locally coherent any more. Its *Money_Withdraw* composite port is not coherent because the primitive port *Money_Transaction* is not connected and the *Money_Dialogue* primitive port is connected. The *CentralBank* component constitutes the $\mathcal{D}_{ATMexample,MemberBank}$ graph and can also be removed. Completeness is researched by selecting and connecting new components. In this example, an *IndependentBank* component is connected to the *ATM* component through its *Money_Transaction* primitive port. At this step, the assembly is not yet complete because all the components are not yet coherent. Indeed, the *IndependentBank* component is not coherent because its *Manage_withdraw* composite port is not coherent. Another component is thus added to the assembly: the *BankIS* component is connected to the *IndependentBank* component through its *Request_Data* primitive port. At that point, the assembly is complete. One can consider that the removed component has been replaced by an assembly composed of the *IndependentBank* and the *BankIS* components[6].

3.4   Implementation and Experimentation

The two processes presented here (automatic component assembly building and dynamic substitution after a component removal) have both been implemented as an extension of the open-source Julia implementation[7] of the Fractal component model [3]. Our dynamic reconfiguration approach has been tested in the same environment we used to test the building process. To do so, we randomly generated the interfaces and ports of generated components, randomly choose functional objectives and then run the building process in order to build full complete assemblies [6]. For example, experiments were run with a library of 38

---

[6] In the example, it is a coincidence that the total number of removed components equals the number of components that are used to complete the assembly.

[7] http://www.objectweb.org

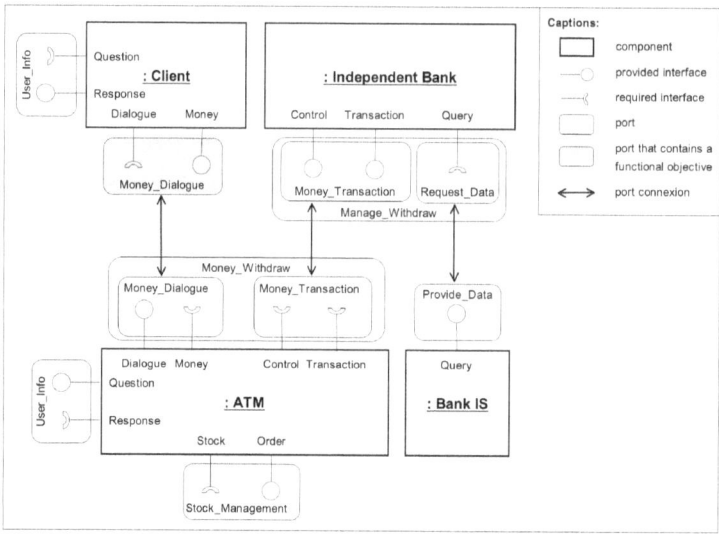

Fig. 5. Dynamic reconfiguration of the assembly

generated components. The search space contained more than 325 000 complete assemblies (complete search stopped after 15 hours). Among those complete assemblies, the largest ones have 48 connections and the smallest ones 18 connections. As a comparison, our optimized building algorithm finds the only minimal architecture composed of 7 connections in less than a second. To test our solution for evolution, a randomly chosen component was removed from a complete assembly and the substitution process was then triggered considering that the removed component was not available anymore. Those experiments showed that our solution provides alternative substitution possibilities (compared to existing one-to-one substitution mechanisms) thus is more flexible because it does not depend on the presence of a component that is able to exactly match the role of the removed one. In these experiments, in most cases, the result of substitution was a one-to-many substitution. We also noticed that the complexity of the mechanism exposed here is not higher than the complexity of the complete building process (which was efficient thanks to optimization strategies and heuristics).

4   Conclusion

The contribution of this paper is double. Firstly, we present an innovative solution for the dynamic replacement of a component from an assembly. This solution is not a component-to-component substitution but allows replacing a single component by a whole set of linked components while guaranteeing there is no functional regression. Secondly, we propose a property to identify useless components that can be removed. The advantage of this approach is that it can increase the number of reconfiguration possibilities by being less constraining. We implemented our solution as an extension of an existing open source implementation of the Fractal component model and successfully tested it on generated components.

The main limitations of this work is that we have not been able to try it on real components[8] but our experimentation framework allowed us to validate our ideas. Another limitation to our approach is that ports need to be added to the components in order to use them in our mechanisms. We believe this limitation is not very strong because ports can be provided by the component designer as an abstract view of the behavioral roles of the components that document the components, generated from protocols (in a design for reuse process) or abstracted from running assemblies that provide execution contexts for the components (in a design by reuse approach).

References

1. Szyperski, C.: Component Software: Beyond Object-Oriented Programming. Addison-Wesley Longman Publishing Co., Inc., Boston, MA (2002)
2. Plásil, F., Balek, D., Janecek, R.: SOFA/DCUP: Architecture for component trading and dynamic updating. In: Proc. of the Int. Conf. on Configurable Distributed Systems, Washington, DC, pp. 43–52. IEEE Computer Society Press, Los Alamitos (1998)
3. Bruneton, E., Coupaye, T., Stefani, J.: Fractal specification - v 2.0.3 (2004), http://fractal.objectweb.org/specification/index.html
4. George, B., Fleurquin, R., Sadou, S.: A substitution model for software components. In: QaOOSE'06. Proc. of the 2006 ECOOP Workshop on Quantitative Approaches on Object-Oriented Software Engineering, Nantes, France (2006)
5. Bures, T., Hnetynka, P., Plásil, F.: Sofa 2.0: Balancing advanced features in a hierarchical component model. In: SERA, pp. 40–48. IEEE Computer Society Press, Los Alamitos (2006)
6. Desnos, N., Vauttier, S., Urtado, C., Huchard, M.: Automating the building of software component architectures. In: Gruhn, V., Oquendo, F. (eds.) EWSA 2006. LNCS, vol. 4344, pp. 228–235. Springer, Heidelberg (2006)
7. Brown, A.W., Wallnau, K.C.: The current state of CBSE. IEEE Software 15(5), 37–46 (1998)
8. Crnkovic, I.: Component-based software engineering—new challenges in software development. Software Focus (2001)
9. Dijkman, R.M., Almeida, J.P.A., Quartel, D.A.: Verifying the correctness of component-based applications that support business processes. In: Crnkovic, I., Schmidt, H., Stafford, J., Wallnau, K. (eds.) Proc. of the 6th Workshop on CBSE: Automated Reasoning and Prediction, Portland, Oregon, pp. 43–48 (2003)
10. Medvidovic, N., Taylor, R.N.: A classification and comparison framework for software architecture description languages. IEEE Trans. Softw. Eng. 26(1), 70–93 (2000)

---

[8] It is not yet possible to find real component bases that are already documented with protocols. We believe that research work aiming at facilitating component reuse will encourage the building of such component repositories and provide us better experimentation frameworks in the future.

11. Inverardi, P., Wolf, A.L., Yankelevich, D.: Static checking of system behaviors using derived component assumptions. ACM Trans. Softw. Eng. Methodol. 9(3), 239–272 (2000)
12. de Alfaro, L., Henzinger, T.A.: Interface automata. In: Proc. of the 8*th* European software engineering conference, pp. 109–120. ACM Press, New York (2001)
13. Mach, M., Plášil, F., Kofron, J.: Behavior protocols verification: Fighting state explosion. International Journal of Computer and Information Science (2005)
14. Wallnau, K.C.: Volume III: A technology for predictable assembly from certifiable components (pacc). Technical Report CMU/SEI-2003-TR-009, Carnegie Mellon University, Pittsburgh, OH, USA (2003)
15. Adamek, J., Plášil, F.: Partial bindings of components - any harm? In: APSEC '04. Proc. of the 11th Asia-Pacific Software Engineering Conference, Washington, DC, pp. 632–639. IEEE Computer Society Press, Los Alamitos (2004)
16. Reussner, R.H., Poernomo, I.H., Schmidt, H.W.: Reasoning on software architectures with contractually specified components. In: Cechich, A., Piattini, M., Vallecillo, A. (eds.) Component-Based Software Quality. LNCS, vol. 2693, pp. 287–325. Springer, Heidelberg (2003)
17. Magee, J., Kramer, J.: Dynamic structure in software architectures. In: SIGSOFT '96. Proc. of the 4th ACM SIGSOFT symposium on Foundations of software engineering, pp. 3–14. ACM Press, New York (1996)
18. Aldrich, J., Chambers, C., Notkin, D.: ArchJava: connecting software architecture to implementation. In: Proc. of ICSE, Orlando, FL, pp. 187–197. ACM Press, New York (2002)
19. Inverardi, P., Wolf, A.L.: Formal specification and analysis of software architectures using the chemical abstract machine model. IEEE Trans. Softw. Eng. 21(4), 373–386 (1995)
20. Allen, R.J.: A formal approach to software architecture. PhD thesis, Carnegie Mellon, School of Computer Science, Issued as CMU Technical Report CMU-CS-97-144 (1997)
21. Matevska-Meyer, J., Hasselbring, W., Reussner, R.H.: A software architecture description supporting component deployment and system runtime reconfiguration. In: WCOP '04. Proc. of the 9*th* Int. Workshop on Component-Oriented Programming, Oslo, Norway (2004)
22. Oreizy, P., Medvidovic, N., Taylor, R.N.: Architecture-based runtime software evolution. In: Intl. Conf. on Software Engineering, Kyoto, Japan (1998)
23. Brada, P.: Component change and version identification in SOFA. In: Bartosek, M., Tel, G., Pavelka, J. (eds.) SOFSEM 1999. LNCS, vol. 1725, pp. 360–368. Springer, Heidelberg (1999)
24. Desnos, N., Urtado, C., Vauttier, S., Huchard, M.: Helping the architect build component-based architectures. In: Rousseau, R., Urtado, C., Vauttier, S. (eds.) LMO2006. Proc. of the 12*th* french speaking conference on Languages and Models with Objets, Nîmes, France, Hermès, pp. 37–52 (in french) (2006)
25. OMG: Unified modeling language: Superstructure, version 2.0 (2002), http://www.omg.org/uml
26. Lobo, A.E., de C. Guerra, P.A., Filho, F.C., Rubira, C.M.F.: A systematic approach for the evolution of reusable software components. In: Black, A.P. (ed.) ECOOP 2005. LNCS, vol. 3586, Springer, Heidelberg (2005)
27. Jones, C.: Systematic Software Development using VDM, 2nd edn. Prentice-Hall, Englewood Cliffs (1990)
28. Abrial, J.R.: The B-Book, Assigning programs to meanings. Cambridge University Press, Cambridge (1996)

Dynamic Adaptation of Aspect-Oriented Components

Cristóbal Costa[1], Jennifer Pérez[2], and José Ángel Carsí[3]

[1,3] Department of Information Systems and Computation
Polytechnic University of Valencia, Camino de Vera s/n, 46022 Valencia, Spain
[2] Department of Organization and Information Structure
Polytechnic University of Madrid, Ctra. Valencia, km7, 28051 Madrid, Spain
ccosta@dsic.upv.es, jeperez@eui.upm.es, pcarsi@dsic.upv.es

Abstract. Current works address self-adaptability of software architectures to build more autonomous and flexible systems. However, most of these works only perform adaptations at configuration-level: a component is adapted by being replaced with a new one. The state of the replaced component is lost and related components can undergo undesirable changes. This paper presents a generic solution to design components that are capable of supporting runtime adaptation, taking into account that *component type* changes must be propagated to its instances. The adaptation is performed in a decentralized and autonomous way, in order to cope with the increasing need for building heterogeneous and autonomous systems. As a result, each component type manages its instances and each instance applies autonomously the changes. Moreover, our proposal uses aspect-oriented components to benefit from their reuse and maintenance, and it is based on *MOF* and *Reflection* concepts to benefit from the high abstraction level they provide.

Keywords: runtime adaptation, dynamic evolution, component adaptability, reflection, CBSD, software architectures, AOSD.

1 Introduction

Complex software systems frequently undergo changes during their lifetime. This is due to the fact that they are exposed to many sources of variability and also have a dynamic nature. It is very common for unforeseen bugs to appear during system execution, and they will have to be corrected at run-time. In order to address this software adaptability, most approaches modify the subsystem that must be updated offline, and once the modification has been completed, they restart the entire system to reflect the new changes. However, this solution has several disadvantages: (i) the state of the system that is running is lost, unless it has been previously saved; (ii) the shutdown and restart processes of the system could increase the performance cost; (iii) a lot of complex systems cannot stop their activity (such as servers or real-time systems). As a result, a solution that overcomes these disadvantages must be provided.

This work focuses specifically on two approaches of software development that improve the reuse, maintenance and adaptability of software. They are the Component-Based Software Development (CBSD) approach [10, 33] and the

H.W. Schmidt et al. (Eds.): CBSE 2007, LNCS 4608, pp. 49–65, 2007.

Aspect-Oriented Software Development (AOSD) approach [15, 16]. CBSD reduces the complexity of software development and improves its maintenance by increasing software reuse and independence. CBSD decomposes the system into reusable and independent entities called components. By extension, these advantages are provided by software architectures [26, 30] since architectural models are constructed in terms of components and their interactions.

Both software architectures and AOSD facilitate software adaptation. On the one hand, software architectures allow us to focus on changes at the component level instead of changes at the implementation level. Software architecture adaptability is managed in terms of the creation and destruction of component instances and their links. This kind of adaptation is called *Dynamic Reconfiguration* or *Structural Dynamism* [8], which has been explored by a lot of research works [3]. However, most of these works only address dynamic adaptation at the architectural level. The internal adaptation of running components is not considered: a component is adapted offline and then the old component (which is running) is replaced with the adapted one. In several cases, runtime component replacement is not enough if the preservation of the component state is mandatory; for instance, when a component needs to be extended with new properties (such as security, persistence, etc.) and its functional state and properties are not modified. In order to support self-adaptability of software architectures, a solution that allows us to both internally update a component at runtime and to preserve the old state not subject to change must be provided.

On the other hand, Aspect-Oriented Models propose the separation of the crosscutting concerns of software systems into separate entities called *aspects*. This separation avoids the tangled concerns of software and allows the reuse of the same aspect in different entities of the software system (objects, components, modules, etc.). This separation of concerns also improves the isolated maintenance of the different concerns of the software systems. Aspect-Oriented Software Development (AOSD) [15] extends the advantages that aspects provide to every stage of the software life cycle. For this reason, several proposals for the integration of the aspects in software architectures have emerged [5, 6]. AOSD allows us to manage changes from the different concerns in an independent way. This facilitates evolution and provides flexibility to adapt components by adding or removing aspects to software architectures. In addition, interaction policies between different concerns of software architectures can be easily changed by adding or removing aspect synchronizations.

This paper proposes a solution to support the dynamic component adaptation of aspect-oriented software architectures. Specifically, the solution is based on the PRISMA approach, which combines AOSD with software architectures. The dynamic adaptation proposal that is presented in this paper provides mechanisms for dynamically changing the internal structure of PRISMA components. This internal change preserves the component state and minimizes the impact of the change on other components that are connected to the updated component. In addition, this proposal takes into account that *component type* changes must be propagated to each one of its running instances, so the needed mechanisms are also described.

This paper is structured as follows. The PRISMA approach is introduced in section 2. Section 3 presents the two concepts on which our proposal is based: *MOF* and *Computational Reflection*. In section 4, our proposal to support dynamic adaptation of *component types* is presented in detail. Related works that address runtime component adaptation are discussed in section 5. Finally, conclusions and further works are presented in section 6.

2 PRISMA

PRISMA is an approach to develop technology-independent, aspect-oriented software architectures [22]. It integrates software architecture and AOSD in order to take advantage of the two approaches. The PRISMA approach is based on its model [24] and its formal Aspect-Oriented Architecture Description Language (AOADL) [23].

In order to define our software adaptation proposal, we chose PRISMA from the different approaches that combine AOSD and software architectures because of the advantages that it offers. Its main advantages are the following: (1) components and aspects are independent of each other, so they provide good properties for dynamic evolution; (2) the PRISMA model is completely formalised and its AOADL is a formal language, so the evolution requirements of our proposal can be easily formalized; (3) PRISMA software architectures can be automatically compiled for a technological platform and a programming language using code generation techniques; and (4) a PRISMA tool has been developed to cope with the challenge of developing aspect-oriented software architectures following the Model-Driven Development (MDD) paradigm [12, 19].

The PRISMA model introduces aspects as first-order citizens of software architectures. As a result, PRISMA specifies different crosscutting concerns (distribution, safety, context-awareness, coordination, etc.) of the software architecture using aspects. From the aspect-oriented point of view, PRISMA is a symmetrical model [13] that does not distinguish a kernel or core entity to encapsulate functionality; functionality is also defined as an aspect. A concern can be specified by several aspects of a software architecture, whereas a PRISMA aspect represents a concern that crosscuts the software architecture. This crosscutting is due to the fact that the same aspect can be imported by more than one architectural element (i.e. a component or a connector) of a software architecture. In this sense, aspects crosscut those elements of the architecture that import their behaviour (see Figure 1).

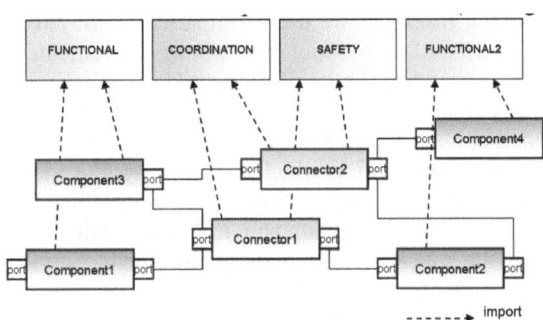

Fig. 1. Crosscutting-concerns in PRISMA architectures

The PRISMA approach takes advantage of the notion of aspect from the beginning of the system definition. The change of a property only requires the change of the aspect that defines it, and then, each architectural element that imports the changed aspect is also updated. A PRISMA architectural element can be seen from two different views: internal and external. In the external view, architectural elements encapsulate their functionality as black boxes and publish a set of services that they offer to other architectural elements (see Figure 2.A). These services are grouped into interfaces to be published through the ports of architectural elements. As a result, ports are the interaction points of architectural elements.

The internal view shows an architectural element as a prism (white box view). Each side of the prism is an aspect that the architectural element imports. In this way, architectural elements are represented as a set of aspects (see Figure 2.B) and their synchronization relationships,which are called weavings. A weaving indicates that the execution of an aspect service can trigger the execution of services in other aspects. The weaving process of an architectural element is composed of a set of weavings.

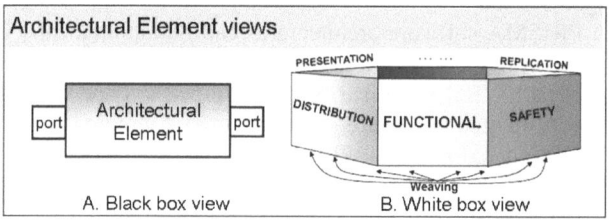

Fig. 2. Views of an architectural element

In PRISMA, in order to preserve the independence of the aspect specification from other aspects and weavings, weavings are specified outside aspects and inside architectural elements. Weavings weave the different aspects that form an architectural element. As a result, aspects are reusable and independent of the context of application, which facilitates their maintenance.

3   MOF+Computational Reflection

In order to illustrate our proposal, we use a simple case study throughout the paper. This case study consists of a robotic arm whose movements are controlled by different joints: Base, Shoulder, Elbow, Wrist and Gripper. These joints are modeled as instances of a Joint *component type*. The specific initialization values of each Joint instance are provided at its instantiation. The behaviour of the Joint is defined by two aspects: (i) a functional aspect, Fun, which defines how the movements are sent to each hardware robotic joint, and (ii) a safety aspect, Saf, which checks that the Joint movements are between the maximum and minimum values that are allowed to ensure the safety of the robotic arm and its environment. Services are exported to other components through the port OperPort.

One of the most important non-functional requirements of the Joint component is that its instances are going to be executed for long periods of time in an high availability software system. Thus, if an update is needed, it will have to be applied at runtime without disturbing the system execution. For this reason, the Joint component provides an evolution infrastructure to support its runtime adaptation without forcing the system to be restarted. In our case study new requirements emerged after the execution of the Joint component, specifically, the inclusion of an emergency service to instantly stop all the robotic movements. This requirement involves the adaptation of the safety aspect. A new *component type*, called Updater, was developed to replace the old safety aspect (Saf) by a new one (Saf2) at runtime.

The evolution infrastructure proposed in this work is based on several key concepts. First, to be able to evolve components, we must distinguish between *component instances* and *component types*, since they are placed at different abstraction levels. The OMG Meta-Object Facility (MOF) specification [20] allows us to clearly distinguish between *types* and *instances* in a proper and elegant way. MOF defines a three-level "architecture" that is focused on Model-Driven Development [19]. Its main purpose is the management of model descriptions at different levels of abstraction and their static modification. The upper layer (M3) is the most abstract one (see M3 layer, Figure 3). This layer defines the abstract language used to describe the entities of the lower layer (metamodels). The MOF specification proposes the *MOF Model* as the abstract language for defining all kind of metamodels, such as UML or PRISMA.

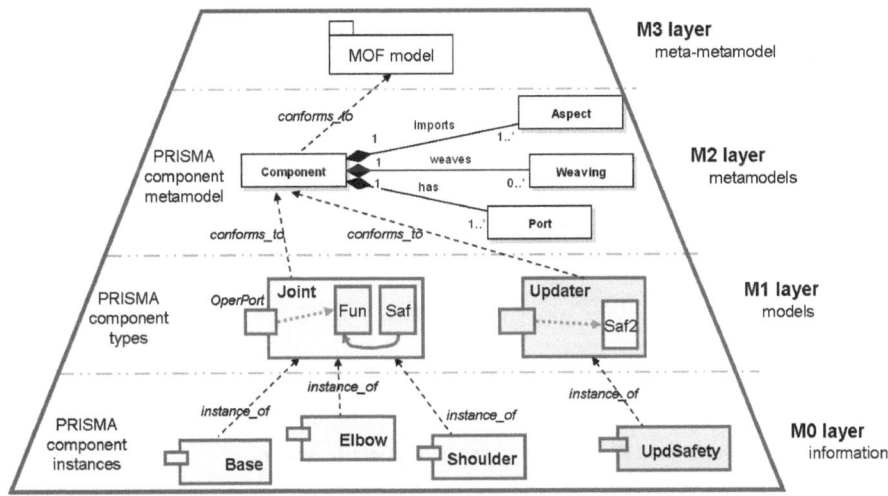

Fig. 3. Meta-Object Facility (MOF) layers and PRISMA Components

The metamodel layer (M2) defines the structure and semantics of the models defined at the lower layer. The PRISMA metamodel is defined at this level: PRISMA components are an aggregation of Aspects, Ports, and Weavings (see M2 layer, Figure 3). Component behaviour is defined by importing aspects and by synchronizying them through the use of weavings. Published services are defined through the use of ports. The M1 layer comprises the models that describe data. These models are described using the primitives and relationships described in the metamodel layer (M2). PRISMA *component types* (i.e.: Joint and Updater) are placed in the M1 layer (see M1 layer,

Figure 3). For instance, the Joint component imports two aspects: a Functional aspect and a Safety aspect (see Fun and Saf aspects, M1 layer, Figure 3), which are synchronized through a weaving. In addition, services from the Functional aspect are provided to other components through a port. Due to the semantics of PRISMA metamodel defined at M2 layer, there is a fourth level, the M0 layer, where PRISMA *component instances* (i.e.: Base, Elbow, UpdSafety, etc.) are placed (see M0 layer, Figure 3). These instances behave as described in the *component type*.

However, the MOF specification was designed to specify and manage technology-neutral metamodels from a static point of view. MOF does not describe how to address the dynamic adaptation of its elements at run-time. For this reason, the *Computational Reflection* concept [17, 31] is used to provide dynamic adaptation to models (in our case, *component types*). *Computational Reflection* is the capability of a software system to reason about itself and act upon itself. In order to do so, a system must have a representation of itself that is editable and that is *causally connected* to itself. Thus, the changes that are made in this representation (which is managed as data) will be *reflected* on the system, and vice versa. Therefore, a system has two different views of itself: the *base-view* and the *meta-view* (see Figure 4.A). The *base-view* "executes" the system business logic behaviour and modifies a set of values that define the process state. The *meta-view* defines how the system behaves; it is a "description" of the system. This view allows the system to change its behaviour by modifying its representation. The process of obtaining an editable representation of the system (the *meta-view*) is called *reification*, and the opposite process is called *reflection* (see Figure 4.A). The main advantage of *computational reflection* is the fact that it describes system self-adaptation in a simple and natural way.

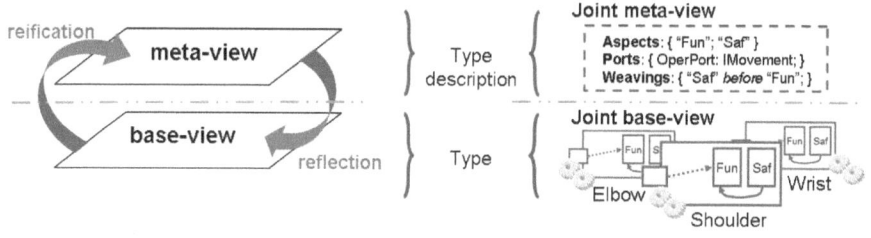

A. Computational Reflection   B. Dual view of the *Joint* component

Fig. 4. Dual views of a reflective system

The PRISMA metamodel describes the component structure and behaviour by means of aspects, weavings, and ports (see M2 layer, Figure 3). For this reason, the *meta-view* of a PRISMA *component type* is an editable data structure (composed of aspects, ports, and weavings) that "describes" the *component type* behaviour. For instance, the *meta-view* of the Joint *component type* describes a component that is made of: (i) the aspects Fun and Saf, (ii) a port OperPort, and (iii) a weaving between the aspects Saf and Fun (see Type description, Figure 4.B). The *base-view* of a PRISMA *component type* is the "execution" of these aspects, ports, and weavings "described" in the *meta-view*. For instance, the *base-view* of the Joint *component type* is the set of all its instances: Base, Elbow, Shoulder, etc. (see Type, Figure 4.B)

The abstraction layers provided by MOF and the capability to describe self-adaptation provided by Computational Reflection allow us to define the necessary infrastructure to dynamically adapt the internal component structure. In this work, we focus only on *component types* (M1 layer) and *component instances* (M0 layer). Each *component type* has a dual view: the *base-view* and the *meta-view*. However, each view is in a different MOF layer (see Figure 5) as described below.

Each *component instance* (i.e.: Elbow, Wrist, …) is a running process which has its own state and behaves as the *component type* (i.e.: Joint) specifies. Thus, the behaviour of the instance is "provided" by the *component type base-view* (i.e. the *running* type, see *base-view$_1$* at M0, Figure 5 below). This behaviour is "described" by the *component type meta-view* at the upper layer (see the *meta-view$_1$* at the M1 layer, Figure 5).

Moreover, the *component type* can be viewed as a running process that also has state and behaviour: (i) the state of the *component type* is its *meta-view* (an editable representation of itself), and (ii) the *component type* behaviour is provided by the *base-view* of the PRISMA Component (see the *base-view$_2$* at the M1 layer, Figure 5). The PRISMA Component *base-view* "provides" the set of evolution services to modify the state of a *component type* (which is the *component type* representation). These evolution services are "described" in the PRISMA Component *meta-view* at the M2 layer (see *meta-view$_2$* at M2, Figure 5).

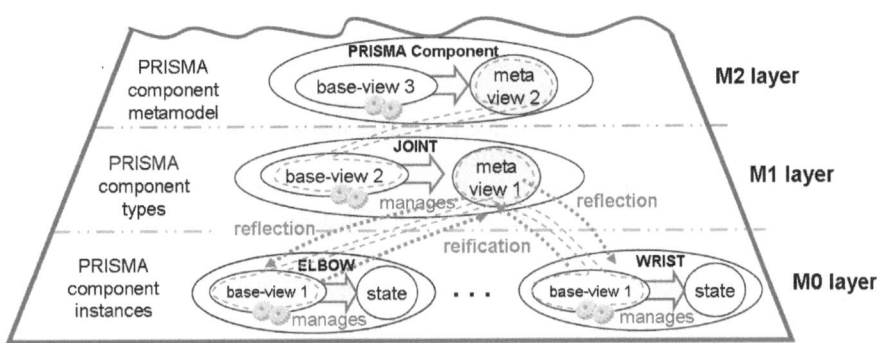

Fig. 5. Dual view of reflective component types

The evolution services are directly provided and executed by each *component type* (in our example, the Joint component), because the PRISMA Component *base-view* is part of each *component type* (see Joint *base-view$_2$*, at the M1 layer, Figure 5). As an evolution service changes the *component type* internal representation (the *meta-view*), those changes are also *reflected* in the *component type base-view*. This means that each *component instance* would have its structure and behaviour updated according to changes made on the *component type meta-view*. For instance, as a consequence of the reflection relationship (see reflection, Figure 5), the execution of the evolution service addAspect("Saf2") on the Joint *component type meta-view* will trigger the addition of the aspect Saf2 on each instance of Joint (i.e.: Base, Shoulder, etc.).

The model described here allows the description of the dynamic adaptation process from a high abstraction level. However, there are some issues in the reification and reflection processes that have to be addressed in each specific implementation. The reification process must take into account how to get the type and its internal structure from a running *component instance*. The reflection process must take into account: (i) how to spread the changes made to a *component type meta-view* to its *component instances*, and (ii) how to change the internal structure of each *component instance* without affecting those parts of the structure that have not been modified. For this reason, in the next section we describe the mechanisms that our evolution infrastructure provides to address these issues.

4   Dynamic Adaptation of Component Types

Once the concepts of *Computational Reflection* and *MOF* have been introduced, we present in detail our dynamic adaptation proposal for aspect-oriented components. The dynamic adaptation of the internal structure of components is triggered when any evolution service provided by a *component type* is invoked. Then, the evolution service modifies the *component type* description (the *component type meta-view*), and the reflection relationship performs the internal adaptation of its instances.

4.1   Evolution of Component Types

Heterogeneous and autonomous systems require that each one of their components implements its own adaptation mechanisms in a decentralized way. For this reason, the main objective of our proposal is to provide internal component adaptation at runtime in a decentralized and autonomous way. Decentralized adaptation is achieved because there is no a centralized evolution manager that maintains and evolves *all* the *component types* of a software architecture. Each *type* is the only entity that is responsible for its instances and is the only one capable of evolving them. Autonomous adaptation is provided in the sense that *instances* provide themselves with the infrastructure necessary to be dynamically evolved in a safe way. Each *instance* mantains its own state and is the only one capable of deciding the best moment to apply the adaptations.

4.1.1   Evolution Services Provided by Component Types

The evolution services that a *component type* provides depend on its internal implementation technology (in an imperative style, or in any declarative or formal language). However, it is possible to identify those parts of the component that are independent of technology. The main technology-independent parts of a component are: (i) behaviour and state; (ii) ports, and (iii) internal interactions between the different processes of the component. In PRISMA, behaviour and state are provided by aspect composition, ports are provided by component ports, and internal interactions are provided by weavings (they synchronize the execution of aspects). Thus, the evolution services that a *component type* should provide are those that modify the main parts of a component. We can distinguish two kinds of evolution services: Type Evolution Services and Introspection Services.

Type Evolution Services are those related to type modification, such as additions and removals of component parts. In PRISMA, some of the Type Evolution Services provided are: `AddAspect()`, `RemoveAspect()`, `AddPort()`, `RemovePort()`, `AddWeaving()`, and `RemoveWeaving()`.

Introspection Services are those evolution services that allow the structure of a component to be known. In PRISMA, some of the Introspection Services provided are: `GetAspects()`, `GetWeavings()`, and `GetPorts()`.

4.1.2 Component Type Reflective Structure

The evolution process can be triggered by the business logic or by a user of the system. Both the business logic of the system and the user are represented in the architecture by means of components. Thus, the need for evolving a specific component emerges from another component that dynamically invokes the evolution services of the component to be updated. In our case study, the UpdSafety instance will invoke the evolution services of the Joint type in order to introduce the new safety requirements of the system.

However, in order to invoke the evolution services, there must be a link from the instance layer (M0) to the model layer (M1), that is, the link between the UpdSafety *base-view* and the Joint *meta-view* (see base and meta views in Figure 5). We call it *reification link* because (i) it is an upward link between layers and (ii) it allows instances to invoke type modification services, which are only available at an upper layer. The *reification link* should be provided by any ADL on which dynamic evolution of *component types* must be supported. There are several ways that a *reification link* could be syntactically expressed. In PRISMA, it is described by

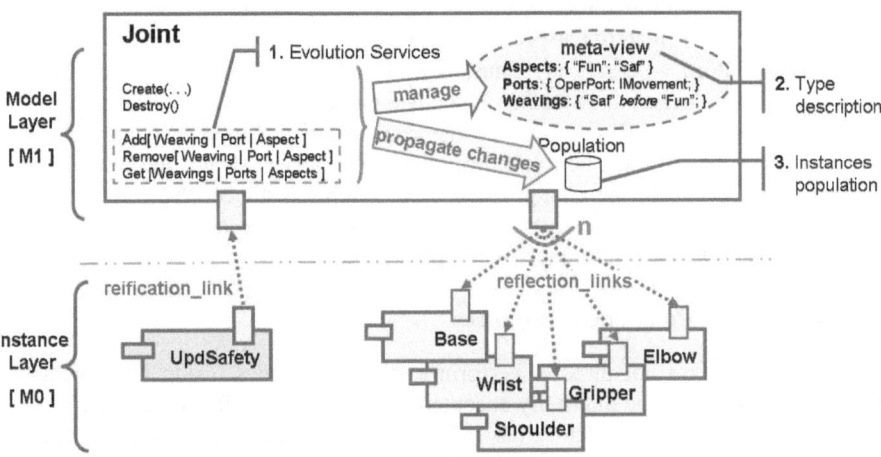

Fig. 6. Reflective infrastructure for component adaptation

specifying the name of the *component type* that has to be evolved, followed by the dot operator "." and the evolution service to be invoked. For instance, the UpdSafety instance adds the aspect "Saf2" to the Joint component this way:

`Joint.AddAspect("Saf2")`

"Joint" is the type to be evolved, and "AddAspect" is the evolution service to be executed. The *reification link* is syntactically expressed by means of the "." operator. We have chosen this syntax because it is self-descriptive: *component types* provide their own adaptation services.

A *component type* is an instance factory: it is responsible for the creation and the destruction of its instances. For this reason, a *component type* manages the population of its instances, that is, a reference to each instance that is running (see note 3, Figure 6). The instance population is usually mantained by the execution platform (i.e. the garbage collector in Java or .NET). However, access to this information is necessary to be able to propagate changes later. In our case study, the population of the Joint component is composed of the instances that have been created in the initial configuration: Base, Elbow, Shoulder, etc.

In addition, a *component type* provides its own evolution services to change itself (see note 1, Figure 6). These services modify (or get information from) the *meta-view* of the *component type* (see note 2, Figure 6). Each *component type* is responsible for keeping the reification of its *meta-view* updated while it is running. Depending on the implementation, the *meta-view* can be represented in an ADL or directly in platform-dependent code (like C#). In our prototype, the reified structure is represented in C# to make its programmed manipulation easy.

Thus, when the UpdSafety instance invokes the AddAspect("Saf2") evolution service (by using a reification link, see Figure 6), the Joint *meta-view* is updated. As a consequence of modifying the *meta-view*, changes are reflected, that is, they are made available to the running system. This is done in two steps. The first step is to store the changes made to the *meta-view* (i.e. the Joint representation) in order to make it persistent, by generating the resulting ADL or platform-dependent code. The immediate effect is that the aspect list {"Fun"; "Saf"} from the *meta-view* is updated by {"Fun"; "Saf2"}. Thus, new instances of Joint will be created (by calling Joint.Create(...)) using the updated type.

The following step is to propagate the changes to the type instances. As with reification links, there must be a link from the model layer (M1) to the instance layer (M0) in order to *reflect* the changes into each running instance. We call these links *reflection links* (see the reflection links in Figure 6). A *reflection link* is created for each *component instance* reference (the population).

4.2 Evolution of Component Instances

Component types do not directly perform evolution changes inside their instances. These changes have to be internally executed by each *instance* for two reasons.

On the one hand, each instance has to decide when and how to execute its changes in order to perform the modification in a safe way. This safe modification is necessary: (i) to ensure that those parts that have not undergone changes are not affected by the modification process; (ii) to guarantee that the modification is executed once the running transactions have finished and all internal processes reach a safe state. For this reason, each component instance (i.e. Base, Elbow, Shoulder, etc.) is provided with an *Evolution Planner* aspect, whose goal is to supervise the update process of the *component instance* to which it belongs.

On the other hand, the adaptation process only makes sense at the instance-level, because state-preserving runtime adaptations are very technology-dependent operations (i.e. stopping threads, modifying memory areas, etc.). For this reason, each instance is composed of two technology-dependent aspects: the *Actuator*, which is the aspect that actually performs the changes on the internal component instance structure, and the *Sensor*, which gives information about what is going on in the *component instance*.

4.2.1 The Evolution Planner

The key aspect to achieving the dynamic adaptation of the internal structure of component instances is to maximize the independence among the internal parts of a component which may undergo changes. In this way, replacing a component internal part has only a minimal impact on the other running parts. Those parts that are dependent to some degree on the part being changed will only need to stop temporarily while changes are being made.

An evolution dependency is defined as a binary relation over the set of internal parts (P) of a component. An internal part $x \in P$ has an evolution dependency with other internal part $y \in P$, defined as $Ev_{DEP}(x,y)$, if any change in x causes a change in y. The total amount of possible evolution dependencies over the set of internal parts P is defined by the mathematical permutation with repetition of P: $|P|^2$. Since a PRISMA component is composed of three kinds of parts (P_{PRISMA} = {*ports, weavings, aspects*}), the set of potential evolution dependencies that a PRISMA component can have is nine (i.e.: Ev_{DEP}={ (port,aspect), (port,weaving), (port,port), ...}). However, due to the high degree of PRISMA reusability, there are actually two evolution dependencies between the internal parts: $Ev_{DEP}(aspect,port)$ and $Ev_{DEP}(aspect, weaving)$. These evolution dependencies are taken into account by the Evolution Planner.

The Evolution Planner (see note 3, Figure 7) is an aspect that has the knowledge about how to adapt the internal structure of a *component instance* in a safe way. For this reason, it is aware of what kind of evolution dependency relationships between the component internal parts can occur when applying a dynamic change. The action to perform is different depending on the type of change to be made: deletions, modifications or additions. In aspect deletions, related ports and weavings need also to be deleted. In aspect replacements or modifications, related ports and weavings need only to be deleted if the dependency points between the aspect and the ports and weavings are modified. In other words: (i) a port will be removed if the interface it publishes is removed from the aspect being changed, and (ii) a weaving will be

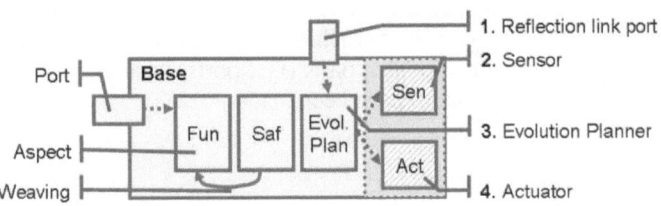

Fig. 7. Internal structure of a component instance

removed if the method it intercepts/triggers is modified in the aspect being changed. Finally, aspects, weaving and port additions can be made without compromising other running component parts or their communications because there is still no relationship among them.

The Evolution Planner *reflects* the changes that are made to the *component type meta-view* to the instance that the Evolution Planner belongs to. For this reason, the Evolution Planner aspect provides the same evolution services as the *component type*, although these services are only applied at instance-level. The adaptation changes to be applied are received through the *reflection links* (see note 1, Figure 7). These changes are the evolution services that the UpdSafety instance has applied on the Joint component *meta-view* and that have been propagated to the Base Evolution Planner through a *reflection link*:

```
RemoveAspect("Saf"); AddAspect("Saf2"); AddWeaving(...)
```

The Evolution Planner will apply these changes by coordinating the actions to be performed by the Actuator and Sensor aspects. This coordination is done in accordance with the correct adaptation protocols that it knows.

4.2.2 Actuator and Sensor

The *Actuator* (see note 4, Figure 7) is the aspect that performs the changes on the running instance: by generating and linking code, by creating dynamic elements, by invoking low-level adaptation mechanisms, etc. It provides additional services to prepare component elements so that changes can be safely made. These services are: `StopAspect()`, `StopPort()`, `StopWeaving()`, `StartAspect()`, `StartPort()`, and `StartWeaving()`. These services are necessary in case an evolution dependency is present, in order to avoid interactions between the part being changed and the dependent parts. The *Sensor* (see note 2, Figure 7) provides services to supervise what is going on: when an aspect has actually been added to the running component instance; when a component part (i.e.: port, aspect, weaving) has been started/stopped; etc. For these purposes, the Sensor provides additional services to get the running state of each element: `GetAspectState()`, `GetWeavingState()`, and `GetPortState()`. Both *Sensor* and *Actuator* are technology-dependent aspects because they perform tasks that rely on how component instances are implemented. The main advantage is that they allow us to abstract from platform-specific details.

The main services provided by the Actuator and the Sensor have been developed on .NET technology [25]. A PRISMA component has been developed as a collection of different objects (aspects, ports and weavings) that: (i) can be dynamically added or removed; (ii) are highly independent on each other; (iii) interact with each other by using asynchronous mechanisms. Asynchronous mechanisms are very important because they allow internal component parts (i.e.: ports, weavings and aspects) to be stopped and restarted after changes have been made.

5   Related Works

In the last few years, there has been greater interest in evolution research in order to reduce the time and the cost of the maintenance process and to provide a solution for dynamic evolution. Thus, many approaches that provide mechanisms to support runtime adaptability have been proposed. Due to space limitations in this paper, we focus on those works related to AOSD and software architectures.

Adaptability works that are proposed by the Aspect-Oriented community usually provide mechanisms to dynamically weave aspects to running *base code*[1]. Some approaches are designed to support AOP for Object-Oriented Programming. These approaches are mainly developed in Java and .NET and are platform-dependent. SetPoint [2] allows for the dynamic addition and removal of aspects. Its weaving is based on the evaluation of logical predicates in which the base code is marked with meta-information that permits the evaluation of such predicates. Rapier-Loom.NET [29] and Eos [28] both allow for the dynamic addition and removal of aspects, but weaving definitions are defined inside aspects, thereby losing their reusability. The work of Yang et al. [34] allows the definition of adaptation rules (i.e. weavings) separately from the code, and the dynamic addition and removal of new code (i.e. aspects) through the evaluation of such rules. However, these approaches (i) weave aspects at the instance-level instead of at the type-level, and (ii) cannot change the base code, they can only extend the base code with new behaviour.

Although there are also several software architecture works that address adaptability at runtime, they are mainly focused on dynamic reconfiguration [3, 7]. Dashofy et al. [9] describe an infrastructure to build self-healing, architecture-based software systems. Their approach consists of dynamically generating a repair plan in order to repair the system. This repair plan is executed by a global Architecture Evolution Manager (AEM). The AEM invokes the needed low-level evolution services that are provided by the runtime infrastructure. The runtime infrastructure performs the required changes in the whole system. The Rainbow Framework [4] also describes an architecture-based approach to provide the self-adaptation of running systems. The Architecture Layer is responsible for the adaptation process from the moment a change requirement is detected until the change is executed. However, these approaches use external and centralized adaptation mechanisms. These mechanisms are appropriate for small to medium-size systems. However, large systems need their adaptation to be managed in a decentralized way, i.e., each subsystem must provide its own adaptation mechanisms. In this sense, Georgiadis et al. [11] describe a decentralized infrastructure to support self-organization. However, since each component instance stores a copy of the global architecture, the infrastructure does not support scalability.

Hardly any of these approaches take into account the runtime internal adaptation of components: the old running components are replaced by the new ones, thereby losing their previous state. MARMOL [7, 8] is a formal, meta architectural model that provides ADLs with *Computational Reflection* concepts [17]. The main idea is to provide the system with an editable representation of itself. Thus, the changes made to this representation are reflected to the running system. However, this work only formalizes the required *Reflection* concepts but it does not describe the necessary infrastructure to support these concepts. The ArchWare project [18, 21] provides a prototype based on a formal language and offers a complete support for the dynamic

---

[1] The base code is composed of the software units (modules, objects, components) of an application, which have been obtained as a result of a functional decomposition.

evolution of software architectures. Runtime adaptability is performed by the Evolution Meta-Process Model [1]. Each ArchWare component is composed of a production process (which provides the component behaviour), and an evolution process. This evolution process evolves and controls the production process of the component. ArchWare supports *programmed evolution*, by providing the specification of the production process to the evolution process. It also supports *ad-hoc evolution* by using *hyper-code* abstraction. However, there is no evidence about how the ArchWare evolution process is able to evolve *component types*. All the examples are always based at the instance-level.

There are approaches that provide dynamic evolution and also combine AOP and software architectures. JAsCo [32] introduces the concept of connectors for the weaving between the aspects and the base code, which permits a high level of aspect reusability. In addition, it provides an expressive language that permits the definition of relationships among aspects. However, due to the fact that aspects are woven in a referential way, this proposal requires an execution platform to intercept the target application and then insert the aspects at runtime. In a similar way, CAM/DAOP [27] is a component-based software architecture approach that introduces aspects as special connectors between components. It supports the separation of concerns from the design to the implementation stages of the software life cycle. However, even though it supports the dynamic weaving of aspects, it does not support the addition of new aspect types at runtime.

Kephart [14] describes the Autonomic Computing (AC) vision, where software systems are able to manage themselves, following a goal-driven approach. An autonomic element is an entity that provides functions to *monitor*, *analyze*, *plan* and *execute* control operations for a managed resource. AC is mainly focused on the IT-management of resources, performance concerns and security concerns. The main contribution of AC is that it establishes the need to build autonomous and heterogeneous software systems to address the software complexity problem.

6   Conclusions and Further Work

This paper has presented a novel approach to support the runtime adaptability of aspect-oriented components. This work takes the advantages of AOSD in software architecture to benefit from its reuse and maintenance, which are fundamental properties for developing complex systems. Dynamic adaptability is provided by using computational reflection concepts, since they provide a natural way to define self-modifying systems. In addition, this proposal describes the needed mechanisms to modify both *component types* and *component instances*. Thanks to the evolution infrastructure provided, running instances can trigger the modification of *component types*, so that their running instances are self-adapted dynamically according to the modifications required. Moreover, the self-adaptation process of *component instances* is possible because it only affects those parts of the instance that are undergoing the changes, thanks to the independence of PRISMA elements. The adaptation process acquires major relevance when it is applied to non-synchronized, multi-threaded components; for instance, two non-woven aspects of a PRISMA component are not aware of changes in each other.

This infrastructure provides the mechanisms needed to *plan* and *execute* adaptations. Thus, as soon as a *component type* is asked to make an adaptation, both the *component type* and its instances *plan* when the changes can be performed and then *execute* them. However, in order to provide the complete functionality of self-adaptable components, the mechanisms to *monitor* and *analyze* component adaptations should be provided by the infrastructure. These two mechanisms are future works that will be dealt with in the future. Some future works that we plan to complete in the short term are the following: (i) to define constraints for *component type* evolution; for example, it could be useful to limit the addition of new aspects or to limit the deletion of specific ports; and (ii) to ensure that a *component type* can only be dynamically evolved by authorized components (security). We are currently working on the self-adaptability capabilities of component instances in order to provide a complete framework for the self-adaptability of aspect-oriented software architectures. In addition, it is important to note that the main adaptation services described in this paper are *additions* and *removals*. However, from a runtime perspective, *replace* operations should also be adressed.

Acknowledgements. This work is funded by the Department of Science and Technology (Spain) under the National Program for Research, Development and Innovation, META project TIN2006-15175-C05-01. This work is also supported by a FPI fellowship from Conselleria d'Educació i Ciència (Generalitat Valenciana) to C. Costa.

References

1. Balasubramaniam, D., Morrison, R., Kirby, G., et al.: A Software Architecture Approach for Structuring Autonomic Systems. In: DEAS 2005. Proc. of Workshop on the Design and Evolution of Autonomic Application Software, St. Louis, Missouri, pp. 1–7 (2005)
2. Braberman, V.: The SetPoint! project (2006), http://setpoint.codehaus.org
3. Bradbury, J.S., Cordy, J.R., Dingel, J., Wermelinger, M.: A Survey of Self-Management in Dynamic Software Architecture Specifications. In: WOSS'04. Proc. of 1st ACM SIGSOFT Workshop on Self-Managed Systems, Newport Beach, California, pp. 28–33 (2004)
4. Cheng, S., Garlan, D., Schmerl, B.: Making Self-Adaptation an Engineering Reality. In: Babaoğlu, Ö., Jelasity, M., Montresor, A., Fetzer, C., Leonardi, S., van Moorsel, A.P.A., van Steen, M. (eds.) Self-star Properties in Complex Information Systems. LNCS, vol. 3460, pp. 158–173. Springer, Heidelberg (2005)
5. Chitchyan, R., Rashid, A., Sawyer, P., et al.: Report Synthesizing State-of-the-Art in Aspect-Oriented Requirements Engineering, Architectures and Design. Technical Report AOSD-Europe Deliverable D11, AOSD-Europe-ULANC-9. Lancaster Univ., UK (2005)
6. Cuesta, C.E., Romay, M.d.P., Fuente, P.d.l., Barrio-Solárzano, M.: Architectural aspects of architectural aspects. In: Morrison, R., Oquendo, F. (eds.) EWSA 2005. LNCS, vol. 3527, pp. 247–262. Springer, Heidelberg (2005)
7. Cuesta, C.E.: Dynamic Software Architecture Based on Reflection. PhD Thesis, Department of Computer Science, University of Valladolid (In Spanish) (2002)
8. Cuesta, C.E., Fuente, P.d.l., Barrio-Solárzano, M.: Dynamic Coordination Architecture through the use of Reflection. In: Proc. of 2001 ACM Symposium on Applied Computing, Las Vegas, Nevada, pp. 134–140 (2001)

9. Dashofy, E.M., van der Hoek, A., Taylor, R.N.: Towards Architecture-Based Self-Healing Systems. In: WOSS'02. Proc. of First Workshop on Self-Healing Systems, Charleston, South Carolina, November 18-19, 2002, pp. 21–26 (2002)

10. D'Souza, D.F., Wills, A.C.: Objects, Components, and Frameworks with UML: the Catalysis Approach. Object Technology Series edn. Addison-Wesley, Reading (1998)

11. Georgiadis, I., Magee, J., Kramer, J.: Self-Organising Software Architectures for Distributed Systems. In: WOSS'02. Proc. of First Workshop on Self-Healing Systems, Charleston, South Carolina, November 18-19, 2002, pp. 33–38 (2002)

12. Greenfield, J., Short, K., Cook, S., et al.: Software Factories: Assembling Applications with Patterns, Models, Frameworks and Tools. Wiley, Chichester (2004)

13. Harrison, W.H., Ossher, H.L., Tarr, P.L.: Asymmetrically vs. Symmetrically Organized Paradigms for Software Composition. Technical Report RC22685 (W0212-147), Thomas J. Watson Research Center, IBM (2002)

14. Kephart, J.O., Chess, D.M.: The Vision of Autonomic Computing. In: Computer, vol. 36(1), pp. 41–50. IEEE Computer Society Press, Los Alamitos (2003)

15. Kiczales, G., Hilsdale, E., Hugunin, J., Kersten, M., et al.: An overview of AspectJ. In: Knudsen, J.L. (ed.) ECOOP 2001. LNCS, vol. 2072, pp. 327–353. Springer, Heidelberg (2001)

16. Kiczales, G., Lamping, J., Mendhekar, A., Maeda, C., et al.: Aspect-Oriented Programming. In: Aksit, M., Matsuoka, S. (eds.) ECOOP 1997. LNCS, vol. 1241, pp. 220–242. Springer, Heidelberg (1997)

17. Maes, P.: Concepts and Experiments in Computational Reflection. In: SIGPLAN Not., vol. 22(12), pp. 147–155. ACM Press, New York (1987)

18. Morrison, R., Kirby, G., Balasubramaniam, D., Mickan, K., et al.: Support for Evolving Software Architectures in the ArchWare ADL. In: WICSA'04. Proc. of 4th Working IEEE/IFIP Conference on Software Architecture, Oslo, Norway, June 12-15, 2004, pp. 69–78 (2004)

19. Object Management Group (OMG): Model Driven Architecture Guide (2003), http://www.omg.org/docs/omg/03-06-01.pdf

20. Object Management Group (OMG): Meta-Object Facility (MOF) 1.4 Specification. TR formal/2002-04-03 (2002), http://www.omg.org/technology/documents/formal/mof.htm

21. Oquendo, F., Warboys, B., Morrison, R., Dindeleux, R., et al.: ArchWare: Architecting evolvable software. In: Oquendo, F., Warboys, B.C., Morrison, R. (eds.) EWSA 2004. LNCS, vol. 3047, pp. 257–271. Springer, Heidelberg (2004)

22. Pérez, J.: PRISMA: Aspect-Oriented Software Architectures. PhD Thesis, Department of Information Systems and Computation, Polytechnic University of Valencia (2006)

23. Pérez, J., Ali, N., Carsí, J.A., Ramos, I.: Designing Software Architectures with an Aspect-Oriented Architecture Description Language. In: Gorton, I., Heineman, G.T., Crnkovic, I., Schmidt, H.W., Stafford, J.A., Szyperski, C.A., Wallnau, K. (eds.) CBSE 2006. LNCS, vol. 4063, pp. 123–138. Springer, Heidelberg (2006)

24. Pérez, J., Ali, N., Carsí, J.A., Ramos, I.: Dynamic Evolution in Aspect-Oriented Architectural Models. In: Morrison, R., Oquendo, F. (eds.) EWSA 2005. LNCS, vol. 3527, pp. 59–76. Springer, Heidelberg (2005)

25. Pérez, J., Ali, N., Costa, C., Carsí, J.A., Ramos, I.: Executing Aspect-Oriented Component-Based Software Architectures on. NET Technology. In: Proc. of 3rd International Conference on. NET Technologies, Pilsen, Czech Republic, June 2005, pp. 97–108 (2005)

26. Perry, D.E., Wolf, A.L.: Foundations for the Study of Software Architecture. ACM SIGSOFT Software Engineering Notes 17(4), 40–52 (1992)
27. Pinto, M., Fuentes, L., Troya, J.M.: A Dynamic Component and Aspect-Oriented Platform. In: The Computer Journal, vol. 48(4), pp. 401–420. Oxford University Press, Oxford (2005)
28. Rajan, H., Sullivan, K.: Eos: Instance-Level Aspects for Integrated System Design. In: Proc. of 9th European Software Engineering Conference held jointly with 11th ACM SIGSOFT International Symposium on Foundations of Software Engineering, Helsinki, Finland, September 2003, pp. 297–306. ACM Press, New York (2003)
29. Schult, W., Polze, A.: Speed Vs. Memory Usage-an Approach to Deal with Contrary Aspects. In: Proc. of 2nd Workshop on Aspects, Components, and Patterns for Infrastructure Software (ACP4IS), International Conference on Aspect-Oriented Software Development (AOSD), Boston, Massachusetts (2003)
30. Shaw, M., Garlan, D.: Software Architecture: Perspectives On An Emerging Discipline. Prentice-Hall, Englewood Cliffs (1996)
31. Smith, B.C.: Reflections and Semantics in a Procedural Language. PhD Thesis, Laboratory for Computer Science, Massachusetts Institute of Technology (1982)
32. Suvée, D., Vanderperren, W., Jonckers, V.: JAsCo: An Aspect-Oriented Approach Tailored for Component Based Software Development. In: AOSD. Proc. of 2nd International Conference on Aspect-Oriented Software Development, Boston, Massachusetts, pp. 21–29 (2003)
33. Szyperski, C.: Component Software: Beyond Object-Oriented Programming. ACM Press/Addison-Wesley Publishing Co., New York (1998)
34. Yang, Z., Cheng, B.H.C., Stirewalt, R.E.K., et al.: An Aspect-Oriented Approach to Dynamic Adaptation. In: WOSS'02. Proc. of First Workshop on Self-Healing Systems, Charleston, South Carolina, November 18-19, 2002, pp. 85–92 (2002)

Component Based Game Development – A Solution to Escalating Costs and Expanding Deadlines?

Eelke Folmer

Game Engineering Research Group
University of Nevada, Reno
89503 Reno, Nevada, USA
research@eelke.com

Abstract. Expanding deadlines and escalating costs have notoriously plagued the game industry. Although the majority of the game development costs are spent on art and animation, significant cost reductions and more importantly reductions in development time can be achieved when developers use off the shelf components rather than develop them from scratch. However, many game developers struggle with component integration and managing the complexity of their architectures. This paper gives an overview of developing games with components, presents a reference architecture that outlines the relevant areas of reuse and signifies some of the problems with developing components unique to the domain of games.

Keywords: Games, COTS, Game architectures.

1 Introduction

Developing games is an expensive and risky activity. Computer games have evolved significantly in scale and complexity since the first game –Pong— was developed in the seventies [1]. Technological advances in console technology, e.g. advances in processor speed, storage media, memory size and graphic cards have facilitated increasingly complex game play and large quantities of realistic graphics. A natural consequence of these advances is that the cost for game development has skyrocketed. Estimates about the average costs for developing a console game range between 3 and 10 million dollar [2]. In addition development time and team size nearly doubled the last decade [3]. An additional problem that developers have to face is the observation that the games is predominantly hits driven; a UK demographics study revealed that the top 99 titles (only 3.3% of development) account for 55% of all sales [3]. The price of computer games, on the other hand, has stayed about the same over the last 10 years and has only slightly increased (from $50 to $60) for 3rd generation (Xbox 360 / Playstation 3) games.

As the game industry continues on a path towards longer development times and larger budgets, developers need to find ways to either sell more games or reduce the cost of building games. One way to reduce the cost of games is to reuse particular

H.W. Schmidt et al. (Eds.): CBSE 2007, LNCS 4608, pp. 66–73, 2007.

game components. Rather then reinventing the wheel when developing a 3d engine, a physics engine or a network component, game developers can choose to use an existing Commercial of the Shelf (COTS) Component. The primary motivation for an organization to use COTS is that they will:

- Reduce overall system development costs and development time because the components can be bought of the shelf instead of having to be developed from scratch. Buying the component is usually cheaper as the development costs for the component are being spread out over the multiple game titles in which the component is incorporated.
- A higher quality of components is to be expected as one can assume that these components are being used in different games, in different environments; more rigidly testing and stressing the quality of the component than in a single game setting.
- In addition a COTS based approach benefits the game industry as a whole as successful COTS developers can focus on one particular aspect of a game e.g. physics or 3d engines. This allows them to advance this technology at a faster rate than when they were building games. These advances are then available for more games to use [1], creating a win-win situation for everybody.

COTS development is not new trend in the games industry. In the past a significant number of games have been built upon existing technologies. Especially in the first person shooter (FPS) genre tech is heavily being reused. FPS engines like the Doom™ engine by ID games and the Unreal™ engine by epic games have spawned numerous successful games. However COTS have predominantly focused on the 3d rendering engine technology and or well understood sub domains such as audio and networking. Ten years ago only a handful of commercial game engines were available and only a small number of libraries for audio and networking. Because of the rapid evolution of games the last decade, game developers now can choose from a plethora of components dealing with various aspects of games e.g. rendering, object management, physics, artificial intelligence and so on. Being able to choose from a multitude of components (some of which are open source and hence free) is good for the game development community as it will allow significant cost reductions and time to market and will allow game developers to concentrate on the features of their game rather than on generic features common to all games. However the success of component based development as can be concluded from other domains such as the web domain, will largely depend on how easy game developer can incorporate such components in their games. In this paper we explore COTS based game development and identify some of the issues that developers face when adopting COTS based game development. The remainder of this paper is organized as follows. In the next section, we present a reference architecture that allows us to identify relevant areas for reuse. Section 3 discusses the relevant areas of reuse. Section 4 discusses some of the problems that hamper component based game development and discusses some research questions worth investigating. Section 5 concludes this paper.

2 A Reference Architecture for Games

Before we discuss the different components available to game developers we need to provide a common vocabulary with which to discuss different game implementations and commonalities between those game implementations. In order to understand which parts of a game are specific and which are general we propose a reference model that allows us to understand the separations and relations between the different parts of a game design. The highest level abstraction of any software system is called the software architecture i.e. the fundamental organization of a system, embodied in its components, their relationships to each other and the environment, and the principles governing its design and evolution [4]. The software architecture is an important artifact in the development of any system as it allows early analysis of the provided quality of a system such as performance, maintainability. This activity is important as these qualities are to a certain extent restricted by its architecture design and during architecture design one can still cost effectively change design decisions. As a specific domain of software systems ages and matures, more and more systems are developed from different organizations, and their functionality, structure, and behavior become common knowledge e.g. abstractions or software architectures will surface that represent their common denominator [5]. Such an abstraction is called reference architecture, which in essence is a software architecture, at a higher level of abstraction. A reference architecture does not contain any implementation details so it can be used as a template solution for designing new systems. Another benefit of having a reference architecture is that it can point out potential areas for reuse.

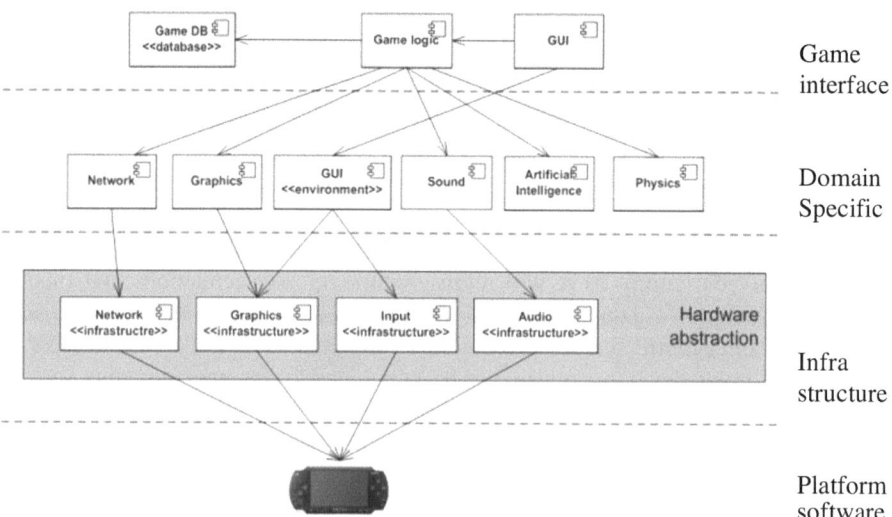

Fig. 1. A reference architecture for the games domain

We derived a reference architecture (RA) from two published game architectures [1, 6], an RTS system which has been published [7] of which we extracted an architecture design and a number of unpublished/ undisclosed systems. Our reference architecture is inspired by the layered reference architecture for component-based development as proposed in [8]. Their layered reference model consists of five layers; the interface, application, domain, infrastructure and platform layer and it puts the most specific components in the highest layer and the more general reusable components in the lower layers. To create our reference architecture we looked at different game architectures, we analyzed their components, and we then analyzed the commonality of these components across different game architecture implementations -and different game genres. Finally these components were organized according to the layered architecture reference model proposed in [8]. We left out the application specific layer form their model. This has resulted in the reference architecture displayed in Figure 1. Our reference architecture consists of four layers:

- *Game interface layer*: the top layer in our reference architecture is comprised of objects and components, which encapsulate the game logic. In this layer all the game specific objects are found such as models and textures. The game user interface, the game logic and a set of specific game objects (models, textures) usually stored in a file system or database. The objects in the database are part of this layer but the database functionality is provided by components from the infrastructure layer. For reasons of simplicity we didn't make this connection explicit.
- *Domain specific layer*: This layer is comprised of components, which encapsulate the interface to one, or more classes, which are specific to the domain of games. Examples of such components are usually graphics, physics, network, sound etc. These components are generally used from multiple places within the game. Behavior of game objects such as determined by the AI or physics is usually controlled by scripting languages such as lua or python that are part of the infrastructure layer.
- *Infrastructure layer:* This layer is made up of bespoke components that are potentially re-usable across any domain, providing general-purpose services such as input/output, persistence, database management, scripting communication, hardware abstraction etc.
- *Platform software*: this is comprised of standard or commonplace pieces of software that are brought in to underpin the game.

The validity, accuracy and completeness of this RA are open for discussion. Our RA has only been based on a limited number of available game architectures, which might not represent an accurate cross section of all possible game architectures. The architectures we derived this from did fit in this RA. Game companies tend not to disclose the architectures of their games. Usually a RA also defines stakeholders, different views and supported qualities and usually the RA is analyzed for its support of those qualities. In this paper we merely outline the RA to sketch out commonalities between different game architecture implementations and point out potential areas for reuse.

3   Areas of Reuse

As can be seen in our reference architecture six areas of reuse can be found in the domain specific layer:

- **Network** - Focuses on the communication between games and servers.
- **Graphics** – A collection of subsystems all related to visualizing the game.
  - ○ **Rendering** - Provides basic 2 or 3 dimensional rendering (producing pixels) functionality.
  - ○ **Modeling** - Focuses on abstract representations of game objects and managing those objects e.g. scene graphs.
  - ○ **Animation:** functionality related to creating moving images.
  - ○ **Texturing& effects:** functionality related to applying textures and light effects to particular models.
- **GUI** – Provides the functionality to build game interfaces.
- **Artificial intelligence** - Provides functionality related to produce the illusion of intelligence in the behavior of non-player characters (NPCs), such as path finding.
- **Physics** - Provides physics related functionality such as collision detecting e.g. game objects should adhere to Newton's laws of dynamics.
- **Sound** – libraries for modifying / generating sounds playing mp3's etc.

Usually a game engine provides a number of such components combined in one, however game engines are usually designed for a particular game and might not be suitable for what your game needs. Numerous third party components can be found which provide a plethora of functionality. We don't provide an overview in this paper but a complete overview can be found on http://www.gamemiddleware.org. To provide a complete picture another important area of reuse should be mentioned that are not included in the reference architecture.

- **Tools** – Tools (such as exporters and importers between different graphic applications) are not part of the game itself but are reused between games. The tools side of game development is unique and important .The tools may require twice the amount of code and are a huge detail given the number of content producers teams have these days. Usually numerous content generation tools such as 3D studio Max or Maja are used but developers often end up having to write numerous plugins and converters to be able to port models/ graphics from such tools to their game engines, which is quite cumbersome.

4   Problems with COTS Development

We identified the following problems possibly limiting the success of COTS.

4.1 Components Versus Frameworks

The success of component based development in the domain of games will depend on how easy developers will be able to integrate existing components into their games. Looking at other domains such as web-based systems, COTS were never as successful as they were claimed to be. COTS were considered to be the "silver bullet" [9] of software engineering during the nineties but the development with components came with many not so obvious trade-offs; Overall cost and development time were reduced, but often at the expense of an increase in software component integration work and a dependency on a third-party component vendors. As a result, COTS were gradually absorbed into higher granularity building blocks, i.e. application frameworks such as .NET or J2EE which don't come with integration problems but also do not offer much flexibility in the choice of components. A similar argumentation holds for the game industry; game engines for FPS were among the first reusable components. As the game industry matured more and more highly specialized components became available for specific sub areas such as physics and artificial intelligence. We are at a point now that if you want to build a game from components a large number of components need to be integrated --which is not an easy task. There seems to be a movement in the game industry towards developing frameworks. The obvious tradeoffs that need to be made here is that building from smaller pieces gives more control but using a large framework usually gives you the tools and less hassle with integration. More research needs to be done to provide developers with guidelines on how to successfully integrate components.

4.2   Complexity and Architecture Design

Another complicating factor is that games have increased in complexity, a 3d engine 10 years ago was an order of magnitude simpler to understand than it is nowadays. One reason for this complexity might be because more and more components are used. Since COTS developers try to design their component in such a way that it might provide a best overall fit for a large number of games, it means that thick glue layers may be needed to make up for the poor fit that the COTS provides for your game. An example of a glue code is for example the code required to perform data conversions between game components such as rendering or physics who require data to be in a specific format [10]. Glue layers usually become a bottleneck when performance is critical, as lots of data needs to be converted runtime. In addition game architectures are overly complex and do not provide maintainability and flexibility because of the spaghetti of dependencies that exist between COTS [1]. Components such as a renderer, physics, audio and artificial intelligence all need their own local data management model (with varying degrees of detail) such as binary spatial tree where the state of game objects is stored. When the state of a game object changes in any of the models this needs to be updated in all the associated models, leading to a synchronization and overhead between components. Another complicating factor is the object centric view that most games adopt [5]; Games are composed of game objects such as entities like cars, bullets, people representing real life objects. Game objects are responsible for all their own data manipulation and most COTS are just functional libraries that help the object do what its supposed to do. With the increase in complexity of this functionality the COTS objects become large and complex and unwieldy [1]. Current game architectures do not support COTS development very well and possible alternatives such as data driven or black board game architecture as proposed in [1] need to be further investigated with regard to performance, scalability and the desired maintainability and flexibility for component based game development.

4.3 The "emerging" Architecture

Usually game developers pick a game engine and write the necessary glue code to incorporate the desired COTS. If we develop our game like this a software architecture "emerges" rather than is designed upfront. An architecture consists of components and connectors and usually some design rationale. An architecture is mainly used as a tool to communicate design decisions to software engineers and it highlights the system's conceptual properties using high level abstractions which allows early analysis of quality requirements. In this model COTS can be used as solutions which facilitate such a design. The danger with randomly assembling a game using components is that the resulting architecture might not be the most optimal given the games quality requirements. There are still some degrees of freedom with regard to component composition that are often unexplored. Software Connectors play a fundamental role in determining system qualities; e.g. the choice to use shared variables, messages, buffers, calls or table entries has a big effect on the qualities of the game such as performance, resources utilization and reliability. Abstracting and encapsulating interaction details may help fulfill properties such as scalability, flexibility and maintainability, which may help reduce the complexity of game architecture designs. With regard to game design this area needs to be further explored.

4.4 The Buy or Build Decision

Because incorporating COTS is difficult and game architecture are complex, deciding which component to select to use in your game is a difficult decision. Especially for game related components usually deep technical knowledge is required to understand how to successfully use and integrate the COTS [10]. Game development requirements are very volatile and change frequently as a result some game developers end up rewriting most of the functionality that they need from the component and they would have been better of building the component themselves in the end. In order for a COTS to be successful it needs to be designed in such a way that it facilitates many needs, so it can be used in many different games. But as it is often impossible to fulfill everyone's needs the COTS need to provide a most common denominator of the required functionality that might not be the best fit for what your game needs. It will take some time to understand the component yet there is no guarantee the COTS will actually speed up the development if after a long investigation the COTS proves to be a poor fit and so much functionality needs to be rewritten that it was better to develop such a component from scratch and avoiding things like ad hoc programming and design erosion. Guidelines for analyzing components and strict interface agreements might mitigate some of this risk but need to be further explored.

5 Conclusions and Future Research

Developing games with components has the potential to minimize development costs and speed up development time. However, currently game developers struggle with a number of problems such as how to successfully integrate the component in their game. Deciding whether the component provides what is required for the game. Managing the complexity of their game architectures and analyzing whether the architecture that results from component composition meets the required quality requirements. Our future research will take a closer look at component composition by doing a comparative study on the relative ease of integration for a number of open source components for a Real time strategy game engine for AI research that is currently being designed at the University of Nevada. These experiences will allow us to develop a set of guidelines and or a game architecture that might facilitate developing games with components.

References

1. Plummer, J.: A Flexible and Expandable Architecture for Electronic Games. Vol. Master Thesis. Arizona State University, Phoenix (2004)
2. Grossman, A.: Postmortems from Game Developer. CMPBooks, San Francisco (2003)
3. DTI: From exuberant youth to sustainable maturity: competitive analysis of the UK games software sector. (2002)
4. IEEE Architecture Working Group. Recommended practice for architectural description IEEE (1998)
5. Avgeriou, P.: Describing, Instantiating and Evaluating a Reference Architecture: A Case Study. Enterprise Architect Journal, Fawcette Technical Publications (2003)
6. Andrew Rollings, D.M.: Game Architecture and Design. Coriolis Technology Press, Arizona (2000)
7. Michael Buro, T.F.: On the Development of a Free RTS Game Engine. GameOn'NA Conference, Montreal (2005)
8. Mark Collins-Cope, H.M.: A reference architecture for component based development
9. Brooks, F.: The Mythical Man-Month; Essays on Software Engineering; Twentieth Anniversary Edition. Addison-Wesley, Reading (1995)
10. Blow, J.: Game Development: Harder than you think. ACM Queue (2004)

Performance Assessment for e-Government Services: An Experience Report

Yan Liu[1], Liming Zhu[1], and Ian Gorton[2]

[1] National ICT Australia
[2] Pacific Northwest National Laboratory
Jenny.liu@nicta.com.au, liming.zhu@nicta.com.au,
ian.gorton@pnl.gov

Abstract. The transformation and integration of government services, enabled by the use of new technologies such as application servers and Web services, is fundamental to reduce the cost of government and improving service outcomes to citizens. Many core Government information systems comprise applications running on legacy mainframes, databases and transaction processing monitors. As Governments worldwide provide direct access over the Internet to these legacy applications from the general public, they may be exposed to workloads well above the origin design parameters of these back-end systems. This creates a significant risk of high profile failures for Government agencies whose newly integrated systems become overloaded. In this paper we describe how we conducted a performance assessment of a business-critical, Internet-facing Web services that integrated new and legacy systems from two Australian Government agencies. We leveraged prototype tools from our own research along with known techniques in performance modeling. We were able to clearly demonstrate that the existing hardware and software would be adequate to handle the predicted workload for the next financial year. We were also able to do 'what-if' analysis and predict how the system can perform with alternative strategies to scale the system. We conclude by summarizing the lessons learnt, including the importance of architecture visibility, benchmarking data quality, and measurement feasibility due to issues of outsourcing, privacy legislation and cross-agency involvement.

Keywords: performance, e-Government, services, and J2EE.

1 Introduction

Government agencies worldwide are increasingly improving their service levels by allowing the general public to access their systems over the Internet. These so-called e-Government services save considerable cost and time by providing useful services directly to the general public. They also greatly increase the flexibility and quality of service provision in the eyes of the public.

Typical of large enterprises, Government IT infrastructures have grown over 30-40 years and comprise an ever-evolving, complex heterogeneous mix of new and legacy systems and technologies. In addition, individual government agencies have generally

H.W. Schmidt et al. (Eds.): CBSE 2007, LNCS 4608, pp. 74–89, 2007.

developed their applications in isolation, to address their own specific requirements. This leads to *stovepiped* agency-based systems that are not designed to integrate with other agencies and external systems [3].

To implement e-Government services, technologies such as application servers supporting component-based development and Web services are used to provide new facades to existing legacy backend systems. These legacy systems include mainframe-based applications, databases and transaction processing monitors such as CICS (Customer Information Control System), which have been designed for known maximum user loads based on the number of internal agency operators and users.

However, applications on the Internet may attract concurrent user loads that greatly exceed the numbers these legacy systems have been designed for. This situation creates the risk of high-profile failures of key Government systems. An example of this is the failure of the Australian Government's new Customs systems in 2005 [1, 2]. This system brought the processing of goods at Australian ports to a standstill for several days due to a lack of processing capacity in a legacy system.

In this paper we describe our experiences in working with two large Government agencies to assess the performance potential of a new, high-profile e-Government service. The service allowed Australian tax payers to retrieve their medical costs for a given tax year directly from an Internet-based application used for lodging a tax return. (In the rest of this paper, we refer to this service as Medical Tax Statement Retrieval service (MTSR)). While the tax return lodgment application, e-Tax, had been available for several years, it had never previously integrated with the medical costs systems which resided in another government agency.

The implementation of this new service was extremely complex, requiring:

- The integration of eight major new and legacy applications across the two agencies
- Passing requests and data between the different security domains used by the two agencies
- Matching incompatible data formats across the two agencies due to different database schemas, with no common unique keys due to privacy legislation

It was also known from previous usage profiles of the e-Tax that the request load increased significantly on the day before the deadline for lodging tax returns. In 2006, a peak workload of more than seven thousands requests per hour was expected on this date (October 31st). This load was also expected to greatly increase in subsequent years as online lodgment becomes more and more prevalent.

The two agencies were able to comprehensively test the various components of the new service in isolation. Some component combinations within each agency could also be easily integrated and tested. It was however prohibitively difficult within the project time frame to perform a full end-to-end test to fully validate the maximum request load that the MTSR service would be able to sustain.

To help mitigate this performance risk, we worked with the two agencies to build an analytical model of MTSR and to populate the model's parameter with values obtained from performance testing. In the process, we adapted our model driven capacity planning approach [7] to work around the many practical issues we encountered. As a result, we were able to predict the maximum request load that the MTSR service would be able to sustain. We also identified the key bottlenecks in the service implementation. The results of our work gave the agencies greatly increased confidence that the implementation would be adequate for 2006 workloads, and gave them a basis for planning enhancements to provide the necessary processing capacity in future years.

2   Performance Prediction Pragmatics

To address this risk, we worked with teams from two Government agencies to build an analytical model of the system so we could predict its performance and scalability. The following describes the major issues we had to address.

2.1   Complexity of Service Architecture

The overall architecture of the MTSR system was not documented in detail, and was in fact difficult to construct. The system integrates a number of new and legacy systems across agencies, and includes:

- communications across secure inter-agency links,
- authentication systems at both ends,
- multiple firewalls,
- pass-through proxies,
- clusters of J2EE application servers,
- transaction processing servers
- database servers

It became a major exercise to bring together a group of 10 people from both agencies to reconstruct an accurate architecture model of the Web service. It was also difficult to get clarification on many issues so that we could confidently abstract away non-performance significant details of the architecture in our model.

2.2   Complexity of the Web Service Scenarios

We needed to construct usage scenarios of the Web service so the behavior of each component within the architecture could be understood. These scenarios are key to modeling the Web service behavior. Their accuracy greatly affects the construction of analytical performance models in terms of assumptions made and the techniques used to model component behavior.

The MTSR system was originally designed to handle batch operations at specific off peak times. These batches were accumulated from over-the-counter and over-the-phone requests throughout a business day. Hence, workload patterns were well understood and controlled. Introducing online access changed this completely, creating a much more complex workload pattern distributed over 24/7 operations.

In addition, the batch operation allowed data mismatches, caused by input errors or incorrect data to be resolved offline by an operator. With an online system, these problems will be returned immediately to the user as a message indication the errors. The user may attempt to correct the problem and resubmit the query. As this is a new system, no frequency data was available before production commenced. However, depending on the number of user resubmissions, the system will perform differently.

The Web service implementation also shares software and hardware resources with a number of other core business services. Thus, in order to predict performance, understanding the workload and background resource usage of these systems was critical.

2.3 Compositional Performance Assessment

Each Government agency was able to comprehensively test the various components of the new service in isolation. Some component combinations within each agency could also be easily integrated and tested, and performance measurements for each service component were available. It was however prohibitively difficult within the project time frame to perform a full end-to-end test to fully validate the maximum request load that the MTSR service would be able to sustain. This necessitates the need for the performance assessment method to be applied at the integration level of services in a compositional manner. A compositional performance assessment method means in this context that the method can operate with different levels of abstraction of the system description. This is because the integrated service was composed with components and legacy applications that were designed, developed and maintained in isolation.

2.4 Difficulties in Performance Measurement

In this complex production environment, obtaining relevant, accurate and detailed performance measurements turned out to be extremely difficult. This had significant impact on how we built the prediction model in terms of both making assumptions in the model and populating model parameters. The challenges we faced in measurement include the following.

- There are significant differences between the test environment and the production systems. Performance measurements in the test environment did not capture a number of significant factors in the production environment. For example, the Web service shared resources with a number of other systems in the production environment. Knowledge of the resource usage of these systems was very limited. We therefore had to take this resource usage into account while working with the test environment data.
- The granularity of the measurements available was very coarse. In most cases, only an average value (e.g. response time) was provided rather than a distribution or time-series based data. This was problematic as workload characterization relies on fine-grained measurement of request profiles. This data was simply not available.
- Operation of some parts of the system is outsourced. This is common in IT environments. Obtaining on-site performance data for these outsourced systems was extremely difficult, as these actions did not fall within the agreed outsourcing contract. Hence we had to proceed with estimated performance data obtained from appropriate generic benchmarks.
- Due to the diversity of the integrated Web service test environment and the different people and tools involved in collecting benchmark data, there were significant discrepancies in measurement and estimation from different sources. Even controlled performance tests presented some difficulties as, they were

performed at different times under different conditions. Correlation between these measurements was very hard, but is a crucial activity in prediction model building and result interpretation.

We overcome some of these challenges through our approach, as described in the next section. Other challenges can be only addressed by having better integration between measurement and prediction as discussed in section 5.

3   Our Approach

We utilized the principles and techniques of our research on model driven capacity planning [6-8]. This enabled us to construct and solve analytical performance models in the context of an e-Government service environment.

Our previous research on capacity planning focused on a methodology for performance prediction and evaluation of alternative architectural solutions of component-based systems at the design level [5]. Performance models were built from UML architecture design models with performance-related annotations. We also built a prototype tool to automate benchmark generation from design artifacts, in order to collect performance measurements for populating the model parameters. These method and tools helped reduce the costs and effort in applying performance engineering techniques in early stages of software development to evaluate architectural alternatives.

Applying our techniques to the MTSR project required us to modify the approach, as the Web service was already built using J2EE components and was about to enter production. Our aims were to predict the maximum request load that the end-to-end Web service would be able to sustain and identify any potential bottlenecks in the architecture. So while the fundamental principles of performance modeling and benchmarking could still be applied, there were problems, as described in the previous section that exacerbated the project complexity. Hence we modified our approach to address these explicitly, and we describe the steps taken in the following sub-sections.

3.1   Defining the Project Goals

The first step of quantitative analysis entails obtaining an in-depth understanding of the Web service under study. This includes understanding the business goals, the architecture, the key usage scenarios and the workload patterns. To obtain the necessary information, we acted as performance analysts and organized workshops and interviews with various service stakeholders. These included the business managers, the Web service architects, the development teams and the performance testers.

The performance goals were defined within the context of the major MTSR scenario of retrieving a medical tax statement, namely:

- Undertake a performance assessment on whether the existing MTSR system would be adequate to handle the predicted peak workload for the next tax year.
- Identify any architecture bottlenecks
- Develop guidelines for scaling the Web service in future years.

3.2 Understanding the Web Service Architecture

In the course of the workshops with the technical stakeholders, the software and hardware components that execute the key scenario were identified. From these discussions and working with the project documentation, we derived an initial architecture model. We then presented the model to the stakeholders for feedback and comments. Over three iterations, an architecture model was agreed, and a simplified version of this is shown in Figure 1.

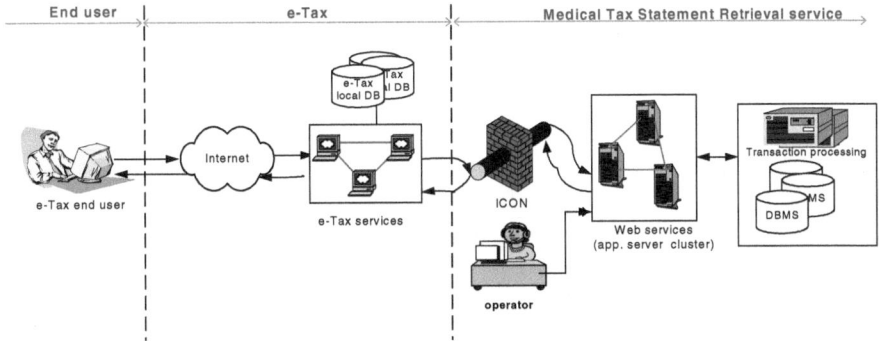

Fig. 1. The MTSR architecture

Briefly, the Web service behaves as follows. A user request for medical costs traverses the Internet and reaches the e-Tax server. e-Tax interprets the request and delegates the processing to the MTSR system to retrieve medical cost records. The request first passes over the dedicated private network, and after authentication, the business method of a Web services hosted in the J2EE application server cluster is invoked. The business logic attempts to validate the data in the request, and if valid, invokes a mainframe transaction to retrieve the medical cost records and writes a log record into a database.

3.3 Understanding the Web Service Workload

The MTSR application went into production on July 1st 2006. Application monitoring was used to record the arrival of requests at the MTSR Web service to retrieve medical cost records. So that we could analyze the workload, the performance engineers aggregated 19 daily history logs for requests, as presented in Figure 2. The 24 lines each represent the requests in a given hour over the 19 day period.

The data shows a correlation between 'load' and 'demand', and requests increase from the second week after the system was online. More requests occur on week days rather than weekends. The peak workload each day occurs during evening hours from 6-10pm.

We observed that the maximum request arrival rate during the monitored period was 356 requests between 8pm to 9pm on July 17th. This gives an average request arrival rate of one request per 10.11 seconds. We refer to this as the inter-arrival time.

Note that the requests received at the MTSR Web service do not come directly from the e-Tax users sitting at their PC. The requests are actually issued by the e-Tax server component. This will only process a fixed maximum number of requests concurrently, as it uses a fixed thread pool to handle simultaneous requests. This indicates that the execution of the MTSR Web Service forms a closed system from a performance modeling perspective [3]. Therefore workload characterization techniques such as the customer behavior graphic model [12] based on the assumption that the system is open are not applicable in this case.

Based on this analysis, the workload can be modeled by two parameters, the number of concurrent requests per second (N) and inter-arrival time (T_{think}). Using Little's law [3], we can understand the relationship between arrival rate λ and average response time R as

$$\lambda = \frac{N}{(T_{think} + R)} \tag{1}$$

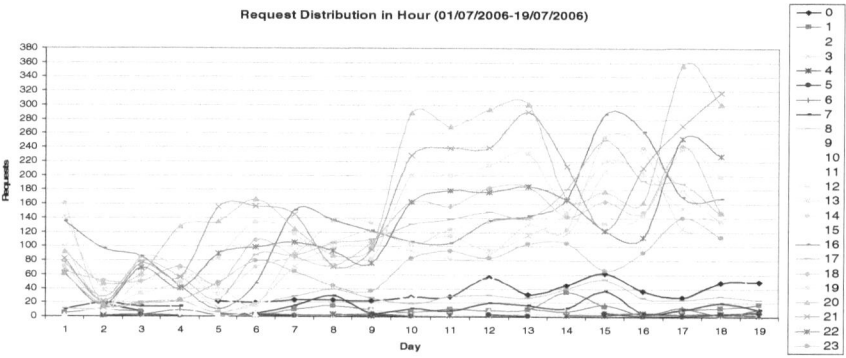

Fig. 2. Request arrival history from the production system

The transaction of the MTRS system completes with either a MTS (Medical Tax Statement) returned or only a message returned without a MTS. For example, a successful request will pass through the whole MSTR architecture shown in Figure 1. However, a request with errors of user input that causes a date of birth mismatch will not call the transactions to retrieve the medical cost records and only a message indicating the error is returned. Consequently, such a kind of requests have a directly impact on the service time for processing a request, and their effect must be built in to the performance model.

As a result of this analysis, we clustered the Web service workload into seven classes. These were the successful transactions plus the six groups (see Figure 3), based on their execution paths and the time spent executing the Web Service, database and transaction processing operations. From a performance modeling perspective, the individual classes impose a specific load on the software and hardware components in the architecture, each with a different ratio of visits and resulting service demands.

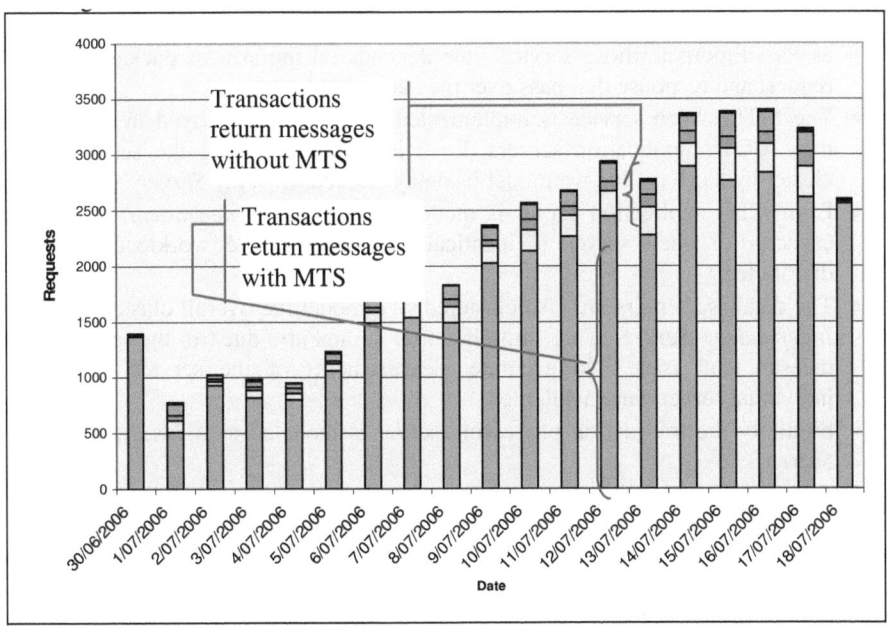

Fig. 3. Distribution of transactions

3.4 Constructing the Compositional Performance Model

In order to meet the need for a compositional approach to performance assessment, we developed a performance model based on a Queueing Network Model (QNM), which is a proven theory for modeling computer system performance [3] (chapter 8 and 9). In addition, a QNM can be constructed at different levels of abstraction, namely system level and component level, to capture the fundamentals of compositional reasoning techniques [9]. For example, at the system level, elements in a model can be represented as black boxes with their performance behavior characterized by input and output distributions, while at the component level, the details of individual elements can be modeled, including their scheduling policy, queue size and so on.

To create a performance model, the software and hardware components in the MTSR architecture need to be mapped to performance model elements. The QNM abstracts the layered architecture in Figure 1. We built the performance model (see **Figure 4**) as follows:

- Concurrent requests from the e-Tax system are the direct work load on MTSR. These are modeled as *Delay Servers* with the service time T_{think} which equals the inter-arrival time between sequential requests. The number of concurrent requests is annotated as N.

- The dedicated network between the e-Tax system and MTSR service is modeled as Fast Ethernet whose service time depends on the size of packages of each request and response that pass over the network.
- The MTSR Web service is implemented in Java and deployed in a cluster of three COTS application servers. Load is balanced among the servers in the cluster by a proxy, and we model its delay effect as a *Delay Server*.
- Each J2EE application server is modeled as a *Load Independent Server*. The capacity of each server is identical. We assume the workload is evenly distributed.
- The database servers are also clustered. We model the overall cluster as a *Load Independent Server*. This simplification is mainly due to the performance measurement issue. No accurate measurements of the service demand of individual server were available.
- Similarly the transaction processing server is modeled as a *Load Independent Server*.

The service time of the application servers, database servers and transaction processing servers are all actually load dependent in nature. Here however we model them as *Load Independent Servers*. This simplification is due to the fact that the service times in the production system are measured under a certain workload (e.g. the number of concurrent sessions), but there is no way for us to correlate the service demand measured with the number of concurrent sessions at any given time. Therefore it was impossible to obtain the service demand metrics under different workloads, which is required for solving models with Load Dependent Servers. (This simplification actually matches the service demands obtained by the performance engineers who developed the MTSR service, which were an average value from their regression analysis.)

As the MTSR system is deployed in a shared resource environment, other applications are also running while MTSR is available during business hours from 9am to 5pm. The MTSR serivce performance engineers observed from history data that these applications didn't cause significant resource contention. Fortunately, our performance assessment was more focused on periods with peak workload that occurred in the evenings, so the performance impact of other shared resource applications could be safely ignored. The same simplification was made for the batch jobs that ran after 3am each day.

The model could be extended to model the effects of other applications and batch jobs, simply by adding servers and queues into the QNM. However, obtaining the parameters value to calibrate these extra performance model elements would require significant engineering effort. In this project the benefit of having a more comprehensive performance model were limited at this stage.

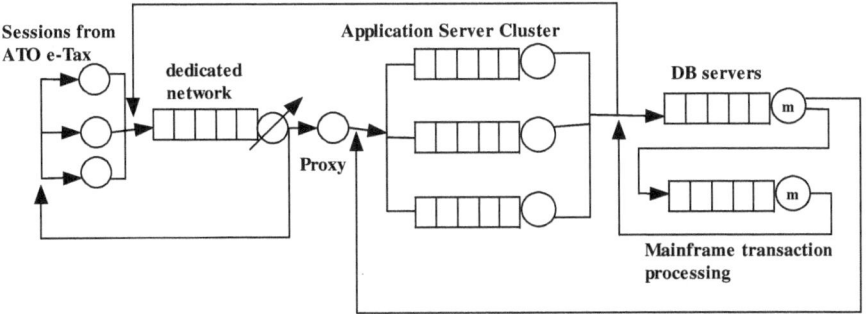

Fig. 4. The MTSR performance model

3.5 Obtain Parameter Values

Note that the performance model is actually built at a coarse grained level. A fine grained performance model could more closely represent the behavior of the system. However, performance modeling must take into account the issues involved in obtaining parameter values. With the MTSR system we did not have access to the full set of parameter values required for solving a more complex performance model. Given these constraints, we simplified the model accordingly.

The critical parameter values required included the service demand and visit ratio of each server in the QNM for every class of workload (characterized in section 4.3). For the dedicated network, we also need to know the network latency and the overhead of sending a byte of data. Other parameters include the average size of Web Service request and response messages.

The performance parameters required to solve the performance models were provided by MTSR performance engineers. The values were either measured from the production system (e.g. the average service time for the Web Service in the J2EE cluster), or calculated from logs. Some values were necessarily estimated by the performance engineers and architects, for example the service time to insert a log record into the database.

3.6 Analyzing the Results

We analyzed the predicted performance from the model in three ways, as explained below.

3.6.1 Boundary-Based Performance Prediction

Equation (1) represents the relationship between the number of concurrent requests per second (N) submitted from e-Tax sessions, the inter-arrival time (T_{think}) and the arrival rate . As discussed in section 4.3, N and T_{think} actually quantify the workload submitted to the MTSR service and the contention for computing capacity, such as CPU and disk usage. By changing the values of N and T_{think}, we can simulate different levels of workload submitted to MTSR service.

From the monitored performance data (Figure 2), the maximum request arrivals were 356 requests within one hour. This gives an average inter-arrival time as 10.11 seconds. Using this data, we first set N = 1 and T_{think} = 10 seconds, and solved the performance model. This gave the average response time for MTSR requests of 685ms. The actual measurements from the performance engineers showed the average response time during the monitored period was 653ms. Hence the error of modeling was within 5%, which was a highly satisfactory result. We presented this result to the stakeholders and they were impressed with the accuracy of the prediction.

We next modified the value of N and T_{think} to predict the service performance and scalability under heavier workloads. We scaled N from 1 to 50 and set $T_{think} = 1$ and 10 second to create different workloads. This simulated the scenario that in which the e-Tax system needs to handle more than 10,000 online customer requests within one hour, which was above the anticipated peak workload. (Note that N and T_{think} are estimated at this stage, as no actual production workloads of this intensity had been experienced. However, these values can be obtained from on-going monitoring of the production systems, and the real measure can be used by the performance engineers to validate the predictions.)

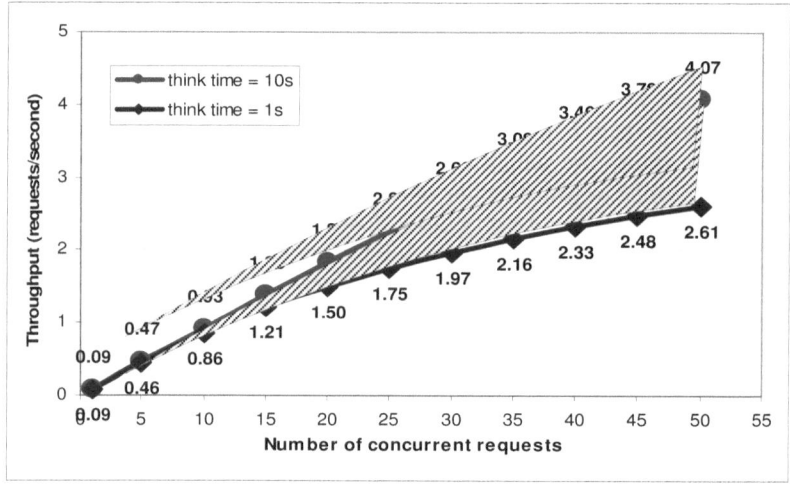

Fig. 5. Predicted throughput

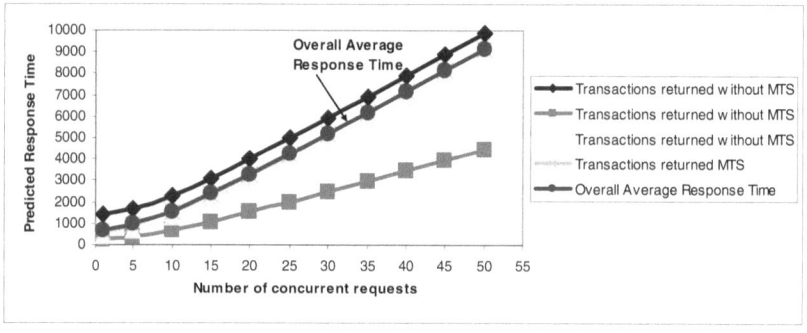

Fig. 6. Predicted response time ($T_{think} = 1s$)

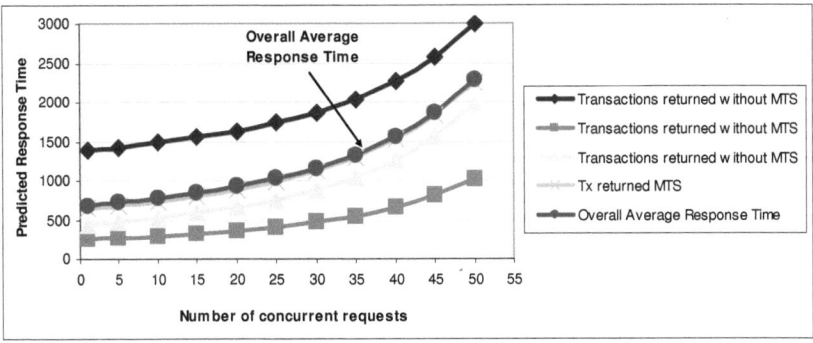

Fig. 7. Predicted response time ($T_{think} = 10s$)

We solved the performance model and the summarized results are in Figure 5, Figure 6 and Figure 7. Figure 5 shows the overall system throughput. Figure 6 and Figure 7 show the response time of each class of request and the overall average response time for $T_{think} = 1s$ and 10s respectively.

In Figure 5, the upper curve is with $T_{think} = 10s$ and lower curve is with $T_{think} = 1s$. These actually form the boundary of the throughput when the number of concurrent requests scales from 1 to 50. We applied boundary analysis to estimate the arrival rates of requests that the services can handle given the simulated workload. At the point of N= 50 and $T_{think} = 1$, from Figure 5 the throughput is 2.61 requests per second. We can therefore predict that the systems can handle 2.61 * 3600, approximately 9396 requests per hour with the average response time as approximately 9 seconds as shown in Figure 6.

Similarly, we can predict that the system can handle approximately 4.07* 3600 = 14,652 requests per hour with the average response time approximately 2 seconds when $T_{think} = 10s$. Using this analysis we can further infer that if the measured arrival rate of requests per second falls in the shaded area, we can roughly estimate that its average response time is between 2 to 9 seconds.

We presented the results to the stakeholders, and their response was that the results from the performance model were in line with current observations from the production system. Hence this performance assessment provided them with increased confidence that their architecture could handle the estimated peak workload of approximately 7000 requests per hour.

3.6.2 Scaling Guidelines
There are generally two ways of scaling hardware resources, namely upgrading the hardware with a more powerful configuration or adding another machine to share the workload. Here we illustrate our analysis for the latter option.

Assuming an identical database server cluster is added to share the load, we can extend the model with a *Load Independent Server* to represent the database server cluster. Figure 8 shows the predicted throughput when scaling the database servers. It clearly shows that the throughput increases for both workload scenarios of $T_{think} = 1s$ and $T_{think} = 10s$. However, the scaling is below a factor of 2. This is due to the fact that adding a new database server cluster also introduces more contention at the transaction processing servers, which prevents the throughput from scaling linearly.

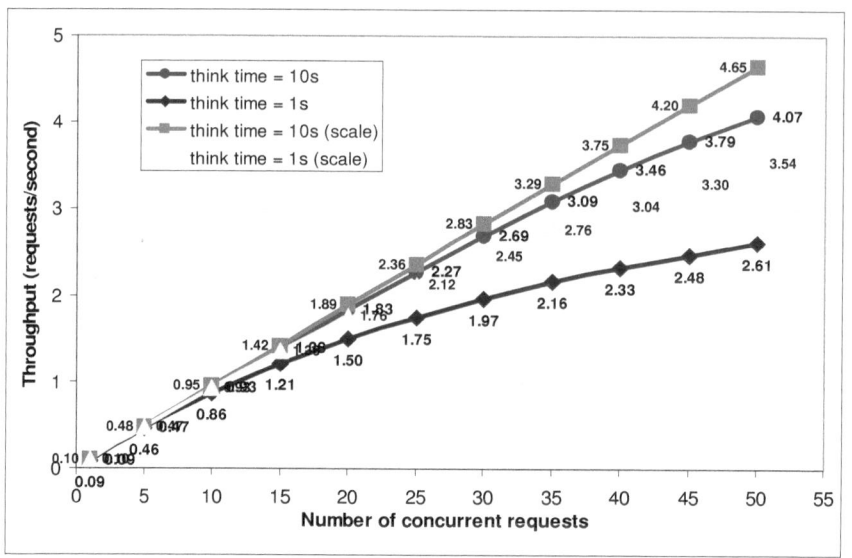

Fig. 8. Throughput of scaling database servers

4 Lesson Learnt

Conducting this project has given us considerable insights in to various facets of capacity planning for cross-agency e-Government services. The following discusses these insights. They are organized into two categories, namely *prediction* and *measurement*.

4.1 Prediction

1) Limited model validation opportunities
Due to the limited duration of this project, the performance model only was validated by data measured during a specific period of time. Monitoring data, calibrating the model, predicting performance and validating predictions are iterative tasks. The more data collected, the more opportunities to validate and refine the model accuracy. However, this also requires more engineering effort and project management. Hence there is a trade-off between the cost and accuracy of the performance modeling process.

2) Work with coarse-grained data
The granularity of measurements used for workload characterization was hourly based. Finer grained minute or second resolution data would've provided a more accurate snapshot of the system's behavior. On the other hand, having fine grained data monitoring and collection will incur extra monitoring overheads at runtime and demands additional engineering effort.

3) Work with incomplete measurement data
Some parameter values were estimated by performance engineers, for example the service time of a database server to insert a log record. This was simply because there was no easy way to obtain this data within the project timeframe. This may reduce the accuracy of the predictions if the estimates are incorrect, and consequently these estimated values need to be closely scrutinized.

4) Work with limited architecture visibility
Modeling a complex system, requires abstraction in the model to make the project tractable. An overly detailed model of the systems may create complex modeling issues that are hard to solve, and an overly abstract model may miss important performance characteristics. In this project, we only modeled the software servers as queueing network components, and did not consider details of the internal server behavior. This black box approach is appropriate for simplifying modeling, and from our experience on this project, still captures the performance characteristics of the overall system.

4.2 Measurement

1) A flexible test data generation tool is required
Due to privacy legislation in the government, gaining full access to any real data for measurement is prohibited, even for the agency software engineers. Using generated test data is therefore the only option. To represent the system as realistically as possible and reduce testing effort, we need flexible test data modeling and generation tools to produce high quality data for a large number of requests types and their combinations. The existing performance tools used in the agencies have scripting and test recording features, but they lack the test data modeling capabilities and are extremely limited in features for test data generation. We were able to use our MDABench prototype in the measurement planning phase. We created test data models along with transaction mix requirements using the UML 2.0 Testing profile. We then used the model to communicate the essential measurements to the MTSR software engineers. However, deploying MDABench directly to the environment would be more efficient.

2) A high degree of measurement and prediction integration is required
The most time consuming activity in the project was dealing with the heterogeneous computing environment and data collection tools for acquiring the necessary measurements to populate parameters in the prediction model. Having the ability to directly integrate measurement data with constructing the performance model would greatly streamline the capacity planning process. Most of the existing tools on the market focus either on measurement or prediction, making the whole process more complex.

3) A distributed unified measurement utility is required
The complexity of the Web service architecture and test environment created difficulties in data measurement. Most measurements were performed at different times, under different runtime conditions and using different tools. Correlating

between these measurements hence became very difficult. A unified measurement utility that can collect all necessary measurements at the same time would significantly increase the usability of the collected data.

4) Time series data is essential for interpreting results
The ability to correlate analysis with external stimulus is important for predicting potential problems. However, most of the performance data we had were averages with a coarse granularity. Distribution and time series based graphs were not available until much later in the project. When we later acquired time series based data, it turned out to be very useful in interpreting the results.

5 Conclusion and Future Work

The performance evaluation results were produced seven weeks before the anticipated peak workload occurs at the time close to the deadline of online e-Tax lodgment. It was later verified that the results from the performance evaluation were in line with observations from the production system. This demonstrates that the performance evaluation results are an independent source of information that corroborate the initial MTSR performance evaluation conducted by the two Government agencies individually. This increases confidence in business planning for future service uses.

The MTSR project has provided us with considerable insights in to the issues of applying performance prediction techniques to large, complex heterogeneous systems. We are encouraged by the fact that we were able to use, with appropriate modifications, some of the techniques and tools developed in our research. This experience will be valuable in guiding our future research efforts towards solution for some of the problems we encountered.

Acknowledgement

National ICT Australia is funded through the Australian Government's Backing Australia's Ability initiative, in part through the Australian Research Council.

References

[1] Almes, G.T., Lazowska, E.D.: The behavior of Ethernet-like computer communications networks. In: SOSP '79. Proceedings of the 7th ACM Symposium on Operating Systems Principles, pp. 66–81. ACM Press, New York (1979)
[2] Bushell, S.: Customs Failure A Catastrophe of IT Governance, http://www.cio.com.au/index.php/id;723894471;fp;4;fpid;21
[3] Menascé, D.A., Almeida, V.: Capacity Planning for Web Services: metrics, models, and methods. Prentice Hall, Englewood Cliffs (2001)
[4] Hohpe, G., Woof, B.: Enterprise Integration Patterns: Designing, Building, and Deploying Messaging Solutions. Addison-Wesley, Reading
[5] Liu, Y., Fekete, A., Gorton, I.: Design-Level Performance Prediction of Component-Based Applications. IEEE Transactions on Software Engineering 31(11), 928–941 (2005)

[6] Zhu, L., Gorton, I., Liu, J., Bui, N.B.: Model Driven Benchmark Generation for Web Services. In: IW-SOSE '06. Proceedings of the 2006 International Workshop on Service Oriented Software Engineering (2006)

[7] Zhu, L., Liu, J., Gorton, I., Bui, N.B.: Customized Benchmark Generation Using MDA. In: Proceedings of the 5th Working IEEE /IFIP Conference on Software Architecture, IEEE Computer Society Press, Los Alamitos (2005)

[8] Management-Advisor-Committee, Connecting Government - Whole of Government Reponses to Australia's Prioirty Challenges. I. T. a. t. A. Department of Communications (2004)

[9] Hissam, S., Moreno, G., Stafford, J., Wallnau, K.: Packaging Predictable Assembly with Prediction-Enabled Component Technology. (CMU/SEI-2001-TR-024)

[10] Davidson, P.: Australia Customs - More Flak Than Facts? In: Information Age (2006)

[11] Hayes, S.: Customs Knew System Would not Compute. In: ITM News (2005)

[12] Almeida, V., Menascé, D.A.: Capacity Planning: an Essential Tool for Managing Web Services. IEEE IT Professional, July/August 2002, pp. 33–38. IEEE Computer Society Press, Los Alamitos (2002)

An Approach for QoS Contract Negotiation in Distributed Component-Based Software

Mesfin Mulugeta and Alexander Schill

Institute for System Architecture
Dresden University of Technology, Germany
{mulugeta,schill}@rn.inf.tu-dresden.de

Abstract. QoS contract negotiation enables the selection of appropriate concrete QoS contracts between collaborating components. The negotiation is particularly challenging when component's QoS contracts depend on runtime resources or quality attributes to be fixed dynamically. This paper proposes a QoS contract negotiation approach by modeling it as a constraint solving problem. Important to our approach is the classification of the negotiation in multiple phases - *coarse-grained* and *fine-grained*, which are concerned with the negotiation of coarse-grained and fine-grained component properties respectively. We present negotiation algorithms first in a single-client - single-server scenario and later generalize it to a multiple-clients scenario. The contract negotiation is illustrated using an example from a video streaming scenario.

1 Introduction

Component-Based Software Engineering (CBSE) allows the composition of complex systems and applications out of well defined parts (components). In today's mature component models (e.g. EJB and .NET), components are specified with syntactic contracts that provide information about which methods are available and limited non-functional attributes like transaction properties. This under-specifies the components and limits their suitability and reuse to a specific area of application and environment. In [3], component contracts have been identified in four different levels: syntactic, behavioral, synchronization, and QoS. The explicit consideration of component QoS contracts aims at simplifying the development of component-based software with non-functional requirements like QoS, but it is also a challenging task.

For applications where the consideration of non-functional properties (NFPs) is essential (e.g. Video-on-Demand), a component-based solution demands the appropriate composition of the QoS contracts specified at the different ports of the collaborating components. The ports must be properly connected so that the QoS level required by one must be matched by the QoS level provided by the other. When QoS contracts are known statically, the developer or assembler can select the right concrete (provided and required) QoS contracts of each component and compose the whole application during design, implementation, or deployment time. But, for composing QoS contracts that depend on runtime

H.W. Schmidt et al. (Eds.): CBSE 2007, LNCS 4608, pp. 90–106, 2007.

resources (e.g. network bandwidth, CPU time) or quality attributes fixed dynamically, and for loose coupling between components, the selection of appropriate QoS contracts must be carried out at runtime by the process of *QoS Contract Negotiation*. In our approach, the component containers perform the contract negotiation at runtime. In this paper, we present QoS contract negotiation algorithms first in a single-client - single-server scenario and later generalize it to a multiple-clients scenario both in an environment where there may be resource constraints at the client, server, and the network.

A component's QoS contract is distinguished into *offered QoS contract* and *required QoS contract* [10]. We use CQML$^+$ [12][7], an extension of CQML [1], to specify the offered- and required-QoS contract of a component. CQML$^+$ uses the *QoS-Profile* construct to specify the NFPs (provided and required QoS contracts) of a component in terms of what a component requires (through a *uses* clause) from other components and what it provides (through a *provides* clause) to other interacting components, and the resource demand by the component from the underlying platform (through a *resource* clause). Due to its dynamic nature, QoS contract is specified with multiple QoS-Profiles as illustrated in Section 5.

The rest of the paper is organized as follows. Section 2 details the modeling of QoS contract negotiation as a constraint solving problem. In Section 3 we explain the need for coarse-grained and fine-grained negotiations and propose heuristic algorithms for these negotiation types in a single-client - single-server setting. Section 4 is devoted to discussions for a multiple-clients scenario. In Section 5, we illustrate the presented ideas based on an example scenario. The paper closes with an examination of related work, a summary, and outlook to future work.

2 Problem Formalization

The QoS contract negotiation can be formulated as a constraint satisfaction problem (CSP) as follows. A CSP consists of variables whose values are taken from finite, discrete domains, and a set of constraints on their values. The task is to assign a value to each variable satisfying all the constraints [14]. We take the variables to be the QoS-Profiles of the collaborating components (Fig. 1). The domain of each variable is the set of all QoS-Profiles specified for a component. The constraints are classified as *conformance, user's* and *resource*.

The conformance constraint is defined for two connected components (e.g. C_1 and C_2 in Fig. 1). Conformance [5] exists between two QoS-Profiles of interacting components when the server's provided-QoS contract conforms to the client's required-QoS contract. For example, the constraint *delay* < 5 conforms to the constraint *delay* < 10. The user's constraint is specified between a front-end component's provided QoS contract and the user's QoS requirement. The resource constraint is specified for three groups: components deployed on the client, on the server, and for those connected across containers (Fig. 1). For instance, the resource demand of profiles of components deployed in the client container must not be greater than the available resource in the client node. The

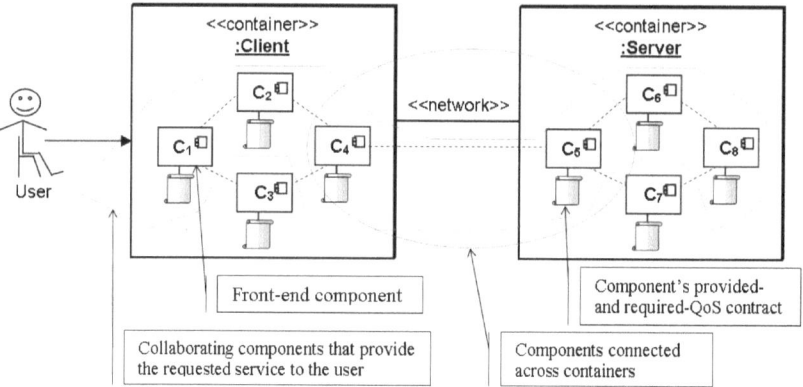

Fig. 1. Components deployed in a client and server container to provide a service to the user

influence of the network must be incorporated in the conformance constraint for those components connected across containers. For example, we assume delay in the network to be a constant for the period the negotiation agreement is valid.

Several solutions may satisfy all the constraints in a CSP. In a QoS contract negotiation, it is required to select a good solution according to some goal (e.g. user's satisfaction). To address this issue, a Constraint Satisfaction Optimization Problem (CSOP) framework [14] would be helpful. A CSOP is defined as a CSP together with an optimization (or objective) function f that maps every solution to a numerical value. The task in a CSOP is to find the solution with the optimal (minimal or maximal) value with regard to the objective function f.

As an objective function, f, we use a utility function. A utility [8] represents varying satisfaction with QoS changes of an application. It is represented by mapping quality points to real numbers in the range $[0, 1]$ where 0 represents the lowest and 1 the highest quality. We refer to A as a "better" solution when compared to another solution B if A's utility is higher than that of B. The successive improvement on a "better" solution would ultimately lead to an optimal solution, which is a solution that gives the highest utility.

Fig. 1 depicts a *single-client - single-server* scenario. There are more general scenarios of the problem like the case with (i) multiple-clients, (ii) multi-tier (multiple servers), and (iii) peer-to-peer. In this paper we discuss the single-client and multiple-clients scenarios.

3   Single-Client - Single-Server Scenario

While investigating QoS contract negotiation in various componentized application scenarios, we realize that the negotiation process is complex and less efficient unless phasing is applied. The complexity arises from the dependency exhibited by component properties and from the different nature of some properties. For instance, compression algorithms affect the QoS contract of components because of resource trading. Moreover, separating protocol negotiation between components and between multiple containers simplifies the negotiation process. Based on this phasing, we classify properties of a component as coarse-grained and fine-grained.

A coarse-grained property is a component implementation's property that can be associated with one or multiple fine-grained properties. This association is created by the fact that for a certain value of the coarse-grained property the fine-grained properties can possibly take different values depending on the allocated resources. As an example, in a video streaming scenario, coding type and protocol can be categorized as coarse-grained properties while frame rate and resolution as fine-grained properties. Moreover, a security goal specified for a component's interface represents a coarse-grained property while associated security mechanisms are fine-grained properties. *Coarse-grained negotiation* is the negotiation on coarse-grained properties while *fine-grained negotiation* is the one on fine-grained properties. A dependency exists between the two negotiation types in that the negotiation on fine-grained properties should be performed if there is an agreement on the associated coarse-grained property. A detailed discussion of these negotiation types is given next.

3.1   Coarse-Grained Negotiation

A coarse-grained property is generally assumed to be specified with multiple values, which are ordered. Ordering is followed to associate a preference with the various values. In our video streaming application scenario, video coding type is taken as a coarse-grained property for the interacting components. A VideoPlayer component's coding type property may be specified as: h264 (most preferred) and h263 (least preferred) while the specification for VideoServer may be h263 (most preferred) and MPEG (least preferred). For two interacting components, the list and preference of values specified for a certain coarse-grained property might not match. In our present strategy, we first consider the client's preference and give priority to it.

Coarse-grained negotiation is successful when offer and expectation of the interacting components *conform* on the concerned property. In general, a conformance relationship is defined for each property to test whether the values of the corresponding properties match to each other. Algorithm 1 outlines the steps to be executed in the coarse-grained negotiation between a client and server component. The algorithm must be applied for each coarse-grained property individually. The input to Algorithm 1 is a property's specification for a client and server component while the output is the agreed value(s) of a property stored in coarseAgreementList.

After executing Algorithm 1, coarseAgreementList may: (i) be empty - the whole negotiation process terminates with no agreement; or (ii) have a single value - final decision has been reached on the property's value at this phase; or (iii) have multiple values - final decision on the property's value will have to be postponed until after the fine-grained negotiation.

Algorithm 1. Coarse-grained negotiation algorithm between a client and server component

```
/* N is the total number of values specified for the coarse-grained
   property in the client component */

List coarseAgreementList;

void CoarseGrainedNegotiation()
{
   Initialize coarseAgreementList to empty;
   for(int i = 1; i <= N; i++) {
      Take the i-th preference of the client component;
      if(there exists a conformant value specified for the server component)
         Store the value into coarseAgreementList;
   }
}
```

3.2   Fine-Grained Negotiation

Fine-grained negotiation is the second and last phase of the contract negotiation process performed on the fine-grained properties such as frame rate, resolution, delay, and security mechanisms corresponding to the agreed values of the coarse-grained properties in the first phase of the negotiation. It is responsible for finding a "better" solution in addition to just picking a solution that satisfies all the constraints. A CSOP framework would be helpful to accomplish this task as explained in Section 2. We use a branch and bound (B&B) [14] technique to tackle the problem modeled as a CSOP.

B&B is a very general framework. To completely specify how a process that applies B&B proceeds, we need to define policies concerning selection of the next variable and selection of the next value. We must also specify the objective and heuristic functions. The heuristic function, h, maps every partial labeling (assignment) to a numerical value and this value is used to decide whether extending a partial labeling to include a new label would result in a "better" solution. We propose below a B&B technique for the fine-grained negotiation by explaining the schemes we used to define: (i) variable and value selection policies, (ii) objective function, f, and (iii) heuristic function, h.

A variable and value ordering is a general purpose heuristics used to solve CSPs efficiently [14]. In this method, the variable to assign next is appropriately selected. After choosing the variable for assignment, the value to assign to must also be appropriately picked out. In our case, the variables (QoS-profiles) are ordered for assignment by topologically sorting the network of cooperating components. By such ordering, the front-end component (e.g. C_1 in Fig. 1) becomes the minimal element. The assignment starts from the minimal element and from there continues to the connected components, and so on. We assume that the cooperating components form only a tree. The possible values of each variable, i.e. the QoS-profiles specified for each component, must be ordered from lower to higher quality. As contracts might involve multiple QoS properties, the ordering is based on the user's relative preference toward each QoS property.

Algorithm 2. Fine-grained negotiation algorithm for components deployed in client and server containers

```
   List<QoSProfiles> selectedQoSProfiles;
   enum CG { On_Client, On_Server, Across_Containers } // component's group

   boolean FineGrainedNegotiation()
 5 {
      if(ConformanceCheck() == false) return false;
      Initialize selectedQoSProfiles to Empty;
      Initialize BOUND to users QoS requirement;
      for(int i=0; i<components[0].profiles.size(); i++) {
10       if((provided QoS contract of the ith profile of Components[0])>=BOUND){
            if(FindAppropriateProfiles()) {
               update selectedQoSProfiles with the newly selected QoS-Profiles;
               update BOUND with the newly computed BOUND;
            }
15          else break; // this is a termination condition
         }
      }
      if(selectedQoSProfiles is Empty) return false else return true;
   }
20 int FindAppropriateProfiles()
   {
      FindConformantProfiles(CG.On_Client);
      if(CheckResourceConstraints(CG.On_Client)) {
         FindConformantProfiles(CG.Across_Containers\CG.On_Client);
25       if(CheckResourceConstraints(CG.Across_Containers)) {
            FindConformantProfiles(CG.On_Server\CG.Across_Containers);
            if(CheckResourceConstraints(CG.On_Server))
               return 1; // success
            else return 0;
30       } else return 0;
      } else return 0;
   }
```

The objective function, *f*, is taken as the utility function. There are two utility values that we should differentiate: *application utility* and *system utility* [8]. Application utility represents the quality of the provided service as perceived by a user while system utility is defined for the overall system, with multiple applications or clients. As applications can involve multiple QoS-dimensions, the utility function of an application is defined as a weighted average of the dimension-wise utility values. The weights define the relative importance of each QoS-dimension.

To define the heuristic function, *h*, we make use of the fact that at any point during the assignment of values to variables, the QoS property of the partially completed solution can be taken as the provided-QoS contract of the front-end component. Hence, *h* can be calculated based on the utility function by taking the QoS points in the provided-QoS contract of the front-end component. Because of the ordering strategy of variables we followed, *h* needs to be computed only at the beginning of each iteration, that is, when the front-end component is assigned a new value. If the new assignment to the front-end component violates the user's constraint, the choice is retracted and the sub-tree under the particular assignment will be pruned. The process will then re-start with a new assignment.

Since the components are distributed in a client and server containers, one approach to follow in the algorithm would be to first find QoS-Profiles of components deployed in the client container, which satisfy the three constraints and at the same time give a "better" solution. The same procedure is then applied to components connected across containers and lastly to components deployed in the server container. Such an approach would lead to more backtracking if the *bottleneck resource* were either the network bandwidth or server resources. To avoid this drawback, the algorithm finds conformant profiles for components deployed in both containers iteratively from low to high quality - in search of a "better" solution. At each iteration the resource constraints are checked at three instances: for components deployed in the client container, connected across containers, and deployed in the server container. When a bottleneck resource is found, the algorithm stops.

We will next give the algorithm together with some descriptions. The inputs to Algorithm 2 are: (i) the QoS-Profiles of each component that are ordered from low to high quality. The collaborating components are also ordered as explained previously; (ii) User's QoS requirements; and (iii) available resources at the client and server nodes and the end-to-end bandwidth. The output of Algorithm 2 is a QoS-Profile for each component that satisfies the user's, conformance, and resource constraints. In addition to fulfilling all the constraints, the solution obtained gives at least the utility that is required by the user. The following is a short description of the variables and functions used in Algorithm 2.

- selectedQoSProfiles (Lines 1, 7, 12, 18) is a list data structure that stores the QoS-Profiles of all components, which fulfill all the constraints. If the list is empty after the execution of the algorithm, then there exists no solution that satisfies all the three constraints, which is an over-constrained situation.
- CG.On_Client, CG.On_Server, and CG.Across_Containers (Lines 2, 22-27) refer to components on the client, on the server, and connected across containers respectively (Fig. 1).
- ConformanceCheck() (Line 6) performs conformance consistency check to every connected pair of components. It returns false if there cannot be conformance between at least two connected components.
- BOUND (Lines 8, 10, 13) is initialized to the user's QoS requirement as the algorithm aims at finding a solution that meets the requirement or even a better one. In Line 10, provided QoS contract of the front-end component is taken as the value of the heuristic function, h.
- components[0] (Lines 9, 10) refers to the front-end component. In Line 9, components[0].profiles.size() denotes the total number of QoS-Profiles specified for components[0]. The list data structure profiles, which is contained within each component, stores the specified QoS-Profiles.
- FindConformantProfiles() (Lines 22, 24, 26) finds QoS-profiles, which are conformant to one another for all the components specified in the input argument. At each iteration this function improves the solution by one step based on the specified QoS-profiles.
- CheckResourceConstraint() (Lines 23, 25, 27) returns true when there are enough resources for the current selection.

A component may belong to two groups in CG (Line 2). For example, a component deployed on the client container and that also communicates across containers belongs to On_Client and Across_Containers. The notation \ in Algorithm 2 is read as "less".

As explained earlier, the whole negotiation is performed in two phases: coarse-grained and fine-grained. The following algorithm combines these two phases.

Algorithm 3. Negotiation algorithm for components deployed in client and server containers

```
void Negotiation()
{
    CoarseGrainedNegotiation();  // Algorithm 1
    if(there is agreement on the value of the coarse-grained property) {
        for(each agreed value in the coarse-grained negotiation) {
            FineGrainedNegotiation();  // Algorithm 2
        }
        Compare the utility of the solutions obtained and choose
        the one that gives the highest utility;
    }
}
```

3.3   Algorithm Termination and Complexity

FineGrainedNegotiation() in Algorithm 2 iteratively searches for a "better" solution. At each iteration, the conformance checking between two connected components (C_i, C_j) where C_i is the parent[1] of C_j is performed as follows. Starting from (C_1, C_2) where C_1 is the front-end component, a new QoS-Profile is chosen for C_1 at the beginning of the iteration each time selecting a QoS-Profile with a better quality (Lines 9-10). Not all of C_2's profiles have to be checked for conformance with the chosen profile of C_1. The checking begins from the profile of C_2 selected in the previous iteration and moving to higher index of the array of profiles (from lower to higher quality). For (C_i, C_j), a profile for C_j is chosen using a similar procedure provided that a profile for C_i has been selected in the previous steps. The termination of the algorithm is guaranteed because of the fact that the network of components constitutes a tree and the number of QoS-Profiles of each component is finite.

ConformanceCheck()(Line 6) in Algorithm 2 performs a conformance consistency check to connected components: (C_i, C_j) where C_i is the parent of C_j. This consistency checking runs from $j = n$ down to 2 for the components $C_1, C_2, ..., C_n$. This step removes QoS-profiles from the domain of C_i for which no conformant profiles have been specified in C_j. The purpose of ConformanceCheck() is to achieve node- and arc-consistency in terms of the user's and conformance constraints and thus enables the remaining part of the algorithm to run with no backtracking. It has been proved that a search in a binary CSP is backtrack-free if the constraint graph of a problem forms a tree and both node- and arc-consistency are achieved in the problem [4]. Note that

---

[1] C_i's *uses* interface is connected to C_j's *provides* interface.

Table 1. QoS levels in a premium and normal service class

	premium service class (resolution, frame rate in s^{-1})	normal service class (resolution, frame rate in s^{-1})
1.	352x288, 30	176x144, 30
2.	352x288, 25	176x144, 15
3.	352x288, 20	176x144, 10
4.	352x288, 15	176x144, 5

in the algorithm design, we assumed the collaborating components form a tree. Assuming the total number of components is n and the number of QoS-Profiles specified for each component is d, the complexity of `ConformanceCheck()` is $O(nd^2)$. The complexity of finding a solution in `FineGrainedNegotiation()` is $O(nd^2 + nd^2) = O(nd^2)$. The solution obtained has the highest utility concerning the most preferred QoS-dimension.

4   Multiple-Clients Scenario

The multiple-clients scenario poses new challenges that haven't existed in our single-client scenario. Some of these are: (i) new clients constantly send requests for a service, which might follow a particular pattern or even occur in bursts. During this time, some clients' contracts haven't yet expired while certain clients leave the system; (ii) multiple clients usually have varying requirements and expectations about the QoS delivered by the service provider; and (iii) there is a need to consider new parameters such as contract duration and time of service delivery.

The first and third characteristics mentioned above have an impact on the server's decision making process during negotiation. We address these issues through an appropriate resource allocation strategy as will be explained shortly. To handle the second characteristic that is concerned with offering differentiated QoS, various approaches have been suggested in the literature [9]. One such approach uses the notion of a service class, which specifies a service with common functionality but different quality.

We can define service classes based on the QoS-Profiles of the collaborating components as follows. Considering our video streaming scenario (section 5), let's assume only a `VideoServer` component is deployed in the server container. If the QoS-Profiles of `VideoServer` are specified for a combination of 4 different frame rates and 4 different resolutions, there are 16 different QoS-Profiles. The 16 QoS-Profiles can be grouped into 4 service classes. As an example, we see two such service classes: *premium* and *normal*, in Table 1. Each service class defines a range of quality levels where selected QoS points may vary within the range to reflect the load conditions on the server. The service provider has the obligation of providing at least the minimum qualities in each service class.

The overall system utility, U, where $U = \sum_{clients} \alpha_i U_{s_i}$, as given by a service provider is defined as a weighted average of the utilities of each client. U_{s_i} represents the utility of the service class s_i. The weight, α_i, assigned to the different service classes capture the importance of each service class to the service provider. The required analytical solution is to find the QoS levels in the service class for each client that maximize U. This solution must be found under the following conditions: (i) the user's, conformance, and resource constraints are satisfied (as in the single-client scenario); and (ii) a service provider's negotiation goal is taken as efficient resource utilization while at the same time fulfilling user's minimum QoS requirements in each service class. The second assumption reconciles the conflicting interests of a client and server. Problems of this type are known to be NP-hard [8]. To cope with this difficulty, we resort to a heuristic solution. Before proposing an algorithm for the multiple-clients scenario, we discuss a resource allocation strategy and policy constraints, which address the challenges explained previously.

4.1   Resource Allocation

The resource allocation should depend on a number of factors: the total number of clients requesting the service, the rate of new client arrivals, the existing active contracts, and future agreed contracts, if there are any. When only few clients make requests and there is abundant resource, services are offered at maximum quality. On the other hand, when there are many clients and the available resource is scant, services are offered with lesser quality.

The maximum number of clients, N, supported by the service provider concurrently depends among others on the type of service class selected and the service mix (how many clients from each service class). Suppose a server's bandwidth capacity is 100 Mbps, and premium and normal class' minimum bandwidth requirement as in Table 1 are 2 and 0.3Mbps respectively. If only premium class is supported, $N = 50$ while $N = 333$ for only normal class clients. N falls between 50 and 333 when mixing service classes. N has been estimated here only based on the bandwidth requirement of each service class. Nevertheless, N can be determined by the CPU requirement as the case in CPU-bound applications. The resource that determines the size of N is termed as the bottleneck resource.

In light of the dynamic nature of load conditions, it would be appropriate to discuss resource allocation under different load conditions and dynamics. For this reason, we consider the following three cases: (i) light-load, (ii) conditions where the clients' request rate is known, and (iii) over-load.

Light-Load Case. Light-load is a situation where few clients make requests and there is enough server resource for all of them. During this condition, the total number of clients making requests and those already accepted is much less than N. All clients are allocated the maximum resource based on their service class. Referring to Table 1, for premium clients, the offered quality is 352x288, 30fps and for normal clients this is 176x144, 30fps.

Known Clients' Request Rate Case. Under the light load case, the offered qualities might not last the whole contract period. The rate of new client requests may increase to the point where resources will no longer be sufficient. Related to this, some questions to be addressed are: do we have to re-negotiate already established contracts whenever new clients arrive? To what quality level should we re-negotiate established contracts? How important is it for the server to know how many clients are anticipated in the future? Answering these questions improves the overall negotiation process. Simply doing negotiations for all clients (requesting and existing), whenever new clients arrive or with some periodicity, could make the system less stable due to the frequent changes in the offered QoS.

The answers to some of the aforementioned questions depend on the request rate of clients and the contract duration. A given service class' resource requirement depends on the selected QoS level. Let the maximum resource requirement for a particular service class be R_{max} and the minimum be R_{min}. If we assume a service uses m different resource types (e.g. CPU, network bandwidth), then $R_{max} = (r_{1,max}, r_{2,max}, ..., r_{m,max})$ and $R_{min} = (r_{1,min}, r_{2,min}, ..., r_{m,min})$. If R_{cap} is the server's available total capacity, $R_{cap} = (r_{1,cap}, r_{2,cap}, ..., r_{m,cap})$.

Let's assume the clients' request rate, $C_{req-rate}$ (in min^{-1}), and contract duration, D (in min) are constants. The maximum number of contracts active at any one time can then be computed as: $C_{req-rate} \times D$. If r_k represents the bottleneck resource (e.g. network bandwidth in a video streaming application), then a condition for the request rate, where maximum quality can be offered for all clients is: $C_{req-rate} \leq \frac{r_{k,cap}}{D \times r_{k,max}}$. If this condition is satisfied, then: (i) all clients can be allocated the maximum resource, and (ii) there is no need of re-negotiating established contracts at any time.

If $\frac{r_{k,cap}}{D \times r_{k,max}} \leq C_{req-rate} \leq \frac{r_{k,cap}}{D \times r_{k,min}}$, then all client requests can be fulfilled with no request waiting. But, the offered qualities can be as low as the minimum in each service class. Some of the clients can however be offered a quality higher than the minimum. This can be decided through policing that may favor one client over another. If $C_{req-rate} > \frac{r_{k,cap}}{D \times r_{k,min}}$, not all clients' requests can be served immediately, even with the minimum quality. This condition leaves the system in an overloaded situation where some clients must be rejected.

Over-Load Case. Over-load is a situation where the capacity of the service provider isn't sufficient to establish contracts with all of the clients requesting service. Under this condition, the total number of clients making requests and those whose contracts haven't expired is greater than N.

If the number of requesting and existing clients is N' where $N' > N$, $(N' - N)$ clients must wait for some period until they get the required service. If the size of the queue length (in number of clients) is S, then the maximum waiting time before a client's request is served is computed as:$(S/N) \times D$. If $N' - N > S$, then $N' - N - S$ clients must be rejected. Before rejecting these clients, multiple offers must be proposed to the S clients. The offers include the interval clients must wait before getting the service in addition to the QoS. The component containers decide on whether or not to accept the offer provided that a user's preference on waiting time has been available.

When the system transitions its state from a light-load to over-load condition in an abrupt manner, which may be a result of sudden increase in new client requests, the already established contracts in all service classes must be re-negotiated to the minimum quality in each class. The reason for this is during light-load conditions maximum resources are allocated to each client. When the system already anticipates overload conditions beforehand, some appropriate re-negotiations times must be chosen.

In general, during the over-load case, termination of some contracts may need to be made in order to create contracts with higher priority service classes. If the utility functions incorporated contract termination costs, we could decide on what benefits the service provider most. But, this may create bad impressions to certain clients and thus, the parameters that determine termination should not solely be made in terms of monetary benefits. This is one interesting area that needs further research.

4.2   Policy Constraints

There are certain behaviors that cannot be captured in utility functions. We model these behaviors by policy constraints, which can be defined as an explicit representation of the desired behavior of the system during contract negotiation and re-negotiation. Some of the different policies that need to be incorporated in the negotiation process concern the following areas.

1. How to make a choice on the proportions of the various service classes to negotiate during over-load conditions? Some possible options are: (i) to follow a strict priority policy where higher priority class always takes precedence over lower priority classes, or (ii) to take a more responsive policy that shares the resources among the various service classes according to a certain criteria.
2. How to move from one quality level into another when the system gradually transitions from light-load to over-load conditions? The various options could be: (i) not to change levels by choosing the minimum quality from the start, (ii) choose maximum first then at some point choose minimum, and (iii) go through all or part of the available levels starting from maximum to minimum.
3. How to favor among clients of the same class when re-negotiating contracts? This case is relevant when some resources are released and re-negotiations can be done so as to increase the quality levels of existing contracts.

4.3   Algorithm

The following algorithm is based on our discussion in subsections 4.1 and 4.2 together with the negotiation algorithms developed for the single-client scenario.

Fig. 2 shows one possible interaction scenario in Algorithm 4. It focuses on how the client and server containers interact to select concrete contracts (i.e. on the decision making process). The negotiation is started when a client makes a request for a particular service. Only a few of the existing clients is shown in the diagram. Client_i and Client_k are new clients while Client_x is a client that has already established a contract with the server. The particular negotiation scenario in Fig. 2 results in establishing contracts for Client_i and Client_k

Algorithm 4. Negotiation algorithm between multiple clients and a server

---

1) Clients send requests for a service
2) Server container performs policy constraint checks (subsection 4.2)
   if there is a need to re−allocate resources to active contracts.
3) Server allocates resources to the new clients (subsection 4.1).
4) Server makes a one to one negotiation with the new clients and also
   with existing clients whose contracts have to be re−negotiated
   using Algorithm 3 (subsection 3.2). This would result in establishing
   contracts between the collaborating components and between the
   user and service provider.
5) If there are clients waiting in the queue, the server proposes an
   offer that contains the quality and the maximum waiting time to
   these clients. If any client would not accept the offer, it is
   rejected. All clients that cannot be allocated resource are rejected.

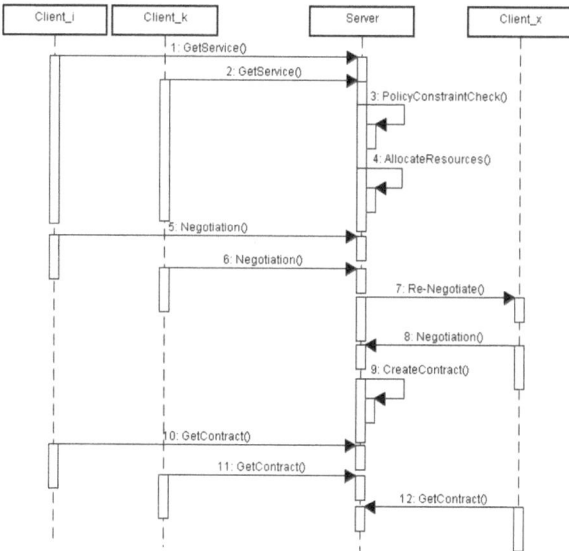

Fig. 2. Possible interaction between multiple clients and a server

and a re-negotiated contract for `Client_x`. Steps 3 and 4 are based on the discussion in subsection 4.1 and 4.2 while steps 5, 6, and 8 use Algorithm 3.

5   Example

We consider a video streaming application scenario that involves a `VideoServer` component deployed in a server container and a `VideoPlayer` component deployed in a client container (Fig. 3). We use the COMQUAD component model [7] that supports streams as special interface types and allows to specify non-functional properties for them. `VideoPlayer` implements two interfaces: a *uses* interface `ICompVideo` and a *provides* interface `IUnCompVideo` while `VideoServer`

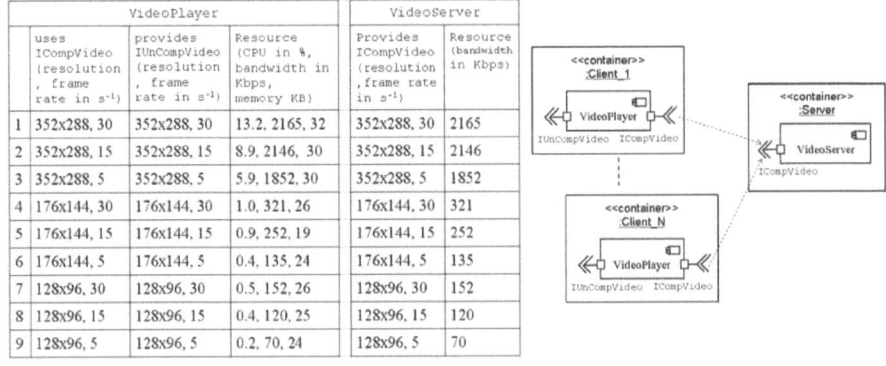

	VideoPlayer			VideoServer	
	uses ICompVideo (resolution, frame rate in s⁻¹)	provides IUnCompVideo (resolution, frame rate in s⁻¹)	Resource (CPU in %, bandwidth in Kbps, memory KB)	Provides ICompVideo (resolution, frame rate in s⁻¹)	Resource (bandwidth in Kbps)
1	352x288, 30	352x288, 30	13.2, 2165, 32	352x288, 30	2165
2	352x288, 15	352x288, 15	8.9, 2146, 30	352x288, 15	2146
3	352x288, 5	352x288, 5	5.9, 1852, 30	352x288, 5	1852
4	176x144, 30	176x144, 30	1.0, 321, 26	176x144, 30	321
5	176x144, 15	176x144, 15	0.9, 252, 19	176x144, 15	252
6	176x144, 5	176x144, 5	0.4, 135, 24	176x144, 5	135
7	128x96, 30	128x96, 30	0.5, 152, 26	128x96, 30	152
8	128x96, 15	128x96, 15	0.4, 120, 25	128x96, 15	120
9	128x96, 5	128x96, 5	0.2, 70, 24	128x96, 5	70

Fig. 3. QoS-Profiles of VideoPlayer and VideoServer implementations

implements a *provides* interface `ICompVideo`. `VideoPlayer`'s `ICompVideo` is connected to `VideoServer`'s `ICompVideo` to receive video streams for a playback at the client's node.

We conducted an experiment to specify the QoS-Profiles of `VideoPlayer` and `VideoServer`. The `VideoPlayer` component was implemented using Sun's JMF framework and the `VideoServer` component abstracts the video media file that has been pre-encoded into many files with differing frame rates, resolutions, protocols, and coding algorithm. Fig. 3 depicts some of the measured QoS-Profiles of `VideoPlayer` and `VideoServer`, with UDP protocol and mp42 coding. Such specifications are declaratively available to the containers that perform the negotiation. Note that these QoS-Profiles depend on the content of the video. During the measurements, average bandwidth and CPU percentage time have been considered. The bandwidth requirement of `VideoServer` is taken to be the same as that of `VideoPlayer`. The measured CPU requirements of `VideoServer` are too small (in the range of 0.1%) and hence have been left out from Fig. 3.

Let's consider clients of only one service class (e.g. normal class in Table 1). This assumption can be relaxed if the proportion of the server capacity allocated to each class is given in the policy constraints. Let the total bandwidth capacity at the server's side, $r_{i,cap}$, be 100Mbps, the contract duration for each client, $D = 4min$, and the bandwidth requirement of the maximum quality in the given service class, $r_{i,max}$ be 320Kbps while $r_{i,min}$ be 135Kbps. We assume that the network bandwidth is the bottleneck resource in the considered application.

- If $C_{req-rate} \leq 100/(4 \times 0.32) = 78min^{-1}$, all clients can be offered the maximum service with no need of contract re-negotiations. The maximum number of active contracts is: $4 \times 78 = 312$.
- Suppose there are only 50 clients currently having active contracts with the server (light-load condition). Let's assume that the 50 clients have all been allocated the maximum resource, i.e. 320Kbps. Now suddenly a burst of clients send request to the server. If the total number of clients - both requesting

and existing - exceeds $100/.320 = 312$, then the already established contracts must be re-allocated resource to the minimum quality, i.e. 135Kbps or some intermediate level depending on the policy constraints and the total number of new clients. The new clients will also not be allocated the maximum resource but lower values.
- Once, resources are allocated to each client, a one-to-one negotiation takes place between the server and the client using Algorithm 3. If the server container is the one responsible for the negotiation, it has to obtain all the input data as required by Algorithm 1 and 2.

6   Related Work

The work in [6] offers basic QoS negotiation mechanisms in only a single container. It hasn't pursued the case of distributed applications where components are deployed in multiple containers. Moreover, no strategies have been proposed for a multiple-clients scenario. In [11] QoS contract negotiation is applied when two components are explicitly connected via their ports. In the negotiation, the client component contacts the server component by providing its requirement; the server responds with a list of concrete contract offers; and the client finally decides and chooses one of the offers. This approach covers only the protocol aspect of the negotiation process. It hasn't pursued the decision making aspects of the negotiation. QuA [13] aims at defining an abstract component architecture, including the semantics for general QoS specifications. QuA's QoS-driven Service Planning has similarities to our concept of QoS contract negotiation. Complexity issues, however, haven't been accounted for in the service planning.

When multiple clients are involved in the contract negotiation, the key question is how to allocate resources to each client. In the literature, we find many resource allocation approaches for QoS-aware distributed systems [8][2][9]. In [8], end users' quality preferences are considered when system resources are apportioned across multiple applications such that the net utility that accrues to the end-users is maximized. In [2] a communication server architecture that maximizes the aggregate utility of QoS-sensitive connections for a community of clients including the case of over-load has been proposed. In [9], a resource allocation strategy is discussed for a clustered web-service environment. There are basically two reasons that make our work different from those mentioned above. Firstly, none of them approached the problem in the context of CBSE. Secondly, the focus of most related approaches is the allocation of server resources. Clients' properties haven't been considered together with the servers' properties.

7   Conclusions and Outlook

We approached the QoS contract negotiation problem by first modeling it as a constraint satisfaction optimization problem (CSOP). As a basis for this modeling, we assumed that the provided and required QoS as well as resource demand are specified at the component level. We have argued that the use of multiple phases simplifies the QoS contract negotiation process. Pertaining to this, we presented algorithms comprising coarse-grained and fine-grained negotiations for collaborating components deployed in distributed nodes in a single-client - single-server and multiple-clients scenarios.

This paper has proposed a two-phased negotiation approach. But, we want to extend this in the future to include more phases with the aim of reducing the complexity of the search in the negotiation. We are also currently examining the nature of utility functions in order to be able to analytically find globally optimal solutions. Defining a utility function is a difficult task due to the inter-dependency of QoS-dimensions. Furthermore, more parameters need to be incorporated into a utility function for our multiple-clients scenario. Some parameters we intend to include concern: how to differentiate two clients of the same service class during over-load case, and contract termination costs.

References

1. Aagedal, J.Ø.: Quality of Service Support in Development of Distributed Systems. PhD thesis, University of Oslo (2001)
2. Abdelzaher, T.F., Shin, K., Bhatti, N.: User-level QoS-adaptive resource management in server end-systems. IEEE Transactions on Computers 52(5), 678–685 (2003)
3. Beugnard, A., Jézéquel, J.-M., Plouzeau, N., Watkins, D.: Making components contract aware. IEEE Computer 32(7), 38–45 (1999)
4. Freuder, E.C.: A sufficient condition for backtrack-free search. Journal of the ACM (JACM) 29, 24–32 (1982)
5. Frolund, S., Koistinen, J.: Quality-of-Service specification in distributed object systems. IOP/BCS Distributed Systems Engineering Journal (1998)
6. Göbel, S., Pohl, C., Aigner, R., Pohlack, M., Röttger, S., Zschaler, S.: The COMQUAD component container architecture and contract negotiation. Technical Report TUD-FI04-04, Technische Universität Dresden (April 2004)
7. Göbel, S., Pohl, C., Röttger, S., Zschaler, S.: The COMQUAD Component Model— Enabling Dynamic Selection of Implementations by Weaving Non-functional Aspects. In: AOSD'04. 3rd International Conference on Aspect-Oriented Software Development, Lancaster, March 22–26, 2004 (2004)
8. Lee, C., Lehoczky, J., Rajkumar, R., Siewiorek, D.P.: On quality of service optimization with discrete qos options. In: IEEE Real Time Technology and Applications Symposium, p. 276. IEEE Computer Society Press, Los Alamitos (1999)
9. Levy, R., Nagarajarao, J., Pacifici, G., Spreitzer, M., Tantawi, A., Youssef, A.: Performance management for cluster based web services. In: IM 2003. Proceedings of 8th IFIP/IEEE International Symposium on Integrated Network Management, Colorado Springs, IEEE Computer Society Press, Los Alamitos (2003)
10. Object Management Group. UML profile for modeling quality of service and fault tolerance characteristics and mechanisms, v1.0. OMG Document (May 2006) URL http://www.omg.org/docs/formal/06-05-02.pdf

11. Ritter, T., Born, M., Unterschutz, T., Weis, T.: A QoS metamodel and its realization in a CORBA component infrastructure. In: Proceedings of the Hawaii International Conference on System Sciences (2003)
12. Röttger, S., Zschaler, S.: CQML$^+$: Enhancements to CQML. In: Bruel, J.-M. (ed.) Proc. 1st Int'l Workshop on Quality of Service in Component-Based Software Engineering, Toulouse, France, June 2003, pp. 43–56. Cépaduès-Éditions (2003)
13. Staehli, R., Eliassen, F., Amundsen, S.: Designing adaptive middleware for reuse. In: ARM '04. Proceedings of the 3rd workshop on Adaptive and reflective middleware, pp. 189–194. ACM Press, New York (2004)
14. Tsang, E.P.K.: Foundations of Constraint Satisfaction. Academic Press, London and San Diego (1993)

A Study of Execution Environments for Software Components

Kung-Kiu Lau and Vladyslav Ukis

School of Computer Science, The University of Manchester
Manchester M13 9PL, United Kingdom
{kung-kiu,vukis}@cs.man.ac.uk

Abstract. Software components are deployed into an execution environment before runtime. The execution environment influences the runtime execution of a component. Therefore, it is important to study existing execution environments for components and learn how they influence components' runtime execution. In this paper, we undertake such a study. We show that deploying components into different execution environments may incur runtime conflicts, which, however, can be detected before runtime.

1 Introduction

The execution environment for a software component controls the component's lifecycle, beginning with component instantiation through runtime management to shutdown. Currently, there are two widely used execution environments for components [13]: desktop and web. The problem we set out to investigate in this paper is: Given a component, how can we determine which execution environments it can be deployed into?

This problem becomes more acute when components are developed by component developers but used by system developers independently [2]. In such a situation, on the one hand, the component developers develop components without the knowledge of the execution environments they will be deployed into; and, on the other hand, the system developers deploy the components into specific execution environments not knowing if the chosen components are suitable for these environments. In this situation, it is important for the system developers to be able to check if a component is suitable for running in a particular execution environment. Current component models do not allow for this kind of checking. In this paper, we make a study of execution environments to enable that.

The work in this paper builds on the work we presented in [9]. In that paper we considered how deployment contracts for components can be defined, and used to check mutual compatibility between components. In this paper, we consider how the deployment contracts for components can be used to check a component's compatibility with its execution environment. Preliminary checking of this kind was introduced in [9]. In this paper we undertake a thorough study of what is involved when checking a component's compatibility with its execution environment. The results of the study enable us to extend our Deployment Contracts Analyser Tool [9] to automatically check a component's compatibility with its execution environment.

H.W. Schmidt et al. (Eds.): CBSE 2007, LNCS 4608, pp. 107–123, 2007.

2   Execution Environments

In this section we study widely used execution environments for components. In general, when we talk about the execution environment in this paper we do not mean component containers as they are not necessarily present in current component models. In fact, despite widely used component models such as EJB [6] and JavaBeans [3] employing containers for component execution, the majority of current component models do not use containers [12].

The distinction between a container and an underlying component execution environment can be seen clearly in Fig. 1.

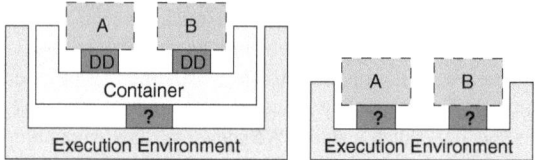

Fig. 1. Component deployment in an execution environment with and without container

On the left hand side in Fig. 1, components A and B are deployed into a container. This is typically done using so-called Deployment Descriptors (DD) [1] that describe the relationship between a component and the container. The container itself, however, is deployed into an execution environment in our sense. The question mark between the container and the execution environment denotes the question of compatibility of the container with the environment.

On the right hand side in Fig. 1, components A and B are deployed directly into the execution environment (without the container). That is, the execution environment is there regardless of the existence of container and impacts component runtime execution. The question marks between the components and the execution environment denotes the uncertainty of compatibility of the components with the environment.

In order to investigate execution environments that are widely used, we turned our attention to platforms widely used for software development in practice [5]. These are the J2EE [14] and .NET [16] platforms. The platforms allow for the development of software that can be deployed into two different execution environments: desktop and web (server). These execution environments are ubiquitous today [13]. In this paper, we want to undertake an analysis of them to find out their characteristics and differences that should lead us to the answer to the question we posed in section 1: Given a component, how can we determine which execution environments it can be deployed into?

The analysis we want to undertake in this paper will be implemented in a tool that will automatically check a component's suitability to run in a particular execution environment. In order to implement the tool we need to know the properties of interest of current component execution environments first.

2.1 Properties of Interest

Let us consider a binary component deployed into an execution environment. Such a component is shown in Fig. 2. The component is ready made and ready for execution. It may access some resources from the execution environment in order to be able to run [9]. Furthermore, it may have some specific threading model implemented inside [9].

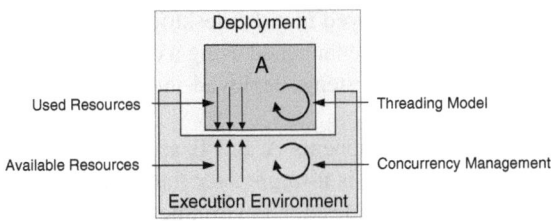

Fig. 2. Properties of interest in an execution environment

Therefore, in order to find out how a component execution environment can influence the runtime execution of the component, we have to find out which resources can be available as well as what the concurrency management is in the execution environment, in general.

For instance, in Fig. 2 the component A at deployment time has some environmental dependencies and a threading model, and is deployed into an execution environment. In order to find out how the execution environment influences runtime execution of the component A, we have to know the resources offered by the environment and the concurrency management of the environment.

Additionally, we need to know how the execution environment manages transient state [15,7] of the component. The transient state of the component, unlike persistent state, can exist only for the lifetime of a component instance. It is shared by requests to the instance, and disappears when the instance vanishes. Transient state is inherently connected to concurrency because it is the state which is shared by multiple threads operating concurrently in the component and has to be protected from corruption by thread synchronisation primitives.

In summary, we need to know the following properties of an execution environment to be able to assess its impact on the component executing in it: *Transient State Management, Concurrency Management, Availability of Resources*. In the following section we investigate these properties for the desktop environment based on an analysis of the J2EE and .NET platforms.

3   Desktop Execution Environment

The desktop environment is an execution environment for systems deployed on a desktop. Known examples of desktop applications are Adobe Acrobat Reader, Ghost Viewer etc. They provide a Graphical User Interface (GUI) to enable the user to interact with the system. Moreover, small programs like UNIX commands, e.g. ls or ps, also

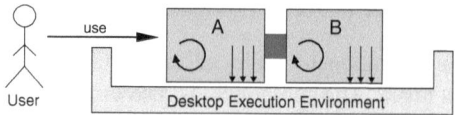

Fig. 3. A system deployed into a desktop environment

represent examples of systems deployed into the desktop environment. These systems do not provide a GUI interface but are launched using a command shell.

A typical user interaction with systems deployed into the desktop environment is shown in Fig. 3.

A system consisting of the components A and B assembled together is deployed into the desktop environment. There is a *single user* interacting with the system. It is a distinguishing characteristic of the desktop environment that it enables a single user to interact with a system instance. (We consider a system to reside on one machine and not to be distributed over several computers)

In the following, we consider Transient State Management, Concurrency Management and Availability of Resources, the properties we identified to be important in Section 2.1, in the desktop environment.

3.1 Transient State Management

If a system is deployed into the desktop environment, it is instantiated by it on the system startup and destroyed on the system shutdown. If in the meantime, i.e. in the time when requests are placed to the system, a component accumulates state,[1] the desktop environment does not interfere.

This is shown in Fig. 4. The component A is deployed into the desktop environment.

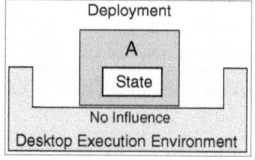

Fig. 4. Transient state management in the desktop environment

It holds transient state, and therefore can be referred to as stateful component. The desktop execution environment does not have an influence on the component A's state.

3.2 Concurrency Management

In general, it is possible to deploy both single-threaded and multithreaded systems into the desktop environment. If the system is single-threaded, it uses the main thread, provided by the desktop environment, to process requests. If the system is multithreaded,

---

[1] We mean "transient state" when referring to "state" in this paper.

it spawns other threads in addition to the main thread for request processing. The distinguishing characteristic of the concurrency management in the desktop environment is that *the main thread is guaranteed to be the same* for every request placed to a system instance during its lifetime.

This is illustrated in Fig. 5.

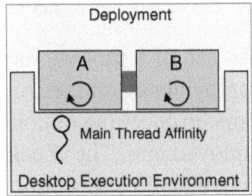

Fig. 5. Concurrency management in the desktop environment

The system AB consists of two components A and B. Each of the components has its own threading model. Depending on the threading model of either component, the system may be single- or multithreaded. In any case, the system makes use of the main thread provided by the desktop environment. It is ensured by the desktop environment for the system AB that the main thread remains the same for the lifetime of a system instance.

This has implications on the elements in components, which require thread affine access. In the desktop environment, such elements can be safely used from the main thread since it is guaranteed to be the same for all requests placed to the system.

3.3 Resource Availability

An execution environment can contain a set of resources that can be used by components deployed in it. In order to find out which resources can be found in the set, we studied the APIs of the J2EE and .NET frameworks that provide access to them. The results of our investigation are shown in Fig. 6. The resource set is as applicable to the desktop environment as it is to the web environment (see later).

The categories of resources in Fig. 6 are self-explanatory. Detailed descriptions of the categories can be found in [10]. Each resource from the categories may or may not be available in a particular execution environment. Therefore, when deploying a component into an execution environment, it is necessary to check if the resources required by the component are available in the execution environment.

Execution Environment				
Resource Set				
Input/Output Devices	Network	File System	Residential Services	Registry Storage
Message Queues	Databases	Event Logs	Performance Counters	Directory Services

Fig. 6. Resources in an execution environment

The resources we discovered are restricted to and complete with respect to the APIs of the J2EE and .NET frameworks. However, the comprehensiveness and wide applicability of the investigated frameworks should imply the same for the derived results.

3.4 Deploying Components into Desktop Execution Environment

In this section, we show an example of components deployed into the desktop environment.

To show the example, we make use of a tool we have developed and initially presented in [9,8]. The tool is the Deployment Contract Analyser (DCA). One of the purposes of the tool is to enable automated checking of compatibility of a component with the execution environment it is deployed into. The checking is done statically on binary components when they are at deployment time (as opposed to instantiated components at runtime).

The DCA implements the properties of the desktop and web execution environments we present in this paper. It takes as input binary components that are augmented with deployment contracts [9,10]. A deployment contract of a component indicates the component's threading model and usage of resources in the execution environment. It is manually defined by component developer. Knowing a component's deployment contract and its execution environment (specified using a graphical tool that can be seen in [8]), the DCA can detect conflicts of the component with the execution environment and present them to the user. Consider the example shown in Fig. 7.

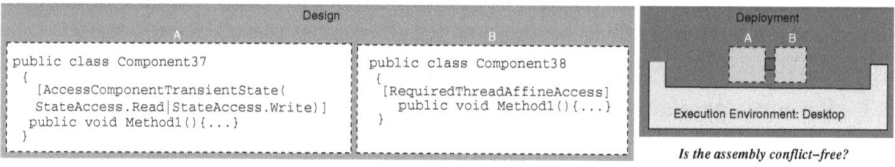

Fig. 7. Example 1

Component A is designed in a way that its method "A.Method1" accesses component's transient state in Read/Write mode. Component B is designed in a way that its method "B.Method1" requires thread affine access. This can be seen from their deployment contracts in Fig. 7.

Suppose at deployment time, a system AB is created. In the system, components' methods are connected so that there is one connection: *Connection 1: method "A.Method1" is invoked prior to the method "B.Method1"*. The system AB is deployed into the desktop environment. Resources available in the execution environment are irrelevant in this case.

Deployment contracts analysis performed by the DCA for the system AB is shown in Fig. 8.

Neither for the component A (Component37 in Fig. 8), nor for the component B (Component38 in Fig. 8) has the DCA found any problem. Therefore, the system AB is conflict-free and can execute safely at runtime.

```
Check Each Component's Deployment Contract against Execution Environment's Resources:

Component 'Component37':
Summary: Component 'Component37' - OK

Component 'Component38':
Summary: Component 'Component38' - OK


Check Components' Deployment Contracts For Mutual Compatibility with Respect to Usage of Resources in the Execution Environment:

Component Connection 'Request 1':
Summary: Component Connection 'Request 1' - OK


Check Components' Deployment Contracts For Mutual Compatibility with Respect to Components' Threading and State Models in Consideration of the Execution
Environment:

Component Connection 'Request 1':
Summary: Component Connection 'Request 1' - OK
```

Fig. 8. Deployment contracts analysis for the Example 3

In the following section we consider properties of the web execution environment and try deploying the assembly AB in it.

4   Web Execution Environment

The web execution environment is an environment for systems deployed on a web server. Known examples of such systems are web portals like Amazon or search engines like Google.

A typical user interaction with such systems is shown in Fig. 9.

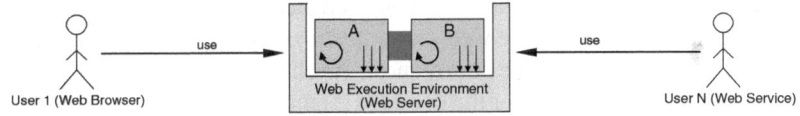

User 1 (Web Browser)   Web Execution Environment   User N (Web Service)
                                  (Web Server)

Fig. 9. System in web execution environment

A system AB consisting of two components A and B is deployed into the web environment. There are *many users*, possibly simultaneously, interacting with the system. It is a distinguishing characteristic of the web environment that it enables many users to interact with a system instance. A user typically uses a web browser to interact with a system deployed into the web environment, but it can also be accessed by web services (Fig. 9).

In the following, we consider Transient State Management and Concurrency Management, the properties we identified to be important in Section 2.1, in the web environment.

4.1   Transient State Management

The distinguishing characteristic of the web environment is that the user interacts with the system on the web server using Hyper Text Transfer Protocol (HTTP) [4]. The

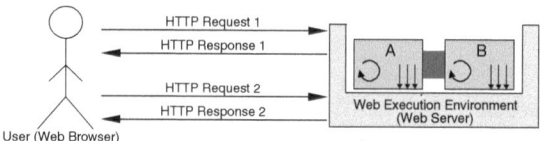

Fig. 10. Request-Response interaction mode using HTTP protocol

HTTP Protocol implements an interaction mode referred to as Request-Response mode [13]. This is shown in Fig. 10.

The user places an HTTP Request 1 to the system and receives a result. Subsequently, the user places another HTTP Request 2 to the system and receives a result to it. An important characteristic of the HTTP protocol is that it does not maintain any transient state between HTTP requests. It is therefore referred to as a stateless protocol. In fact, an HTTP request does not maintain any relationship to previous requests issued to the system on the web server. For instance, in the example from Fig. 10, at the beginning of the interaction, the HTTP Request 1 is sent to the web server, processed by the system and a result is returned to the user. The user is now completely disconnected from the web server. The web server, in turn, does not maintain any transient state about the Request 1 placed by a user. It, indeed, has "forgotten" about it. Now, the user places another request to the system, HTTP Request 2. This request does not maintain any relationship to Request 1 and is processed by the system without any transient state related to Request 1.

However, why did the web server "forget" about Request 1? The truth is that the HTTP protocol's Request-Response interaction mode operates in a way that for each HTTP request the client establishes a new connection to the web server. The web server, in turn, creates a new system instance. The newly created system instance processes the request and generates a result. The web server *destroys* the system instance and sends the result back to the client. On the next request, the chain of the events is repeated etc.

This is exemplified in Fig. 11 for the two HTTP requests we considered before.

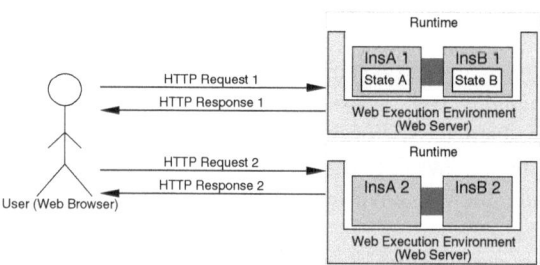

Fig. 11. Request-Response interaction mode and system instantiation

At the time when the user places Request 1 to the system AB, a system instance actually does not exist. It is only created by the web server when the request arrives there. The newly created system instance processes the request and generates a result. Subsequently, the web server destroys the system instance and sends the result back to the user. The user is now not only disconnected from the system, which processed Request 1, but the system instance actually does not physically exist any more. The web server does not maintain any information about Request 1 either. Now, the user places another request, Request 2, to the system AB. Again, no system instance exists till the request arrives at the web server, which creates a new system instance. The system instance processes the Request 2 and generates a result. After that the web server destroys the instance and returns the result. Again, no system instance exists till another request to the system AB hits the web server.

In such an environment, any component transient state cannot be retained between requests to the system. For instance, assuming components in Fig. 11 hold transient state. The component A holds 'State A', whereas the component B hold 'State B'. These transient states exist only for the lifetime of a system instance. Since the web server destroys the instance at the end of a request processing and creates another one at the beginning of the processing of the next request, the states 'State A' and 'State B' exist only during processing of Request 1 and do not exist during processing of Request 2.

Components that do not hold state, i.e. *stateless components*, can be deployed into and smoothly run in the web environment. They are immune to instance creation and destruction by the web server since they process each request individually without reliance on state information from previous requests. They, therefore, represent ideal candidates for the web environment. By contrast, components that do hold state, *stateful components*, pose a problem in the web environment since it, unlike the desktop environment, does not retain component state in between requests to the system.

In order to deal with the statelessness of the web environment, different technologies for web application development have been put forward. For instance, the J2EE Platform contains Java Server Pages (JSP) technology for web application development. Furthermore, .NET platform has Active Server Pages (ASP.NET) technology for the same purpose. These technologies allow for state retention in components on the web server. More traditional techniques for web application development such as Common Gateway Interface (CGI) scriptsfollow the Request-Response model of the HTTP protocol explained above and do not retain state on the web server side. JSP and ASP.NET are technologies that are representative and widely used in practice. We undertook a thorough analysis of them in [11]. For lack of space, we only present the essential findings of the analysis here.

4.2   Transient State Management in Java Server Pages

JSP from J2EE platform is a technology for building web applications. It is based on Java Servlet Technology, which is also part of the J2EE platform.

Java Servlet Technology provides a special container running on the web server. The container hosts and manages components referred to as "Servlets". The servlet container prevents servlets from being created and destroyed by the web server on each request processing cycle. It ensures that there is always one instance of component system to process all requests from all users. This is illustrated in Fig. 12.

Users place, possibly simultaneous, requests to the system AB. A system instance is running in the servlet container, which, in turn, is running on the web server. The container makes sure that the web server does not destroy the instance at the end of

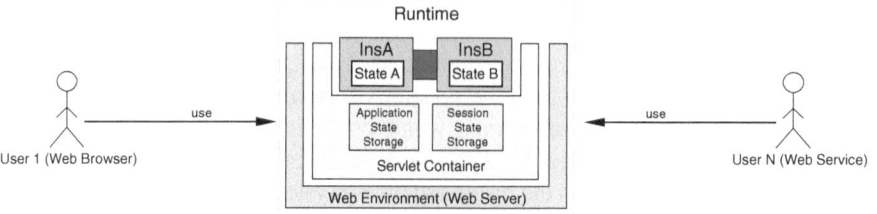

Fig. 12. Servlet Container

each request processing. Therefore, the components A and B can safely hold state and make use of it for request processing.

In addition, the servlet container offers two types of storage to component developers. That is, *application and session state storage*. On the one hand, application state storage can store information for the lifetime of a system instance. Moreover, it is shared among all users of a web application. On the other hand, session state storage stores information for the lifetime of a user or browser session. The session state storage is therefore user-specific. A user, or browser, session embraces a specific number of requests from a web browser instance to the system on the web server.

If a system in the web environment is going to have a large number of concurrent users, it is inefficient to have a single system instance process all user requests. Therefore, the Java Servlet Technology provides another mode of system instantiation referred to as Single Thread Model. With this model, the servlet container instantiates not only one but a fixed, configurable, number of more than one system instances that process user requests. If the user requests are concurrent, the load is distributed among available system instances.

With the Single Thread Model, the container guarantees that a system instance is accessed by one and only one thread per request, and not concurrently. However, the container does not guarantee that all requests from a user will be processed by the same system instance. This makes state management in the system complicated. Indeed, a user request may be processed by a system instance. The system instance may accumulate some transient state during the request. Then, another request from the same user may be processed by another system instance, whose component instances do not hold the data created on the previous request. It becomes even more complicated to hold some global data in the system. However, for all these cases, the usage of application and session state storage provides a solution to cope with state retention issues.

Now we consider how state is managed with another technology – ASP.NET.

4.3 Transient State Management in Active Server Pages

Active Server Pages (ASP.NET) from .NET platform is another technology for developing web applications. It provides a special environment referred to as ASP.NET environment. The ASP.NET environment runs on a web server and hosts .NET components. This is shown in Fig. 13.

Components A and B are running inside the ASP.NET environment, which in turn runs on a web server. The default behaviour of the ASP.NET environment, unlike servlet

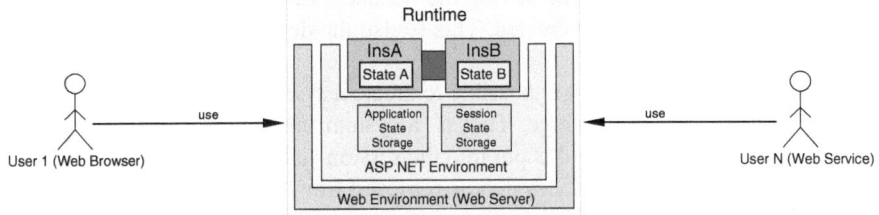

Fig. 13. ASP.NET Environment

container, with respect to system instantiation is that it follows the Request-Response model of HTTP protocol. That is, the ASP.NET environment creates and destroys a system on each request processing cycle. However, like the servlet container, it offers application and session state storage to component developers to deal with state retention issues.

Overall, the web environment, unlike the desktop environment we learnt in Section 3, has great influence on state inside components of a system. The influence depends on the technology used as summarised in Table 1.

Table 1. Transient state management in the web environment

	Request–Response Mode (CGI)	ASP.NET	JSP
System transient state management	System state is not retained among requests to the system.	1) Default: System state is not retained. 2) Application and Session state storage available.	1) Default: state is retained 2) Application and Session state storage available. 3) Single Thread Model: state is not retained.

4.4 Concurrency Management

A system deployed on a web server is exposed to, theoretically, an unlimited number of concurrent users. Therefore, concurrency issues are inherent in such an environment. A web server spawns a thread for every request it receives. Following this, we can conclude that in the web environment *the main thread is not guaranteed to be the same* for every request placed to a system instance during its lifetime. The handling of a request depends on the technology used for web application development, i.e. CGI, JSP or ASP.NET. Moreover, it depends on the way a technology is used. In particular, concurrency management in the web environment depends on the chosen system instantiation mode. Below, we undertake a brief categorisation of system instantiation modes in the web environment. Full details can be found in [11].

4.5 System Instantiation Modes

With CGI, Request-Response mode imposed by the HTTP protocol is used. That is, a system instance is created at the beginning of a request processing and destroyed after the request has been processed by the instance. In other words, in this mode *a system instance per request* is created. This is also the default mode of operation with ASP.NET.

Moreover, with ASP.NET, it is possible to create *a system instance per user session* by using the session state storage. That is, a system instance is created on the first request from a specific user and is put into the session state storage. On all subsequent requests from the same user, the system is retrieved from the session state storage and used for request processing.

Furthermore, with JSP, by default, the servlet container creates a system instance which processes all requests to the system. Therefore, in this mode there is *a system instance for all requests*. The same behaviour can be achieved with ASP.NET by using the application state storage. That is, a system instance is created on the first request and is put into the application state storage. On all subsequent requests, the system is retrieved from the application state storage and used.

Finally, with the servlet container using Single Thread Model, a pool of system instances is created. The container guarantees that a system instance is accessed by only one thread during a request processing. In other words, in this mode *a pool of synchronised system instances for all requests* is created.

In summary, we can identify the following four system instantiation modes in the web environment: *A System Instance Per Request*, *A System Instance Per User Session*, *A System Instance For All Requests*, *A Pool Of Synchronised System Instances For All Requests*. They correspond to the individual technologies for building web applications in the way shown in Table 2.

Table 2. System instantiation modes in the web environment with corresponding technologies for building web applications

	System instance per request	System instance per user session	System instance for all requests	Pool of synchronised system instances for all requests
CGI	default	not available	not available	not available
JSP	not available	not available	default	Single Thread Model
ASP.NET	default	use of session state storage required	use of application state storage required	not available

Observations on Concurrency Management in Web Environment. An inherent property of the web environment is that it enables a system to be accessed by, potentially concurrent, multiple users. As a corollary, the web environment itself may impose threading issues on a system instance by exposing it to multiple threads. Moreover, the concurrency management in the web environment depends heavily on the system instantiation mode used. During the analysis of the concurrency management in the web environment [11], we encountered the following three problems:

State Corruption Problem – This problem occurs when multiple threads concurrently access state of a component, which is not protected by a thread synchronisation primitive.

Lack of Thread Affinity Problem – This problem occurs when a component containing thread affine elements is not always accessed by one and the same thread.

Shared Statics and Singletons Problem – For this problem to occur, the following conditions must be met: (i) A component in a system must contain static variables (statics) or singletons, (ii) The system must be instantiated more than once in an operating system process, (iii) Created system instances must be executed concurrently to each other by the execution environment. This means that a system instance itself may not be executed concurrently but process requests sequentially. However, other system instances are also executed at the same time, (iv) The statics or singletons are not used by a thread-safe component part.

In this case, the statics or singletons are shared by component instances that are executed concurrently. Since they are unprotected from concurrent access by multiple threads, state corruption in them will occur. This problem, indeed, boils down to the state corruption problem described above. However, since it has far more conditions to emerge we can treat it as a problem in its own right.

With these problems defined, in the Table 3 we show occurrences of them depending on the system instantiation mode used.

Table 3. System transient state and concurrency management depending on system instantiation mode in the web environment

	System instance per request	System instance per user session	System instance for all requests	Pool of synchronised system instances for all req.
Concurrency management	A system instance is accessed by one thread	A system instance can be accessed by mult. threads sequentially	Concurrent access of a system instance by multiple thr.	A system instance can be accessed by multiple threads sequentially
System transient state managment	System state is not retained among requests	System state is retained during a user session	System state is retained among all requests	System state is not retained among requests
State Corr. Problem	No	No	Yes	No
Lack of Thread Affinity Problem	No	Yes	Yes	Yes
Shared Statics and Singletons Problem	Yes	Yes	No	Yes

With the system instantiation mode "system instance per request", a system instance is accessed by only one thread provided by the web environment. Therefore, the lack of thread affinity problem cannot occur here. Furthermore, the system state is not retained among requests to the system. Therefore, in this case the state corruption problem cannot occur. However, the shared statics and singletons problem may occur here if different users place their requests to different system instances concurrently.

Furthermore, with the system instantiation mode "system instance per user session", a system instance can be accessed by multiple threads but only sequentially. System state is retained during a user session. However, since no threads operate concurrently in a system instance, no state corruption problem will occur. On the other hand, due to the access of the system by multiple threads, lack of thread affinity problem may occur. Moreover, since in this mode a system instance is created for each user and they all reside in a single operating system process, shared statics and singletons problem may occur.

Additionally, with the system instantiation mode "system instance for all requests", a system can be accessed concurrently by multiple threads. System state is retained among requests. Therefore, the state corruption problem may occur here. Furthermore, since the system is not always accessed by one and the same thread, lack of thread affinity problem may occur. As to the shared statics and singletons problem, it cannot occur here since there is only one system with this system instantiation mode.

Finally, with the system instantiation mode "pool of synchronised system instances for all requests", a system instance can be accessed by multiple threads but only sequentially. System state is not retained among requests. Following this, there is also no state corruption problem. Moreover, there is no guarantee of the thread affinity of the main thread for a system instance. Therefore, the lack of thread affinity problem may occur. Since there are several system instances all residing in the web server process, the shared statics and singletons problem may occur here as well.

4.6 Deploying Components into Web Execution Environment

In this section we show how the system AB from the Section 3.4 can be deployed into the web execution environment.

Example 1. Consider the system AB from the Section 3.4 deployed into the web environment with the system instantiation mode 'system instance per user session' (Fig. 14).

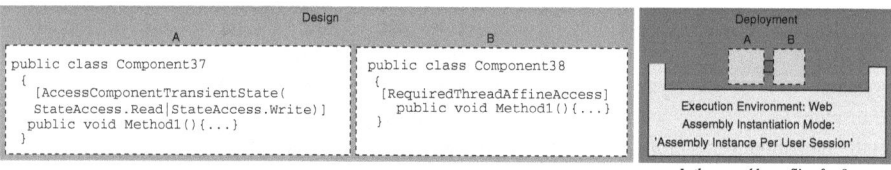

Fig. 14. Example 1

Deployment contracts analysis performed by the DCA for the system AB is shown in Fig. 15.

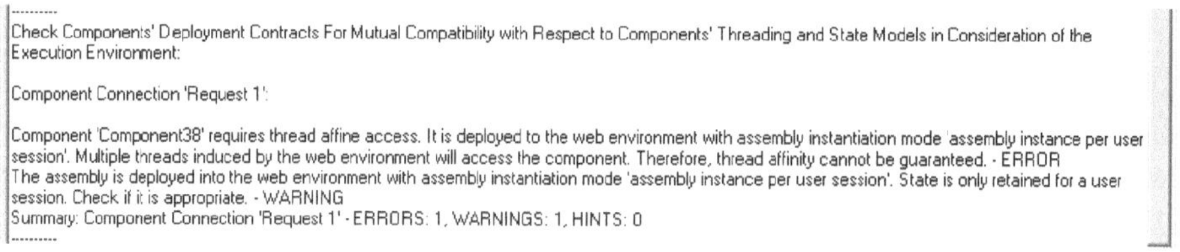

Check Components' Deployment Contracts For Mutual Compatibility with Respect to Components' Threading and State Models in Consideration of the Execution Environment:

Component Connection 'Request 1':

Component 'Component38' requires thread affine access. It is deployed to the web environment with assembly instantiation mode 'assembly instance per user session'. Multiple threads induced by the web environment will access the component. Therefore, thread affinity cannot be guaranteed. - ERROR
The assembly is deployed into the web environment with assembly instantiation mode 'assembly instance per user session'. State is only retained for a user session. Check if it is appropriate. - WARNING
Summary: Component Connection 'Request 1' - ERRORS: 1, WARNINGS: 1, HINTS: 0

Fig. 15. Deployment contracts analysis for the Example 1

For component B (Component38 in Fig. 15), the DCA finds out that the requirement of the method "A.Method1" cannot be satisfied due to the concurrency management of the environment the system AB is deployed to, namely absence of thread affinity of the main thread.

Moreover, in this environment, state is only retained for the duration of a user session. This is relevant for the component A (Component37 in Fig. 15). Assume that this is acceptable for the system the system developer is building.

Deployment contracts analysis of the system AB has shown 1 error. Therefore, the system AB is not conflict-free and cannot execute safely at runtime. Component B has to be replaced by another one in the system AB.

Example 2. Consider the system from Section 3.4 deployed into the web environment with the system instantiation mode 'system instance for all requests'. Resource available in the execution environment are irrelevant in this case (Fig. 16).

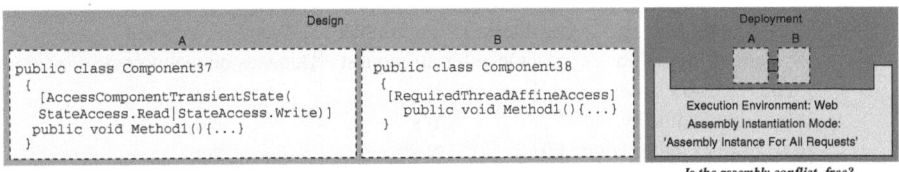

Fig. 16. Example 2

Deployment contracts analysis performed by the DCA for the system AB is shown in Fig. 17.

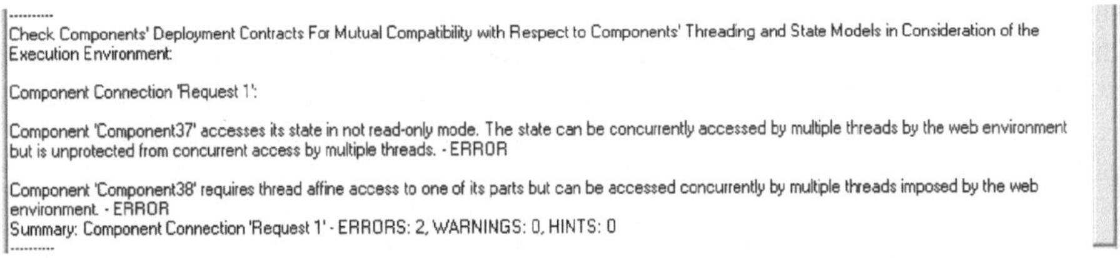

Check Components' Deployment Contracts For Mutual Compatibility with Respect to Components' Threading and State Models in Consideration of the Execution Environment:

Component Connection 'Request 1':

Component 'Component37' accesses its state in not read-only mode. The state can be concurrently accessed by multiple threads by the web environment but is unprotected from concurrent access by multiple threads. - ERROR

Component 'Component38' requires thread affine access to one of its parts but can be accessed concurrently by multiple threads imposed by the web environment. - ERROR
Summary: Component Connection 'Request 1' - ERRORS: 2, WARNINGS: 0, HINTS: 0

Fig. 17. Deployment contracts analysis for the Example 2

For component A (Component37 in Fig. 17), the DCA finds out that component's state will be accessed concurrently in the system's execution environment. Since the state is unprotected from concurrent access by multiple threads, state corruption problem will occur.

For component B (Component38 in Fig. 17), the DCA finds out that the requirement of the method "A.Method1" cannot be satisfied due to the concurrency management of the environment the system AB is deployed to, namely concurrent access of the system by multiple threads.

Deployment contracts analysis of the system AB has shown 2 errors. Therefore, the system AB is not conflict-free and cannot execute safely at runtime.

5   Discussion and Concluding Remarks

As we have seen in Sections 3 and 4, desktop and web environments differ substantially with respect to the management of state and concurrency of systems deployed in them. The major differences are: *system instantiation*, *handling of component state*, *allocation of the main thread for a system instance* and *the way a system instance is exposed to the users*.

Table 4 shows how these criteria are handled in the desktop and web execution environment.

Table 4. Comparing the properties of the desktop and web execution environment

	Desktop Environment	Web Environment
System instantiation	Once for all requests	Depends on technology
State retention issues	No	Yes
Main thread affinity	Yes	No
Exposure to multiple threads	No	Yes

In the desktop environment, system instantiation is done at system start. The created system instance processes all requests to the system. By contrast, in the web environment, the used technology greatly influences the handling of system instantiation. It can range from a system instance per request through a system instance for all requests.

Furthermore, in the desktop environment, there are no state retention issues due to the fact that a single system instance processes all requests to the system. Contrary, in the web environment, it requires an effort to retain state among requests to the system since it is by far not a common case that a single system instance processes all requests. Rather, different technologies deal with system instantiation differently making it complicated to maintain state among requests.

Moreover, in the desktop environment, the main thread for a system instance is guaranteed to be always one and the same. However, this does not hold true for the web environment. Again, the issue of main thread affinity depends on the technology used for building web applications.

Additionally, in the desktop environment, a system instance is never exposed to multiple threads induced by the environment. Unlike the desktop environment, the web environment makes it possible for a system instance to be concurrently accessed by multiple users, thus exposing the instance to the concurrent access of multiple threads.

The main contribution of this paper is the analysis of what is involved in deploying a component into different execution environments. The study of the execution environments undertaken in this paper has enabled us to extend our DCA tool to perform compatibility checks of components with their execution environments.

As a matter of fact, such checks are not performed by any of current component models [12]. However, in sections 3.4 and 4.6 we showed that neglecting these checks leaves systems go into runtime with conflicts that impair runtime system execution. We also showed how these conflicts can be checked at deployment time, before runtime, using the Deployment Contracts Analyser [8] tool we have developed and extended since its initial presentation in [9].

Our future work will consist in investigating the OSGI framework to extract more expressive deployment contracts for components. Furthermore, we will implement a tool that help the component developer apply the contracts to their components.

Finally, full details of the study of component execution environments and more examples can be found in [8].

References

1. Bachmann, F., Bass, L., Buhman, C., Comella-Dorda, S., Long, F., Robert, J., Seacord, R., Wallnau, K.: Volume II: Technical Concepts of Component-Based Software Engineering. Technical Report CMU/SEI-2000-TR-008, Carnegie Melon University (2000)
2. Crnkovic, I., Schmidt, H.W., Stafford, J.A., Wallnau, K.C.: Automated Component-Based Software Engineering. Journal of Systems and Software 74(1), 1–3 (2005)
3. Englander, R.: Developing Java Beans. O'Reilly & Associates (1997)
4. Fielding, R., Gettys, J., Mogul, J., Nielsen, H., Berners-Lee, T.: Hypertext transfer protocol HTTP/1.1, 1997. RFC 2068 (1997)
5. Fowler, M., Box, D., Hejlsberg, A., Knight, A., High, R., Crupi, J.: The great J2EE vs. Microsoft .NET shootout. In: OOPSLA '04: Companion to the 19th annual ACM SIGPLAN conference on Object-oriented programming systems, languages, and applications, pp. 143–144. ACM Press, New York (2004)
6. Haefel, R.M.: Enterprise Java Beans, 4th edn. O'Reilly (2004)
7. Heineman, G.T., Councill, W.T. (eds.): Component-Based Software Engineering: Putting the Pieces Together. Addison-Wesley, Reading (2001)
8. Lau, K.-K., Ukis, V.: A Reasoning Framework for Deployment Contracts Analysis. Preprint 37, School of Computer Science, The University of Manchester, Manchester, M13 9PL, UK ISSN 1361 - 6161 (June (2006)
9. Lau, K.-K., Ukis, V.: Defining and Checking Deployment Contracts for Software Components. In: Gorton, I., Heineman, G.T., Crnkovic, I., Schmidt, H.W., Stafford, J.A., Szyperski, C.A., Wallnau, K. (eds.) CBSE 2006. LNCS, vol. 4063, pp. 1–16. Springer, Heidelberg (2006)
10. Lau, K.-K., Ukis, V.: Deployment Contracts for Software Components. Preprint 36, School of Computer Science, The University of Manchester, Manchester, M13 9PL, UK, ISSN 1361 - 6161 (February 2006)
11. Lau, K.-K., Ukis, V.: On Characteristics and Differences of Component Execution Environments. Preprint 41, School of Computer Science, The University of Manchester, Manchester, M13 9PL, UK, ISSN 1361 - 6161 (February 2007)
12. Lau, K.-K., Wang, Z.: A taxonomy of software component models. In: Proceedings of the 31st Euromicro Conference, pp. 88–95. IEEE Computer Society Press, Los Alamitos (2005)
13. Lee, D., Baer, J.-L., Bershad, B., Anderson, T.: Reducing startup latency in web and desktop applications. In: 3rd USENIX Windows NT Symposium, Seattle, Washington, July 1999, pp. 165–176 (1999)
14. Sun Microsystems. Java 2 Platform, Enterprise Edition. http://java.sun.com/j2ee
15. Szyperski, C., Gruntz, D., Murer, S.: Component Software: Beyond Object-Oriented Programming, 2nd edn. Addison-Wesley, Reading (2002)
16. Wigley, A., Sutton, M., MacLeod, R., Burbidge, R., Wheelwright, S.: Microsoft.NET Compact Framework (Core Reference). Microsoft Press (January 2003)

Monitoring Architectural Properties in Dynamic Component-Based Systems*

Henry Muccini[1], Andrea Polini[2], Fabiano Ricci[1], and Antonia Bertolino[2]

[1] Dipartimento di Informatica
University of L'Aquila
Via Vetoio, 1 – L'Aquila, Italy
[2] Istituto di Scienza e Tecnologie dell'Informazione - "Alessandro Faedo"
Area della Ricerca del CNR di Pisa
Via Moruzzi, 1 – 56124 Pisa - Italy
muccini@di.univaq.it, andrea.polini@isti.cnr.it,
fabiano.ricci@di.univaq.it, antonia.bertolino@isti.cnr.it

Abstract. Modern systems are increasingly required to be capable to evolve at run-time, in particular allowing for the dynamic plugging of new features. It is important that this evolution happens preserving some established properties (which can concern the structure, the interaction patterns, or crucial extra-functional properties, such as reliability or security), and due to dynamicity this needs to be checked at run-time, as the changes occur.

In this work we consider evolving component-based systems formed by a kernel architecture to which new components can be plugged in at run-time, and introduce the MOSAICO approach for the run-time monitoring of architectural properties. MOSAICO uses Aspect-oriented technologies for instrumenting and monitoring the system according to selected architectural properties. MOSAICO can handle evolving black-box component systems since it continuously watches the events occurring at the extension points of the kernel architecture.

The application of a prototype implementation of MOSAICO, capable to handle interaction pattern properties, is illustrated on the NewsFeeder case study.

1 Introduction

An increasingly important requirement for modern software-intensive systems is the ability of changing over time, to address the need to dynamically add/remove features, and to protect the system from incoming attacks or run-time malfunctions. However, this newly acquired level of dynamicity makes it more complex to guarantee certain qualities of the system. This problem even exacerbates in the context of component-based systems (CBSs).

Being a CBS an assembly of reusable components designed to meet the quality attributes identified during the architecting phase, the quality of a CBS strongly relies on

---

* This work has been partly supported by the EU FP6-2005-IST EU Project PLASTIC (Providing Lightweight and Adaptable Service Technology for pervasive Information and Communication) and by the national FIRB Project ART DECO (Adaptive InfRasTructures for DECentralized Organizations).

H.W. Schmidt et al. (Eds.): CBSE 2007, LNCS 4608, pp. 124–139, 2007.

the selection of the right architecture. Analysis techniques and tools have been introduced for verifying and validating the architectural compliance to expected properties (see, e.g., in [1,2]); however, most of them suppose the existence of a static architecture.

Due to the new requirement of dynamicity, components can be added and removed at run-time so giving rise to dynamic, evolving, and unpredictable architectures, implemented via middleware-based technologies, plugin-based infrastructures, or service oriented paradigms. Therefore, the focus moves from validating the designed architectural configuration to validating the changing over-time architecture. While in static architectures the verification can be done once and for all before deployment, for dynamic architectures validation becomes a perpetual activity to be performed during system execution.

This research work focusses on a specific type of dynamism: we consider dynamically evolving CBSs in which, given a core set of architecturally connected black-box components (hereafter referred as the *kernel architecture*), new components can be plugged in at run-time (hereafter referred as *run-time components*). We propose the MOSAICO (MOnitoring SA In COmponents) approach with two main goals: *to verify that a system derived by assembling black-box components satisfies certain architectural properties*, and *to verify that by modifying some existing components or adding new black box components dynamically, those original properties still hold*.

The main contribution of this work consists in proposing the MOSAICO approach (an its associated tool) to monitor dynamically evolving architectures while verifying that interesting properties still hold on the modified CBS. While traditional approaches focus on one-time analysis of static systems, MOSAICO focusses on perpetual analysis of evolving systems. What the MOSAICO approach foresees hence is to first validate the kernel architecture for compliance to some architectural properties, and then to perpetually observe (through monitoring) the system execution and check weather the dynamically evolving architecture continues to comply to the initially verified properties. The properties this paper will consider are scenario-based temporal properties, identifying wanted/unwanted execution flows. Other types of properties, such as security and performance, will be the subject of future work.

The next section provides a high-level introduction to the approach, while a detailed description of the developed solution is presented in Section 3. Section 4 introduces the NewsFeeder case study and applies the approach over it. Section 5 discusses related work, while Section 6 concludes the paper and provides future research directions.

2 MOSAICO: A SA Property-Driven Monitoring Approach

The MOSAICO approach consists in monitoring the run-time execution of a dynamically evolving CBS in order to analyze its perpetual compliance to selected properties. This section provides a first glimpse on the approach, while details are provided in Section 3.

1. **Definition of the SA:** In our approach we assume the availability of such specification and base on it all the following steps. In our hypothesis the architecture describes the relations among a set of components belonging to the kernel. At the same time, it specifies how it is possible to dynamically extend the system at run-time.

2. **Definition of Relevant Architectural Properties:** In this phase the engineer defines which are the architectural properties that a real implementation of the system must satisfy. Some of the properties could be verified statically on the SA definition, for instance by a model-checker. Nevertheless, the presence of black box components should generally suggest to complement static verification with run-time techniques. A simple example could be a certain communication pattern among components that must hold at run-time.

3. **Instrumentation and Monitoring:** This step requires to put in place mechanisms to monitor the flow of messages among the components. In general the term "monitoring" refers to watching a system while it is running. This comprehends various activities, as detailed below, and might become a quite critical and expensive process [1].

   First of all, the events to be observed at run-time so to check the defined properties must be identified. Then, the system needs to be instrumented accordingly and monitored. In the MOSAICOapproach the instrumentation is carried on using Aspect Oriented Programming (see Section 3.3 for detail). Nevertheless, other approaches are possible based for instance on the use of mechanisms provided by the platform. It is worth noting that the presence of concurrent processes could make the observation of message order tricky [4].

4. **Definition of the Analyser Engine:** This is the mechanism that reveals if a property has been fulfilled or not. All the information collected must be reported to this engine. In general not all the observed events are relevant for verification purpose, as we discuss in 3.4. Clearly, if the analyser detects a violation, it should report it to some recovery system that can bring the system back to a correct state or gracefully stop it. This final step is certainly important but is outside the scope of the present paper.

Through the described steps and the artifacts correspondingly derived, the MOSAICO approach perpetually re-iterating steps three and four permits to continuously check the compliance of the system to the properties. In particular, whenever the architecture evolves as consequence of the insertion/removal of components, the approach permits to immediately highlight violated properties.

The basic assumption of our approach is that it is possible to trace architectural components to real components. Thanks to this assumption, it is possible to identify the interfaces allowing for the cooperation among the real components in the implementation, and to trace such interactions back to the architectural definition. Figure 1 shows our assumption on matching among architectural components (ACx in the picture) and real components (Cx).

3   The Approach

We now detail each of the steps introduced in Section 2. In particular for each step we describe techniques and tools that have been used and integrated to make some initial experimentation with the proposed approach.

---

[1] For a comprehensive survey on monitoring and related taxonomy we refer to [3].

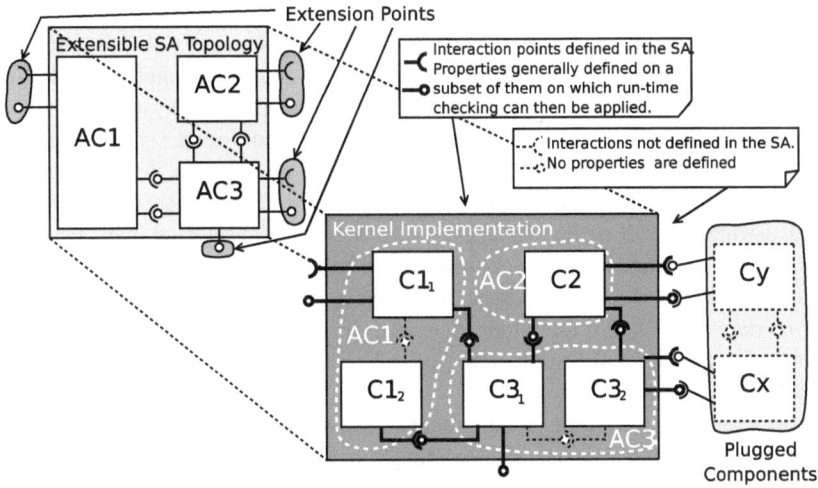

Fig. 1. Extensible Architecture Example

3.1 SA Specification

Scope of this work is architectural validation of dynamically evolving CBS. As said, we focus on extensible architectures composed by a kernel (some core components representing the system skeleton) plus a few dynamically pluggable components (in the specific, run-time evolving services).

In this context, the following development scenario is assumed: the specification of the kernel architecture is available (as usually happens in plugin-based CBS or middleware) and implemented possibly through black-box components, while dynamically pluggable components are black box (since produced and integrated by third parties) and can interact with the kernel through precisely defined extension points. Figure 1 describes a plug-in based architecture and possible extension points. In the picture the kernel part is specified by a precise description to which the real components and their interactions can be mapped. The architecture specifies also the extension points, even if the behaviour of the at run-time plugged components cannot be foreseen a priori.

3.2 Properties Specification

While architectural properties can be of various nature (e.g., security, reliability, performance, usability and others [5]), within the context of this paper we deal with scenario-based temporal properties, identifying how components are supposed to interact in order to satisfy a pre-defined pattern or a needed service, by specifying wanted/unwanted execution flows among architectural elements.

In order to model such properties, we make use of the Property Sequence Charts (PSC) [6,7] notation, a scenario-based graphical language. PSC is an extended graphical notation of a subset of UML2.0 sequence diagrams, which is used for specifying the interaction between a collection of component instances that execute concurrently. It has a formally defined syntax and semantics.

In Figure 2 we show all the PSC graphical elements. Three types of special messages can be specified: *Regular, Required*, and *Fail*. Regular messages (labeled with e : *msg name*) constitute the precondition for a desired (or an undesired) interaction. Required messages (labeled with r : *msg name*) must be exchanged by the system and are used to express mandatory interactions. Fail messages (labeled with f : *msg name*) should never be exchanged and are used to express undesired interactions. A *strict* operator is used to explicitly specify a strict ordering between a pair of messages. A *loose* ordering, instead, assumes any other messages can occur between the selected ones. *Constraints* are introduced to define restrictions on what can happen between the message containing the constraint and its predecessor or successor. PSC also uses the *parallel, loop, simultaneous, complement* operators for specifying parallel merge (i.e., interleaving), iteration, simultaneity and complement (i.e., all possible messages but a specified one), respectively.

We adopt PSC since it aims at balancing expressive power and simplicity of use, by building on results and experience of existing valuable proposals in literature.

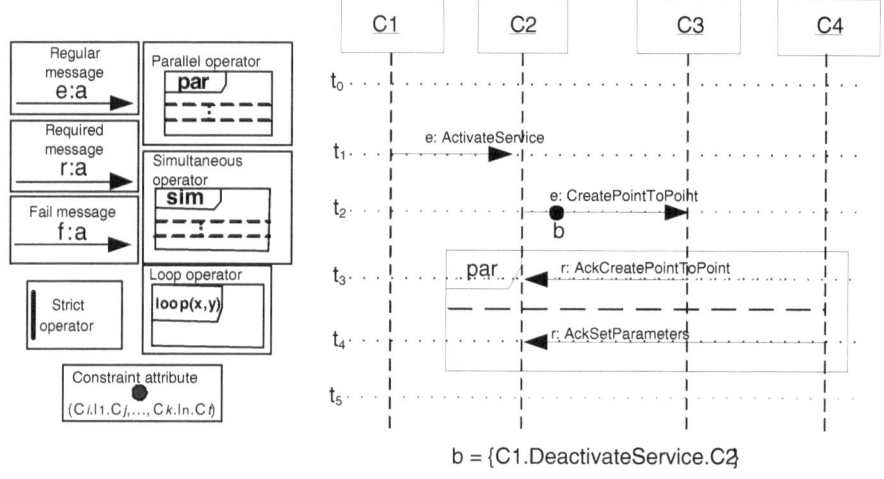

PSC graphical elements   **PSC Example**

Fig. 2. The PSC Graphical Notation

3.3   The AOP Instrumentation and Monitoring Approach

As well known, Aspect Oriented Programming (AOP) is a programming paradigm improving modularity. The main concepts in AOP are: *cross-cutting concerns, aspects, joint point*, and *weaving*. A cross-cutting concern represents a feature which cannot be located in a single component, but instead needs to be spread over a number of modules. Thus, one concern can be spread through many objects, and one object can implement many concerns. That means changing one module entails understanding all the tangled concerns. A typical example is security: making a system secure requires to consider security concerns all over the system implementation. An aspect is a crosscutting concern, with the main goal of being transversal to the system structure. Through aspects, crosscutting features can be created and automatically imported into the system, without modifying existing modules. A joint point represents the locations where the aspect is joined into the code, through a weaving process. A weaver is the engine which merges together the aspect and the target application, according to the identified joint point. The weaving process can be static (compile time) or dynamic (run-time).

Our approach employs AOP techniques for instrumentation. In particular, we use the AspectJ language used for monitoring J2EE applications.

The process is shown in Figure 3 (rounded boxes represent algorithms and applications, irregular boxes represent artifacts, colored boxes represent algorithms or artifacts developed by us).

In a property-driven monitoring approach based on SA definition, the identification of the events to monitor is somehow straightforward. In order to validate the properties at run-time we need to observe all the invocation that are "mentioned" at least in one PSC. In turn PSCs are defined using messages defined in the interfaces of the architectural components.

A parser application (written in Java) parses the PSC xml file so to identify those objects and interfaces to be monitored (the `PropertyParser` box in Figure 3). The `ProfiledInput` parser output contains information on which component/method/interface we are interested to monitor, as described in the PSC.

Next step consists in creating the aspect for monitoring the selected PSCs. For this purpose, the `AspectCreator` takes in input the `AspectTemplate` file (a parameterized aspect written for monitoring purposes) and the profiled information, and produces the property-dependent aspect, by instantiating the `AspectTemplate` document according to the PSCs. Joint points are identified according to the PSC document and embedded in the aspect. The aspect is stored into a ".aj" file and successively compiled through the AspectJ compiler. The compiled aspects and the target application are then weaved so to create an instrumented target application which allows the system monitoring according to the identified properties. The monitoring system is composed by a J2EE instrumented application. When it is run, the execution of PSC components/methods/interfaces are collected and stored in a monitored traces file.

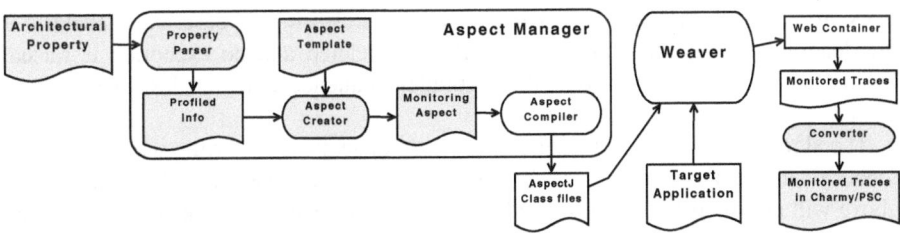

Fig. 3. The MOSAICO AOP Approach

3.4   The Analyzer Engine

On receiving the information from the instrumented system interfaces the Analyser Engine must be able to verify at run-time if a property has been satisfied or not. The derivation of such an engine, for the case of properties defined using PSC, is not easy. In particular the analyzer must be able to check, for each notified event, if it is relevant in the context of any defined property. Moreover in case of PSC specifying time constraints it will be necessary to set up deadlines for the observation of an event.

The engine we developed takes in input all the PSC defining the properties to be validated at run-time, and organises this information in suitable data structures. When an event is notified, the following algorithm is followed:

1. the property database is searched looking for any property specifying that event as the first event in a sequence.
2. for each property identified, a Property Validation Context (PVC) is opened. This is a data structure that contains all the information concerning the next expected events (or a set of it in case the alternative operator was specified) and the set of events that should not be observed (in case at least a fail message is specified in the sequence). PVCs are grouped according to the JVM threads that started it. In case of events to be observed within a time frame a deadline is fixed. When the deadline expires the event is considered not happened and in case of an expected event an exception is raised.
3. for all PVCs already open and related to the thread whose ID is associated to the notified event, the analyzer checks if the event is in the set of expected or forbidden events. In the latter case, an exception is raised. An exception is also raised if the next event expected in the PVC was specified using the "strict" operator and it does not match with the notified one.
4. for all PVCs associated to the thread for which the event matches with the expected one (or is in the set of expected one) the set of expected and denied events are replaced with the new sets found in the next step of the related PSC. In case there is no next event specified in the PSC the property has been satisfied and the PVC is closed.

Using PSC it is also possible to specify a sequence of events that shall "not" be observed. This case is treated in a dual way with respect to expected sequences. Deadlines are fixed for each next event in the sequence also in this case. Nevertheless, if the deadline expires the corresponding PVC is deleted and no exception is raised. Instead an exception is raised if the forbidden sequence until the last event is observed.

The algorithm needs to consider also the case of sequences starting with two occurrences of the same event such as for instance *aab*. In this case, the algorithm shown above will erroneously open a second PVC when the second *a* event is notified. Such PVC will probably lead to an incorrect exception. To avoid this situation, additional checks are added to the algorithm verifying that a PVC is not open for the same thread on the same PSC.

4   The NewsFeeder Case Study

The NewsFeeder case study consists of a Web application which manages a newsletter. Such newsletter makes use of the Feed Rss web formats used to publish frequently updated digital content, such as blogs, news feeds or podcasts.

As in a traditional newsletter, three are the main system actors: a *generic user*, who can access the feed Rss archive and see the list of available web services; a *newsfeeder*, who can create his profile, add up to six Rss feeds, change its data, search info on the db; an *administrator*, who can add and remove feeds, manage feed categories, and users. As soon as an Rss feed is inserted, it is parsed and validated. If valid, an Rss feed preview is created through an XSLT file and visualized on a web browser. Rss feed are aggregated according to user profiles, and thanks to the Formatting Objects (XSL-FO) a pdf file is created and sent to the user.

Daily, the system updates the Rss feeds with the daily news in the db, creates the pdf file for each existing profile and send it to all the newsfeeder who created their own profile. In such a way, each newsfeeder daily receives an email with attached the news conforming with its profile.

New services can be dynamically added to the NewsFeeder system.

4.1   The NewsFeeder Software Architecture Specification

The NewsFeeder is implemented through the J2EE framework. This application is three-tiered, composed by a Client tier (the presentation layer), a Middle tier (containing the business logic), and a Data tier (the database). The NewsFeeder application resides on the middle tier and is composed by three (main) layers, as shown in Figure 4.

The Presentation Layer is responsible of the presentation logic. It includes three main components: the `CommonActions` implements generic actions; the `NewsFeederAction` implements the actions associated to the newsfeeder (profile management, feed addition to the selected profile, personal data management); the `AdminActions` includes the actions associated to the administrative area (e.g., feed management, feed categories management). The `Transformation` component includes features for feed validation, and preview and pdf file creation. The Presentation Layer controller is implemented through STRUTS, while the GUI is implemented via JSP.

The Business Layer is responsible of implementing the computational features. The `BusinessFactory` abstract class acts as a bridge between the presentation and the business layers. At deployment time, an instance of this class is created. At each time a request to the business layer arrives, the `Factory` component creates a new `NewsFeederDelegate` or `FeedDelegate` components. Such delegate components access the database through Data Access Object (DAO) objects. The Business Layer is implemented through POJOs business services.

The Integration Layer is responsible for the database connection. The `NewsFeederDAO` and `FeedDAO` components take the data from the DB, and create a Transfer Objet (TO) component depending on the resulting data. The TOs components provide data to respond to the presentation layer actions. The Integration Layer uses JDBC library to connect the Business tier with the Data tiers.

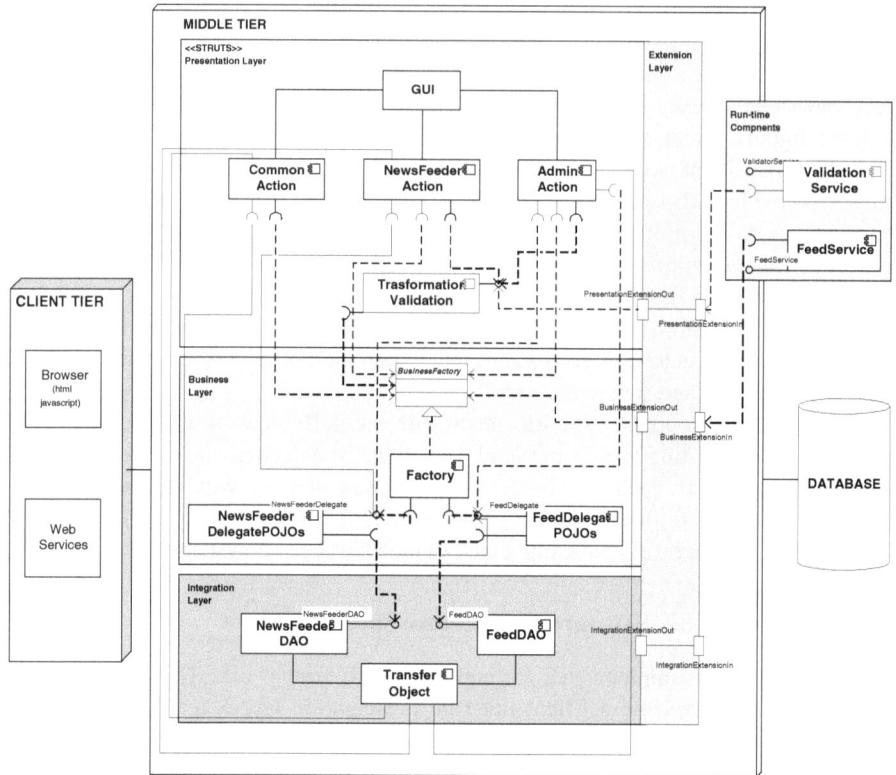

Fig. 4. The NewsFeeder Case Study Kernel Architecture and Run-time Components

The NewsFeeder Architecture Dynamicity. The NewsFeeder architecture is extensible at run-time through the addition or modification of run-time components. Such components reside on the Run-time Components layer and can be attached to the kernel architecture through the extension points depicted in Figure 4. In the web application we are taking into consideration, two are the black box components we added at run-time: one implementing the Rss feed validation feature (`ValidationServices`), and the Rss feed search and visualization features (`FeedServices`). In order to make some further monitoring analysis, we also added a mutated faulty version of the validation web service, referred in the following as `BadValidationServices`.

Tool Support. The software architecture specification of the NewsFeeder application has been modeled inside the Charmy framework [8]. Charmy allows the specification of the SA topology in terms of components, connectors and relationships among them, using a UML-based notation (stereotyped class diagrams for the topology and state diagrams for the behavior). The internal behavior of each component is specified in terms of state machines. Once the SA specification is available, a formal executable prototype in Promela [9] can be automatically generated.

4.2   The NewsFeeder Properties Specification

Two are the main classes of properties we are interested to monitor in this paper: Pattern-oriented properties, and Feature-oriented properties.

A J2EE application can make use of several patterns: Model View Controller, Singleton, Factory, Business delegate, Transfer Object, and Data Transfer Object [10]. Each of them imposes constraints on how component (types) can be assembled and on how they can communicate.

By considering the NewsFeeder application, we focussed mainly on two patterns: the Factory and Data Transfer Object patterns. The *Factory pattern* deals with the problem of creating components' objects[2] without specifying the exact class or object that will be created. This pattern helps to model an interface for creating a component object which at creation time can let its subclasses decide which class to instantiate. The *Data Transfer Object pattern* manages the connection to the database and creates the "transfer" serializable object to maintain data received by the database. We defined two pattern-oriented properties (POP) out of those two patterns.

POP1 *Direct access to a POJO object (unwanted):* according to the factory pattern, the Business Layer can be accessed only through the creation of a factory class. In the NewsFeeder architecture, this property is expressed by saying that in order to access the Business Layer, (see Figure 4, Middle Tier, Business Layer), an instance of the `BusinessFactory` class must be retrieved, and the implementation of this object creates a delegate object responsible for making visible the business layer public interfaces. What the property denies is the direct access to a POJO (delegate) object (i.e., `NewsFeederDelegatePOJOs` and `FeedDelegatePOJO`), without making a call to the `BusinessFactory` (in conformance to the Factory pattern).

POP2 *DAO object creation (unwanted):* according to the Data Transfer Object pattern, the creation of a DAO object (to make the system connecting to the database) has to be done by a POJO object. In the NewsFeeder study, when the application is deployed, it has to create an instance of the *BusinessFactory* so to identify the location of the data source. The `NewsFeederDAO` and `FeedDAO` DAO objects have to be created by the `NewsFeederDelegatePOJOs` and `FeedDelegatePOJO` objects, respectively (see Figure 4). The property we defined negates the possibility of creating a DAO object from an invalid data source (in conformance to the Data Transfer Object pattern).

The implementation of a certain feature, requires the interaction among different components, and may require the satisfiability of different patterns. We analyzed three different feature-oriented properties (FOP).

FOP1 *Business service creation feature:* this property specifies that, when a client makes a service creation request to the system, the system executes the required service and returns the result to the user. In the NewsFeeder system, when a client makes a service request, the STRUTS controller links such a request into an action, which calls an instance of the `BusinessFactory`. The

---

[2] Hereafter we refer to objects as instances of components' classes.

`BusinessFactory` through the `Factory` component creates a delegate object, which makes the service available to the action. The action executes that service and returns the result to the user. This feature requires the application of four different patterns (Factory, Singleton, Business delegate, and Model View Controller) and is activated by a user action;

FOP2 *Web service request features:* this property specifies that, when a client wants to open a connection with the server, the system elaborates its request and eventually returns a SOAP message. In the NewsFeeder architecture, a client web service creates a new ServiceLocator (in the Client Tier) that opens a new connection with the server. At the same time the ServiceLocator creates a stub that will manage the connection for the client. At this point the service client starts interacting with the server using SOAP messages. To satisfy incoming services requests from the client the server creates an instance of the BusinnesFactory and through the `Factory` component creates a delegate object which satisfies those requests. Finally a SOAP message is sent back to the client.

FOP3 *Remote validation service feature:* as in the description above the client service creates a ServiceLocator (in the Client Tier) that creates a stub to interact with the server. Using the connection an URL is sent to the server. The server parses the stream of that URL, validates it, and creates a report which is sent back to the system, and then to administrators through a dedicated news feeder.

Tool Support. PSC is implemented as a Charmy plugin. An example on how property POP1 looks like is shown in Figure 5.

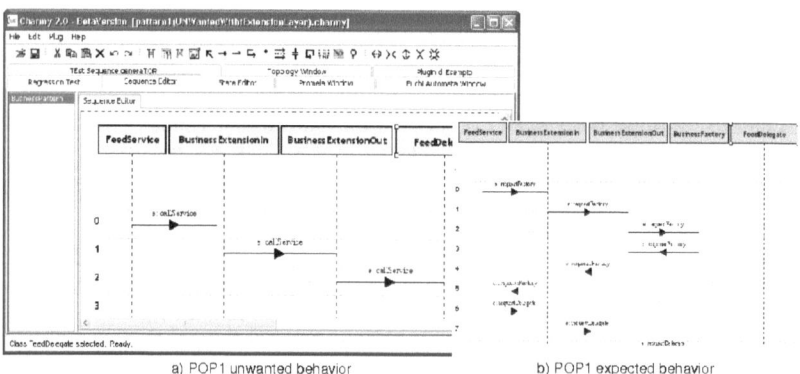

a) POP1 unwanted behavior   b) POP1 expected behavior

Fig. 5. The POP 1 PSC Specification

4.3   The NewsFeeder Instrumentation and Monitoring

Input to the AOP instrumentation and monitoring approach are a set of architectural properties (specified in PSC) and the target application. According to what introduced in Section 3.3 and summarized in Figure 3, five are the main steps to be applied over the given inputs: i) property parsing, ii) aspect creation, iii) aspect compilation, iv)

weaving, v) system execution and trace capture, vi) monitored trace conversion to PSC. Being steps iii), iv) and v) realized through traditional AOP technologies and tools, we here focus on the application of the complementary steps.

During property parsing, the XML representation of the five selected PSC properties are parsed so to obtain the list of messages and components to be monitored.

The aspect template we built for monitoring purposes is then instantiated with the information coming from the profiled information document. The aspect template file is a 123 lines of Java code, extending the *AspectWriter* class. It accepts one vector parameter (containing the result of the property parsing) and contains mostly *println* commands to store information on executed methods or interfaces. The output of the aspect creator process automatically generates an aspect (*public aspect Tracer{...}*). The AspectJ weaving process allows the creation of an instrumented J2EE application to be run.

When running the instrumented application, execution traces are captured, according to what of interest from the PSC properties. A monitored trace lists the all instrumented methods covered during system execution.

Monitoring the NewsFeeder Architecture Dynamicity. Being the NewsFeeder a dynamic system, it allows the addition of new components at run-time. While the previous step monitored the kernel architecture compliance to selected properties, the AOP monitoring system needs to keep working in perpetual way to monitor the run-time changing architecture. In our experiment, three components have been dynamically added to the kernel architecture: the `ValidationServices`, the `FeedServices`, and the faulty `BadValidationServices` components (the first two are shown in Figure 4).

To monitor dynamically evolving CBS, instead of static systems, we need to watch constantly the interfaces from the kernel to the external world (i.e., the extension points used for attaching plugins at run-time). This requires a small change to the property parser and introduces a small monitoring overhead, but gives a great flexibility to the monitoring system. Since the monitoring system captures any call going through the extension points, any call made by the added plugin is monitored without needing to change or even re-start the instrumented target application. In the specific case of the NewFeeder application, we monitor since the beginning the interfaces in the Extension Layer.

In case new properties need to be monitored after a run-time component is added, the Property Parser is launched again (to identify the new events to be monitored), the Aspect Creator creates the new monitoring aspect (taking into consideration the new events), which is successively compiled and weaved together with the target application. So far, this process requires to shut down and restart the application. This is due to a technical restriction of AspectJ, which does not allow run-time weaving.

In summary, the run-time addition of a black box component to the kernel architecture does not require any change to the monitoring system. At any time a new component is added, the monitoring system is transparent to the user, who can continue its execution without interrupts. In other terms and considering other classes of properties, e.g. security, the user can continue executing the updated system, while the software security policies are still verified.

Tool Support. Three are the main modules we developed in order to automatize the AOP instrumentation and monitoring process: a property parser, an aspect creator, and a converter (as shown in Figure 3). The property parser extracts from the PSC XML representation information on components, methods or interfaces which must be monitored, according to the property under analysis. The aspect creator takes the property parser input and uses it for instantiating an aspect template. The converter tool shows the execution traces as sequence diagrams inside the Charmy framework.

4.4   The NewsFeeder Analyzer Engine

Next step in the MOSAICO approach is the analysis of the deployed system to verify that it conforms to the architectural specification. This last step also provides the opportunity of verifying that MOSAICO works as expected, correctly identifying at run-time the violation of specified properties.

In order to test MOSAICO we used then a mutated version of the various Newsfeeder components. In particular, we inserted in the mutated components some interactions breaking the rules defined by the various patterns, for which properties were defined as illustrated in subsection 4.2.

Particularly interesting are properties related to the interactions involving components added at run-time to the system. For instance with reference to POP1 we inserted a *FeedService* component that directly accessed an existing POJO instance, which reference was provided by an external component, without first calling the *BussinessFactory* component instance. In this case MOSAICO correctly reported the violation having observed an invocation to the POJO from a component which did not invoke the *BusinessFactory* before. Clearly, though the approach seems to provide promising results, its validation as exposed here is still preliminary, and we plan to carry on more formal experimentation.

Tool Support. During run-time analysis the algorithm described in Section 3.4 is applied. In the real implementation the events are not directly notified by the probes inserted by the aspects. Instead, they are retrieved monitoring the different files in which the events are logged using the *inotify* Linux file system event-monitoring mechanism, that permits to be alerted when a line to file is inserted. Using the information stored in these files it is possible to reconstruct the execution traces. In particular, the information stored in the file concern the package and the object type receiving the method invocation, and the thread ID to which the invocation belongs.

5   Related Work

Many papers are related to the topic of monitoring and specifically Aspect Oriented monitoring. The distinguishing contribution of this work is the focus on architectural properties in monitoring of CBSs. In the following a set of approaches and tools are overviewed with respect to their objective and supporting technology.

AOP monitoring of CBSs:

In [11] Kiviluoma and coauthors describe an approach for the run-time monitoring of what they call the architecturally significant behaviors. A UML profile is utilized to specify the system. The behavioral profile consists of three stereotyped elements: <<ClassRole>> defines the participants role (e.g. Client e Server), <<OperationRole>> defines the operations of a ClassRole, and <<AttributeRole>> defines the attributes of roles. The behavioral role together with a model which maps roles to classes in the target application are utilized for creating AspectJ aspects successively weaved inside the target application. The target application is then run and differences among the modeled system and the one under execution are captured.

Java Logical Observer (JLO) [12] makes use of aspects for the verification of temporal assertions at run-time. In JLO, temporal properties are specified in LTL and inserted into java bytecode through Java 5.0 annotations. Successively, the annotated Java code is compiled and the resulting bytecode is inputted to the JLO tool which creates the aspects and verifies at run-time properties previously identified. Differently from our approach, JLO requires to annotate Java code, thus assuming code availability. Moreover, it cannot be considered a monitoring approach, rather a way to reason about behavior at run-time.

In [13] Xiaoguang et May introduce a framework for integration testing of component-based systems using aspect oriented technologies. Aspects are used for introducing testing-related cross cutting concerns to black box components. Collaboration and interaction among components are monitored using AspecJ. Similarly to our approach, execution traces are collected through monitoring, even if for different purposes.

The Reverse Engineering tool ARE [14] permits a dynamic analysis of Java code and uses AspectJ for creating execution traces. The tool permits to improve the dynamic analysis of a target application, by capturing and successively analyzing execution traces. Differently from our approach, it is not architectural and focusses on Java code, instead of CBSs.

The Glassbox Ispector [15] is an application monitor which combines AspectJ and the Java Management Extensions for performance tracing by extracting execution traces; Bugdel [16] is an Eclipse plug-in for Java applications debugging which allows the definition of aspects in a easy way, through a wizard procedure which hides some of the AOP complexity. Katz [17] introduces an approach for automatically verifying wether an aspect can introduce an unexpected problem in the original target application.

Analysis of Dynamic architectures

Software architectures may change over time, due to the need to provide a more dependable system, the need to remove identified deficiencies, or the need to handle dynamically-evolving collections of components at run-time [18].

Some research has investigated SA evolution, especially at run-time. In [19] the authors analyze how an architecture may change at run-time (in terms of component addition, component removal, component replacement, and run-time reconfiguration) and how tool suites may be used to cope with such evolution. In [20] the authors describe an approach to specify architectures that permits the representation and analysis of dynamic architectures. In [21] the authors analyze the issues of dynamic changes to a software configuration, in terms of component creation and deletion, and connection and disconnection. The CBabel (Building applications by Evolution with Connectors) architectural language allows the specification of dynamic architectures supporting reconfiguration [22]. CBabel makes use of the Maude model checker so to model-check LTL properties.

6 Conclusions and Future Work

Component-based systems are becoming self-adaptable, self-reconfiguring, and their architecture evolves at run-time. Pre-deployment validation techniques become inadequate in this dynamic context and must be complemented with run-time perpetual validation techniques. This paper has proposed the MOSAICOapproach (and its associated tool) for validating wether CBSs maintain the compliance to some architectural properties when subject to dynamic evolution. The dynamically evolving system is perpetually monitored for identifying unforeseen errors introduced while adding, modifying or removing components.

Manifold are the directions for future work.

The performance of the monitoring system needs to be carefully analyzed. This is an ongoing activity which is requiring the MOSAICO application to different systems.

The monitored properties can be of various nature, as outlined in Section 3. While this paper has focussed on component integration properties, in future work we are planning to extend the set of properties including also security and architectural style related properties.

As shown, the approach yields ample room for the development of automatic support. This paper has shown a set of tools supporting some of the steps foreseen by MOSAICO, nevertheless some of these steps are still carried on manually, like the manual elicitation of properties.

So far, the Analyzer Engine permits to validate the conformance among the monitored trace and the expected property. The definition of failure localization, recovery and repairing mechanisms in terms of the notifications raised by the analyzer has not been considered.

Finally, this paper has taken into consideration a static architecture capable of evolving at run-time. The kernel architecture is a known assembly of components (typically black box), and run-time components can be added. In a purely dynamic architecture, instead, a kernel is designed so to only provide routing features (e.g., like in Peer to Peer architectures) and the architectural configuration is created and evolves at run-time. We are investigating how our approach can be extended to deal with such situation.

References

1. Muccini, H., Hierons, R. (eds.): ROSATEA 2006: The Role Of Software Architecture in Testing and Analysis. ACM Digital Library. ACM Press, New York (2006)
2. QOSA Conferences on the Quality of Software Architectures, Lecture Notes on Computer Science (2005-2007)
3. Delgado, N., Gates, A.Q., Roach, S.: A taxonomy and catalog of runtime software-fault monitoring tools. IEEE Trans. Softw. Eng. 30(12), 859–872 (2004)
4. Bertolino, A., Muccini, H., Polini, A.: Architectural verification of black-box component-based systems. In: RISE2006. Proc. Int. Workshop on Rapid Integration of Software Engineering techniques, vol. to appear as LNCS (2006)

5. Kazman, R., Abowd, G., Bass, L., Clements, P.: Scenario-based analysis of software architecture. IEEE Softw. 13(6), 47–55 (1996)
6. Autili, M., Inverardi, P., Pelliccione, P.: A scenario based notation for specifying temporal properties. In: SCESM'06, Shanghai, China, May 27, 2006, ACM Press, New York (2006)
7. PSC home page: http://www.di.univaq.it/psc2ba (2005)
8. CHARMY Project. Charmy Web Site. (http://www.di.univaq.it/charmy)
9. Holzmann, G.J.: The SPIN Model Checker: Primer and Reference Manual. Addison-Wesley, Reading (2003)
10. Crawford, W.C., Kaplan, J.: J2EE Design Patterns. O'Reilly (2003)
11. Kiviluoma, K., Koskinen, J., Mikkonen, T.: Run-time monitoring of architecturally significant behaviors using behavioral profiles and aspects. In: ISSTA'06. Proc. Int. Symposium on Software Testing and Analysis, Portland, Maine, pp. 181–190 (2006)
12. Bodden, E.: A lightweight ltl runtime verification tool for java. In: Companion to the 19th annual ACM SIGPLAN conference on Object-oriented programming systems, languages, and applications, pp. 306–307. ACM Press, New York (2004)
13. Xiaoguang, M., May, J.: A framework of integration Testing using AspectJ. In: WAOSD. Int. Workshop on Aspect-Oriented Software Development, Beijing, China (2004)
14. Gschwind, T., Oberleitner, J.: Improving dynamic data analysis with aspect-oriented programming. In: CSMR '03. Proc. 7th European Conference on Software Maintenance and Reengineering, Washington, DC, p. 259. IEEE Computer Society Press, Los Alamitos (2003)
15. Bodkin, R.: AOP@Work: Performance monitoring with AspectJ (September 2005) IBM: http://www-128.ibm.com/developerworks/java/library/j-aopwork10/
16. Usui, Y., Chiba, S.: Bugdel: An aspect-oriented debugging system. In: APSEC '05. Proc. 12th Asia-Pacific Software Engineering Conference, Washington, DC, pp. 790–795. IEEE Computer Society Press, Los Alamitos (2005)
17. Katz, S.: Diagnosis of Harmful Aspects Using Regression Verification. In: FOAL workshop in AOSD 2004 (2004)
18. Garlan, D.: Software Architecture: a Roadmap. In: Finkelstein, A. (ed.) ACM ICSE 2000, The Future of Software Engineering, pp. 91–101. ACM Press, New York (2000)
19. Oreizy, P., Medvidovic, N., Taylor, R.: Architecture-Based Runtime Software Evolution. In: ICSE 98. Proc. Int. Conf. on Software Engineering, Kyoto, Japan (1998)
20. Allen, R.J., Douence, R., Garlan, D.: Specifying and Analyzing Dynamic Software Architectures. In: Astesiano, E. (ed.) ETAPS 1998 and FASE 1998. LNCS, vol. 1382, Springer, Heidelberg (1998)
21. Kramer, J., Magee, J.: Analysing Dynamic Change in Software Architectures: A case study. In: Proc. 4th IEEE Int. Conf. on Configurable Distributed Systems, IEEE Computer Society Press, Los Alamitos (1998)
22. Rademake, A., Braga, C., Sztajnberg, A.: A rewriting semantics for a software architecture description language. ENTCS 130, 345–377 (2005)

A Modeling Approach to Analyze the Impact of Error Propagation on Reliability of Component-Based Systems[*]

Vittorio Cortellessa[1] and Vincenzo Grassi[2]

[1] Dipartimento di Informatica, Universita' dell'Aquila
cortelle@di.univaq.it
[2] Dipartimento di Informatica Sistemi e Produzione, Universita' di Roma "Torvergata"
vgrassi@info.uniroma2.it

.

Abstract. We present a novel approach to the analysis of the reliability of a component-based system that takes into account an important architectural attribute, namely the error propagation probability. This is the probability that an error, arising somewhere in the system, propagates to other components, possibly up to the system output. As we show in the paper, this attribute may heavily affect decisions on crucial architectural choices. Nonetheless, it is often neglected in modeling the reliability of component-based systems. Our modeling approach provides a useful support to the reliability engineering of component-based systems, since it can be used to drive several significant tasks, such as: (i) placing error detection and recovery mechanisms, (ii) focusing the design, implementation and selection efforts on critical components, (iii) devising cost-effective testing strategies. We illustrate the approach on an ATM example system.

Keywords: component-based systems, reliability, state-based model.

1 Introduction

Emerging paradigms of software development, like component-based software engineering and COTS-based software development, stress the idea of building a software system as an assembly of pre-existing and newly developed components.

Assessing the quality (with respect to both functional and non functional properties) of such systems is not straightforward, as it can depend in non trivial ways on the quality of their components and on how they are assembled. In this paper, we focus on *reliability*, defined as a probabilistic measure of the system ability to successfully carry out its own task as specified, and provide a modeling approach for reliability analysis. Our approach exploits information about the reliability properties of each component, as well as architectural information about how components are assembled. Using this information, we show how to get an estimate of the overall system reliability and of its sensitivity with respect to variations in the reliability properties of its components.

---

[*] This work has been partially supported by the PLASTIC project (EC 6th Framework Programme). http://www.ist-plastic.org

H.W. Schmidt et al. (Eds.): CBSE 2007, LNCS 4608, pp. 140–156, 2007.

Being model-based, our approach can be used to perform early reliability analysis, thus driving the actual system implementation. It can be used for "what if" experiments to predict the impact of architectural changes needed to adapt the system to new or changing requirements. In particular, the sensitivity analysis supported by our approach provides useful insights for system design, development and testing. Indeed, it can be used to drive the placement of error detection and recovery mechanisms in the system. Moreover, from the viewpoint of project and resource management, it can be used to convey consistent project resources on the most critical components (i.e. the ones with the highest sensitivity). It can also be used to focus the testing efforts on those components where a small change in the failure characteristics may lead to considerable variations in the overall system reliability.

Architecture-based analytic approaches to the reliability analysis of component-based systems have been already presented in the literature (see Section 2.3). The main novelty of our work, that distinguishes it from most of the existing analytic approaches, consists in taking into account an important architectural aspect, namely the *error propagation* from component to component. As the results of our experiments show, neglecting this aspect may lead, at the best, to overly pessimistic predictions of the system reliability, that could cause unnecessary design and implementation efforts to improve it. Worse yet, if reliability analysis is used to drive the selection of components, it could lead to wrong estimates of the reliability of different component assemblies, thus causing the selection of an assembly which is actually less reliable than others.

The paper is organized as follows. In section 2 we first provide a brief overview of basic reliability concepts, then we introduce our component-based system failure model, and finally we review related work on reliability analysis of component-based systems. In section 3 we present our approach to the reliability analysis of component-based systems and provide an analytic solution for the reliability estimate that takes into account the error propagation probabilities. Based on the results of section 3, we provide in section 4 analytic solutions for the sensitivity of the system reliability with respect to the reliability properties of each component. In section 5 we apply our results to an example of Automated Teller Machine (ATM) and show the relevance of the newly introduced parameters. Finally, we draw some conclusions and give hints for future work in section 6.

2   Background

2.1   Basic Concepts

According to [3], a *failure* consists in the deviation of the service provided by a system from the correct service. An *error* is the part of the system state that leads to the occurrence of a failure, and is caused by a *fault*. However, not all faults cause an error, and not all errors lead to a failure. For example, a bug in the code that implements a software component is an internal fault that causes an error in the component internal state only if that code is actually executed. This error leads to the occurrence of a component failure only if it reaches the interface of the component (this might not happen, for example, if the error is overwritten by other internal computations). In turn, a component failure does not necessarily implies a failure of a system consisting of an assembly

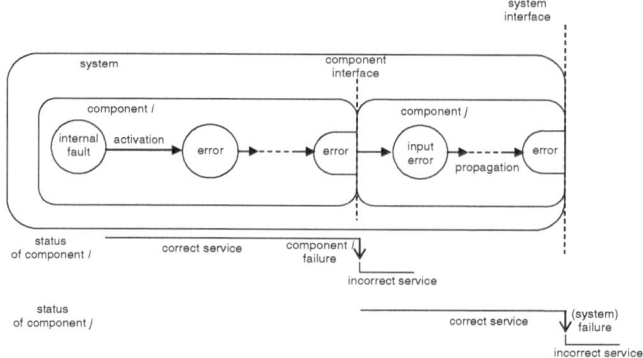

Fig. 1. Error propagation in a component assembly

of components. A system failure occurs only if the generated error propagates through other components up to the external interface of the system. Figure 1 exemplifies this propagation chain [3].

From this brief discussion it emerges that the reliability of a component-based system, defined as the probability that no system failure occurs, strongly depends on the following factors:

- the *internal failure probability* of each component, that is the probability that the component generates a failure caused by some internal fault;
- the *error propagation probability* of each component, that is the probability that the component propagates to its output interface an erroneous input it has received;
- the *propagation path probability* of the component assembly, that is the probability of each possible error propagation path from a component up to the system output.

The former two factors are intrinsic characteristics of each component taken in isolation. The latter factor instead depends on the system architecture, i.e. on the topology of the component connections and the likelihood of possible component interaction patterns.

None of these factors should be neglected to get a significant estimate of the reliability of a component-based system. However, most of the existing analytic approaches (see section 2.3) do not consider the error propagation factor.

2.2   Component-Based System Failure Model

In Figure 2 we give a visual representation of our component-based system failure model, along with the parameters involved in the computation of the system reliability that is denoted in figure as REL.

In our model we consider an application consisting of C interacting components. Each interaction corresponds to a control transfer from a component i to a component j, that also involves the transfer to j of some data produced by i. In [24] the distinction between data flow and control flow is discussed with respect to the integration of module

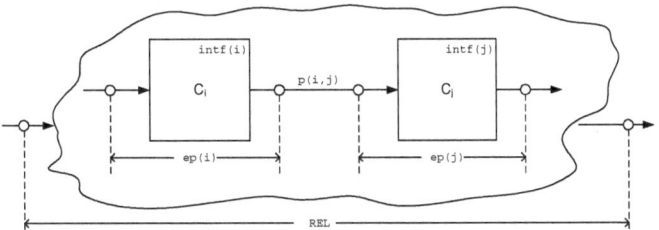

Fig. 2. The component-based system failure model and its parameters

and system performance. In our approach, we do not distinguish the two aspects, and we assume that data errors always propagate through the control flow [11].

We assume that the operational profile of each component i is known, and it follows the Markov property. Hence, it is expressed by the probabilities $p(i, j)$ $(1 \leq i, j \leq C)$ that, given an interaction originating from i, it is addressed to component j [12,29]. It holds the obvious constraint that $(\forall i) \sum_j p(i, j) = 1$. Self-transitions are not forbidden in our model, namely it may occur that $p(i, i) \neq 0$.

Besides its operational profile, each component i is also characterized by its internal failure probability $intf(i)$. $intf(i)$ is the probability that, given a correct input, a failure occurs during the execution of i causing the production of an erroneous output. In this definition, "erroneous" refers to the input/output specification of i taken in isolation. $intf(i)$ can be interpreted as the probability of component failure per demand [12].

However, the occurrence of a failure within a component does not necessarily affect the application ability of producing correct results as outlined in Section 2.1. To take into account this effect, we introduce in our failure model the additional parameter $ep(i)$, that denotes the error propagation probability of component i, that is the probability that i does not mask but rather propagates to its output a received erroneous input.

We assume that $intf(i)$ and $ep(i)$ are independent of each other. This is in accordance with the literature on the analysis of the error propagation characteristics of a system, where this aspect is considered independently from the reliability of each system component (see, for example, [1,15]). We point out that, as a consequence of this independence assumption, $ep(i) < 1$ for some component i implies an increase of the system reliability with respect to the case $ep(i) = 1$, as in the former case there is a non-zero probability that i does mask an error received from other components.

2.3   Related Work

A crucial element in any model-based approach to reliability analysis is the meaningful estimate of the model parameters. As it can be argued from the above discussion, these parameters concern the internal failure and error propagation probabilities for each component, and the probability of each possible propagation path. In the following, we first review proposed methodologies for their estimate. Then, we review existing architecture-based analytic approaches to reliability analysis of component-based systems.

An interesting classification of potential sources of data that may be relevant for reliability estimation of software architectures can be found in [25]. Four classes of sources are defined, two for newly developed software and two for reused software.

Methods for the estimate of the probability of failure of a single component are extensively reviewed in [12], and have been also reviewed in [11]. Hence, we refer to those papers for a wide discussion on this issue.

With regard to estimate of the error propagation probability for each single component, relevant work has been recently presented in [1,15]. In [15] an error permeability parameter of a software module is defined, which is a measure providing insights on the error propagation characteristics of the module. A methodology is devised to extract this parameter from an existing software system through fault injection. In [1] an analytical formula for the estimate of the error propagation probability between two components is provided. This estimate derives from an entropy-based metrics, which basically depends on the frequencies of component interactions and the injectivity degree of the function calculated by each component. Another approach based on fault injection to estimate the error propagation characteristics of a software system during testing was presented in [26,27].

With regard to the estimate of the propagation path probabilities, the basic information exploited by all the architecture-based methodologies is the probability that component i directly interacts with component j. At early design stages, where only models of the system are available, this information can be derived from software artifacts (e.g. UML interaction diagrams), possibly annotated with probabilistic data about the possible execution and interaction patterns [8].

A review and discussion of methodologies for the interaction probability estimate can be found in [11,12]. A more recent method has been discussed in [23], where a Hidden Markov model is used to cope with the imperfect knowledge about the component behavior.

Once the interaction probabilities are known, the probability of the different error propagation paths can be estimated under the assumption that errors propagate through component interactions. According to the classification proposed in [12], most of the existing approaches can be broadly categorized as: (i) *path-based* models, where the probability of the possible component execution paths is explicitly considered; (ii) *state-based* models, where probabilistic control flow graphs are used to model the usage patterns of components.

These two types of approaches are conceptually quite similar. One of the main differences between them emerges when the control flow graph of the application contains loops. State-based models analytically account for the infinite number of paths that might exist due to loops. Path-based models require instead an explicit enumeration of the considered paths; hence, to avoid an infinite enumeration, the number of paths is restricted in some way, for example to the ones observed experimentally during the testing phase or by limiting the depth traversal of each path. In this respect, we adopt here a state-based model.

Moving to the analysis of the overall system reliability, a thorough review of existing model-based approaches can be found in [12], whereas a more recent approach appeared in [22]. However, albeit error propagation is an important element in the chain that leads to a system failure, all existing approaches ignore it. In these approaches, the only considered parameters are the internal failure probability of each component and the interaction probabilities, with the underlying assumption that any error that arises in a component immediately manifest itself as an application failure, or equivalently that it always propagates (i.e. with probability one) up to the application outputs.

Only few paper have considered the error propagation problem within a system-level reliability model. In [15] an experimental approach to the analysis of the system reliability is presented, based on the monitoring of the error propagation phenomena in deployed systems. At the best of our knowledge, the only analytical model for reliability analysis of component-based systems that considers the error propagation has been presented in [21]. In this model it is assumed that each error arising within a component always causes a system failure and, at the same time, it can also propagate to other components affecting their failure probability. In our opinion this failure model, based on the contemporary assumption of immediate failure and propagation to other components, deserves further investigation about its soundness. Indeed, the immediate failure assumption seems to make irrelevant (or contradictory) to reason about the propagation of errors to other components. The model we present in section 3 is based on a different assumption.

An important advantage of architectural analysis of reliability is the possibility of studying the sensitivity of the system reliability to the reliability of each component, as said in the Introduction. Although this advantage is widely recognized [11,19,28], few model-based approaches for computing the sensitivity of the system reliability with respect to each component reliability have been developed [6,10]. A basic work for the sensitivity analysis of the reliability with respect to some system parameter was presented in [5], but it does not address specifically architectural issues. Moreover, all these models do not take into account the error propagation attribute.

With respect to the existing literature, the original contributions of this paper can be summarized as follows:

- We define a state-based architectural model for the analysis of reliability, where the error propagation factor is taken into account, and derive an analytic solution for the reliability evaluation.
- We derive analytic expressions for the evaluation of reliability sensitivity with respect to the error propagation and the failure probability of each component.
- The above modeling results can be exploited in component-based development processes to place error detection and recovery mechanisms, to focus the design, implementation and selection efforts on critical components, and to devise cost-effective testing strategies.

3   Embedding the Error Propagation in a Reliability Model

In this section we provide the mathematical foundations of our model, and in the following section we perform a sensitivity analysis with respect to the model parameters.

The operational profile of a component-based software application is expressed by a matrix $\mathbf{P} = [p(i,j)], (0 \leq i,j \leq C+1)$, where each entry $p(i,j)$ represents the probability that component i, during its execution, transfers the control to component j. The rows 0 and $C + 1$ of $\mathbf{P}$ correspond to two "fictitious" components that represent, respectively, the entry point and the exit point of the application [29]. These components allow to easily model: (i) the stochastic uncertainty among application entry points, by means of $p(0, j)$ probabilities $(0 \leq j \leq C)$, (ii) the completion of the application by means of the first control transfer to component $C + 1$.

Given this model, the application dynamics corresponds to a discrete time Markov process with state transition probability matrix $\mathbf{P}$, where the process state i represents the execution of the component i, and state $C + 1$ is an absorbing state. Figure 3 depicts the structure of $\mathbf{P}$, where $\mathbf{Q}$ is a $(C + 1) \cdot (C + 1)$ sub-stochastic matrix (with at least one row sum < 1), and $\mathbf{c}$ is a column vector with $C + 1$ entries.

Hence, the entries of the k-step transition probability matrix $\mathbf{P}^k = [p^{(k)}(i, j)]$ of this process represent the probability that, after exactly k control transfers, the executing component is j, given that the execution started with component i. We recall that $\mathbf{P}^k$ is recursively defined as $\mathbf{P}^0 = I$ (the identity matrix) and $\mathbf{P}^k = \mathbf{P} \cdot \mathbf{P}^{k-1} (k \geq 1)$. Figure 3 also depicts the structure of $\mathbf{P}^k$, where $\mathbf{c}^{(k)}$ is a column vector.

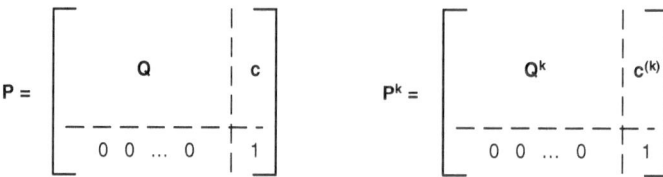

Fig. 3. The structures of $\mathbf{P}$ and $\mathbf{P}^k$ matrices

Let us denote by Rel the application reliability, that is the probability that the application completes its execution and produces a correct output (as defined in Figure 2). In order to model Rel we introduce the following probabilities in addition to $intf(i)$ and $ep(i)$ defined in section 2.2 [1]:

- $err(i)$: probability that the application completes its execution producing an erroneous output, given that the execution started at component i $(0 \leq i \leq C)$;
- $err^{(k)}(i, j)$: probability that the execution reaches component j after exactly k $(k \geq 0)$ control transfers and j produces an erroneous output, given that the execution started at component i $(0 \leq i, j \leq C)$.

Using these definitions we can write the following equations:

$$err(i) = \sum_{k=0}^{\infty} \sum_{h=0}^{C} err^{(k)}(i, h)p(h, C + 1) \tag{1}$$

$$Rel = 1 - err(0) \tag{2}$$

Equation (1) derives from the assumption that the application completion is represented by the first occurrence of a transition to state $C + 1$. Equations (1) and (2)

---

[1] By definition, we assume $intf(0) = intf(C + 1) = 0$ and $ep(0) = ep(C + 1) = 1$.

emphasize that $err^{(k)}(i,j)$ probabilities are key elements for the evaluation of the system reliability. These probabilities can be evaluated using simple decomposition arguments. Let us consider a component i that has been reached after k component-to-component transitions. Two mutually exclusive events may take place at i: either an internally generated failure occurs or it does not occur. In the former case, i transmits an error to the next component irrespective of whether it has received or not an erroneous input from the previous component. In the latter case, it transmits an error to the next component only if it has received an erroneous input from the previous component and this error propagates through i up to its interface. Based on these arguments, we may write the following recursive equations, which relate $err^{(k)}()$ with $err^{(k-1)}()$:

$$err^{(k)}(i,j) = p^{(k)}(i,j) \cdot intf(j) + ep(j) \cdot (1 - intf(j)) \cdot \sum_{h=0}^{C} err^{(k-1)}(i,h)p(h,j) \quad (3)$$

where we assume $err^{(k)}(i,j) = 0$ for $k < 0$ [2].

For computational purposes, it is convenient to put the above equations in matrix form. In [14] we have proven that $err(0)$ in equation 2 is the 0-th element of the column vector $\mathbf{e} = [err(i)](0 \leq i \leq C)$, which is defined by the following closed-form matrix expression:

$$\mathbf{e} = (\mathbf{I} - \mathbf{Q})^{-1} \cdot \mathbf{F} \cdot (\mathbf{I} - \mathbf{Q} \cdot \mathbf{R} \cdot (\mathbf{I} - \mathbf{F}))^{-1} \cdot \mathbf{c} \quad (4)$$

where $\mathbf{Q}$ and $\mathbf{c}$ are the ones appearing in Figure 3 and:

- $\mathbf{F} = [f(i,j)](0 \leq i,j \leq C)$, a diagonal matrix with $f(i,i) = intf(i)$, and $f(i,j) = 0$ ($\forall i \neq j$);
- $\mathbf{R} = [r(i,j)](0 \leq i,j \leq C)$, a diagonal matrix with $r(i,i) = ep(i)$, and $r(i,j) = 0$ ($\forall i \neq j$);
- $\mathbf{I}$ is a $(C+1)$ sized identity matrix.

Equation 4 represents the basis of the sensitivity analysis that is performed in the next section.

4   Sensitivity Analysis of Reliability

In this section we show how the analytic model developed in section 3 can be used to analyze the sensitivity of the system reliability with respect to the internal failure and error propagation probabilities of its components [3].

For this purpose, let us define the following notations:

- $de\_err(i; l)$: the partial derivative of $err(i)$ with respect to $ep(l)$ ($1 \leq i, l \leq C$);

---

[2] Note that this basic assumption corresponds to $err^{(0)}(i,j) = intf(j)$ ($\forall i = j$) and $err^{(0)}(i,j) = 0$ ($\forall i \neq j$), namely the probability of an erroneous output from component j without any transfer of control is its own probability of *internal failure*.

[3] For sake of readability, we do not report mathematical proofs in this section, while they can be found in [9].

- $de\_err^{(k)}(ij;l)$: the partial derivative of $err^{(k)}(ij)$ with respect to $ep(l)$ ($1 \leq i,j,l \leq C$);
- $di\_err(i;l)$: the partial derivative of $err(i)$ with respect to $intf(l)$ ($1 \leq i,l \leq C$);
- $di\_err^{(k)}(ij;l)$: the partial derivative of $err^{(k)}(ij)$ with respect to $intf(l)$ ($1 \leq i,j,l \leq C$);

We first consider the derivative of Rel with respect to $ep()$'s and then with respect to $intf()$'s.

4.1 Sensitivity with Respect to $ep()$'s

From equation (2), the sensitivity of the application reliability with respect to $ep(l)$ can be expressed as:

$$\frac{\partial}{\partial ep(l)} Rel = -\frac{\partial}{\partial ep(l)} err(0) = -de\_err(0;l) \tag{5}$$

Hence, our goal here is to calculate $de\_err(0;l)$. By differentiating equations (1) and (3) with respect to $ep(l)$ we get, respectively:

$$de\_err(i;l) = \sum_{k=0}^{\infty}\sum_{h=0}^{C} de\_err^{(k)}(ih;l)p(h,C+1) \tag{6}$$

$$de\_err^{(k)}(ij;l) = ep(j)(1 - intf(j))\sum_{h=0}^{C} de\_err^{(k-1)}(ih;l)p(h,j)$$
$$+ I\{j=l\}(1 - intf(l))\sum_{h=0}^{C} err^{(k-1)}(i,h)p(h,l) \tag{7}$$

where it is assumed that $de\ err^{(0)}(ij;l) = 0$, and $I\{e\}$ is the indicator function defined as: $I\{e\} = 1$ if condition e is true, 0 otherwise.

By defining $\hat{\mathbf{e}} = [\hat{e}(l)]$, ($0 \leq l \leq C$), with $\hat{e}(l) = de\_err(0;l)$, in [9] we prove that:

$$\hat{\mathbf{e}} = \mathbf{D}(\mathbf{I} - \mathbf{F})(\mathbf{I} - \mathbf{QR}(\mathbf{I} - \mathbf{F}))^{-1}\mathbf{c} \tag{8}$$

where $\mathbf{D}$ is a diagonal matrix obtained as follows: given the matrix $\mathbf{N} = [n(lj)]$, $\mathbf{N} = (\mathbf{I} - \mathbf{Q})^{-1}\mathbf{F}(\mathbf{I} - \mathbf{QR}(\mathbf{I} - \mathbf{F}))^{-1}\mathbf{Q}$, then

$$d(jj) = n(0j)$$
$$d(lj) = 0, \forall l \neq j$$

Equation 8 is finally plugged in 5 to study the sensitivity of Rel with respect to $ep()$'s.

4.2 Sensitivity with Respect to $intf()$'s

Analogously to what done in section 4.1, from equation (2) the sensitivity of the application reliability with respect to $intf(l)$ can be expressed as:

$$\frac{\partial}{\partial intf(l)}Rel = -\frac{\partial}{\partial intf(l)}err(0) = -di\_err(0;l) \tag{9}$$

Hence, our goal here is to calculate $di\_err(0;l)$. By differentiating equations (1) and (3) with respect to $intf(l)$ we get, respectively:

$$di\_err(i;l) = \sum_{k=0}^{\infty}\sum_{h=0}^{C} di\_err^{(k)}(ih;l)p(h,C+1) \tag{10}$$

$$di\_err^{(0)}(ij;l) = I\{i=j \wedge j=l\} \tag{11}$$

$$di\_err^{(k)}(ij;l) = ep(j)(1-intf(j))\sum_{h=0}^{C} di\_err^{(k-1)}(ih;l)p(h,j)$$

$$+ I\{j=l\}(p^{(k)}(il)-ep(l)\sum_{h=0}^{C} err^{(k-1)}(i,h)p(h,l)) \tag{12}$$

By defining $\tilde{\mathbf{e}} = [\tilde{e}(l)]$, $(0 \le l \le C)$, with $\tilde{e}(l) = di\_err(0;l)$, in [9] we prove that:

$$\tilde{\mathbf{e}} = (\mathbf{A} - \mathbf{DR})(\mathbf{I} - \mathbf{QR}(\mathbf{I} - \mathbf{F}))^{-1}\mathbf{c} \tag{13}$$

where $\mathbf{A}$ is a diagonal matrix obtained as follows: given the matrix $\mathbf{M} = [m(ij)]$, $\mathbf{M} = (\mathbf{I} - \mathbf{Q})^{-1}$, then

$$a(jj) = m(0j)$$
$$a(lj) = 0, \forall l \ne j$$

Equation 13 is finally plugged in 9 to study the sensitivity of Rel with respect to $intf()$'s.

5 Results and Analyses

Each entry of $\hat{\mathbf{e}}$ and $\tilde{\mathbf{e}}$ (defined in Section 4) represents, respectively, the sensitivity of the overall system reliability with respect to the error propagation probability and the internal failure probability of a specific component. Hence, by calculating these vectors, we obtain the reliability sensitivity with respect to the error propagation and internal failure probability of all the system components.

We have used an ATM bank system example to validate our reliability model, taken from [29] and illustrated in Figure 4 [4]. Shortly, a GUI is in charge of triggering the identification task that is carried out through the interaction of the Identifier and a DBMS.

---

[4] The system architecture differs from the one used in [29] only by one component that we have not duplicated as we do not consider fault-tolerance in our approach.

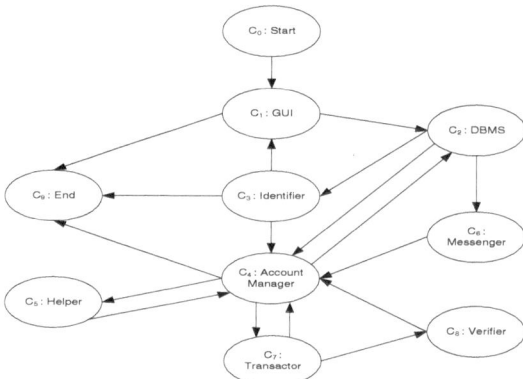

Fig. 4. The ATM architecture

Then the control goes to the Account Manager that is the core of the system. The latter, by interacting with all the other components (i.e. Messenger, Helper, Transactor and Verifier) and by using the data in the DBMS, manages all the operations required from the user during an ATM working session. Without the fictitious *Start* and *End* components, the system is made of components C_1 through C_8.

We devise two sets of experiments on this architecture to show the application of our model. In the first set, based on the results presented in section 3, we compare the reliability prediction we get by neglecting the error propagation impact with the prediction we get when this impact is taken into consideration. In all the experiments, the reliability values where error propagation is neglected have been obtained by setting to 1 the error propagation probabilities of all components. We call this setting as "perfect" propagation. In the second set of experiments, based on the results presented in section 4, we analyze the sensitivity of the system reliability to the error propagation and internal failure probabilities of its components. We have obtained all the results presented in this section using a standard linear system solver [30].

5.1 Impact of the Error Propagation: Experimental Results

Table 1 shows the values we have considered for the model parameters, that match the ones used in [29]. In Table 2 the value Rel of the system reliability obtained from equations (2) and (4) is reported (in the bottom row) while varying the error propagation probability $ep(i)$ of all the components (in the top row). In this experiment we have assumed the same $ep()$ value for all components. The first column (i.e. $ep(i) = 1.0$) represents a perfect propagation setting, where each component propagates to its output all the errors that it receives as input. This corresponds to the setting of all the existing reliability models where error propagation is not considered. For sake of giving evidence to the impact of "non-perfect" error propagation, from the second column on we decrease the $ep(i)$ value by the same quantity (i.e. 0.1) for all the components.

It is easy to observe that the perfect propagation assumption brings to heavily underestimate the system reliability. In fact, a decrease of only 10% of the error propagation

Table 1. Initial values of model parameters

		C_0	C_1	C_2	C_3	C_4	C_5	C_6	C_7	C_8	C_9 (c)	$intf(i)$
C_0		0	1	0	0	0	0	0	0	0	0	0
C_1		0	0	0.999	0	0	0	0	0	0	0.001	0.018
C_2		0	0	0	0.227	0.669	0	0.104	0	0	0	0.035
C_3		0	0.048	0	0	0.951	0	0	0	0	0.001	0
C_4		0	0	0.4239	0	0	0.1	0	0.4149	0	0.0612	0.004
C_5		0	0	0	0	1	0	0	0	0	0	0.01
C_6		0	0	0	0	1	0	0	0	0	0	0
C_7		0	0	0	0	0.01	0	0	0	0.99	0	0
C_8		0	0	0	0	1	0	0	0	0	0	0.1001
C_9		0	0	0	0	0	0	0	0	0	1	0

Table 2. System reliability vs component error propagation

$\forall i, ep(i)$	1.0	0.9	0.8	0.7	0.6	0.5	0.4	0.3	0.2	0.1
Rel	0.4745	0.8261	0.8989	0.9399	0.9494	0.9617	0.9710	0.9784	0.9848	0.9906

probability of each component (i.e. from 1.0 to 0.9) brings a 74% increase in the whole system reliability (i.e. from 0.4745 to 0.8261).

In order to show the negative effects of such underestimation on the component selection activity in a software development process of component-based systems, let us assume that an alternative component $C_{4.1}$ is available for the Account Manager. $C_{4.1}$ is functionally equivalent to the one adopted in the initial configuration, whereas its failure characteristics are: $intf(4.1) = 0.008$, $ep(4.1) = 0.9$. If we adopt a failure model that does not take into consideration the error propagation, then the new component cannot apparently improve the system reliability, as its internal failure probability doubles the one of the original component. In fact, the system reliability with the new value of $intf(4.1) = 0.008$ would be $Rel = 0.4594$, which corresponds to an apparent net decrease of 3% with respect to $Rel = 0.4745$ obtained with C_4. This would induce a system designer to not considering the new component in a component selection activity based on reliability characteristics. But if we adopt our model that embeds the error propagation probability, then the system reliability with the new values of $intf(4.1) = 0.008$ and $ep(4.1) = 0.9$ will be $Rel = 0.7094$, which corresponds to a net increase of 49%. Our model brings to the evidence at the system level the ability of the new component to mask more errors with respect to the old one, which is expressed in its lower $ep()$ value. Thus, although $C_{4.1}$ worsens the internal failure probability of C_4, its role of core component in the system architecture (i.e., propagation paths traverse this component with high probability) brings to prefer the former, as it propagates the errors with a lower probability.

5.2   Sensitivity Analysis: Experimental Results

We start this sensitivity analysis from the derivative of Rel in the parameter setting of Table 1 that brought to $Rel = 0.4745$, as shown in the previous section. The derivative

Table 3. System reliability derivatives for the initial values of model parameters

	C_1	C_2	C_3	C_4	C_5	C_6	C_7	C_8
$ep(i)$	1	1	1	1	1	1	1	1
$\frac{\partial Rel}{\partial ep(i)}$	-0.0199	-1.7830	-0.4360	-4.2732	-0.4246	-0.2001	-1.6031	-1.5853
$intf(i)$	0.018	0.035	0	0.004	0.01	0	0	0.1001
$\frac{\partial Rel}{\partial intf(i)}$	-0.5051	-2.1502	-0.4705	-3.8948	-0.3864	-0.2159	-1.4442	-1.5870

values of Rel are summarized in Table 3 along with the component parameters $intf()$'s and $ep()$'s [5].

From Table 3 it straightforwardly appears that the failure characteristics of certain components (i.e. probability of internal failure and error propagation probability) affect the system reliability much more severely than the characteristics of other components. In particular, high absolute values for both derivatives are obtained for components C_2, C_4, C_7 and C_8. This means that variations in their failure characteristics would affect the system reliability more than variations in the characteristics of the remaining components.

The set of critical components that have emerged is not surprising, as from the transition matrix $\mathbf{Q}$ in Table 1 they appear to be the most intensely visited components (due to the number and probabilities of their entering edges). In other words, the majority of the propagation paths traverse these components, therefore a change in their failure characteristics would affect the majority of the system results.

These data, that have been obtained from our matrix expressions in Section 4, can be very relevant to support decisions during the component-based development process. For example, a system developer may decide to concentrate the efforts on critical components to improve their failure characteristics. In fact, small gains in those components would lead to large gains in the whole system reliability. We support with a numerical example this consideration.

We first assume that $ep(2)$ drops to 0.9, while all the other error propagation probabilities remain unchanged. This change brings the system reliability Rel from 0.4745 to 0.6078, with an increase of 28%. If we instead drop the value of a non-critical component, for example $ep(6)$, to the same value 0.9, while leaving unchanged the other ones, then Rel goes from 0.4745 to 0.4939, with an increase of only 4%.

With a similar logic, if we assume that $intf(8)$ decreases by the 20% of its value, that is from 0.1001 to 0.0801, then we obtain an improvement of Rel by 7% from 0.4745 to 0.5085. On the contrary, if we decrease $intf(5)$ (i.e. a non-critical component one) by the same percentage, from 0.01 to 0.008, then we obtain only a 0.17% improvement of Rel from 0.4745 to 0.4753.

This example highlights that the gain (in terms of system reliability) brought by improving a component ability either to mask errors or to not failing heavily depends on the considered component. Our model captures this aspect.

In Figures 5(a) and 5(b) we report the derivatives of the system reliability with respect to the internal failure probabilities over their ranges, partitioned respectively as critical components (i.e., C_2, C_4, C_7 and C_8) and non-critical ones (i.e., C_1, C_3, C_5

---

[5] C_0 and C_9 are not reported because they represent fictitious components.

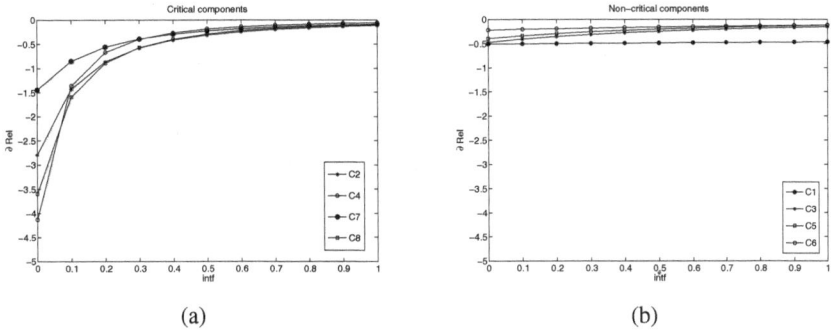

Fig. 5. Derivatives of system reliability vs probability of failure

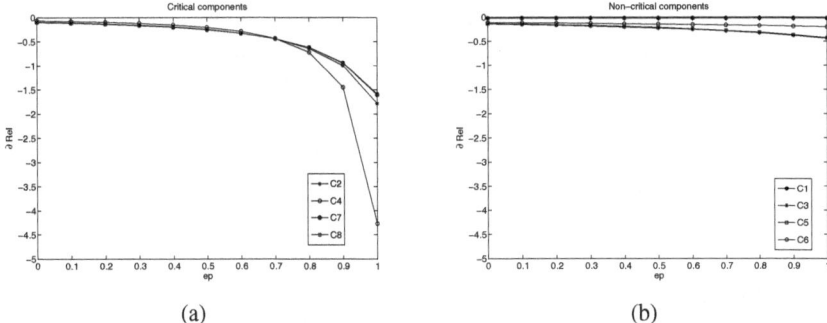

Fig. 6. Derivatives of system reliability vs error propagation probability

and C_6). Each curve has been obtained by varying the value of $intf(i)$ from 0 to 1 with a 0.1 step for all the components.

Similarly, in Figures 6(a) and 6(b) we report the derivatives of the system reliability with respect to the error propagation probabilities over their ranges.

In general, it is interesting to note that, for all the components, the function $\frac{\partial Rel}{\partial ep(i)}$ is monotonically decreasing whereas $\frac{\partial Rel}{\partial intf(i)}$ is monotonically increasing. This brings to find the highest absolute values of derivatives, respectively, near the value $ep(i) = 1$ for $\frac{\partial Rel}{\partial ep(i)}$ and near the value $intf(i) = 0$ for $\frac{\partial Rel}{\partial intf(i)}$.

$\frac{\partial Rel}{\partial intf(i)}$ for critical components in Figure 5(a) indicates that it is worth to work on the internal failure of a component when its probability falls close to 0, because large improvements can be induced on the system reliability in that subrange. On the contrary, it is not worth spending any effort to decrease the internal failure probability of components with high values of $intf(i)$ (i.e. close to 1), because no large gains can be obtained on the whole system reliability in that subrange. Figure 5(b) shows that the derivatives for non-critical components are almost always flat and very close to 0, thus changes in these components would never bring perceivable effects on the system reliability.

$\frac{\partial Rel}{\partial ep(i)}$ for critical components in Figure 6(a) indicates that it is worth to work on the error propagation of a component when its probability falls close to 1, because large improvements can be induced on the system reliability in that subrange. On the contrary, it is not worth spending any effort to decrease the error propagation probability of components with low values of $ep(i)$ (i.e. close to 0), because no large gains can be obtained on the whole system reliability in that subrange. Figure 6(b) shows that the derivatives for non-critical components are almost always flat and very close to 0, thus changes in these components would never bring perceivable effects on the system reliability also in this case.

From the software designer viewpoint, with modern testing techniques it is practically always possible to produce a software component with an internal failure probability lower than 0.001. Thus, it is very likely to find and build software components with values of $intf()$ in the range where the absolute value of the Rel derivative is very high if they are critical components (see Figure 5(a)). This means that it would be worthwhile to spend ever more testing effort on these components, as slight variations in their internal failure probability may heavily affect the whole system reliability. Likewise, it is very likely to find and build software components with values of $ep()$ very close to 1 [15], that is in the range where the absolute value of the Rel derivative is very high if they are critical components (see Figure 6(a)). Therefore, techniques that decrease the error propagation probability would similarly be suitable to sensibly affect the system reliability.

6 Conclusions

We have proposed a modeling approach to the reliability analysis of a component-based software system that takes into account the impact of the error propagation characteristics of each component on the overall system reliability. We have shown that neglecting this impact may cause an imprecise prediction of the system reliability, with consequently wrong decisions about the most suitable component assembly. Moreover, our sensitivity analysis results can help in identifying the most critical system components, where the implementation and testing efforts should be focused, and where the placement of error detection and recovery mechanisms could be more effective. The results that we have obtained are very promising, as our model easily captures error propagation effects that are instead omitted in other models.

Several open issues remain as future work, toward the goal of building a fully comprehensive reliability model of a component-based software system.

A first issue concerns the definition of a more complete model where, besides components, also connectors are taken into account.

A second issue concerns the adoption of a more comprehensive failure model. Given our focus on the analysis of the error propagation impact, we have only considered failures that generate erroneous output. However, other kinds of failures could affect the overall system reliability, like "stopping failures" that lead to a complete system stop [18], or hardware failures. We have not considered these two issues in the model presented in this paper mainly because our intent has been to keep it as simple as possible in order to make our main contribution (i.e. error propagation modeling) clearly emerging. We point out that in a previous work [13] we have proposed an architectural model that embeds connectors and stopping software/hardware failures, without keeping into account error propagation. We are working towards the merging of the model presented in [13] an the one presented in this paper.

A third issue concerns the trade-off between model tractability and model refinement. In this respect, it is worth investigating the most suitable granularity level in reliability modeling, in particular modeling the individual offered service reliability and behavior versus averaging them into component-level parameters.

Finally, we certainly believe that empirical validation of our model would bring to consolidate the theory that we have presented here. Proving that theoretical models can be used in practice is a great contribution to the adoption of modeling techniques in industrial contexts, as it has been done in a recent report of successful applications of reliability models in industry [17].

References

1. Abdelmoez, W., Nassar, D.M., Shereshevsky, M., Gradetsky, N., Gunnalan, R., Ammar, H.H., Yu, B., Mili, A.: Error Propagation in Software Architectures. In: METRICS'04. Proc. of 10th International Symposium on Software Metrics (2004)
2. Allen, R., Garlan, D.: A formal basis for architectural connection. ACM Trans. on Software Engineering and Methodology 6(3), 213–249 (1997)
3. Avizienis, A., Laprie, J.C., Randell, B., Landwehr, C.: Basic Concepts and Taxonomy of Dependable and Secure Computing. IEEE Trans. on Secure and Dependable Computing 1(1), 11–33 (2004)
4. Bass, L., Clements, P., Kazman, R.: Software Architectures in Practice. Addison-Wesley, Reading (1998)
5. Blake, J.T., Reibman, A.L., Trivedi, K.S.: Sensitivity analysis of reliability and performability measures for multiprocessor systems. In: Proc. of SIGMETRICS'88 (1988)
6. Cheung, R.C.: A user-oriented software reliability model. IEEE Trans. on Software Engineering 6(2), 118–125 (1980)
7. Cinlar, E.: Introduction to Stochastic Processes. Prentice-Hall, Englewood Cliffs (1975)
8. Cortellessa, V., Singh, H., Cukic, B., Gunel, E., Bharadwaj, V.: Early reliability assessment of UML based software models. In: WOSP'02. Proc. of 3rd ACM Workshop on Software and Performance, ACM Press, New York (2002)
9. Cortellessa, V., Grassi, V.: Role and impact of error propagation in software architecture reliability, Technical Report TRCS 007/2006, Dipartimento di Informatica, Universita' dell'Aquila http://www.di.univaq.it/cortelle/docs/internalreport.pdf
10. Gokhale, S., Trivedi, K.: Reliability Prediction and Sensitivity Analysis Based on Software Architecture. In: ISSRE'02. Proc. of 13th International Symposium on Software Reliability Engineering (2002)
11. Gokhale, S., Wong, W.E., Horgan, J.R., Trivedi, K.: An analytical approach to architecture-based software performance and reliability prediction. Performance Evaluation (58), 391–412 (2004)
12. Goseva-Popstojanova, K., Mathur, A.P., Trivedi, K.S.: Architecture-based approach to reliability assessment of software systems. Performance Evaluation (45), 179–204 (2001)
13. Grassi, V.: Architecture-based Reliability Prediction for Service-oriented Computing. In: de Lemos, R., Gacek, C., Romanovsky, A. (eds.) Architecting Dependable Systems III. LNCS, vol. 3549, pp. 279–299. Springer, Heidelberg (2005)

14. Grassi, V., Cortellessa, V.: Embedding error propagation in reliability modeling of component-based software systems. In: NetObjectDays'05. Proc. of International Conference on Quality of Software Architectures (2005)
15. Hiller, M., Jhumka, A., Suri, N.: EPIC: Profiling the Propagation and Effect of Data Errors in Software. IEEE Trans. on Computers 53(5), 512–530 (2004)
16. Inverardi, P., Scriboni, S.: Connectors Synthesis for Deadlock-Free Component-Based Architectures. In: ASE'01. Proc. of Automated Software Engineering Conference (2001)
17. Jeske, D.R., Zhang, X.: Some successful approaches to software reliability modeling in industry. The Journal of Systems and Software (74), 85–99 (2005)
18. Laprie, J.C. (ed.): Dependability: Basic Concepts and Terminology. Springer, Heidelberg (1992)
19. Krishnamurthy, S., Mathur, A.P.: On the estimation of reliability of a software system using reliabilities of its components. In: ISSRE'97. Proc. of 8th International Symposium on Software Reliability Engineering (1997)
20. Mehta, N.R., Medvidovic, N., Phadke, S.: Toward a taxonomy of software connectors. In: ICSE'00. Proc. of 22nd Int. Conference on Software Engineering (2000)
21. Popic, P., Desovski, D., Abdelmoez, W., Cukic, B.: Error propagation in the reliability analysis of component based systems. In: ISSRE'05. Proc. of 16th International Symposium on Software Reliability Engineering (2005)
22. Reussner, R.H., Schmidt, H.W., Poernomo, I.H.: Reliability prediction for component-based software architectures. Journal of Systems and Software (66), 241–252 (2003)
23. Roshandel, R., Medvidovic, N.: Toward architecture-based reliability prediction. In: WADS'04. Proc. of ICSE Workshop on Architecting Dependable Systems (2004)
24. Singpurwalla, N.D., Wilson, S.P.: Statistical Methods in Software Engineering. Springer Series in Statistics. Springer, Heidelberg (1999)
25. Smidts, C., Sova, D.: An architectural model for software reliability quantification: sources of data. Reliability Engineering and System Safety (64), 279–290 (1999)
26. Voas, J.: PIE: A Dynamic Failure-Based Technique. IEEE Trans. on Software Engineering 18(8), 717–727 (1992)
27. Voas, J.: Error propagation analysis for COTS systems. Computing and Control Engineering Journal 8(6), 269–272 (1997)
28. Yacoub, S., Cukic, B., Ammar, H.: Scenario-based reliability analysis of component-based software. In: ISSRE'99. Proc. of 10th International Symposium on Software Reliability Engineering (1999)
29. Wang, W.-L., Pan, D., Chen, M.-H.: Architecture-based software reliability modeling. The Journal of Systems and Software (79), 132–146 (2006)
30. MATLAB http://www.mathworks.com/products/matlab/

Performance-Driven Interface Contract Enforcement for Scientific Components*

Tamara L. Dahlgren

Lawrence Livermore National Laboratory, Livermore, CA 94550 USA
`dahlgren1@llnl.gov`

Abstract. Several performance-driven approaches to selectively enforce interface contracts for scientific components are investigated. The goal is to facilitate debugging deployed applications built from plug-and-play components while keeping the cost of enforcement within acceptable overhead limits.

This paper describes a study of global enforcement using *a priori* execution cost estimates obtained from traces. Thirteen trials are formed from five, single-component programs. Enforcement experiments conducted using twenty-three enforcement policies are used to determine the nature of exercised contracts and the impact of a variety of sampling strategies. Performance-driven enforcement appears to be best suited to programs that exercise moderately expensive contracts.

1 Introduction

Selective, performance-driven interface contract enforcement is intended to help scientists gain confidence in software built from plug-and-play components while retaining their code's high performance. This work is a natural extension of decades of research in component technology and software quality. For the purposes of this work, a *component* is defined as an independent software unit with an interface specification describing how it should be used [3]. Hence, caller and callee are loosely coupled through the callee's interfaces. Thus, logical feature groupings within existing scientific libraries can be wrapped as components.

Interchangeable components based on varying characteristics such as the underlying model, precision, and reliability were key features of the vision published in McIlroy's 1968 seminal paper on software components [4]. Grassroots efforts were begun in the late 1990's by the Common Component Architecture (CCA) Forum [5,6,7,8] to bring component-based software engineering to the high-performance scientific computing community. At present, eleven institutions — consisting of national laboratories, universities, and research-based

* This research was funded under the auspices of the U.S. Department of Energy's Center for Technology for Advanced Scientific Component Software (TASCS) [1] of the Scientific Discovery through Advanced Computing (SciDAC) [2] program by the University of California Lawrence Livermore National Laboratory under contract number W-7405-Eng-48. UCRL-CONF-228332.

H.W. Schmidt et al. (Eds.): CBSE 2007, LNCS 4608, pp. 157–172, 2007.

companies — are actively involved in collaborative efforts to further facets of the organization's goals. This research is part of the CCA's software quality initiative.

The Institute of Electrical and Electronics Engineers (IEEE) [9] defines *quality* as "the degree to which a system, component, or process meets" its specifications, needs, or expectations. Interface contracts are specifications that take the form of preconditions, postconditions, and or invariants that belong to the interface, not the the the underlying implementation(s). *Preconditions* are assertions on properties that must hold prior to method execution. *Postconditions* are assertions that must hold upon method completion. *Invariants* apply before and after method execution. Hence, interface contracts are specifications that are amenable to automated enforcement.

Interface contracts are related to a practice traditionally referred to as "defensive programming". Conscientious developers have long relied on assertions at the top of their routines to protect their software from bad inputs. The basic intent is to catch potential input-related problems before they cause the program to unexpectedly crash. These kinds of checks should always be retained since contracts may not be enforced during deployment. However, interface contracts are broader in scope since they can include constraints on other properties of the input as well as properties of the output, the component, and its state.

Since scientific components are developed by people with different backgrounds and training, it is not safe to assume that everyone uses the same level of rigor in their software development practices — especially in the case of research software. This fact does not preclude the potential advantages for scientists to experiment with different research components providing similar computational services. Defining those services with a common interface specification facilitates the use of different implementations. Executable interface contracts then provide some assurances that interface failures can be caught regardless of the programming discipline used by component implementors.

However, the community's performance concerns could become a roadblock to the adoption of contract enforcement during deployment; hence, the pursuit of performance-driven enforcement policies. Section 2 describes the trade-offs faced by the community. The enforcement infrastructure is summarized in Section 3. Section 4 elaborates on the methodology and subjects used in the study before highlighting key findings. An overview of the most relevant related works is given in Section 5 before the summary of future work in Section 6.

2   Motivation

There is growing interest in leveraging component-based software engineering (CBSE) for the re-use of legacy software as plug-and-play components in multi-scale, multi-physics models. The resulting complexity of these applications — especially when components are implemented in different programming languages — makes testing and debugging difficult. The ability to swap components at run-time increases debugging challenges. At the same time, developers of scientific applications are very concerned with the performance implications of new technologies since computational scientists are typically willing to incur no more than ten percent additional overhead. Effectively balancing these competing demands is a significant challenge.

Applications composed in a plug-and-play manner depend on components implemented and wrapped in accordance with claimed services. However, when using unfamiliar components, there is increased risk of incorrect or unanticipated usage patterns. Furthermore, such applications have the potential of relying on input data set combinations that lead to unexpected component behavior.

Interface contracts can provide clear documentation of service constraints. When specified in an implementation-neutral language, contracts can also serve as a basis for the consistent instrumentation and enforcement of interface constraints, regardless of the underlying implementation language. Pinpointing the exact statement or module in which the computation failed would be ideal; however, the ability to detect violations in the middle of execution can still save many hours to weeks of debugging.

While interface contracts can facilitate testing and debugging applications built of components, contract enforcement is generally perceived as too expensive for deployment. This may be an extension of the idea that programming language-level assertions can have a negative impact on performance. Intuitively, assertions in frequently executed code and tight loops are most likely to be too costly. Consequently, standard practice — specifically in domains and projects that rely on assertions — involves eliminating all checks or disabling at least the more complex or expensive ones. The result, however, is exposing software to unchecked violations. Risks range from spending days to weeks reproducing and debugging errors to making decisions or reporting findings based on erroneous information.

With the growing interest in CBSE for building multi-scale, multi-physics models from legacy software comes the challenge of providing mechanisms to facilitate debugging with minimal performance impact. Hence, this research pursues a compromise solution of performance-driven enforcement within a user-specified overhead tolerance. The basic idea is to throttle enforcement at runtime if and when the limit is reached.

3   Enforcement Infrastructure

The Babel [10] toolkit developed at Lawrence Livermore National Laboratory forms the basis for the enforcement infrastructure. Specifications in the Scientific Interface Definition Language (SIDL) are automatically translated into language interoperability middleware using the Babel compiler. Contracts are supported through optional SIDL annotations, which are mapped to runtime checks embedded in the middleware. An example of an annotated SIDL specification for the vector *norm* method is given below. The remainder of this section describes the toolkit with an emphasis on changes since preliminary investigations [11,12].

```
package vector version 1.0 {
    class Utils {
                        ⋮

        static double norm(in array⟨double⟩ u,
                           in double tol, in int badLevel)
        throws      /* Exceptions */
            sidl.PreViolation, NegativeValueException, sidl.PostViolation;

        require     /* Preconditions */
            not_null: u != null;
            u_is_1d: dimen(u) == 1;
            non_negative_tolerance: tol ≤ 0.0;

        ensure      /* Postconditions */
            non_negative_result: result ≥ 0.0;
            nearEqual(result, 0.0, tol) iff isZero(u, tol);
                        ⋮

    }
}
```

Enforcement decisions are centralized in the experimental Babel toolkit to better control overhead across multiple components. In addition, decisions are made on a finer basis by grouping contracts by locality. For example, the three expressions in the *norm* method's preconditions are treated as a single group while the two postcondition expressions form a second group. Splitting contracts in this manner allows for a wider variety of enforcement options. Previously [11,12] only three options were supported: *Periodic, Random,* and *Adaptive Timing (AT)*. The first two classic strategies were compared to *AT*, which sought to limit the overhead of contract enforcement using runtime timing instrumentation.

Enforcement policies are now based on two parameters: enforcement frequency and contract type. Enforcement frequency determines how often contracts are checked. Contract types further constrain checks to classes of contracts, thereby providing a mechanism for measuring the properties of contracts actually exercised during program execution.

Enforcement frequency can be one of: *Never, Always, Periodic, Random, Adaptive Fit (AF), Adaptive Timing (AT),* or *Simulated Annealing (SA)*. With *Never,* the middleware completely by-passes the enforcement instrumentation. Hence, the software operates as if contracts had never been added to the specification. All contracts (of the specified type) are enforced with the *Always* option. *Periodic* and *Random* support the classic sampling strategies. Enforcement decisions for the remaining three options are based on estimated execution times of methods and their associated contracts. *AF* enforces contracts only if their estimated time will not result in exceeding the user's limit on the cumulative total of program and method cost estimates. *AT* enforces contracts when their estimated times will not exceed the user-specified overhead limit for the method.

Finally, *SA* operates like *AF* but allows the overhead to exceed the user-specified limit with decreasing probability over time. Hence, a total of seven enforcement frequencies are supported, three of which are performance-driven.

Contract types can be one of: *All, Constant, Linear, Method Calls, Simple Expressions, Preconditions, Postconditions, Invariants, Preconditions-Postconditions, Preconditions-Invariants, Postconditions-Invariants,* and *Results.* All types are checked at the specified frequency with the *All* option. For historical and built-in assertion function reasons, complexity options are currently limited to *Constant-* and *Linear*-time, where contracts for a method are considered to be at the level of the highest complexity assertion expression. The *Method Calls* option enforces only contracts containing at least one method call — built-in or user-defined — while the *Simple Expressions* option is used for contracts wherein no method calls appear. *Preconditions, Postconditions, Invariants,* and their combinations enforce contracts conforming to those classical distinctions. Finally, *Results* enforces (postcondition) contracts only when at least one expression contains a result or output argument. When combined with *Always,* statistics using these options can serve as baselines for performance-driven counterparts.

Another new feature is enforcement tracing. When enabled by the program, special instrumentation in the middleware determines the amount of time spent in the program, enforcing preconditions, enforcing invariants before the method call, executing the annotated method, enforcing its postconditions, and enforcing invariants after the method call. The resulting timing data is currently dumped to a file after each invocation before control is returned to the caller. Hence, trace results provide the basis for *a priori* execution cost estimates needed for performance-driven enforcement.

The experimental version of the Babel toolkit automatically translates contract annotations in the SIDL specification into runtime checks embedded in the generated language interoperability middleware. During program execution, enforcement decisions are made globally using the chosen frequency and contract type options that form the enforcement policy. One of seven frequency options — including *Never* and three performance-driven strategies — together with one of twelve contract type options can be active at a time. For simplicity, when any frequency option is combined with *All* contract types, "*All*" is dropped from the name.

4   Experiments

Experiments are conducted on a total of thirteen trials formed from five, single-component programs. Enforcement traces are produced to obtain program, method, and contract execution times for use in enforcement experiments. A variety of sampling strategies are employed for each trial in order to study and compare their effects. Analysis of experiment results reveal several interesting patterns. Before presenting results for performance-driven policies, it is useful to consider the impact of full contract enforcement.

4.1   Subjects

Five, single-component programs along with several input array sizes are used as the basis for thirteen trials. Table 1 describes the programs and selected input array sizes. The first four programs rely on components implementing a community-developed mesh interface standard that defines interfaces supporting multiple mesh access patterns. The specification was established by the Terascale Simulation Tools and Technologies (TSTT) Center [13,14], which is now called the Interoperable Tools for Advanced Petascale Simulation (ITAPS) Center. A single, readily available input file was used with each program. The fifth program is a Babel regression test specifically developed to exercise basic contract enforcement features.

Table 1. Descriptions of the five programs that form the basis for thirteen trials

Component	Abbrev.	Program Description
	MA	Retrieve all faces from the mesh then, for each face, retrieve the adjacent vertices.
Simplicial Mesh	**A**	Retrieve all faces from the mesh in sets based on the size of the input array. Sizes 1, 14587 (10%), and 145870 (100%) were used to reproduce the violation and vary processing.
	AA	Retrieve faces in the same manner as program **A** plus, for each set of faces, retrieve their corresponding adjacent vertices. The same input array sizes were used.
Volume Mesh	**MT**	Exercise and check consistency of five mesh interfaces: core mesh capabilities, single entity query and traversal, entity array query and traversal, single entity mesh modification, and entity array mesh modification.
Vector Utilities	**VT**	Exercise all supported functions to include successful execution; one or more precondition violations; and one or more postcondition violations. Sizes 6 (original), 10, 100, 1000, and 10000 were used to vary processing.

Much as one would expect in the real world, the programs involve predominantly constant-time contracts in a variety of settings. Program **A** exercises only constant-time contracts. Varying the input array size in this case corresponds to different amounts of processing within the method and numbers of loop iterations (to vary sampling opportunities). Program **AA** builds on **A** by adding the adjacency retrieval method and its linear-time postconditions to the loop to vary contract processing times as well. (Input array sizes for both programs were selected to induce a violation discovered in previous work [12].) That same method is the only one invoked within program **MA**'s loop. So the three programs vary not only method and contract processing times with constant- and, in two cases, linear-time contracts, they also provide meager to ample sampling opportunities.

The last two programs — **MT** and **VT** — are test programs that serve other purposes in this study. Program **MT** exercises 1,909,129 contracts using a small input file readily available with the GRUMMP [15] software. **VT**, on the other hand, checks 146 contracts every run regardless of the input array size. Since the program builds multiple vectors, varying input array sizes has a significant impact on the amount of execution time attributed to the program. So the two programs expand on the variety of sampling opportunities or execution cost distributions demonstrated with the first three programs.

Hence, different input arrays sizes for several of the five programs were used to define thirteen trials. The trials varied in terms of the amount of work done in the methods and programs. The numbers of sampling opportunities also varied, ranging from six (with **A-145870**) to 1,909,129 (with **MT**). Finally, although linear-time contracts are checked to some degree in nearly all trials, checked contracts are predominantly constant-time.

4.2   Methodology

The experimental process consists of essentially three phases. In the first phase, execution cost estimates are established in order to guide performance-driven enforcement decisions. The second phase involves conducting the actual experiments. Finally, experiment results are analyzed and compared.

Once annotated contracts are translated by Babel into enforcement checks in the middleware and the software re-built, *a priori* execution time estimates are needed for each annotated method and its associated contracts. The enforcement tracing feature, described in Section 3, is used to estimate those costs. Due to the sizes of the corresponding trace files, each trial is executed five times with tracing and full contract enforcement enabled. Mean execution times are then computed from the traces to obtain trial-specific estimates.

Figure 1 illustrates the resulting enforcement trace results. Preconditions dominate contract costs for trials **MA**, **A-1**, and **AA-1**. The total costs of annotated methods far exceed the times attributed to the other categories for trials **A-14587**, **A-145870**, **AA-14587**, and **AA-145870**; however, contract execution times are dominated by postconditions for the latter two as a result of the linear-time contracts. Only 15-20% of the execution times of trials **VT-6**, **VT-10**, and **VT-100** are attributed to contracts where even less time is spent in the methods. Finally, execution times for trials **VT-1000** and **VT-10000** are almost exclusively spent in the programs. Nearly every trial illustrates a different pattern, or execution profile.

Experiments are then performed by executing each trial multiple times using each enforcement policy under consideration. A total of twenty-three different policies were used to gather data for this study. Seven policies combined the *All* contract types option with each of the seven enforcement frequency options to capture frequency-specific data. Eight more policies combined the *Always* option with basic contract types to provide data on the nature of checked contracts. Finally, the *AF* option was combined with the basic contract types for the last eight policies. The goal was to investigate the impact of performance-driven

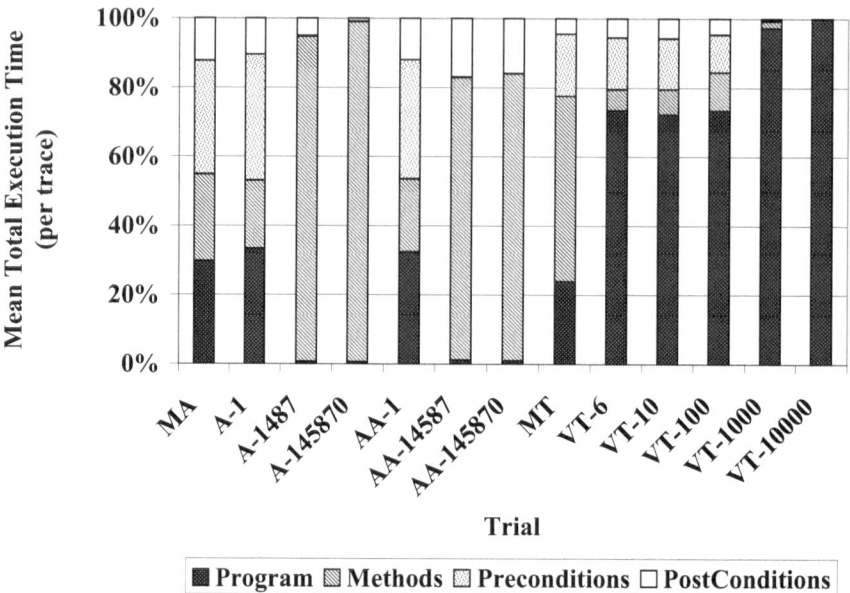

Fig. 1. Trace execution profiles

variants. A 5% overhead limit was used on all performance-driven enforcement policies. Between ten and thirty repetitions of each experiment were performed to mitigate the inherent variations in execution times. Every effort was made to perform experiments, which were executed on a networked machine running Red Hat Linux 7.3, when the machine was lightly loaded.

Baseline data are derived from the results of policies using the *All* types option. Three metrics are computed based on experiment results: enforcement overhead, contract coverage, and violation detection effectiveness. Since the *Never* policy measures the execution time when the instrumentation is by-passed, it serves as the basis for computing overhead. That is, **enforcement overhead** is calculated as the percentage of execution time above that of *Never*. Running trials with the *Always* policy provides baselines for both the total number of contracts checked and total number of detectable violations. **Contract coverage** is then computed as the percentage of the number of checks for a policy versus the number with *Always*. Similarly, **violation detection effectiveness** is the fraction of violations detected with a policy versus with *Always*. Combining the *Always* frequency option with specific contract types provide similar coverage and violation detection baseline metrics for their performance-driven counterparts.

Hence, tracing is used to obtain the program, method, and contract execution cost estimates needed by the middleware to guide performance-driven policies. Enforcement experiments are run by executing each trial numerous times for each enforcement policy to mitigate the inherent variability in execution times.

Baseline metrics are collected using basic policies like *Never* (for overhead) and *Always* (for contract coverage and detected violations).

4.3   Full Enforcement Results

Figure 2 illustrates the overhead with *Always* by percentage of linear-time contracts. Trials **A-14587**, **A-145870**, **VT-1000**, and **VT-10000** incur negligible overhead. Contract enforcement opportunities range from 6 to 146 per run with at least 92% being constant-time contracts. Trial **MT** incurs only 3% overhead despite checking significantly more contracts than any other trial. According to results using the *Linear* policy, only 89 of **MT**'s contracts are linear-time. Trials **A-1**, **AA-1**, and **MA** reflect between 291,740 and 583,484 contract checks per run. While the latter two trials include linear-time contracts, the corresponding output arrays contain only a few entries due to their use of single-element input arrays. Furthermore, trial **AA-1** exercises only constant-time contracts in the first method in its loop so the instrumentation overhead on those invocations is not ameliorated. Trials **AA-14587** and **AA-145870** checked 44 and 8 contracts per execution, respectively, with their linear-time contracts working on several times the number of elements as in their input arrays. Even though all trials with program **VT** check the same number of contracts, trials **VT-6**, **VT-10**, and **VT-100** incur significantly more overhead than any other trial. Judging from the data in the trace profiles shown in Figure 1, this may be attributable to the relatively small amount of time spent in the methods.

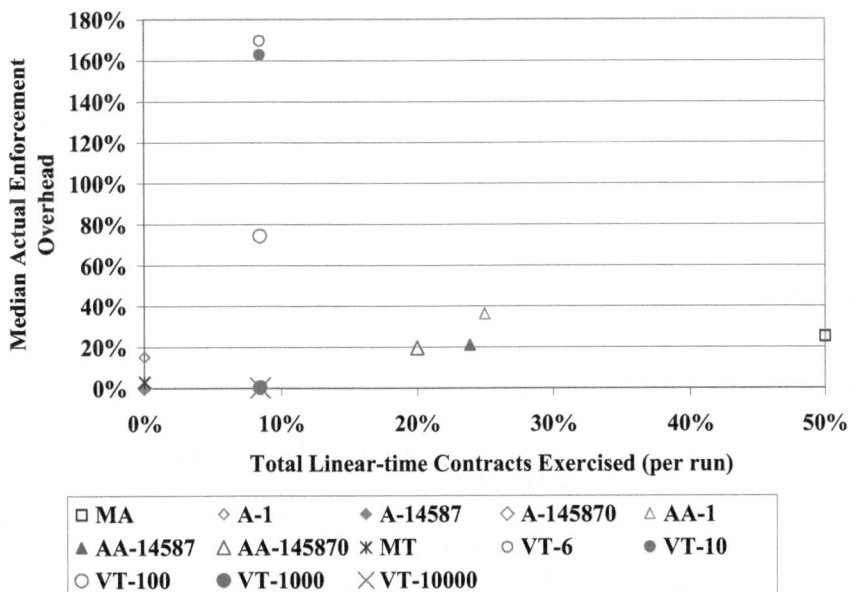

Fig. 2. Median enforcement overhead with *Always* by percentage of linear-time contracts

Trials formed using different input array sizes were deliberately chosen to detect the same violations for each program. Those violations are described in Table 2. Mesh program violations reflect the fact that both the programs and component implementations were initially developed prior to contract definition. Program **VT**, on the other hand, exhibits characteristics of non-compliant programs and implementations as a result of deliberately triggering precondition and postcondition violations.

Table 2. Contract violations detected with *Always*, where the same violations occur regardless of input array size

Program Abbrev.	Description
MA	No contract violations.
A	Final (extra) call returns a null array pointer when no more faces left to retrieve from the mesh. The postcondition (set) is constant-time.
AA	Same violation as in **A**.
MT	Four precondition violations occur in constant-time contracts as a result of the program not pre-allocating two classes of input arrays. The remaining 43 violations, which occur in linear-time postconditions, result from the implementation not properly setting output array values for adjacencies.
VT	A total of 78 violations per run are deliberately triggered with *Always*, where postcondition failures are emulated. In all, 94% of the violations are triggered in constant-time preconditions.

So, with the *Always* policy, only seven of the thirteen trials incur more than 3% overhead. It appears these results can be attributed either to lots of relatively inexpensive contracts in tight loops or to moderately expensive contracts. The trials also illustrate a range of between one and seventy-eight contract violations per run. The numbers of violations are tied to the programs not the trials.

4.4   Performance-Driven Enforcement Results

An analysis of the results indicate performance-driven policies generally perform well relative to *Always* — in terms of performance and detected violations — in 83% of the trials with detectable violations. In half of those trials, at least 43% of the performance-driven policies detect all of the violations with negligible overhead — even in trial **VT-145870** where the overhead of *Always* is 20%. Unfortunately, only *SA* is able to check more than two contracts in trials **A-1** and **AA-1**. The remainder of this section focuses on results using *AF*, *AT*, and *SA* for the six trials where performance-driven enforcement show an improvement over *Always*.

With only 3% overhead for checking all of **MT**'s contracts, all but *SA* cut the overhead by a third while checking only a small fraction of the contracts and generally detecting no more five of the forty-seven violations. Surprisingly, AT detects 94% of the violations while covering only 0.04% of the contracts. Given the algorithm used by the policy, these results indicate those violations occur in relatively cheap contracts.

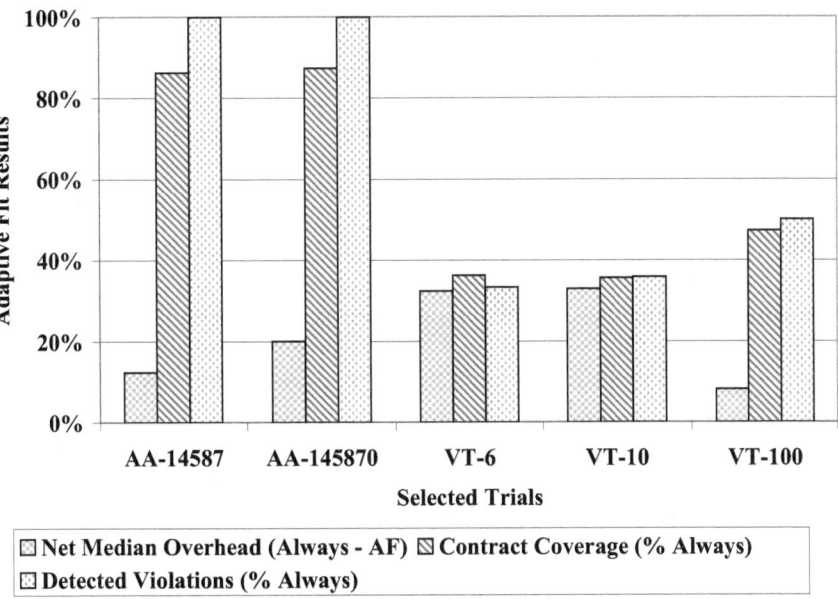

Fig. 3. Enforcement results for *Adaptive Fit (AF)*

Figure 3 illustrates the results for AF on the remaining five trials. The corresponding chart for SA is very similar. While AT checks fewer contracts for the first two trials shown, it always detects the violation at negligible overhead in those cases. However, it is unable to check any contracts for the last three trials, indicating their execution times exceed 5% of their methods'. This information is useful when considering the results for AF and SA.

Both AF and SA cover 86% or more of the contracts for trials **AA-14587** and **AA-145870** and always detect the violation while incurring less than 43% of the overhead of *Always*. The numbers of contracts checked in those trials are forty-four and eight, respectively. So there is less overhead savings for the trial with more contracts.

As shown in Figure 2, the remaining trials incur the most overhead with *Always*. However, the estimated execution time and results of AT indicate all of the contracts exceed 5% of their method's execution times. So it is not surprising that the overhead savings with AF and SA are relatively modest. However, AF is able to detect a third (for **VT-6**) to half (for **VT-100**) of the violations with at least an 8% savings in overhead. SA detects 29% to 36% of the violations in the same trials with 3-4% more savings in overhead in the first two cases. In these cases, the larger the input array size, the lower the overhead and the lower the savings with performance-driven enforcement. However, the larger the input array size, the higher the coverage for a given policy and the more violations it detects.

Three patterns in the results emerged during analysis. First, the instrumentation appears to be too costly for trials that exercise lots of relatively inexpensive contracts; namely, those within tight loops. This is likely attributable to insufficient work performed in the methods to offset those costs. That does not appear to be the case for trials enforcing under two hundred, inexpensive contracts where the overhead is negligible. In general, performance-driven enforcement seems better suited to trials whose traces indicated between 15% and 22% estimated enforcement overhead.

5   Related Work

Associating assertions with software dates to the 1950's [16,17,18]. Applied researchers recognized the value of executable assertions for testing and debugging in the mid-1970's [19,20,21]. Meyer's [22] Design-by-Contract methodology was built on this foundation. Component-level extensions of Meyer's work began appearing in the mid-1990's. This section briefly summarizes seven technologies supporting component contracts and three using or proposing sampling of assertions during deployment.

The Architectural Specification Language (ASL) [23,24] encompasses a family of design languages for CBSE. Its Interface Specification Language (ISL) extends CORBA [25] Interface Definition Language (IDL) with preconditions, postconditions, invariants, and protocol (or states). The Assertion Definition Language (ADL) [26] extends CORBA IDL with postconditions. The goal of ADL is to facilitate formal specification and testing of software components. Hamie [27] advocates extending the Object Constraint Language (OCL), which is a textual language for expressing modeling constraints. He proposes adding invariants to class diagrams. Hamie also proposes adding preconditions, postconditions, and guards to state transition diagrams. The extensions are integrated into specifications for C++ and Java. Similarly, Verheecke and van Der Straeten [28] developed a framework that translates OCL into executable constraints (for Java) using constraint classes. The *ConFract* [29] system adds internal and external composition to the classic contracts, using a rule-based, event-driven approach to runtime verification. The Java Modeling Language (JML) [30] is another example of a language pursuing component contracts — in the form of preconditions and postconditions in comments. Edwards *et al.* [31] also automatically generate wrappers from specifications, with the goal being to separate enforcement from the client and implementation. Their "one-way" wrappers are used to check preconditions. They also have "two-way" wrappers to check preconditions and postconditions, but those are not automatically generated. Heineman [32] employs a Run-time Interface Specification Checker (RISC) for enforcement of preconditions and postconditions.

While the aforementioned technologies pursue component contracts, the most relevant related research efforts identified so far involve sampling assertions. In two efforts, assertions in program bodies are sampled during deployment to reduce enforcement overhead. Liblit *et al.*'s [33,34] statistical debugging relies on (uniform) random sampling of assertions in remotely deployed applications. This facilitates remote application profiling and debugging of arbitrary code using automated instrumentation. Similarly, Chilimbi and Hauswirth [35] focus on rarely occurring errors but within the context of their SWAT memory leak detection tool. Three pre-defined staleness predicates automatically inserted into program bodies are sampled during deployment. Checking is based on tracing infrequently executed code while frequently executed code is sampled at a very low rate to reduce overhead. The sampling rate starts at 100% but decreases — to a minimum — with each check. Leak reports are then generated from trace files after the program terminates. Collet and Rousseau [36] advocate random sampling limited to universal quantification for recently modified classes and their dependents.

Like the first seven technologies, this work leverages component contracts to improve the quality of software. Programming language-neutral SIDL contracts are automatically instrumented for use by implementations in a variety of languages employed in scientific computing; namely, C, C++, Fortran 77/90, Java, and Python since they are supported by Babel. Using implementations in different programming languages can vary the effects on performance; hence, another motivation for pursuing performance-driven heuristics. Sampling of enforcement decisions is similar to the approach taken by Liblit *et al.* and Chilimbi and Hauswirth. However, while they employ basic sampling strategies, this research advocates automatically tuning the sampling level at runtime based on performance-driven heuristics.

6   Future Work

This research lays a foundation for further investigation of both the nature of interface contracts needed for scientific applications and their impact on performance. Additional studies, involving collaborations with component developers and scientists, should yield insights that can be used to refine the current set of techniques as well as develop others. Better techniques are also needed to improve the accuracy of enforcement decisions. In the meantime, the toolkit is being revised to more readily support multi-component contract enforcement and to integrate these new features into the official Babel source code repository. The work is being done in preparation for conducting a study using small, multi-component example programs as part of a CCA collaboration.

7   Summary

This paper presents results from an investigation of the impact of performance-driven policies supported in an experimental version of the Babel language interoperability toolkit. Enforcement decisions are made on a global basis using *a priori* execution costs obtained from enforcement traces.

Results for five single-component programs are presented based on three logical phases. The first phase involves trace experiments to obtain execution times attributable to programs, invoked methods, preconditions, postconditions, and invariants. Baseline enforcement experiments are then used to obtain execution costs when enforcement is by-passed (with the *Never* policy); total numbers of contracts checked and violations detected during normal contract enforcement (with the *Always* policy); and characteristics of the contracts and violations (with basic contract type options). Finally, the impacts of performance-driven enforcement policies are compared to baselines.

In general, performance-driven policies performed as well or better than *Always* while catching significant numbers of violations in 83% of the trials with violations. Performance-driven policies tended to incur at most a few percent overhead in trials where the overhead of *Always* was negligible. The policies were not able to overcome instrumentation overhead issues in trials representing tight loops. However, the more general-purpose, performance-driven policies were able to detect significant numbers of violations at a saving of at least 8% overhead compared to *Always* in trials involving moderately expensive contracts.

Acknowledgments. Thanks go to those who contributed software and or financial support for this work. In particular, Lori Diachin provided the simplicial mesh component and Carl Ollivier-Gooch the GRUMMP volume mesh component. Carl was also responsible for the Mesh Unit Test program. Contracts for the mesh interface specification were defined in collaboration with Lori, Carl, and Kyle Chand. As leads of the project responsible for the Babel toolkit, Tom Epperly and Gary Kumfert supported this work. Many thanks for the useful feedback also go to those who reviewed this paper: Tom Epperly, Prem Devanbu, Steve Dahlgren, and the anonymous reviewers.

References

1. United States Department of Energy: TASCS Initiative: `http://www.scidac.gov/compsci/TASCS.html`
2. United States Department of Energy: SciDAC Initiative. `http://www.osti.gov/scidac/`
3. Meyer, B.: The grand challenge of trusted components. In: ICSE '03. Proceedings of the 25th International Conference on Software Engineering, Portland, OR, May 3-10, 2003, pp. 660–667 (2003)
4. McIlroy, M.D.: Mass produced software components. In: Proceedings of the NATO Software Engineering Conference, October 1968, pp. 138–155 (1968), Also available at `http://cm.bell-labs.com/cm/who/doug/components.txt`
5. Alexeev, Y., et al.: Component-based software for high-performance scientific computing. In: SciDAC 2005. Proceedings of Scientific Discovery through Advanced Computing, San Francisco, CA, June 26-30, 2005 (2005)

6. Armstrong, R., Beholden, D.E., Dahlgren, T., Elswasif, W.R., Kumfert, G., McInnes, L.C., Nieplocha, J., Norris, B.: High end computing component technology (white paper). In: Workshop on the Road Map for the Revitalization of High End Computing, Washington, DC (2003)

7. Bernholdt, D.E., et al.: A component architecture for high-performance scientific computing. International Journal of High-Performance Computing Applications, ACTS Collection special issue (2005)

8. Common Component Architecture (CCA) Forum: Cca, http://www.cca-forum.org/

9. 610.12-1990, I.S.: IEEE Standard Glossary of Software Engineering Terminology. The Institute of Electrical and Electronics Engineers, Inc., 345 East 47th Street, New York, NY 10017, USA (September 1990)

10. Lawrence Livermore National Laboratory: Babel. http://www.llnl.gov/CASC/components/babel.html

11. Dahlgren, T.L., Devanbu, P.T.: Adaptable assertion checking for scientific software components. In: Proceedings of the Workshop on Software Engineering for High Performance Computing System Applications, Edinburgh, Scotland, May 24, 2004, pp. 64–69 (2004)

12. Dahlgren, T.L., Devanbu, P.T.: Improving scientific software component quality through assertions. In: Proceedings of the Second International Workshop on Software Engineering for High Performance Computing System Applications, St. Louis, Missouri, May 2005, pp. 73–77 (2005)

13. Brown, D., Freitag, L., Glimm, J.: Creating interoperable meshing and discretization technology: The terascale simulation tools and technologies center. In: Proceedings of the 8th International Conference on Numerical Grid Generation in Computational Field Simulations, Honolulu, HI, June 3-6, 2002, pp. 57–61 (2002)

14. Ollivier-Gooch, C., Chand, K., Dahlgren, T., Diachin, L.F., Fix, B., Kraftcheck, J., Li, X., Seol, E., Shephard, M., Tautges, T., Trease, H.: The TSTT mesh interface. In: Proceedings of the 44th AIAA Aerospace Sciences Meeting and Exhibit, Reno, NV (January 2006)

15. GRUMMP — Generation and Refinement of Unstructured, Mixed-Element Meshes in Parallel. http://tetra.mech.ubc.ca/GRUMMP/.

16. Hoare, C.A.R.: The emperor's old clothes. Communications of the ACM 24(2), 75–83 (1981)

17. Floyd, R.W.: Assigning meanings to programs. In: Proceedings of the Symposia in Applied Mathematics, Mathematical aspects of Computer Science. American Mathematical Society, vol. 19, pp. 19–32 (1967)

18. Hoare, C.A.R.: An axiomatic basis for computer programming. Communications of the ACM 12(10), 576–580, 583 (1969)

19. Adams, J.M., Armstrong, J., Smartt, M.: Assertional checking and symbolic execution: An effective combination for debugging. In: Proceedings of the 1979 annual conference, pp. 152–156 (1979)

20. Chen, W.T., Ho, J.P., Wen, C.H.: Dynamic validation of programs using assertion checking facilities. In: The IEEE Computer Society's 2nd International Computer Software and Applications Conference, November 13-16, 1978, pp. 533–538. IEEE Computer Society Press, Los Alamitos (1978)

21. Saib, S.H.: Executable assertions — an aid to reliable software. In: Proceedings of the 11th Asilomar Conference on Circuits, Systems and Computers, November 7-9, 1977, pp. 277–281 (1977)

22. Meyer, B.: Object-Oriented Software Construction, 2nd edn. Prentice-Hall, Englewood Cliffs (1997)

23. Bronsard, F., Bryan, D., Kozaczynski, W.V., Liongosari, E.S., Ning, J.Q., Ólafsson, A., Wetterstrand, J.W.: Toward software plug-and-play. In: SSR '97. Proceedings of the 1997 Symposium on Software Reusability, Boston, MA, May 17-20, 1997, pp. 19–29 (1997)
24. Kozaczynski, W.V., Ning, J.D.: Concern-driven design for a specification language supporting component-based software engineering. In: Proceedings of the 8th International Workshop on Software Specification and Design, pp. 150–154 (1996)
25. Object Management Group: CORBA basics.
    http://www.omg.org/gettingstarted/corbafaq.htm
26. Sankar, S., Hayes, R.: ADL — an interface definition language for specifying and testing software. ACM SIGPLAN Notices, IDL Workshop 29(8), 13–21 (1994)
27. Hamie, A.: Enhancing the object constraint language for more expressive specifications. In: APSEC '99. Proceedings of the 6th Asia-Pacific Software Engineering Conference, December 7-10, 1999, pp. 376–383 (1999)
28. Verheecke, B., Straeten, R.V.D.: Specifying and implementing the operational use of constraints in object-oriented applications. In: TOOLS Pacific 2002. Proceedings of the 40th International Conference on Technology of Object-Oriented Languages and Systems, Sydney, Australia, February 2002, pp. 23–32 (2002)
29. Collet, P., Ozanne, A., Rivierre, N.: Enforcing different contracts in hierarchical component-based systems. In: Löwe, W., Südholt, M. (eds.) SC 2006. LNCS, vol. 4089, pp. 50–65. Springer, Heidelberg (2006)
30. Leavens, G.T., Rustan, K., Leino, M., Poll, E., Ruby, C., Jacobs, B.: JML: notations and tools supporting detailed design in Java. Technical Report TR 00-15, Iowa State University, Ames, Iowa (August 2000)
31. Edwards, S.H.: Making the case for assertion checking wrappers. In: Proceedings of the RESOLVE Workshop, Also available as Virgina Tech Technical Report TR-02-11(June 2002)
32. Heineman, G.T.: Integrating interface assertion checkers into component models. In: Proceedings of the 6th ICSE Workshop on Component-Based Software Engineering: Automated Reasoning and Prediction, Portland, OR, May 3-4, 2003 (2003)
33. Liblit, B., Aiken, A., Zen, A.X., Jordan, M.I.: Bug isolation via remote program sampling. In: PLDI '03. Proceedings of the ACM SIGPLAN 2003 Conference on Programming Language Design and Implementation, San Diego, CA, June 9-11, 2003, pp. 141–154. ACM Press, New York (2003)
34. Liblit, B., Aiken, A., Zheng, A.X., Jordan, M.I.: Sampling user executions for bug isolation. In: RAMSS '03. Proceedings of the 1st Workshop on Remote Analysis and Measurement of Software Systems, Portland, OR, May 2003, pp. 3–6 (2003)
35. Chilimbi, T.M., Hauswirth, M.: Low-overhead memory leak detection using adaptive statistical profiling. In: Proceedings of the 11th International Conference on Architectural Support for Programming Languages and Operating Systems, Boston, MA, October 9-13, 2004, pp. 156–164 (2004)
36. Collet, P., Rousseau, R.: Towards efficient support for executing the object contraint language. In: TOOLS 30. Proceedings of the Technology of Object-Oriented Languages and Systems, Santa Barbara, CA, August 1-5, 1999, pp. 399–408 (1999)

Integration of Time Issues into Component-Based Applications

Sébastien Saudrais, Noël Plouzeau, and Olivier Barais

IRISA France, Triskell Project*
{ssaudrai, barais, plouzeau}@irisa.fr

Abstract. In this paper we describe a technique for specifying time related properties on traditional software components. We apply the separation of concerns paradigm to allow independent specification of timing and to integrate time-checking specialized tool support into conventional software design processes. We aim at helping the designer to specify time contracts and at simplifying the introduction of time properties in the component behaviour description. We propose to handle timing issues in a separate and specific design activity, in order to provide means of formal computation of time properties for component assemblies without modifying in depth existing design processes.

1 Scope and Objectives

Component based design is now at the heart of many modern applications. A rather important category of these applications must manage time, for instance because they interact with users in a time controlled manner (e.g. media players, group cooperation environments, etc) or because they are highly distributed (e.g. applications based on a bunch of Web services from diverse origins). Yet mainstream design techniques often emphasize type centric interactions between components: the component models they use offer powerful notations and tools for defining, refining and checking data types. Time properties are not explicitly taken into account by these models. At the source code level, programming languages and their associated frameworks also include some time characteristics [8]. Again, time propeties such as the maximum duration of an operation execution are treated as second class concepts: there are no time type systems. To overcome this deficiency, timeliness and other quality of service properties are sometimes specified using meta-attributes of programming languages (e.g. C# or Java). From a static validation point of view, these attributes are often treated like structured comments. These comments may be used to generate runtime monitors but their semantics is usually too weak to allow reasoning about time properties.

At the design level, several research results have shown the usefulness of specific languages to describe component based software architectures. Thanks to the precise semantics of such languages, tools suites have been developed to analyze the consistency of a software architecture and to prototype it. For example, SOFA [17] provides a specific language that extends the OMG IDL to describe the architecture of component based software. It also provides a process algebra to specify the external behaviour

---

* This work was funded by ARTIST2, the Network of Excellence on Embedded Systems Design.

H.W. Schmidt et al. (Eds.): CBSE 2007, LNCS 4608, pp. 173–188, 2007.

of component. However, using SOFA the architect cannot describe the required and provided QoS of components. The AADL standard [26] is one of the first ADL that provides mechanism to specify the QoS into the component interface, also identified as the fourth level of contract [7]. However, AADL is a low abstraction model, strongly connected with the implementation. Besides, AADL is not yet connected with tools that use the QoS information to analyze the consistency of the architecture. In the domain of model driven engineering, modeling languages such as the UML use profiles to add time and performance dimensions [25]. Many profiles exist for designing real time systems: SPT-UML from OMG, MARTE [1]. These profiles define concepts for modeling real-time system but without precise semantics [15]. All these diverse time models are not formal enough to allow reasoning on time properties of software modules. Working with time properties of software components' assemblies is even more difficult, because loosely defined time notions do not compose well and they cannot be used to build quality of service contracts. On a more theoretical point of view, many formal systems exist to describe timed behaviours and reason about them. For instance, timed automata models support well-defined composition operations. Therefore they can help to specify precise component interfaces, which include types, logical conditions, behaviour and time specifications. Furthermore, tool chains provide automated means to check timed automata against time properties, e.g. timed logic formulas.

In this paper, we argue that time properties must be defined in a component interface. We propose a technique to manipulate time as a separate dimension of component-based software design in order to improve the modularity when the architect defines its architecture. It uses formal time conceptual tools based on temporal logic with quantitative timed automata. This time model can be used at design time to check a component's design against a specification and to compute the properties of component assemblies. The time model is also used to generate monitors that test and supervise component implementations.

The rest of this paper is organized as follows: Section 2 presents an overview of our meta-model for components. Section 3 details the time formalism and how to add timed information into components. Finally, Section 4 describes related work. Section 5 concludes and discusses future work.

2   Analysis and Design

Our approach extends a component based design process and relies on a set of artifacts. In this section we describe these artifacts together with a global overview of the process.

2.1   Artifacts of the Process

The component design process uses or produces the following artifacts:

A *service specification* describes what can be requested from a component, using type definitions and operations to request service execution. Operations can carry constraints such as type, pre and postconditions, behavioural and time related properties. Our interpretation of the notion of service bears some resemblance to the Web service notion: a service is defined as a public capability to perform a rather specialized set of

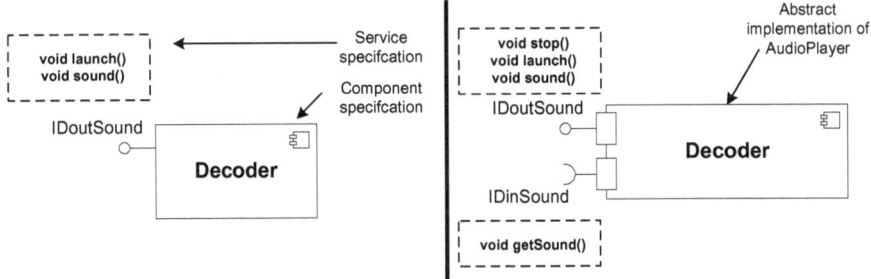

Fig. 1. Example of artifacts

tasks (e.g. hotel room booking service). A given service provide means to solve one application domain's precise concern.

A component specification groups a set of services supported by the component implementations. A component specification is more than a bundle of services: a component specification gives additional constraints that pertain to the coordination of the services. This resembles the specification of a compound Web service (a choreography) built with an orchestration of other Web services.

An abstract implementation of components must adhere to a component specification in order to implement a set of services. This abstract implementation publishes additional information, such as the set of required services that the implementation relies upon in order to perform its tasks, and bounds to quantitative properties of the services that the component implementation provides. These bounds usually depend on quantitative properties of the environment. An abstract implementation hides all platform-specific details: it is a description suited to formal validation of composition, and to computation of the properties of a composition. In other words, the abstract implementation must contain all information needed to check for properties of individual component and component assemblies while hiding all other details not needed by these property checks.

A concrete component implementation is a code level entity that is runnable in a component runtime environment. A concrete implementation must provide the services of its associated abstract component implementation, together with the associated properties.

Each level (service specification, component specification and component implementation) conforms to languages or metamodels that define the fundamental constraints and properties of service and component models (for the sake of simplicity we merge the concept of metamodel and language here). Fig 1 illustrates the three first levels in UML2. In our tool chain implementation, we have selected languages and metamodels that (1) support simultaneously constraints ranging from traditional type compatibility up to real-time properties (e.g. timeliness), (2) are semantically sound, (3) are supported by tools for validation, (4) allow for COTS implementation.

In order to define a notation suitable for timed specifications and abstract implementation, we have extended a subset of UML 2.0. We base our subset on existing component based architecture concepts (components, ports, interfaces and connectors) of the UML and extend them with time related features. The resulting notation (metamodel) is resembling those used by other approaches such as [23]. The design model is organized in two main parts:

1. the service specification describes services that components will implement, including time constraints;
2. the abstract implementation describes a component based architecture and provides a definition of the component behaviour.

Every component metamodel must deal with a clear, sound and complete definition of composition. In the UML 2.0, the composition semantics is not complete enough to support formal definitions of component interactions.

A common notion of component compatibility relies on type compatibility models derived from object-oriented programming: two ports can be connected when the port providing service exposes an interface subtyping the interface exposed on the port requiring service. However, this type model has already shown its limits [24]. The compatibility between two operation prototypes cannot guarantee their correct use. To overcome these limits, we rely on a "rich" black box model that includes timed behaviour descriptions. These specification enrichments are commonly used in Design by Contract software development techniques. They guarantee every component of a system lives up to its expectations. In our approach, according to [7], we identify four levels of contracts. The first level of contracts is based on classical type compatibility. The second level deals with behavioural contracts and it strengthen the level of confidence in a sequential context. A behavioural contract is a set of constraints defined as pre and post conditions on an operation. The third level deals with synchronization contracts. This level provides coordination rules in distributed or concurrency contexts, by explicit specification of the observable behaviours of a component. The fourth level deals with quantitative contracts, quantifies quality of service and the relevant contracts are usually parameterized through a negotiation.

The designer should be able to design each level independently and should be able to ensure at the design stage that the architecture obeys the component's contracts.

In the UML 2.0 world, a service is associated with the definition of a provided interface that specifies the operations that can be invoked. An abstract component specification is a set of services. It declares the interfaces provided by a component. These interfaces are enriched with four levels of contracts. Several approaches have worked on the first three levels. In section 3.2, we lay out a set of mechanisms to define and integrate the fourth level related to the quality of service.

2.2   Abstract Implementation of an Architecture

The next step in the software development life cycle is the abstract implementation of the component. By abstract implementation we mean the description of the component implementation where we omit all details that are not necessary to understand how a component interact with its environment along the time dimension axis. This step also defines either a component's internal structure (an assembly of other components) or its behaviour and temporal specification. This section presents the structural concepts for defining the architecture and the formalisms for the behavioural and the temporal properties of components.

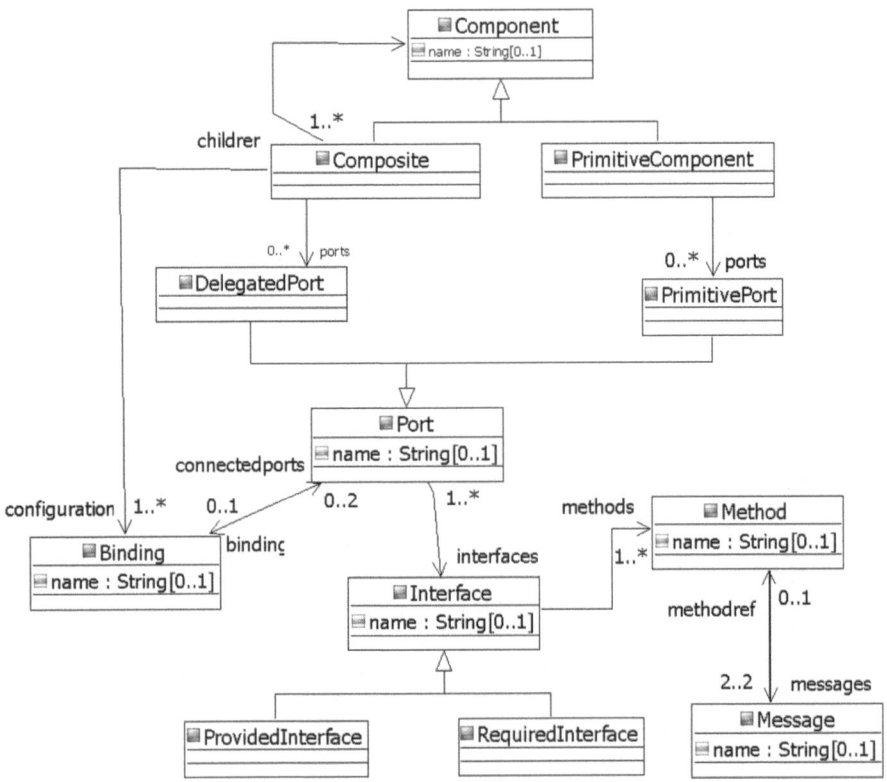

Fig. 2. Structural part of the component's Metamodel

Structural Elements of the Component Model. The structural part of our component model is largely derived from the UML 2.0 architecture metamodel concept. However, contrary to the UML 2.0, we define an abstract model with fewer concepts to limit the complexity of the language that the architect has to manipulate, and to remove all the semantic variation points existing in UML 2.0.

Consequently, in our component model, a *component* provides *methods* and may require some services from other components. Services can only be accessed through explicitly declared ports. A *port* is a binding point on a component that defines two sets of interfaces: *provided* and *required* ones.

Our component model distinguishes between two kinds of components: *primitives* and *composites*. *Primitives* contain executable code and are basic building blocks in component assemblies. *Composites* are used as a mechanism to deal with a group of components as a whole, while potentially hiding some of the features of the subcomponents. Our component model does not impose any limit on the levels of composition. There are, therefore, two ways to define the architecture of an application: using a *binding* between components ports or using a composite to encapsulate a group of components. A connector associates a component's port with a port located on another component. Two ports can be bound with each other only if the interfaces required by one port are provided by the other, and vice versa. This constraint on binding is the classical type compatibility (level 1 contracts). The services provided and required by the child components of a composite component are accessible through *delegated ports* which are the only entry points of a composite component. A delegated port of a composite component is connected to exactly one child component port. The structural part of the component model is presented in Fig. 2.

Behaviour Specification. With the interface and method definitions, a component declares structural elements about provided and required services. The behaviour specification defines the component's interactions with its environment. This behaviour is declared by a process algebra with the In and Out Automaton model [21] to check the system.

Process algebra. To specify a component behaviour, we use a reduced process algebra inspired by FSP [22]. This process algebra is based on an expression describing a set of traces (sequences of events). When applied to components, an event is an abstraction of a method call or response to a call. For example, a call of $m1$ on the interface $i1$ of the port $p1$ is captured as $p1.i1.m1$, a response to the call as $p1.i1.m1\$$. Every event is emitted by a component and accepted by another component. Calling $m1$ via the interface $i1$ of the Port $p1$ is seen as the emission of $!p1.i1.m1$ by the component $C1$ (denoted by an event token of the form $!C1.p1.i1.m1$); at the same time the reception of $p3.i2.m1$ is accepted by $C2$ (denoted as $?C2.p3.i2.m1$ from the perspective of $C2$).

The operators employed in behaviour protocols are: $\rightarrow$ for sequencing, $|$ for alternative choice and $*$ for a finite repetition. This algebra is used to represent the behaviour of primitive components only.

The I/O automaton model. Besides a process algebra, we use an I/O automaton formalism to perform checking.

Definition 1. *(I/O automaton)*
An Input/Output automaton is a tuple (S, L, T, s_0) where:

- *S is a finite non empty set of states,*
- *L is a finite non empty set of labels. $L = I \bigcup O$ where I is a set of inputs and O the outputs and $I \bigcap O = \emptyset$,*
- *$T \subseteq S(L \bigcup \{\tau\})S$ is the finite set of transitions where τ is an non observable internal action.*
- *s_0 is an initial state, an element of S.*

Composition of I/O automata. The composition of components in our system is based on the synchronization of an output of a component with the input of a connected component[10].

The composition of I/O Automata is associative and commutative. When the architect composes several components, the composition order is irrelevant.

This process algebra can be seen as a textual representation of a subset of the sequence diagram where the roles, identified in the diagram, are the port of the component.

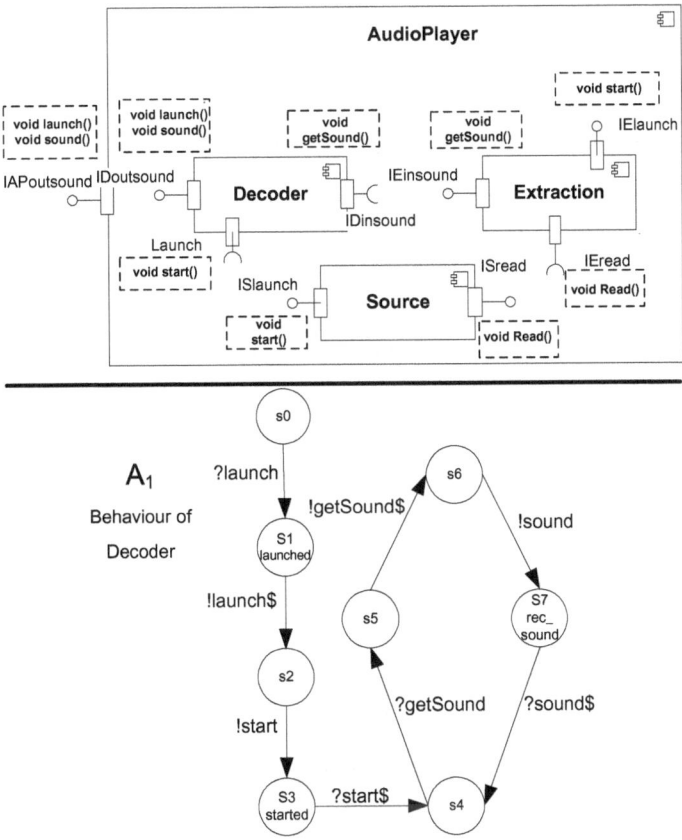

Fig. 3. Example of an audio player component

Example. Figure 3 illustrates the model with an example of component Audio-Player. The AudioPlayer component provides an IAPoutsound interface that contains methods launch and sound. It is composed of 3 components: Decoder, Extraction and Source. The top side shows the structural representation of the component in UML 2.0. The bottom of Figure 3 shows an automaton A_1 describing all possible behaviours of the Decoder.

3   Adding Time Properties into Components

After defining all functional properties in the component, the designer may add some extra-functional properties into it. These extra-functional properties include dense time properties. In order to add time properties to the components we will modify add time information in two different places: on behaviour specifications and on contracts attached to required interfaces. These two places represent what the component provide and require and are used during the composition of components. In order to add time to component behaviour, we use the Timed Automata theory [5]. Furthermore, we define time patterns to help the designer with the definition of time contracts. Our formalism for such contracts is based on a timed temporal logic (Timed Computation Tree Logic [4]).

3.1   Adding Time into Component's Behaviour

While time logic is used to specify contracts, one also needs a means to specify the time properties of abstract implementation of components. Since automata are already used to describe component behaviours, we rely on timed automata (TA) to add precise timing constraints on these behaviours.

Timed Automata.   A timed automaton is an automaton extended with clocks, which are a set of variables increasing uniformly with time. Formally, a timed automaton is defined as follows:

Definition 2. *(Timed   Automaton)   A   timed   automaton   is   a   tuple A $=<$ $S, X, L, T, \iota, P >$ where:*

 - *S is a finite set of locations,*
 - *X is a finite set of clocks. To each clock, we assign a valuation $v \in V$, $v(x) \in R^+$ for each $x \in X$.*
 - *L is a finite set of labels,*
 - *T is a finite set of edges. Each edge t is a tuple $< s, l, \psi, , s' >$ where $s, s' \in S$, $l \in L$, $\psi \in \Psi_X$ is the enabling condition. Ψ_X is the set or predicates on X defined as $x \sim c$ or $x - y \sim c$ where $x, y \in X$ and $\sim \in \{<, \leq, =\}$ and c in$N$.*
 - *ι is the invariant of A. $\iota \in \Phi_X$ where Φ_X is the set of functions $\phi : S \to \Psi_X$ mapping each location s to a predicate ψ,*
 - *P associates a set of atomic propositions to each location.*

A state of an automaton is a location and a valuation of clocks that satisfies the invariant of that location. Two different types of state transition exist: discrete transitions and timed transitions.

Timed Patterns.   In order to ease the addition of time constraints to behaviour, we have defined a set of time patterns based on those partially defined in [14]: response time, delay, execution time, period of service call, duration, etc. We explain hereafter two of these timed patterns: response time and execution time.

Response time.   The *response time* pattern enables the expression of a response time with a timed automaton. The response time is the delay between a service call and its acknowledgment. For example, to express a response time on the getSound service, one needs to initialize a clock when calling getSound; to receive the acknowledgment, one checks if the clock value is correct with respect to a defined value. This pattern requires three parameters: the service call *service*, the operator $\sim \in \{<, \leq, =, \geq, >\}$ and the value c. The RT automaton on Figure 4 represents the generic response time pattern. The pattern consists in three locations, two transitions and one clock. The clock is initialized on the first transition with the service call and checked in the second one with the acknowledge of the service. The second location has the property

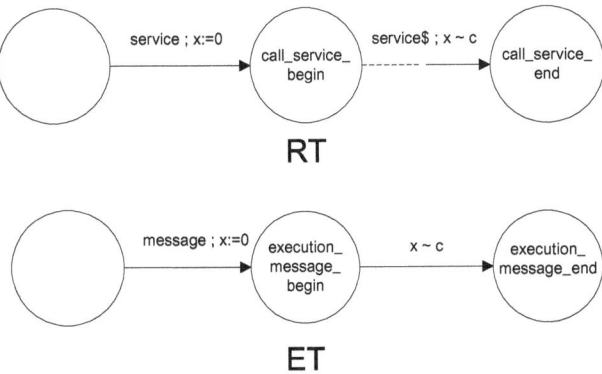

Fig. 4. Response time and execution time patterns

call_service_begin and the third one *call_service_end*. These properties will be used for checking contracts. When the pattern will be added to the component's behaviour, the two transitions need be not consecutive, other transitions can be inserted between them. This is represented on *RT* by the dotted line between the second location and the second transition.

Execution time. The execution time pattern is used to represent an execution with a timed automaton. The execution time is the time used to do a processing. For example, after receiving the response to a service call, the component requires some processing time. The pattern has three parameters: message *message*, operator $\sim$ and value c. The automaton *ET* on Figure 4 represents the generic execution time pattern. The pattern consists in three locations, two transitions and one clock. The clock is initialized on the first transition with the message to be processed and checked in the second transition without any message. The second location has the property *execution_message_begin* and the third one *execution_message_end*. These properties will be used to check TCTL formulas. In contrast with the response time pattern, the two transitions must be consecutive because the component is used by the processing and cannot compute something else. This is why the second transition and the third location do not exist in the component's behaviour; they will be created when the pattern will be applied. This way of adding the pattern is not the only one, we can define an execution time pattern where the clock check is added to every outgoing transition of the second location.

Timed Behaviour. After defining a set of patterns, we will add them to the component's behaviour. The designer selects the different patterns with their parameters. They will be automatically integrated to the component's behaviour. We will illustrate this design process by adding two timed patterns to the component's behaviour of the example. First, we select the timed pattern response time with the *getSound* service call, the $<$ operator and the value 4. For this pattern we add a clock $x1$ to an automaton. This clock is initialized on the ?*getSound* transition from the location $s5$. The *call_getSound_begin* property is added to the targeted location of this transition, in location $s5$. Then we select the transition !*getSound*$ add the guard $x1 < 4$ and add

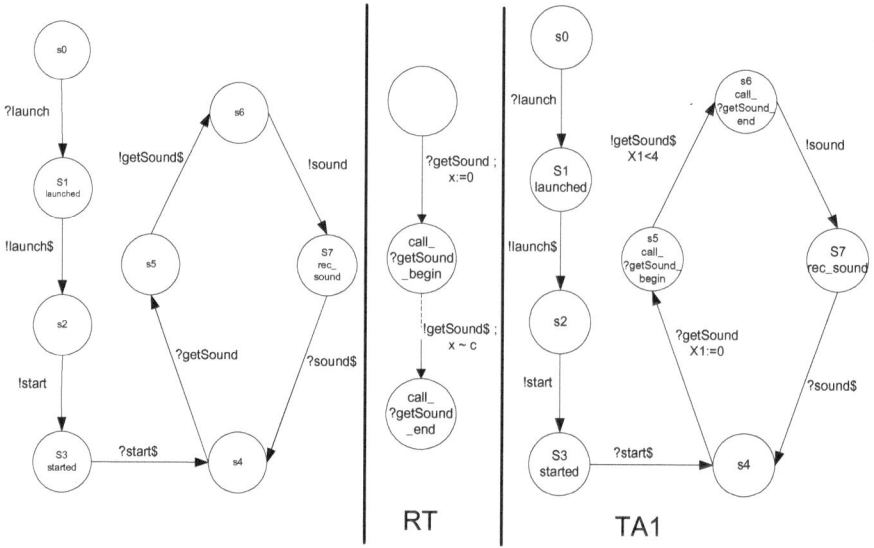

Fig. 5. Adding response time patterns to component's behaviour

the property *call_getSound_begin* to the target of the transition. The result is shown on the *TA*1 of figure 5.

Second, we add the pattern execution time with message !*getSound*$, operator < and value 2. A second clock $x2$ is added to the automaton and it is initialized on the transition !*getSound*$. We add a new location *s6_exec* and a transition between *s6* and *s6_exec* with the guard $x2 < 2$. The outcoming transitions of *s6* of *TA*1 become the outgoing transitions of *s6_exec*. The properties *execution_!getSound$_begin* and *execution_!getSound$_end* are respectively added to *s6* and *s6_exec*. The new automaton of the component is shown on the *TA*2 of figure 6. The new behaviour of the component does not change with respect to the original one : you can obtain A_1 from TA_2 by removing the clock and the transition without a label.

3.2 Adding Time into a Component Contract

Component contracts are part of a component specification; they are bound to ports to describe type, state and behaviour properties that must be enforced by component implementations. In this section we show the addition of time contracts expressed with a timed temporal logic named TCTL [4]. These new contracts will be checked during the composition phase against the timed automata to validate the compatibility between two components.

TCTL. TCTL is an extension of CTL [13] with quantitative temporal operators.

In CTL, a formula $\exists \Diamond p$ is satisfied if and only if predicate p can become true along some computation path, without any information about the instant p evaluates to true. The TCTL extension is able to handle quantitative constraints: for example formula

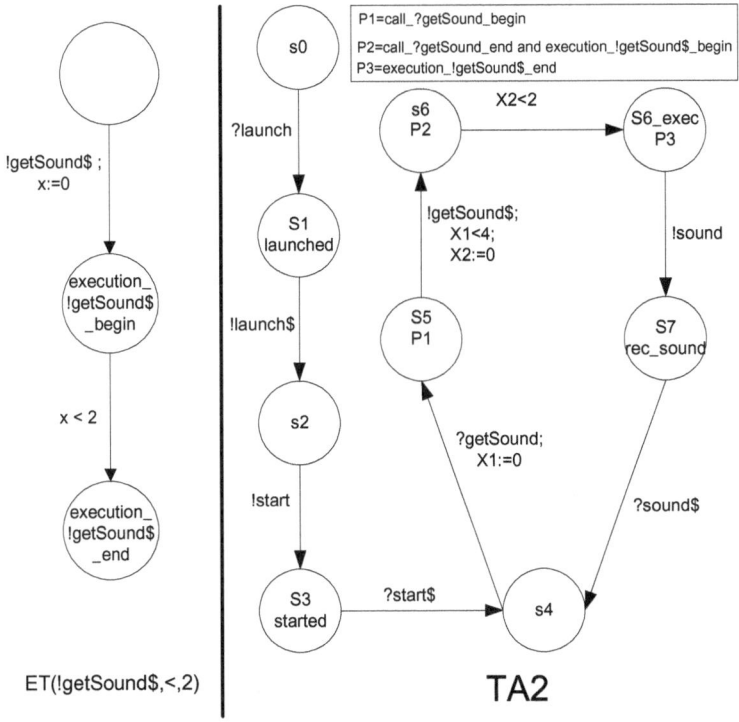

Fig. 6. Adding execution time patterns to component's behaviour

$\exists\lozenge_{<5}p$ is true if and only if along some computation path property p becomes true within 5 time units.

Let P be a set of properties and N be the set of natural numbers:

Definition 3. *(Syntax) The formulas ψ of TCTL are defined as follows:*

$$\psi := p\,|\,false\,|\,\psi_1 \rightarrow \psi_2\,|\,\exists\psi_1 U_{\sim c}\psi_2\,|\,\forall\psi_1 U_{\sim c}\psi_2$$

where $p \in P$, $c \in N$, and $\sim\,\in \{<, \leq, =, \geq, >\}$.

Abbreviations are defined by:

- $\exists\lozenge_{\sim c}\psi$ for $true\exists$ (possibility),
- $\forall\lozenge_{\sim c}\psi$ for $true\forall U_{\sim c}\psi$ (all locations along all computations),
- $\exists\square_{\sim c}\psi$ for $\neg\forall\lozenge_{\sim c}\neg\psi$,
- $\forall\square_{\sim c}\psi$ for $\neg\exists\lozenge_{\sim c}\neg\psi$ (some locations along all computations).

We prohibit the use of more than one clock in a given expression in order to avoid the forward analysis problem[9].

Timed Contract. The timed contracts are attached to the required interfaces of a component, like the three other types of contract. To use the definition of these timed contracts, we define a set of patterns based on [19]. These contract patterns are skeletons, which must be completed by the designer. A designer may also write contracts directly in TCLT. To create a new timed contract, the designer selects the appropriate pattern and provides parameter values. Some examples of patterns are:

- time response of c of service call $foo : call\_foo\_begin \rightarrow \forall\Box(\forall\Diamond_{\sim c}call\_foo\_end)$
- period of c of the property $p : \forall\Box(\forall\Diamond_{\sim c}p)$
- time of c between two property $p1$ and $p2 : p1 \rightarrow \forall\Box(\forall\Diamond_{\sim c}p2)$

Other contracts are automatically created when timed patterns are added by the designer. For example, if the response time pattern is chosen with an external service call, (e.g. service $?getSound$), the contract is implicitly included in this pattern. The formula in TCTL is created with the parameters of the timed pattern.

3.3   Checking Time Properties When Composing Components

As described in the previous sections, we use timed logic for specification of components and timed automata to describe abstract implementations of these components. Since we use formally defined notations, we are able to use software tools for validation of implementations against specifications. To check the time properties during the composition process, we use the Kronos tool [11], which is able to evaluate TCTL formulas on timed automata. The behaviour of each primitive component is modeled by timed automata and the timed contracts are expressed in the real-time temporal logic TCTL. When a timed automaton does not satisfy a formula, Kronos identifies the locations where the formula does not hold. For instance, if the environment's contracts are :

- receive $sound$ periodically with 7 units of time : $\forall\Box(\forall\Diamond_{<7}rec\_sound)$
- receive $sound$ at least 5 units of time after sending $launch$:
  $launched \Rightarrow \forall\Box(\forall\Diamond_{<5}rec\_sound)$

Kronos answers $true$ when provided with the timed automaton and the first formula. When we provide Kronos the second formula, the tool answers that the formula does not hold and gives the previous locations of where rec_sound is true.

4   Related Work

Architecture level timing analysis will not come as a replacement for lower-level timing analysis that can be performed once all the detailed design step is achieved. It aims at validating the system early in the development process. To perform such an analysis, an abstract model of the internal behaviour of the components must be known (including estimation of computing times, which can be obtained from a WCET analysis for pre-existing components and by a first evaluation for other ones). In this section, we discuss the different existing models that can be used to describe time properties in a the component behaviour. Next, this section comes back on the issue of the separation of concerns between time properties and functional properties in software modeling.

UML Profiles, ADLs and Component Models

There are several component based models dedicated to the design of real-time applications. For example, in the UML community several profiles have been proposed to add time information at the modeling level. CQML [3] is a lexical language designed for QoS specification. It can be integrated with UML and can be used at different levels of abstraction. However, CQML is poorly tooled. Consequently, it can not be efficiently used in a software development process. The OMEGA project [2] provides formal methods to check the consistency of UML 2.0 models. The OMEGA approach deals with the specification level only but without link to component-based applications. In the domain of component-based software architecture, the AADL is a new international standard for predictable model-based engineering of real-time and embedded software [26]. Mainly inspired by MetaH [29], its fields of application are automotive, avionics, space and industrial control systems. AADL is a lower-level modeling language than UML or other component models used at the modeling level. Main concepts manipulated by this language are components, ports, threads, communication bus, *etc*. AADL models describe software topologies bound to execution platform topologies. AADL is interesting for two reasons. Far-off the concern of this article, it provides a mechanism of *mode* to model the reconfiguration of statically-known systems. Secondly, more relevant for this paper, it was one of the first ADL to model the quality of service in a component based software architecture. It can model times properties or latency. Nevertheless, AADL is a low-level ADL, directly connected to the implementation. Besides, there is currently no way to help the designer to integrate time properties in an existing component based software architecture.

Several toolboxes for real-time modeling exist. Uppaal [20] is an integrated tool environment for the modeling, the validation and the verification of real-time systems defined as networks of timed automata. Uppaal is able to evaluate CTL formulas on timed automata but can not check TCTL formulas. Consequently, it cannot be used to evaluate QoS contracts expressed on the component interfaces but can be used for the third level.

All the models presented in this section support the description of the architecture and aim at validating the architecture of a system with respect to its timing requirements (e.g. basic and end-to-end deadlines, throughput, etc.). However, two main problems limits their use in a concrete system development process. First, most of these models are not connected to a concrete component platform. Consequently, analysis performed at design time are lost to the implementation. Secondly, due to a lack of separation of concerns in the software development process, time properties and functional properties has to be managed at the same time.

To solve the issue of the gap between the modeling stage and the development stage, BIP [6] provides a framework to model heterogeneous components. The BIP component model is the superposition of three layers: the lower layer describes the *behaviour* of a component as a set of *transitions*; the intermediate layer includes *connectors* describing the *interactions* between transitions of the layer underneath; the upper layer consists of a set of *priority* rules used to describe scheduling policies for interactions. BIP components can be extended with clock variables, but the time model is then a discrete and simulated one. For instance, BIP can not embed time contracts such as TCTL contracts. Besides, BIP does not provide any mechanism to handle contract violations.

Separation of Concerns

Improving the separation of concerns in a component based software architecture comes from a very natural analogy: Just like in an house architecture we have distinct *view/plan/blueprints* describing distinct concerns of the same house (walls and spaces, electrical wiring, water conducts), it seems reasonable to conceive a software architecture description as the composition of several concerns specifications reflecting several perspectives of the same software system. With this kind of analogy, it seems natural to view time as a separated concern that must be integrated with the rest of the architecture.

In this trend, the Accord methodology proposed in [28] defines a technique based on aspect oriented design to support separation of concerns in real-time component based architectures. The associated component model is tuned to allow the computation of worst case execution time of woven parts rather than general analysis techniques on abstract components.

Klein et al. propose a semantic-based weaving of scenarios [18], where the weaving is based on the dynamic semantics of the models used. This work relies on Message Sequence Charts (MSC) as a language of scenarios, but MSC and I/O automata used to specify the behaviour are similar languages for the weaving operator point of view. Nevertheless, the weaving operator can help the designer to integrate aspect behavioural specification but it does not support timed automata and the integration of QoS in the component specification. Our approach can be seen as a first step to support the weaving of time, although currently we do not provide any pointcut language to specify integration of our time based patterns.

5 Conclusion and Perspectives

The separation of concerns make the design easier, improve the testability and the software maintainability. The separation of concerns is often used to modularize in separated units some technical concerns like security, persistence or traceability. This paper addresses time as a concern and proposes mechanisms to help the designer to integrate time QoS information during the specification and the design of a component based software. For example, this approach highlights patterns for the behaviour and the contracts definition.

The work presented in this paper is a part of a global approach that aims to decrease the gap between the specification model and the implementation [27]. It proposes a unified approach to the design and implementation of component based systems. This approach aims at assisting architects in the design and in the implementation of real-time systems by providing a set of tools that check the consistency of the artifacts used to create these systems. This approach is based on an extension of the UML 2.0 standard used to design the services provided by components, to specify components and to give a first abstract implementation of the systems. Using a Model Driven Engineering style, the approach provides code generation capabilities that clearly separate functional part based on the Fractal Component Model [12] and QoS part based on the Giotto framework [16]. The patterns proposed in this paper are mainly useful at the design stage. They allow to design the software without QoS information and add these information in a second stage.

We are currently working on implementing these patterns as an aspect at the model level. The goal is to design a new primary artifact at the model level to be able to reuse QoS models. Besides, we want to define a expressive pointcut language to simplify the integration of the same QoS model into several component based software architectures. It will also allow the QoS layer to be composed with other aspects of the architecture.

References

1. MARTE UML profile RFP. voted at OMG.
   http://www.omg.org/cgi-bin/doc?realtime/2005-02-06
2. Webpage of the OMEGA IST project. http://www-omega.imag.fr/
3. Aagedal, J.O.: Quality of Service Support in Development of Distributed Systems. PhD thesis, Department for Informatics, University of Oslo (June 2001)
4. Alur, R., Courcoubetis, C., Dill, D.L.: Model-checking in dense real-time. Information and Computation 104(1), 2–34 (1993)
5. Alur, R., Dill, D.L.: A theory of timed automata. Theor. Comput. Sci. 126(2), 183–235 (1994)
6. Basu, A., Bozga, M., Sifakis, J.: Modeling heterogeneous real-time components in bip. In: SEFM '06. Proceedings of the Fourth IEEE International Conference on Software Engineering and Formal Methods, Washington, DC, pp. 3–12. IEEE Computer Society Press, Los Alamitos (2006)
7. Beugnard, A., Jézéquel, J.-M., Plouzeau, N., Watkins, D.: Making components contract aware. Computer 32(7), 38–45 (1999)
8. Bollella, G., Gosling, J.: The real-time specification for java. Computer 33(6), 47–54 (2000)
9. Bouyer, P.: Untameable timed automata! In: Alt, H., Habib, M. (eds.) STACS 2003. LNCS, vol. 2607, pp. 620–631. Springer, Heidelberg (2003)
10. Bouyer, P., Petit, A.: Decomposition and composition of timed automata. In: Wiedermann, J., van Emde Boas, P., Nielsen, M. (eds.) ICALP 1999. LNCS, vol. 1644, pp. 210–219. Springer, Heidelberg (1999)
11. Bozga, M., Daws, C., Maler, O., Olivero, A., Tripakis, S., Yovine, S.: Kronos: A model-checking tool for real-time systems. In: Vardi, M.Y. (ed.) CAV 1998. LNCS, vol. 1427, Springer, Heidelberg (1998)
12. Bruneton, E., Coupaye, T., Leclercq, M., Quéma, V., Stefani, J.-B.: An open component model and its support in java. In: Crnković, I., Stafford, J.A., Schmidt, H.W., Wallnau, K. (eds.) CBSE 2004. LNCS, vol. 3054, pp. 7–22. Springer, Heidelberg (2004)
13. Clarke, E.M., Emerson, E.A., Sistla, A.P.: Automatic verification of finite-state concurrent systems using temporal logic specifications. ACM Trans. Program. Lang. Syst. 8(2), 244–263 (1986)
14. Graf, S., Ober, I.: A real-time profile for UML and how to adapt it to SDL. In: Reed, R., Reed, J. (eds.) SDL 2003. LNCS, vol. 2708, Springer, Heidelberg (2003)
15. Graf, S., Ober, I.: How useful is the UML real-time profile SPT without semantics. In: SIVOES 2004, associated with RTAS 2004, Toronto Canada (submitted for publication) (April 2004)

16. Henzinger, T.A., Kirsch, C.M., Horowitz, B.: Giotto: A time-triggered language for embedded programming. Proceedings of the IEEE 91(1), 84–99 (2003)
17. Kalibera, T., Tuma, P.: Distributed component system based on architecture description: The sofa experience. In: Meersman, R., Tari, Z. et al. (eds.) CoopIS 2002, DOA 2002, and ODBASE 2002. LNCS, vol. 2519, pp. 981–994. Springer, Heidelberg (2002)
18. Klein, J., Hélouët, L., Jézéquel, J.M.: Semantic-based weaving of scenarios. In: Proceedings of the 5th international conference on Aspect-oriented software development, pp. 27–38 (2006)
19. Konrad, S., Cheng, B.H.C.: Real-time specification patterns. In: Inverardi, P., Jazayeri, M. (eds.) ICSE 2005. LNCS, vol. 4309, pp. 372–381. Springer, Heidelberg (2006)
20. Larsen, K.G., Pettersson, P., Yi, W.: Uppaal in a Nutshell. Int. Journal on Software Tools for Technology Transfer 1(1-2), 134–152 (1997)
21. Lynch, N.A., Tuttle, M.R.: An introduction to input/output automata. CWI Quarterly 2(3), 219–246 (1989)
22. Magee, J.: Behavioral analysis of software architectures using ltsa. In: Proceedings of the 21st international conference on Software engineering, pp. 634–637. IEEE Computer Society Press, Los Alamitos (1999)
23. Medvidovic, N., Taylor, R.N.: A classification and comparison framework for software architecture description languages. IEEE Transactions on Software Engineering 26, 23 (2000)
24. Meyer, B.: Applying design by contract. Computer 25(10) (October 1992)
25. Object Management Group OMG. UML Profile for Schedulability, Performance, and Time Specification, Version 1.1. (January 2005)
26. As-2 Embedded Computing Systems Committee SAE. Architecture Analysis & Design Language (AADL). SAE Standards n^o AS5506 (November 2004)
27. Saudrais, S., Barais, O., Duchien, L.: Using model-driven engineering to generate qos monitors from a formal specification. edocw 0, 45 (2006)
28. Tesanovic, A.: Aspects and components in real-time system development: Towards reconfigurable and reusable software. Journal of Embedded Computing 1(1), 17–37 (2005)
29. Vestal, S.: Fixed-priority sensitivity analysis for linear compute time models. IEEE Transactions on Software Engineering 20(4) (1994)

Slicing of Component Behavior Specification with Respect to Their Composition[*]

Ondřej Šerý[1] and František Plášil[1,2]

[1] Charles University in Prague, Faculty of Mathematics and Physics
Department of Software Engineering
Malostranske namesti 25, 118 00 Prague 1, Czech Republic
{sery, plasil}@dsrg.mff.cuni.cz
http://dsrg.mff.cuni.cz
[2] Academy of Sciences of the Czech Republic
Institute of Computer Science
plasil@cs.cas.cz
http://www.cs.cas.cz

Abstract. Being an important means of reducing development costs, behavior specification of software components facilitates reuse of a component and even reuse of a component's architecture (assembly). However, since typically only a part of the components' functionality is actually used in the new context, a significant part of the behavior specification may be superfluous. As a result, it may be hard to see (and filter out) the actual interplay among the components in their behavior specification. This paper targets the problem in the scope of behavior protocols. It presents a technique for slicing behavior protocols with respect to a given context (composition), designed to remove the unused behavior from a behavior specification. The technique is based on a formal foundation, generic enough to support slicing with respect to a property expressed as a predicate. To demonstrate viability of the proposed approach, a positive experience with behavior specification slicing applied in real-life case study is shared with the reader (along with a short description of a prototype).

Keywords: Components-based software engineering, Behavior specification, Software architecture reuse.

1 Introduction

When reusing a software component (such as a COTS component) in a component-based application, it is likely that only a part of its functionality will be actually used. Assuming a behavior specification of the component is available, a significant part of it may be superfluous in the given application. As a result, it is hard to read and comprehend the actual interplay among the components from their behavior specification. A similar issue arises when reusing a component architecture

---

[*] This work was partially supported by the Grant Agency of the Czech Republic project 201/06/0770. The results will be applied in the ITEA/EUREKA project OSIRIS Σ!2023.

H.W. Schmidt et al. (Eds.): CBSE 2007, LNCS 4608, pp. 189–202, 2007.

(assembly) in a new environment, employing only a part of the provided functionality. In order to make the behavior specification relevant only to the specific application and, as a pleasant side effect, facilitate human comprehension of the actual interplay among the components, it is desirable to find methods for slicing the behavior specification to make it contain only the parts really used in a specific component composition and/or environment. This also helps clarify the actual roles of individual components.

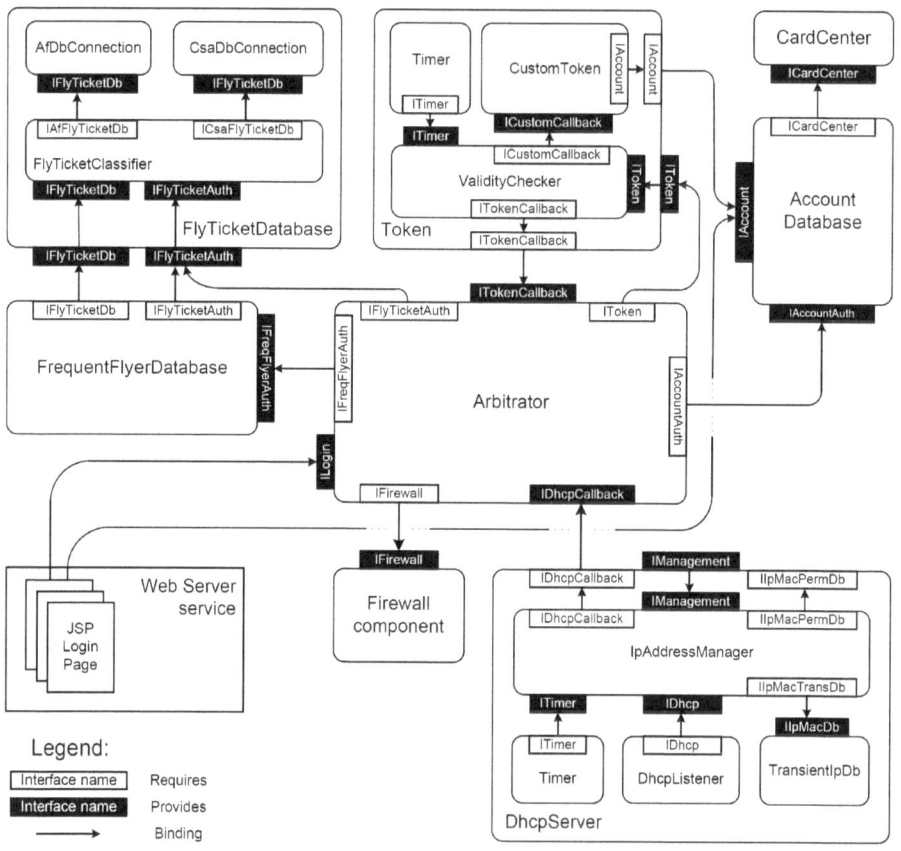

Fig. 1. Architecture of the demo component application, the airport internet providing service

The problem can be illustrated on a demo component application (Fig. 1), designed as a part of the Fractal Component Reliability Extension (CRE) project [7]. The aim of the project was to enhance Fractal component model by behavior specification and to provide tools for its analysis. The demo application constitutes an airport service for providing a wireless internet connection (to the owners of first or business class tickets, to the frequent flayer and credit card holders). As to the top-level components, Firewall realizes the firewall for blocking unauthorized internet connections by redirecting them to the login web page. The FlyTicketDatabase and

`FrequentFlyerDatabase` components mediate access to the databases of airlines companies. `CardCenter` communicates with the bank credit card services and `AccountDatabase` encapsulates accounts with prepaid internet connection. The `Token` component is a dynamically created entity representing a single logged user. All communication is orchestrated by `Arbitrator`, while `DhcpServer` manages dynamic IP address allocation with support for use of the permanent IP address database. This database, mapping Mac to IP addresses, could be connected via the `IIpMacPermanentDb` interface and its use be triggered on via the `IManagement` interface. However, both these interfaces are left unbound, since permanent IP address allocation is not used in the application. The behavior of about twenty components was specified via the formalism of behavior protocols [17] and, using a behavior protocol checker, the behavior compliance of these components was verified.

Assume now an internet provision service in a public garden (payment by credit card only). Evidently, the component architecture in Fig. 1 can be reused for such a purpose. A necessary modification involves simplification of `DhcpServer` (no permanent addresses), and of `Arbitrator` (no airport-specific logins). Obviously, it would be very confusing to see any `FlyTicketDatabase` and `Frequent-FlyerDatabase`-related behavior in the specification of these modified components. Thus, slicing of behavior specification with respect to actual component architecture (composition) is desirable.

1.1 Behavior Protocols

The formalism of behavior protocols [17] was developed for behavior specification of software components. As a behavior, the desired finite sequences of method calls on component's interfaces (their interplay) are considered, abstracting from method parameters and internal data. Behavior protocol specifying behavior of a particular component is called its *frame protocol.*

Being a specific process algebra [3], behavior protocol P is an expression that generates a set of traces of method calls (the language $L(P)$). More precisely, a trace is a sequence of tokens representing atomic events related to method invocations (?a↑ stands for accepting a method invocation, !a↑ issuing an invocation, ?a↓ means accepting the response (end) of a method execution, !a↓ means issuing the response). Syntactically, a behavior protocol is composed of tokens, operators (";" sequencing, "+" alternative, "*" repetition, and "|" parallel interleaving), and abbreviations ?a (stands for ?a↑; !a↓), ?a{P} (stands for ?a↑; P; !a↓), and similarly for !a, and !a{P}.

In Fig. 2, there is a frame protocol of the `DhcpServer` component from Fig. 1. The meaning of the protocol is as follows. On its required interface `IDhcpCallback`, the `DhcpServer` calls `IpAddressInvalidated` (line 2) when an IP address lease expires. The call can be arbitrarily repeated ("*"). In parallel to this ("|"), `DhcpServer` can accept calls on the `IManagement` provided interface (lines 4–15). The `IManagement` interface provides means for mode switching between random IP address assignment and persistent MAC to IP address mapping via the `IIpMacPermDb` interface (`!IIpMacPermDb.GetIpAddress*` at line 7). Since a request for stopping permanent address assignement can come while `!IIpMacPermDb.GetIpAddress*` is in progress ("↑"), this has to be captured by explicitly stating requests and responses of the mode switching calls in order to achieve synchronization.

Behavior protocols introduce special case of parallel composition (known from process algebras), the *consent operator* ∇. Similar to parallel composition, e.g. in CCS, the consent operator produces interleaving of events, while merging the invoke "!" and accept "?" events with the same name into an internal event (prefixed by "τ"). Moreover, the consent operator identifies communication errors: *bad activity* – the issued event cannot be accepted, *no activity* (deadlock) – all of the ready events' tokens are prefixed by "?", and *infinite activity* (divergence) – the composed protocols "cannot reach their final events at the same time", so that the composed behavior would contain an infinite trace (only finite traces are allowed). Technically, these communication errors are reflected by ∇, appending the erroneous traces with error events (!ε, ∅ε, and ∞ε for bad activity, no activity, and infinite activity errors, respectively). For more information, the reader is referred to [1].

```
line#
  1    (
  2        !IDhcpCallback.IpAddressInvalidated*
  3        |
  4        (
  5            ?IManagement.UsePermanentIpDb↑ ;
  6            (
  7                !IIpMacPermDb.GetIpAddress*
  8                |
  9                (
 10                    !IManagement.UsePermanentIpDb↓ ;
 11                    ?IManagement.StopUsingPermanentIpDb↑
 12                )
 13            ) ;
 14            !IManagement.StopUsingPermanentIpDb↓
 15        )*
 16    )
```

Fig. 2. DhcpServer frame protocol

To illustrate use of the consent operator, suppose that the architecture of the composed `DhcpServer` component is to be checked for correctness of its internal communication—*horizontal compliance*. This is achieved by applying the consent operator to the frame protocols of all subcomponents of `DhcpServer` and finding out whether the resulting language: $L(FP_{\text{IpAddressManager}} \nabla FP_{\text{DhcpListener}} \nabla FP_{\text{TransientIpDb}} \nabla FP_{\text{Timer}})$, contains any erroneous trace. If so, the internal communication can generally result in a communication error. Another important task is to check whether the architecture of the composed `DhcpServer` component obeys its frame protocol—*vertical compliance*. For this purpose, the *inverted frame* trick is used, i.e. the frame protocol of `DhcpServer` is inverted ("?" are substituted by "!" and vice versa) and the inverted protocol is composed with the protocol of the architecture: $L\ (FP_{\text{DhcpServer}}^{-1} \nabla FP_{\text{IpAddressManager}} \nabla FP_{\text{DhcpListener}} \nabla FP_{\text{TransientIpDb}} \nabla FP_{\text{Timer}})$. The result is then sought for erroneous traces. The key idea behind the trick is testing the architecture in the most general environment of $\texttt{DhcpServer}$, represented by its inverted frame protocol $FP_{\text{DhcpServer}}^{-1}$. It is worth noting that the consent operator does not correspond to equivalences known from process algebras. It is just a smart parallel composition operator, which can explicitly insert error events ($!\varepsilon$, $\varnothing\varepsilon$, and $\infty\varepsilon$) into resulting traces. Consequently, the vertical compliance corresponds to subtyping, as the internal architecture of a composed component is required to correctly implement (i.e. without communication errors) the behavior specification of the composed component. This relation is not an equivalence between behavior specifications, as it permits the internal architecture to potentially feature additional behavior which is not employed in the environment determined by the frame protocol of the enclosing component.

1.2 Goal and Structure of the Paper

The goal of the paper is to propose a way of reducing frame protocols of components with respect to a particular component composition (architecture/assembly) in order to omit the unused parts of the behavioral specification. This should clarify the actual role of each component in their composition and make understanding of the overall behavior interplay of the components easier.

This goal is reflected in the structure of the paper as follows. Formal foundation of behavior protocol reductions and protocol slicing is provided in Sect. 2, while Sect. 3 introduces slicing with respect to composition and proposes a technique to achieve this kind of protocol reduction. The last sections are devoted to a prototype's description, related work discussion, and a conclusion.

2 Reduction and Slicing of Behavior Protocols

2.1 Reduction Preorder

First of all, it is necessary to formalize the notion of reduction; i.e. to define when a behavior protocol can be considered a reduction of another one. For this purpose, the notion of *substitutability* of components (and their behavior protocols) is crucial. Suppose that a component B working in an environment Env_B without any communication errors (Fig. 3-a) is to be substituted by another component A and each of them is associated with its frame protocol.

Definition 1. A behavior protocol a is *substitutable* for a behavior protocol b, if $L(a \nabla b^{-1})$ does not contain any trace with communication error. A component A is *substitutable* for a component B, if the frame protocol of A is substitutable for the frame protocol of B.

In other words, Def. 1 says that a component A is substitutable for another component B, if by placing A to the most general environment of B (described by the inverted protocol b^{-1}) does not result in any communication error. Thus A can be safely placed into any environment Env_B of B (Fig. 3-b), assuming B is working without any communication errors in this environment.

Having the substitutability defined, the next step is to formalize the reduction itself. The basic idea is as follows: A component B_{red} with a reduced frame protocol b_{red} working in an environment Env_{red}, can be replaced by a component B with the frame protocol b, provided b is substitutable for b_{red} and $L(b_{red}) \subseteq L(b)$, Fig. 3-c. This is captured by defining a *reduction preorder* $\leq_R$ over behavior protocols in Def. 2. For the proof that the relation $\leq_R$ is really a preorder, the reader is referred to [19].

Definition 2. Let b_{red} and b be behavior protocols. b_{red} is *reduction* of b, $b_{red} \leq_R b$, if b is substitutable for b_{red} and $L(b_{red}) \subseteq L(b)$.

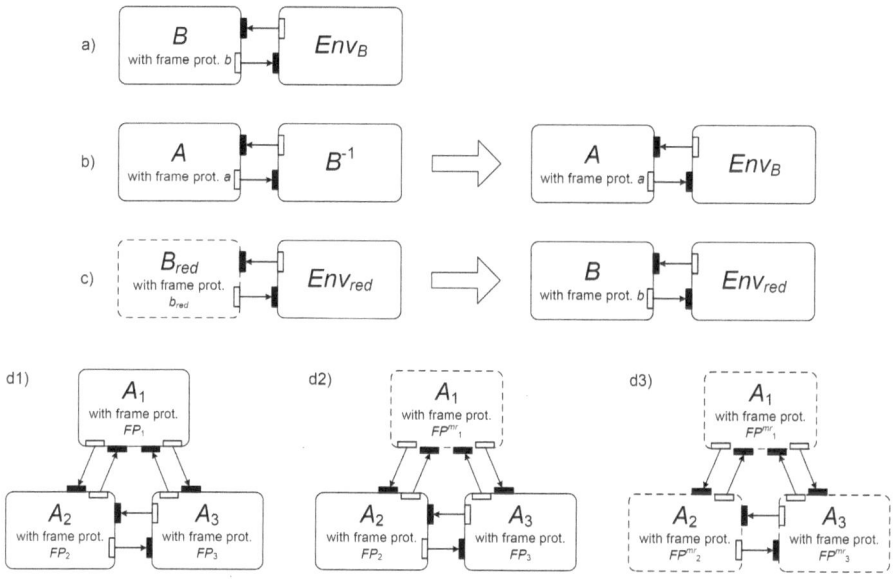

Fig. 3. Motivation for protocol reduction basic definitions

Intuitively, the reduction b_{red} of b is obliged to describe only a subset of the traces described by the protocol b ($L(b_{red}) \subseteq L(b)$). Furthermore, the original protocol b has to be substitutable for its reduction b_{red}. This is required to assure that any architecture (Env_{red}) designed using the reduced virtual component B_{red} can safely use any component B described by the original protocol b instead of B_{red}. Thus the designer can safely use the simpler reduced protocol b_{red} and be sure that the resulting architecture will function correctly even with a component featuring the more complex original protocol b.

2.2 Minimal Reduction

The reduction preorder presented in Sect. 2.1 constitutes a formal instrument for deciding whether a protocol is a valid reduction of another one and for formalizing a set of valid reductions of a given protocol. However, the typical requirement is to find "in some sense" the minimal reduction of a given protocol. Furthermore, there is usually a constraint the resulting reduction should satisfy, so the goal is to find the minimal reduction satisfying the constraint (represented as a predicate C over languages in Def. 3). What the constraint actually is follows from the concrete type of the reduction, e.g. there is a set of important traces that should be preserved in the reduction (the actual constraint predicate for reduction with respect to composition is to be discussed later in Sect. 3). The minimal reduction could be straightforwardly defined as follows.

Definition 3. Let b be a behavior protocol over the alphabet Σ and C a predicate over 2^{Σ^*} (the constraint). A behavior protocol b_{red} is a *minimal reduction* of b satisfying C, if $b_{red} \leq_R b$, $C(L(b_{red}))$ holds, and there is no behavior protocol c such that $c \leq_R b_{red}$, $C(L(c))$ holds, and $L(c) \subset L(b_{red})$.

Even though such a definition seems natural, there are several issues to address: First, the minimal reduction is generally not unique, i.e. more minimal reductions can exist (even infinitely many, since, e.g. $L(a) = L(a+a+...)$). Second, the actual syntactical form of the protocols is not considered—the semantics of reduction is based on the languages generated by the protocols only. Third, if one tries to address the first two issues by requiring the minimal reduction to be the shortest one, then finding such a minimal reduction is a PSPACE complete problem. This follows from the close relation between regular expressions and behavior protocols and the well known fact that minimizing a regular expression is a PSPACE complete problem [9], [12], and [14] (a full-fledged justification is out of scope of the paper).

These observations trigger the need to develop a technique for finding reductions that would: i) assure uniqueness of the result, ii) take the actual syntactical form of the protocols into consideration, iii) be of a "reasonable" computational complexity, and iv) adhere to the reduction preorder as defined in Sect. 2.1. Such a technique— *protocol slicing*—is proposed in Sect. 3. It is based on the *slice* concept:

Definition 4. Let a and b be behavior protocols. We say a is *slice* of b, if a is reduction of b ($a \leq_R b$) and the syntax tree of a is derived by pruning the syntax tree of b.

In other words, the protocol reduction concept is based on the languages generated by the protocols, whereas protocol slicing brings into account also the syntactical form of the protocols by pruning the syntactical tree of the protocol to be reduced. In consequence, given a protocol b and a constraint C, there can be no minimal reduction of b being also a slice of b. For instance, consider the protocol ?a* and the constraint that the method a will be called sequentially three times (more formally, the predicate C is defined as $C(L) \equiv (<?a; ?a; ?a> \in L)$, where L is a language), then the protocol ?a* can be minimally reduced to ?a; ?a; ?a. On the other hand, there are only two slices of the protocol: NULL and ?a*, i.e. it is either sliced to empty protocol (which does not satisfy the constraint of three ?a), or remains unmodified. However, in general, slicing is practically more important than "optimal, language-based" reduction, since the former inherently means simplification of a protocol, while the latter can result in a blow-up of the protocol. For example, consider again the DHCPServer frame protocol in Fig. 2 and assume that the repetition on the lines

4–15 is to be repeated 3 times. The corresponding minimal reduction takes the form depicted in Fig. 4. Obviously, this reduction result becomes hard to read.

Definition 5. Let *a* be a behavior protocol over the alphabet Σ and *C* a predicate over 2^{Σ^*} (the constraint). A behavior protocol *b* is a *minimal slice* of *a* satisfying *C*, if *b* is a slice of *a*, $C(L(b))$ holds, and there is no behavior protocol *c* such that *c* is a slice of *b*, $C(L(c))$ holds, and $c \neq b$.

```
(
  !IDhcpCallback.IpAddressInvalidated*
  |
  (
    (
      ?IManagement.UsePermanentIpDb↑ ;
      (
        !IIpMacPermDb.GetIpAddress*
        |
        (
          !IManagement.UsePermanentIpDb↓ ;
          ?IManagement.StopUsingPermanentIpDb↑
        )
      ) ;
      !IManagement.StopUsingPermanentIpDb↓
    ) ; (
      A repeated here
    ) ; (
      A repeated here
    )
  )
)
```

A

Fig. 4. A minimal reduction of the DHCPServer frame protocol

3   Slicing with Respect to Composition

This section presents a concrete protocol slicing technique—slicing with respect to composition. This technique is the proposed solution addressing the goal articulated in Sect. 1.2, i.e. to develop a method to reduce behavior protocols with respect to their particular composition (reflecting a desired component architecture/assembly) in order to omit the parts of the behavioral specification superfluous with respect to the composition. The technique is based on the formal basis provided in Sect. 2, and the general slicing strategy described in [20], which aims at extending the program slicing paradigm to general slicing of an expression.

Again, the goal is to determine the unused behavior in a composition of given components and eliminate it from the behavior specification. Assuming the behavior of components is specified via their frame protocols $FP_1, FP_2, \dots, FP_n$ and the language of the composition of the components is thus $LC = L(FP_1 \nabla FP_2 \nabla \dots \nabla FP_n)$, it is desirable to find minimal reductions FP^{mr}_1, FP^{mr}_2, ... , FP^{mr}_n of the protocols FP_1, FP_2, ... , FP_n such that $L(FP^{mr}_1 \nabla FP^{mr}_2 \nabla ... \nabla FP^{mr}_n) = LC$. In other words, the composition of the reduced protocols should specify precisely the same behavior as the composition of the original protocols and thus only the unused parts are removed. In terms of Def. 3, the predicate is chosen for each protocol FP_i separately as $C_i(L(FP^{mr}_i)) \equiv (L(FP_1 \nabla ... \nabla FP^{mr}_i \nabla ... \nabla FP_n) = LC)$, which merely formally states the requirement above. Moreover, it would be an advantage to echo this reduction in these frame protocols by their syntactical simplification—to slice them. However minimal reduction cannot be reflected accurately by slicing in general (Sect. 2.2); fortunately, as a compromise, minimal slicing of these frame protocols is achievable—see below. Thus instead of by a minimal reduction FP^{mr}_i, each FP_i is to be replaced by a minimal slice FP^{ms}_i of it, again asking similarly $C_i(L(FP^{ms}_i)) \equiv (L(FP_1 \nabla ... \nabla FP^{ms}_i \nabla ... \nabla FP_n) = LC)$ to hold.

The general expression slicing strategy [20] prescribes slicing to be done in three phases: *parsing* – creation of syntax tree of an expression, *marking* – marking syntax tree nodes that are important with respect to the given slicing criterion, and *outputting* – creating slice of the original expression based on the marks on the syntax tree nodes.

Clearly, the actual logic of a specific slicing technique lies in the design of the phases, namely the second one that determines how the slicing criterion is applied. The first and third phases are highly specific to the nature of the expression being sliced, but they do not influence the actual application of the slicing criterion.

The phases of the proposed slicing with respect to composition are as follows (Fig. 5). First, parsing of the protocols is done using the JavaCC [11] generated parser. The goal of the second phase is to mark the nodes of the syntax trees, which represent the behavior (sub)protocol relevant in the given composition. Basically, this is achieved by traversing the reachable states of the composition state space; all the syntax tree nodes that were used to generate reachable states are marked. This assures that the language of the resulting slice satisfies the constraint C_i articulated above. In the third phase, the slice is acquired by pruning the syntax trees of individual protocols based on the marks on their nodes (the unmarked nodes are removed as well as the operators that are no longer relevant—like a "+" with one operand removed).

By removing all the unmarked nodes, the technique clearly creates as small slices as possible, assuming that the protocols are not redundant, i.e. they do not specify redundantly (as e.g. protocol a? + a? does). This assumption does not cause any harm—real-life behavior protocols are usually not redundant, since redundancy does not introduce any new information into the behavioral specification.

For illustration, slicing of the behavior protocols ?a{!x}* | ?b* and !a{?x + ?y}* with respect to their composition via the consent operator ∇ is depicted in Fig. 5. In the 1st phase, parse trees of these behavior protocols are constructed. Then, in the 2nd phase, the behaviors specified by these protocols are composed via ∇. All the reachable states of the composition state space are sought on-the-fly and all the nodes of the parse trees that were used to generate the reachable states of the composition are marked. Finally, in the 3rd phase, the parse trees are pruned to contain only the marked nodes which make sense (note deletion of the | and + operators, when losing the second operand). The resulting sliced protocols are: ?a{!x}* and !a{?x}*, which are minimal slices (and even minimal reductions, in this special case).

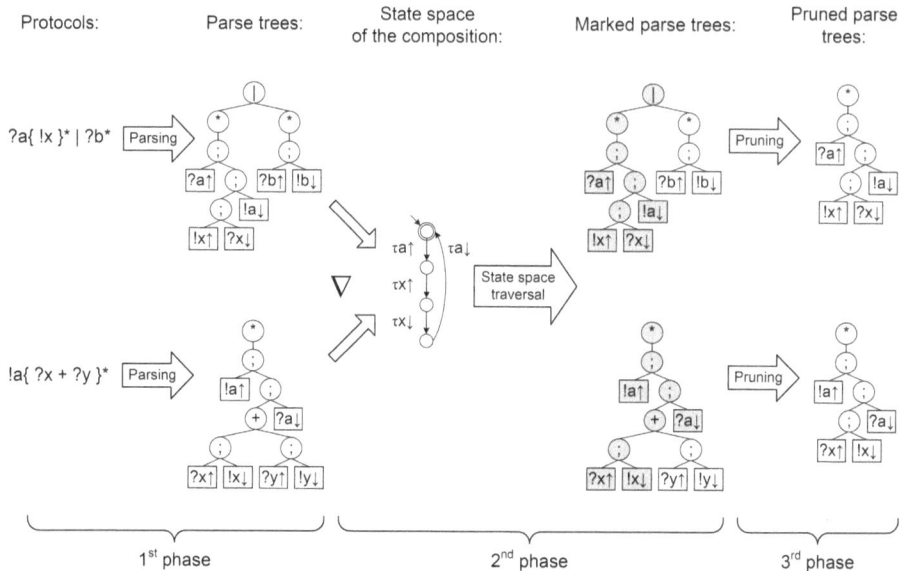

Fig. 5. Three phases of slicing with respect to composition

4   Tools and Case Study

The proposed technique was implemented as a stand alone application BPSlicer, being an extension of the dChecker behavior protocol checker written in Java 1.5, both available at [8].

BPSlicer was applied to the case study mentioned in Sect. 1 (Fig. 1), which was modified (reused) to provide internet access in a public garden, where credit card payment was considered as the only option. The frame protocol representing the environment was manually modified accordingly. Then the frame protocols of the components were sliced with respect to composition by BPSlicer. As expected, the frame protocols of Token, Firewall, CardCenter, and AccountDatabase remained unchanged, since they do not feature any airport specific functionality. On the other hand, the frame protocols of FlyTicketDatabase and Frequent-FlyerDatabase were reduced to a NULL protocol, which means that these components were not used in the new environment and could be safely removed from the architecture. The frame protocols of Arbitrator and DhcpServer were reduced partially: The airport specific login calls were omitted from the frame protocol of Arbitrator. As to DhcpServer, the unused part describing the permanent MAC to IP address association was sliced off (actually this feature was not used even in the original application; note the unbound IManagement and IIpMacPermDb interfaces in Fig. 1).

Technically speaking, the slicing technique proposed in Sect. 3 is implemented as a part of the consent operator evaluation in dChecker, which also uses parse trees and creates on-the-fly the state space of the parallel composition (BPSlicer adds the marking). As an aside, the state space generated by the behavior composition of the top-level components in Fig. 1 features around 4.5 million states and its error-free communication was verified by the dChecker in 126 seconds (Core Duo T2400 2x1.83 GHz, 1 GB RAM, 600 MB for Sun JVM 1.5.0.08, Linux 2.6.17). For comparison, the garden scenario, featured 421 980 states and took 23 seconds to verify the communication and slice the protocols to the size indicated in Table 1 (without slicing, the verification took 18 seconds).

Table 1. Summary of the case study results. Sliced protocols are printed in bold script

protocols	#states	
	original	reduced
Environment	13	13
Arbitrator	15 625	**8 125**
DhcpServer	33	**3**
Token	245	245
Firewall	81	81
AccountDatabase	729	729
CardCenter	3	3
FlyTicketDatabase	7	**1**
FrequentFlyerDatabase	7	**1**

The reduction of state space is a "pleasant" and inherent consequence of slicing, which makes the state space smaller (in contrast to minimal reduction which in general can make the state space even bigger). Obviously, to which extend the state space size is lowered by a reduction very much depends on what kind of operators are removed. For instance, elimination of an unused parallel behavior reduces the size by removing one of the state space "dimensions", i.e. by removing one element of the Cartesian product of the behaviors composed in parallel. In contrast, removing an alternative reduces the state space naturally by a linear factor only. In the case study, slicing the frame protocol of the Arbitrator component removed two alternatives (two airport specific logins) inside one of five basic parallel behaviors of Arbitrator, reducing the number of states from 15 625 to 8 125.

5 Related Work

There are two main areas of related work. The first one includes research sharing our motivation—applying slicing to formal specification and/or the software architecture in order to facilitate its reuse and make its comprehension easier. In [10], Hassine *et al.* apply generalized slicing to functional requirement specification stated in Use Case Map notation. Their goal is to promote reuse of the requirement specification and aid with software maintenance by developing techniques that would help identify feature dependencies and interactions. Although the motivation is very similar to ours, the levels of abstraction differ.

The works by Stafford and Wolf [21] and Zhao [22] target slicing of software architecture description with similar goals. Stafford and Wolf provide the Aladdin tool for slicing of software architecture specified in Rapide [13]. In his work, Zhao describes a technique for reduction of software architecture in Wright [2]. Both these works aim at removing connectors and/or components from the software architecture based on the behavioral description and a slicing criterion. In contrast, our approach goes one-step further, because we can reduce unused behavior at a finer level of granularity—method calls, not being limited to granularity of components and connectors as in [21] and [22].

The second area pertains related work which is focused on component adaptation. In [18], Reussner presents a concept of *parameterized contract* on component interface. The contract specifies which of the provided interfaces of a component can be safely used if specific required interfaces are bound. This approach, in addition to a separate behavior specification on each interface, needs an explicit specification of the contract between the provided and required interfaces (in a different formalism). On the contrary, a frame protocol describes behavioral specification of a component as a whole (the interplay of calls on the proved and required interfaces), so that all the necessary information for adaptation of the specification is available in the protocol. In a similar vein, the relativity of a component's failure with respect to a particular environment it is used in is further discussed in [1].

Bobeff and Noye [4] use the techniques of program slicing and partial evaluation for component (code) specialization (adaptation). They envision delivery of generic components (*component generators*) that would automatically generate components adapted to the environment they are used in. When compared to our approach, [4] works at the code level, requiring it to be known at the time of adaptation. Our technique works solely on the level of behavioral specification and can be applied even when the actual code is not available, which is typical for COTS components. Similar to [4] is the Koala component framework [15], which statically optimizes the architecture for specific parameters. Our solution is more flexible since it takes into account also the behavior (not only static configuration of components).

Finally, Cheung and Kramer [5, 6] aim at mitigating the state explosion problem in the scope of Compositional Reachability Analysis. They use information about context in which a component (process) is employed in the form of interface processes, either automatically generated or user provided, to reduce the size of the state space to analyze. In contrast, our slicing technique captures the actual behavior used in a concrete component environment (context) by modifying the original behavior specification accordingly.

6 Conclusion

In order to help a software designer with reusing software components and even whole component architectures, a technique for slicing behavior protocols, slicing with respect to composition, was presented. Given a composition of components, the technique can remove the unused behavior from the behavior specification, clarifying thus the actual roles of individual components.

Viability of the proposed technique was demonstrated by the prototype implementation and its use in a non-trivial case study in Sect. 4. Moreover, the formal foundation in Sect. 2 was designed to allow for an easy extensibility, so that it can be used as a basis for other slicing techniques than the one described. For example, slicing with respect to property, omitting the parts of the behavior specification irrelevant to a certain user-specified property, could be considered. We also envision the contribution of our work to the problem of modeling component environment for the purpose of code checking of isolated primitive components [16], as the presented technique of slicing with respect to composition can be used to restrict the model of a component's environment, reducing size of the state space to be explored and making code checking more feasible in this way.

Acknowledgements

The authors would like to thank to Pavel Ježek and Jan Kofroň for sharing the CRE demo application architecture diagram, being a basis for Fig. 1 and to Pavel Parízek for valuable comments and suggestions.

References

1. Adamek, J., Plasil, F.: Component Composition Errors and Update Atomicity: Static Analysis. Journal of Software Maintenance and Evolution: Research and Practice 17(5), 363–377 (2005)
2. Allen, R., Garlan, D.: A Formal Basis for Architectural Connection. ACM Transactions on Software Engineering and Methodology 6(3), 213–249 (1997)
3. Bergstra, J.A., Ponse, A., Smolka, S.A.: Handbook of Process Algebra. Elsevier, Amsterdam (2001)
4. Bobeff, G., Noye, J.: Molding Components using Program Specialization Techniques. Eighth International Workshop on Component-Oriented Programming (2003)
5. Chueng, S.C., Kramer, J.: Compositional Reachability Analysis of Finite-State Distributed Systems with User-Specified Constraints. In: Proceedings of the 3rd ACM SIGSOFT Symposium on Foundations of Software Engineering, pp. 140–150. ACM Press, New York (1995)
6. Cheung, S.C., Kramer, J.: Enhancing Compositional Reachability Analysis with Context Constraints. In: Proceedings of ACM SIGSOFT'93 Symposium on Foundations of Software Engineering, pp. 115–125. ACM Press, New York (1993)
7. The CRE project (Component Reliability Extensions for Fractal Component Model), http://kraken.cs.cas.cz/ft/public/public_index.phtml
8. dChecker & BPSlicer, http://dsrg.mff.cuni.cz/projects/dchecker
9. Gramlich, G., Schnitger, G.: Minimizing NFA's and Regular Expressions. In: Diekert, V., Durand, B. (eds.) STACS 2005. LNCS, vol. 3404, pp. 399–411. Springer, Heidelberg (2005)
10. Hassine, J., Dssouli, R., Rilling, J.: Applying Reduction Techniques to Software Functional Requirement Specifications. In: Amyot, D., Williams, A.W. (eds.) SAM 2004. LNCS, vol. 3319, pp. 138–153. Springer, Heidelberg (2005)
11. JavaCC (Java Compiler Compiler), https://javacc.dev.java.net
12. Jiang, T., Ravikumar, B.: Minimal NFA problems are hard. SIAM Journal on Computing 22(1), 1117–1141 (1993)

13. Luckham, D.C., Kenney, J.J., Augustin, L.M., Vera, J., Bryan, D., Mann, W.: Specification and Analysis of System Architecture Using Rapide. IEEE Transactions on Software Engineering 21(4), 336–355 (1995)
14. Meyer, A.R., Stockmeyer, L.J.: The Equivalence Problem for Regular Expressions with Squaring Requires Exponential Space. In: Proceedings of the 13th Annual Symposium on Switching and Automata Theory, FOCS, pp. 125–129 (1972)
15. van Ommering, R., van der Linden, F., Kramer, J., Magee, J.: The Koala Component Model for Consumer Electronics Software. IEEE Computer 33(3), 78–85 (2000)
16. Parizek, P., Plasil, F.: Modeling Environment for Component Model Checking from Hierarchical Architecture. In: FACS'06. Proceedings of Formal Aspects of Component Software, Prague, Czech Republic. ENTCS (2006)
17. Plasil, F., Visnovsky, S.: Behavior Protocols for Software Components. IEEE Transactions on Software Engineering 28(11), 1056–1076 (2002)
18. Reussner, R.H.: Automatic component protocol adaptation with the CoConut/J tool suite, Tools for program development and analysis, vol. 19(5), pp. 627–639. Elsevier Science Publishers, Amsterdam (2003)
19. Sery, O.: Model Checking and Reduction of Behavior Protocols, Master thesis at Charles University in Prague (2006) available at: http://dsrg.mff.cuni.cz
20. Sloane, A.M., Holdsworth, J.: Beyond Traditional Program Slicing. In: ISSTA '96. Proceedings of the 1996 ACM SIGSOFT International Symposium on Software Testing and Analysis, pp. 180–186. ACM Press, New York (1996)
21. Stafford, J.A., Richardson, D.J., Wolf, A.L.: Architecture-level Dependence Analysis for Software Systems. International Journal of Software Engineering and Knowledge Engineering 11(4), 431–451 (2001)
22. Zhao, J.: A Slicing-Based Approach to Extracting Reusable Software Architectures. In: Proceedings of the Conference on Software Maintenance and Reengineering, pp. 215–223. IEEE Computer Society Press, Los Alamitos (2000)

An Execution-Level Component Composition Model Based on Component Testing Information

Gerardo Padilla, Carlos Montes de Oca, and Cuauhtemoc Lemus

Research Center in Mathematics - CIMAT,
Callejón Jalisco S/N. Mineral de Valenciana
36020, Guanajuato, Mexico
{gpadilla, moca, clemola}@cimat.mx
http://www.cimat.mx/ingsoft/index.html

Abstract. Software components and software architectures have emerged as a promising paradigm to improve the construction of software systems. Some attributes, such as reliability, requires evidences about failures in the system. An approach addressing the software reliability estimation problem is based on considering all execution traces collected during the testing process. An execution trace is a sequence of blocks grouping source code statements. Following this approach, early reliability assessment of component assemblies requires addressing an important issue: a precise composition semantics representing the behavior of the assembled components. This paper describes a composition model for sequential component assemblies which uses as basic units of composition a set of empirical evidences generated during the component testing process. These units are named as Component Test Records.

1 Introduction

Software is becoming a critical element nowadays. The range of applications that require software is increased every day since software provides a flexible and easy way to encapsulate complex behaviors [1]. Examples of such complex applications include appliances, automobiles, aircrafts, and medical equipment.

Software Components and Software Architectures have emerged as a powerful paradigm to build complex and larger systems. Several kinds of attribute analyses are performed by using software architectures including performance analysis [2] and reliability analysis [3].

Similarly to other non-software domains, the early assessment of system attributes, such as performance or reliability, provides information to improve the software development process [4]. The term "early" means that the assessment is performed before the actual construction of the system and it is based on evidences of candidate components which will be used in the system. This kind of assessment allows the evaluation of design alternatives and component selection before the actual construction of the system with benefits in the project schedule and project costs.

H.W. Schmidt et al. (Eds.): CBSE 2007, LNCS 4608, pp. 203–210, 2007.
© Springer-Verlag Berlin Heidelberg 2007

Our interest addresses the early reliability assessment of component-based software. Architectural reliability models consider the structure and the internal parts of the system (i.e., components). Depending on the model approach, the information collected from each component is incorporated into the system reliability estimation in different ways [5], [6], [7], [8]. Our approach follows a different strategy since our model is based on performing a low-level composition of reliability-related information before the reliability assessment.

The reliability-related information is composed of test cases, test results, and execution related information (i.e., execution traces). Execution traces are sequences of blocks of statements defined by a regular control-flow static analysis [9] and instrumented before the component testing process [10] (i.e., this instrumentation process enables the monitoring of such execution traces). The reliability-related information is consolidated into an artifact named as Component Test Record.

This paper describes the composition model for sequential assemblies of components based on their component test records. This paper considers as component any reusable part of software that can be characterized by inputs and outputs (i.e., functions, procedures, object methods, or libraries can be seen as components). Even the importance of component models, this paper does not include them. The composition model presented in this paper might be used to formalize some part of a component model.

The paper is organized as follows. Section 2 provides related works in the areas of composition models. Next, Section 3 describes how the reliability-related information is organized by using the Component Test Record artifact. Section 4 describes the formal composition model for component test records assembled sequentially. Finally, Section 5 provides conclusions, future work and final remarks on this paper.

2   Related Works

The problem of defining composition models and their semantics has been addressed by using different formalisms which depend on the purpose of such semantics and the available information. For example, the process algebra formalism has been used for systems where concurrency is a concern [11]. Petri-Nets have been used as foundations for parallel execution allowing the verification of properties such as liveness and safety [12].

Our approach is based on considering execution-level information. This information is modeled by using abstract interpretation of source code [13]. This interpretation defines a high level model of the source code structure and it models the execution using such abstractions. This approach is also named as symbolic execution [14]. The composition model presented in this paper is based on execution traces and the natural dependency found between any execution trace and its corresponding input and output value.

3   Component Test Records

A Component Test Record is an artifact for consolidating the testing and the execution-related information. A component test record is composed of test data (i.e., a set of test cases), test meta-data (i.e., descriptions about the information stored in the component test record), and test results (i.e., verdict about the test case and execution information).

An example of a component test record is shown in Table 1. This example focuses on a component that computes the square root of integer values. Two sections are show in this table. The first section corresponds to the meta-data information about the component including the domain description and the functionality description. The second section includes all test data, test results, and their corresponding execution trace information.

Table 1. Square Root Computation Component Test Record

Component Functionality	Functionality Signature	Domain Description
Square root computation function for integer values	$Sqroot(input): output$	$input \in [0..65535]$ $output \in (0, 300)$

Testing Data				
Test Case Number	Input Value	Expected Output Value	Execution Trace	Test Result
1	1	1	ABCD	PASS
2	43	6.557438	ABBBBBBBCD	PASS
3	49	7	ABBBBBBBCD	PASS
4	55	7.416198	ABBBBBBBCD	PASS
5	56	7.483315	ABBBBBBBCD	PASS
6	58	7.615773	ABBBBBBBCD	PASS
.	.	.	.	.
.	.	.	.	.
.	.	.	.	.

4   A Composition Model for Component Test Records

Intuitively, the composition mechanism for two component test records is shown in Fig. 1. This figure shows the representation of two component test records (A and B) where the notation i_{Aj} denotes the input value of the *j-th* test case contained in the component test record A. Similarly, the notation o_{Aj} denotes the output value of the *j-th* test case and ε_{Aj} denotes the corresponding execution trace. The symbol $[\Rightarrow]$ denotes the test record composition operator. The resulted composed component is generated by finding "compatible" or similar values between the output value of one test case in the first component test record and the input value in the second test record. This matching condition is denoted with the expression $o_{Aj} \cong i_{Bs}$, meaning that there is an input value i_{Bs} that is compatible or equivalent with the output value o_{Aj}.

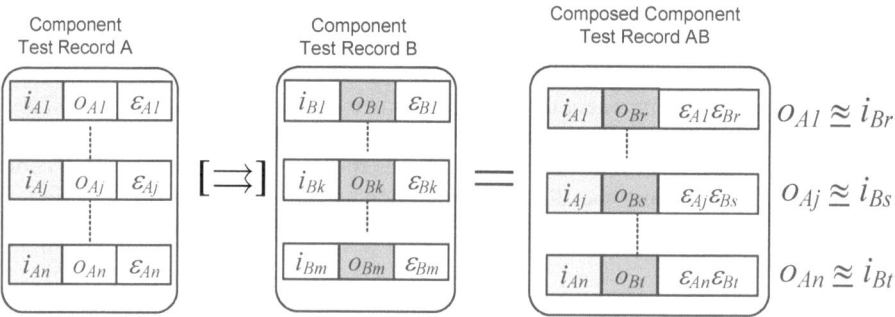

Fig. 1. Composition Mechanism for Two Component Test Records

The basic building blocks defined for this model are:

- **Execution Nodes:** A finite set E of labeled execution nodes.
- **Basic Data Domains:** A set B_D of basic data domains. These domains represents basic data types such as

$$B_D = \{Integer,\ Real,\ Character,\ SEQ(Character)\}[1].$$

The next definitions provide the characterization of the data contained within component test records.

Definition 1. A **Constrained Basic Data Domain**, R_D, is a subset of a basic data type defined in the set of basic data domains. This subset is defined as

$$R_D = \{x \mid istypeof(x) \in B_D \wedge pred(x)=\textbf{TRUE})\}$$

where x represents any element in the subset satisfying two conditions. The first condition states that the data type associated to such element is contained within the set of basic data domains (i.e., using the *istypeof* predicate). The second condition focuses on the specific constraints associated for such subset. These constraints are defined using the *pred* predicate.

Definition 2. A **Complex Data Domain**, C_D, is a tuple of constrained basic data domains such as

$$C_D = <rd_1,\ rd_2,\ rd_3,...rd_n>$$

where rd_1, rd_2, ... rd_n denotes constrained basic data domains. The complex data domain can be seen as the description of an abstract data type without the specification of operations.

Definition 3. An **Input Domain**, $\mathcal{I}$, is a tuple of complex data domain such as

$$\mathcal{I} = <cd_1,\ cd_2,\ cd_3,...cd_r>$$

where cd_1, cd_2, ... cd_r denotes complex data domains. Similarly, an **Output Domain**, $\mathcal{O}$, is a tuple of complex data domain such as

---

[1] The expression, SEQ*(Character),* denotes all possible sequences of characters.

$$O = <cd_1, cd_2, cd_3, ... cd_s>$$

where cd_1, cd_2, ... cd_s denotes complex data domains.

Definition 4. An **Input Domain Instance**, I, is a tuple such as

$$I = <i_1, i_2, i_3, ... i_r>$$

where $i_1 \in_v cd_1$, $i_2 \in_v cd_2$, $i_3 \in_v cd_3$, ... $i_r \in_v cd_r$. This tuple represents a set of actual values (or instances) defined for every constrained basic data domain in every complex domain that it is denoted by the symbol $\in_v$. The definition for the Output Domain Instance, O, follows a similar definition. An **Output Domain Instance**, O, is a tuple such as

$$O = <o_1, o_2, o_3, ... o_s>$$

where $o_1 \in_v cd_1$, $o_2 \in_v cd_2$, $o_3 \in_v cd_3$, ... $o_r \in_v cd_s$.

Definition 5. A **Test Record**, T_P, is a tuple such as

$$T_P = <\mathcal{P}, \mathcal{I}, \mathcal{O}, E>$$

where $\mathcal{I}$ denotes the input domain and $\mathcal{O}$ the output domain. E denotes a set of labeled execution nodes and $\mathcal{P}$ denotes a set of tuples such as

$$\mathcal{P} = <I, O, \mathcal{E}>$$

where I is an input domain instance, O is an output domain instance, and $\mathcal{E}$ represents a sequence of labeled execution nodes where $\mathcal{E} \in \mathrm{SEQ}(E)$.

Next, additional definitions are provided to characterize the matching of information between instances of input and output domains.

Definition 6. Domain Matching Condition. Given an input domain $\mathcal{I}$ and an output domain $\mathcal{O}$. It is said that these domains satisfy a **domain matching condition,** denoted by $\mathcal{I} \Rightarrow \mathcal{O}$, when for every complex data domain, cd_i in $\mathcal{I}$, there is an equivalent complex data domain cd_j in $\mathcal{O}$. Two complex data domains are equivalent when *istypeof*(cd_i) = *istypeof*(cd_j).

Definition 7. Instance Equivalence Condition. Given an input domain instance I and an output domain instance O where their corresponding input and output domain satisfy the domain matching condition. Then, it is said that these instances satisfy an **instance equivalence condition,** denoted by $I \cong O$, when for every instance i_k, and its corresponding match o_j, satisfy the predicate *covered*(i_k, o_j) = TRUE.

The predicate covered (i_k, o_j) is defined as a function that returns true if i_k is mapped to o_j otherwise returns false. The predicate *covered* plays an important part for the composition since it determines which values can be used for the composition. The *covered* predicate is defined on a case basis depending on the characteristics of the specific information.

Definition 8. Execution Trace Composition Operator. Given two execution node sequences, e_1 and e_2, the composition of sequences, denoted by $e_1 \oplus e_2$, is defined as the concatenation of both execution sequences.

We use the notation $T_i(\mathcal{I})$ and $T_i(\mathcal{O})$ to denote the corresponding input and output domain of the T_i test record. The next rule defines the test record composition following an algorithmically approach.

Execution Composition Rule. Given two test records,

$$T_j = <\mathcal{P}_j, \mathcal{I}_j, \mathcal{O}_j, E_j>, \quad T_k = <\mathcal{P}_k, \mathcal{I}_k, \mathcal{O}_k, E_k>,$$

where the output domain of the *jth*-record and the input domain of the *kth*-record satisfy the domain matching condition $T_j(\mathcal{O}) \Rightarrow T_k(\mathcal{I})$. Then, the executable composition of two test records, denoted by $T_j [\Rightarrow] T_k$, is defined as follows:

- A new test record, T_{jk}, is defined. The elements of this test record are instantiated as follows:

$$T_{jk} = <\mathcal{P}_{jk}, \mathcal{I}_j, \mathcal{O}_k, E_{jk}> \text{ where}$$

  $E_{jk} = E_j \cup E_k$, representing the union of both labeled execution node sets.
  $\mathcal{P}_{jk}$, representing the composed tuples $\mathcal{P}_{jk} = <I_c, O_c, \mathcal{E}_c >$ from both test records. This set of tuples is generated following the next algorithm
    - For every $p \in \mathcal{P}_j$, find a tuple $q \in \mathcal{P}_k$ satisfying the instance equivalence condition, such that $p.O \approx q.I$
    - Add a new tuple $<i_c, o_c, e_c >$ in $\mathcal{P}_{jk}$ such that

$$i_c = p.i, \quad o_c = q.o, \quad e_c = p.e \oplus q.e \text{ where } p.i \text{ denotes the input domain instance in } p, q.o \text{ denotes the output domain instance in } q, \text{ and } p.e. \text{ and } q.e \text{ denote the corresponding execution trace.}$$

4.1 Example

We use two component test records to illustrate the concepts defined previously. This example composes two components; one computes the square root of integer values and the second computes the logarithms of real values, denoted as C_{sqr} and C_{log} respectively. The composition $C_{sqr} [\Rightarrow] C_{log}$ is described.

The component test record for defined for the C_{sqr} component is defined as follows

$TP_{sqr} = <\mathcal{P}_{sqr}, \mathcal{I}_{sqr}, \mathcal{O}_{sqr}, E_{sqr}>$, where

$\quad E_{sqr} = \{A, B, C, D\}, \quad \mathcal{I}_{sqr} = <<i_{sqr} \in \text{Integer} >>,$

$\quad \mathcal{O}_{sqr} = <<o_{sqr} \in \text{Real} \wedge [o_{sqr} > 0 \text{ and } o_{sqr} < 300] >>,$ and

$\quad \mathcal{P}_{sqr} = \{<1, 1, \text{ABBBCD}>, <16, 4, \text{ABBBBCD}>, ...\}$

Similarly, the component test record defined for the C_{log} component is defined as follows

$TP_{log} = <\mathcal{P}_{log}, \mathcal{I}_{log}, \mathcal{O}_{log}, E_{log}>$, where

$\quad E_{log} = \{H, I, J, K\},$

$\quad \mathcal{I}_{log} = < < i_{log} \in \text{Real} >>, \quad \mathcal{O}_{log} = < < o_{log} \in \text{Real} >>$, and

$\quad \mathcal{P}_{log} = \{<1,0, \text{HIJK}>, <3.5, 0.544, \text{HIJJJK}>, ...\}$

The composition requires meeting the *domain matching condition*, $\mathcal{I}_{log} \Rightarrow \mathcal{O}_{sqr}$. This condition is satisfied since *istypeof*(Real) = *istypeof*(Real). Next, we need to state the *instance equivalence condition* by defining the predicate *covered*. In this case, the predicate *covered* is defined as follows

$$covered(i, j) = \begin{cases} \text{TRUE} & |i - j| < \xi \\ \text{FALSE} & Otherwise \end{cases}$$

This predicates is simple since it only compares the numeric distance between two elements (i.e., the value selected is the one that is less than a threshold value denoted as ξ). Finally, using this information, the composed test record is described as

$TP_{sqr\text{-}log} = <\mathcal{P}_{sqr\text{-}log}, \mathcal{I}_{sqr\text{-}log}, \mathcal{O}_{sqr\text{-}log}, E_{sqr\text{-}log}>$, where

$\quad E_{sqr\text{-}log} = \{A, B, C, D, H, I, J, K\}, \quad \mathcal{I}_{sqr\text{-}log} = < < i_{sqr\text{-}log} \in \text{Integer} >>$

$\quad \mathcal{O}_{sqr\text{-}log} = < < o_{sqr\text{-}log} \in \text{Real} >>$, and $\mathcal{P}_{sqr\text{-}log} = \{<1,0, \text{ABBBCDHIJK}>, ...\}$

5 Final Remarks and Future Work

This paper has presented a composition model for sequential assemblies of component test records. The core part of the composition is based on selecting matching points meeting an equivalence condition and then, generating a new component test record. The complexity presented in the formal composition model is derived from the incorporation of other composition patterns such as procedure call that is part of our future research.

This composition model assumes the existence of a comprehensive number of test cases. Our research has incorporated predictive models to address the practical issue of having only a limited number of test cases. Experiments have shown promising results after using this composition model in small applications. The reliability assessments are based on an ad-hoc reliability model that is sensible to changes in the internal behavior of the component [15].

References

1. Humphrey, W.S.: Winning with Software: An Executive Strategy. Addison-Wesley, Reading (2002)
2. Sharma, V.S., Trivedi, K.: Architecture Based Analysis of Performance, Reliability and Security of Software Systems. In: WOSP '05. 5th international Workshop on Software and Performance, Palma, Illes Balears, Spain (2005)

3. Rodrigues, G., Rosenblum, D., Uchitel, S.: Using Scenarios to Predict the Reliability of Concurrent Component-Based Software Systems. In: Cerioli, M. (ed.) FASE 2005. LNCS, vol. 3442, Springer, Heidelberg (2005)
4. Bass, L., Clements, P., Kazman, R.: Software Architecture in Practice. Addison-Wesley, Reading (2003)
5. Smidts, C., Sova, D., Mandela, G.K.: An Architectural Model For Software Reliability Quantification. In: 8th International Symposium On Software Reliability Engineering (1997)
6. Goseva-Popstojanova, K., Hamill, M., Perugupalli, R.: Large Empirical Case Study of Architecture-based Software Reliability. In: ISSRE '05. 16th International Symposium on Software Reliability Engineering, Chicago, IL (2005)
7. Yacoub, S.M., Cukic, B., Ammar, H.H.: IEEE Transactions on Reliability 53, 465 (2004)
8. Roshandel, R., Medvidovic, N.: Toward Architecture-Based Reliability Estimation. In: WADS 2004. Twin Workshops on Architecting Dependable Systems, Edinburgh, UK (2004)
9. Allen, F.E.: Control Flow Analysis. In: Proceedings of a Symposium on Compiler optimization, Urbana-Champaign, Illinois (1970)
10. Tikir, M.M., Hollingsworth, J.K.: Efficient Instrumentation For Code Coverage Testing. In: Proceedings of the 2002 ACM SIGSOFT international symposium on Software testing and analysis, Roma, Italy (2002)
11. Wallnau, K., Ivers, J., Nishant, S.: A Basis for Composition Language CL. Software Egineering Institute, Pittsburgh, PA (2002)
12. Anisimov, N.A., Golenkov, E.A., Kharitonov, D.I.: Compositional Petri Net Approach to the Development of Concurrent and Distributed Systems. Program. Comput. Softw. 27, 309 (2001)
13. Debray, S.: Abstract Interpretation And Low-Level Code Optimization. In: Proceedings of the 1995 ACM SIGPLAN symposium on Partial evaluation and semantics-based program manipulation, La Jolla, California (1995)
14. Coward, P.D.: Software Testing for Critical Systems. IEE Colloquium on Software Testing, 2/1 (1990)
15. Padilla, G.: A Test Profile Analysis Framework for Assessing the Reliability of Software Component Assemblies (2007)

Capturing Web Services Provider Constraints – An Algorithmic Approach

Sudeep Mallick and S.V. Subrahmanya

E-commerce Research Lab, Infosys Technologies Ltd.,
Bangalore (NASDAQ: INFY), India 560100
{sudeepm, subrahmanyasv}@infosys.com

Abstract. In the SOA paradigm service composition enables creation of business processes and workflows by assembling together simple or composite services in a particular sequence. In such a distributed architecture possibly involving multiple service providers, optimal selection of service implementations from an existing pool of services, based on QoS and cost factors assumes critical practical relevance. In this paper, we analyze various complex service provider configurations, where multiple business functionalities (comprising a business process) are available as simple or composite services from multiple service providers (some possibly working in coalitions) at varying QoS and cost attribute values. We study the service composition constraints resulting in such a context and propose an algorithm to formally capture these special constraints and represent these into simple weighted multi-stage graphs suitable for subsequent application of various optimization techniques cited in the literature.

Keywords: Oriented Computing, Web services, Quality of Service, Optimization, Graph Theory.

1 Introduction

In the Service Oriented Architecture (SOA) paradigm a service has been defined as a loosely coupled unit of application logic that provides either some business functionality or information to other applications and service consumers through well defined and standardized interfaces [1]. Modularity and independence enabled by SOA brings about tremendous flexibility, reusability and interoperability of legacy and freshy developed application logic. Garnter predicts SOA will be used in more than 50% of new, mission critical applications designed in 2007 and more than 80% by 2010 with 0.7 probability [3]. While internal service implementations are rapidly proliferating the modern day enterprise, publicly available commercial services are also emerging at a fast pace from portals such as www.amazon.com, www.google.com, ww.strikeiron.com, etc. [2][4][5]. Software as a Service (SaaS) products vendors such as salesforce.com, SAP, etc. are basing their new versions on service orientation model.

The distributed nature of the SOA and likely existence of multiple service providers pose challenges with respect to service cost and quality optimization

H.W. Schmidt et al. (Eds.): CBSE 2007, LNCS 4608, pp. 211–226, 2007.

peculiar to this emerging architecture paradigm [6]. Multiple service implementation options – simple or composite - could be available from one or more service providers at varying cost and quality factors. This could lead to quite complex service provider and service implementation configurations and dependencies. Optimal selection of service implementations (concrete services) becomes a challenge in such a scenario in order to accomplish a complete business process at minimum cost and best possible quality of service. In this paper we consider various service provider configurations that could occur in real life scenario and develop an algorithm to formally capture the new constraints resulting out of these special configurations. The output of this algorithm is a formal and structured representation of the services and their dependencies. The structured output could then be used to perform optimal service selection from among the service implementation options available to complete the particular business process under consideration.

In section 2 we briefly discuss the SOA paradigm to enable the reader appreciate the problem under consideration. In section 3 we discuss the formal models used to describe the web services composition problem. In section 4 we identify the special scenarios of practical business concern describing different service provider configurations. In section 5 we propose an algorithm, for formalizing these special business scenarios or constraints. In section 6, we discuss the algorithm implementation developed in Java™ and the architecture of a tool embodying the algorithm implementation. We also discuss the algorithm implementation test results.

2   SOA, Services and Web Services

Services could be categorized as "simple" services made up of a single, unified piece of standalone business logic that could be used independent of others and "composite" ones which embody more complex logic and multiple business steps and are made by composing two or more simple services or other composite services. Services chained together into appropriate sequence could enable business processes or workflows where each service node would represent one business activity step. SOA implementation platforms such as Web services have standards which enable both static composition of services and dynamic composition of services. The exposure of the description of service interface in terms of machine readable standards based description language such as WSDL enables run-time search, selection, binding and composition of services from a pool of available services [6].

A service is described not only by its interface (which describes the business functionality it caters to and also the data input and output structure and semantics) but also by its cost (or price) and Quality of Service (QoS) attributes such as reliability, availability, etc. [7]. When multiple service implementations are available catering to the same business functionality (which could likely happen both in the intra-organization scenario or B2B and B2C scenarios), services are chosen based on these attribute values.

Optimal service selection and composition has been the area of active research, where semantics based techniques have been combined with quantitative optimization techniques to enable optimal service selection and composition. In [6][8][9][10] QoS models for Web services have been developed and various optimization techniques applied for QoS and cost based selection and composition of services from multiple service providers to enable business processes and workflows.

3   Formal Definition of (Web) Services

Formal description of a Web service and service composition for the purpose of optimal service selection from a pool of available services would need to satisfy the following requirements (Fig. 1):

- it should capture the service metadata which would distinguish between services catering to different business functionalities.
- it should capture the service metadata which would distinguish between services catering to the same business functionality but having other distinguishable attributes such as QoS, cost, provider identification and any other attribute relevant for decision making.
- it should capture the sequential dependencies among web services in a composition meant to represent workflows and business processes

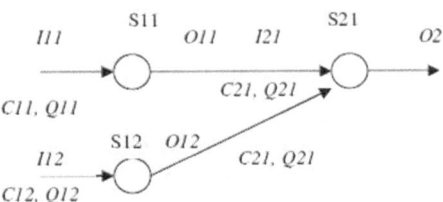

Fig. 1. Services S11 and S21 from provider 1 are sequenced together where O11, the output interface of S11, is compatible or matching with I21, the input interface of S21. Similarly the services S12 and S21 from providers 2 and 1 respectively are compatible. The cost C11, C12, C21 and quality Q11, Q12, Q21 attributes of the respective service implementations are represented accordingly.

An abstract definition of the service (referring to the functionality, interface, dependencies) would actually be implemented by one or more service providers. Hence, a concrete service implementation is an actual instantiation of an abstract service having different QoS, cost attributes and there could be multiple concrete implementations of the same service.

We use the model and representation technique used in [9] to represent a service enabled business process as a weighted multi-stage graph where the weights could represent cost and/or quality depending upon the optimization objective. We also continue to use the concepts of Web services clusters and communities as explained in [9].

Web services cluster represent groups of concrete web services catering to the same functionality. Web services community CM represent group of concrete web services (implementations) catering to the same functionality as well as having the same interfaces (input as well as output). Hence, a Web services cluster could be made up of one ore more Web services communities. Two communities are said to have matching interface if the implementations they contain could be sequenced together in a chain to form a composite service. So service s and s' would be said to have matching interfaces if the input interface of s' is a subset of the output interface of s. Services from the communities having matching interfaces could be chained together to form a complete business process or workflow. The weights on the links between services could represent cost and / or QoS attribute values of the respective services.

Web service s is a tuple $s(p, f, i, o, c, q, m)$

where p = provider; f = functionality; i = input interface; o = output interface; c = cost; q = aggregated quality metric; m = composite number.

Web services cluster CL is a set of concrete services that provide functionality F, i.e.

$$CL(F) = \{s \mid s.f = F\} \tag{1}$$

Web services community CM is a set of concrete services in a cluster that have the same interfaces I, O, i.e.

$$CL(F, I, O) = \{s \mid s E CL(F) \wedge s.i = I \wedge s.o = O\} \tag{2}$$

4 Special Service Provider Configurations

Simple scenarios of concrete services powered business process chains where there are multiple service providers have already been studied in [9]. In this section we discuss more complex service provider configurations and contexts that could occur in real life scenarios and the formalization of the constraints resulting out of such configurations.

Scenario 1

It is possible that the same service is available from the same service provider at different price or QoS attribute value due to reasons such as contractual agreement between the provider and the requestor for a certain number of invocations (bulk procurement) as in the case of commercial services or bulk operations in an intra-organization scenario. This would lead to cost-QoS slabs (or buckets). For example, a scenario is depicted in Table 1.

Table 1. Scenario 1

Service	Provider	Cost of operation (or price)	QoS attribute (reliability)
1 (S11)	1	$1	0.75
1 (S11')	1	$1.1	0.80
1 (S11'')	1	$1.2	0.90
2 (S21)	1	50 cents	0.75
2 (S21')	1	$1	0.90

Scenario 2

It is possible that the same service could be available at a different cost and / or QoS attribute value from the same service provider when bundled (composed) with other interface matching services from the same provider. In other words, the composite service could have a different cost, QoS attribute value than a simple aggregation [references for QoS aggregation techniques] of the values for each participating service in the composite. For example, the following could be a scenario.

As we can seen from Table 2 the cost of the composite service is not $2 and the response time is not 90 + 80 = 170 ms. This is a likely scenario as the response time of co-located service implementations could improve due to lower latency (and possibly even the reliability) and the cost could reduce due to lower operational cost of co-located services (possibly operating on the same physical server). Hence, it appears from this analysis, it is possible that better terms could be available for bundles of services (or composites) than for the individual services participating in the composite.

Table 2. Scenario 2

Service	Provider	Cost of operation (or price)	QoS attribute (response time)
1 (S11)	1	$1	90 ms
2 (S21)	1	$1	80 ms
1-2 (composite – S11C, S21C)	1	$1.75	160 ms

Scenario 3

In this scenario two or more service providers could enter into contractual agreements for preferential deals when operating as a group. The composite services made up of participating service implementations from providers within the group would result into better cost, QoS attribute values than the case, where each of the participating individual service (that made the composite) is made available individually for use as simple service or for composition with other services (available from service providers outside their own group). This scenario can occur for commercial web services where different service providers enter into commercial agreements. The same situation can manifest itself for the case of internal services where services hosted by particular geographical unit or region of the enterprise could have better terms of operation with other services hosted by the same unit or region. In the case of B2B or extended enterprises there could be different terms of operation mutually agreed upon with different business partners, for different mutually useful services. Hence, it may be a requirement to operate the same service at different cost and QoS levels depending upon the nature of the business partner. The scenario has been depicted in Table 3.

Table 3. Scenario 3

Service	Provider	Cost of operation (or price)	QoS attribute (response time)
1 (S11)	1	$1	90 ms
2 (S21)	1	$1	80 ms
3 (S32)	2	$1.5	70 ms
4 (S42)	2	$1.25	85 ms
5 (S52)	2	$1	70ms
1-2-3-4-5 (composite – S11C', S21C', S32C', S42C', S52C')	1,2	$5.40	370 ms
1-2 (composite – S11C, S21C)	1	$1.75	160 ms
3-4 (composite – S32C, S42C)	2	$2.70	150 ms

In Table 3, it is obvious that the composite services created out of services taken from providers 1 and 2 together, is better in terms than the case when they are procured separately – services 1,2,3,4 and 5 taken together turns out to be a better deal than individual services procured separately or even the smaller composite services (1-2, 3-4 along with service 5).

In all the above scenarios it is clear that composite services created from bundles of services from one or more service provider might have different cost and / or QoS attribute values compared to those of the individual participating services due to both business and technical reasons.

5 Specification of the Service Provider Constraints – Algorithmic Approach

In order to optimally select simple and composite services under the above practical architectural scenarios, the following steps are required:

- capture the service provider configurations, coalitions and service composites in a structured manner based on the formal definition of services as explained in Section 3.
- use this formal representation (possibly a graph or matrix) as input to a process of optimal services selection as in [8][9].

The proposed algorithm takes as input basic service details provided by service providers giving details such as in Tables 1, 2 and 3.

Stage 1
From tables such as 1, 2 and 3 provided by the service providers create an equivalent formal representation of the service following these rules:

1. Define the service as a tuple $s(p, f, i, o, c, q, m)$ and create a service description table (SD) representing data related to provider, functionality, input interface, output interface, cost, quality, composite identification.

2. For simple services from the same provider: provided at variable cost-quality combinations create as many service rows in *SD* for each combination with $m = null$ setting appropriate values for p, f, i, o, c, q.

3. For composite services from the same or different provider: provided at variable cost-quality combinations create one row in *SD* for each participating service for each different composite. Give each service participating in a composite the same composite number $m = M$ to uniquely distinguish the row (from the other rows representing the same service but existing as part of other composites). Set appropriate values for p, f, i, o, c, q for each service thus formed.

Stage 2

Once we have the exhaustive listing for services, we proceed with the creation of clusters, communities.

1. Create a service cluster table *CLT(CL, f, g)* representing each cluster, functionality, stage number in the entire business process.

2. Horizontally partition *SD* into service clusters where the value of column *f* remains the same in each partition. Denote each cluster table as CL_i for stage *i* of the business process embodying functionality f_i, where $i = 1$ *to* k (there are k stages in the business process).

3. Make entries into the *CLT.*

4. For each CL_i in *CLT*
   a. horizontally partition the corresponding table into further tables such that they have same values for *i* and *o* columns where $m = null$. Each resulting table is a community denoted by CM_{ij} where $j = 1$ *to* a (assuming there are *a* communities for i^{th} cluster with $m = null$).
      i. Add the CL_i to CM_{ij} mapping in a mapping table *CL-CM (CL, CM)*.
   b. For the remaining rows in CL_i having $m != null$ (m not equal to null)
      i. horizontally partition each row into a separate table each. Each resulting table becomes a community by itself denoted by CM_{ij} where $j = a+1$ *to* b (assuming a total number of communities $a+b$ in the cluster).
      ii. Add the CL_i to CM_{ij} mapping to *CL-CM.*
      iii. Add each such table to a community chain data structure *CC (m, CM, r)* containing the community number *CM*, and *m* and *r* values. If there exists no row with the same value of *m*, mark this row by setting $r = 1$. If there exists another row with the same value of *m*, mark this by setting $r =$(largest value of *r* for rows having the same value of *m*) $+1$.

Stage 3

Once we have the exhaustive listing of clusters and communities, we proceed with the creation of interface matching between communities.

1. For each CL_i in *CLT*
   a. Find the successive CL_{i+1}
   b. For each CM_{ij} of CL_i (from *CL-CM* table)

      a.   If CM_{ij} does not belong to CC or CM_{ij} belongs to CC but is the last position community for a particular value of m then

         i.   For each CM_{ij}'of CL_{i+1} (from CL-CM table)

            1.   If CM_{ij}' does not belong to CC or CM_{ij}' belongs to CC but is the first position community for a particular value of m then

               a.   establish the existence of interface matching between these.

               b.   If matching exists

                   i.   store the community matching in the matching table MT.

2. Consider CC. For each value of m

    a.   For value of $i=2$ to largest value of r for this value of m

       i.   establish the match between community CM_{ij} in CC having rank i-1 and community CM_{ij}' having rank i and add the match to MT

Having established all the service, clusters, communities and interface matching between communities, taking into account all constraints arising out of composite services, we are ready to apply an algorithm such as the one given in [9] to generate the weighted graphical representation taking the tables CLT, CL-CM, CM and MT as input. The generated graph could be subsequently used for optimal service selection.

The usefulness of this algorithm lies in the following aspects:

• it is generic enough to support both simple and composite service spanning one of more stages and one or more service providers.
• composite services are treated as a complete unit during interface matching – the intermediate participating services are not matched with services outside the composite. This is very important as the cost and quality attribute values quoted for the service are possible only during participation in the composite.
• interface matching between pairs of services – simple or composite- is transparently taken care of.
• although the algorithm works on breaking down a composite service into logically simple service unit representing each stage of the business process for computation purpose, the service provider need only specify the input and output interfaces of the entire composite service.

6   Implementation of the Algorithm and the Tool

The algorithm implementation in the form of a tool was developed in Java™, an object oriented language. The data structure used was primarily objects (not table as referred to in the Algorithm section) for convenience. The tool has the following parts – preprocessing covering Stage 1 of the algorithm and core processing covering Stages 2 and 3 of the algorithm, besides the input screen and result formatter (Fig. 2).

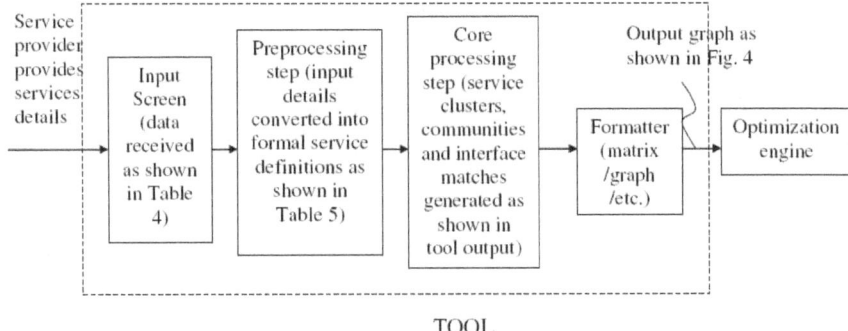

TOOL

Fig. 2. Architecture of the tool implementing the proposed algorithm

The optimization of the service selection falls outside the purview of this work and hence shown outside the scope of the implemented tool.

Preprocessing (Stage 1)

The service provider provides the following input to the tool:

- service interface doc location or document (typically a WSDL file)
- business functionality stage in a publicized business process for which the service is provided (in case of a composite service spanning multiple stages the intermediate service interfaces are not relevant and need not be provided, unless the composite is made of other services which have already been exposed)
- in case of composite service the covered stage numbers, provider details for the particular stage (self or others) and the service numbers of the other participating services and composite identification number (if already generated in an earlier case and is known)
- QoS information for the service
- Cost information for the service

The tool accepts the above basic inputs from the service providers (through a GUI input screen). It then generates the following for each service entry:

- service identification number – and dummy service identification numbers for non-exposed notional services in a composite service (or better called larger grained service catering to multiple business process stages)
- provider identification number
- interface doc identification number linking it to the WSDL location
- input interface and output interface identification numbers and their descriptions
- in case the same service implementation from the same service provider participates in multiple composites, a unique service identification number is generated and all the basic information is replicated. Also, unique service identification numbers would be generated for each case, if the same service

implementation from the same service provider is provided at different combinations of cost and QoS attribute values.

- dummy interface identification numbers for the intermediate input and output interface definitions for the notional non-exposed intermediate services in a composite
- composite identification number for services in a composite (from same or different service providers) – linked to the service identification of the participating services in a composite

The preprocessing tool has some running serial number generators for:

- service identification number (it will implement a technique to generate different numbers for the same service implementation from the same provider, when the service participates in composites or in different cost, QoS combinations). Here we use a simple technique of multiplying the original (a 2-digit number) service identification with 100 and incrementing by 1 after that.
- provider identification number
- composite identification number – each time first among the participating services arrives for entry
- interface doc identification number
- interface identification number – also capable of generating dummy interface identification numbers

After the preprocessing step the each service (simple ones as well as the participating services in a composite) is described by the following items (please refer to service tuple definition in section 3). This forms the output of the preprocessing stage and it is now ready as input for the core processing stage:

- service identification number
- stage number
- interface doc identification number
- input interface identification number
- input interface description
- output interface identification number
- output interface description
- cost value
- quality value
- composite identification number (zero in case of a simple service)

Core Processing (Stage 2 and 3)

After deriving the service in the desired implementation format the Stages 2 and 3 core processing is done. The following Classes definitions were used:

- Cluster (int cluster Id, Vector communities, Vector services) – holds the global collection of services and communities. Corresponds to cluster-community mapping table CL-CM.

- Community (double inputInterfaceId, Vector services) – holds services having the same input and output service interfaces; identified uniquely by the input interface id of the contained services. Corresponds to the community-service mapping table CM.
- Service (int serviceId, Provider provider, Stage stage, int cost, int qos, int compositeId).
- ServiceInterface(double id, String contents, char type) – input / output interface.
- Stage (int stageId, ServiceInterface input, ServiceInterface output).
- Provider (providerId, HashMap counter) – contains running counters dedicated to each stage for which the provider could provide multiple service implementations in different configurations (cost, quality and composites).
- CompositeCommunity(HashMap communities, int compositeId, int rank) – holds the communities forming a composite and running counter to rank the participating communities / services in proper sequence. Corresponds to the rows in composite community chain table CC.
- CommunityMatch(Community firstCommunity, Vector matchingCommunities) – holds the pairs of matching communities for each community. A community in a particular stage could have matching interface with one of more communities in the next stage. Corresponds to a row in MT.

The main program uses the above classes and has the following global data structures in Java™:

- Vector serviceList
- Vector clusters (corresponds to table CLT)
- HashMap compositeCommunityChain (corresponds to table CC, indexed on compositeId)
- HashMap providers (indexed on providerId)
- HashMap communityMatches (corresponds to table MT, indexed on the primary community)

The main program has the following methods operating on the above data structures and classes to :

- createService (it accepts inputs from the preprocessing steps and populates the serviceList global data structure)
- creatClusters (it creates clusters for the different stages and populates clusters global data structure)
- populateClusters (it populates each Cluster with the relevant services)
- createCommunities (it creates Communities for each Cluster by operating on service interface definitions as described in Section 5, and populates the Cluster with the Communities)
- createNewCompositeCommunityAndAddService (in case the service has non-zero composite Id a separate community is made for it, in which it will reside (refer to step 4b of stage 2 of the algorithm); this community holding a single service is added to the corresponding Cluster)

- matchCommunities   (it matches the interface of the neighboring communities which are not part of composites or are part of composites but occur towards the beginning or end of a composite chain – refer to step 1 of Stage 3 of the algorithm)
- matchCompositeCommunities   (it established matching among the neighboring communities participating in a composite – refer to step 2 of Stage 3 of the algorithm)
- printObjects   (it generates the matching among the different services from the different providers, at various stages in the form of matrix or equivalent graphical representation – the entries in the matrix table and weights on the links in the graph are the cost / quality attribute values of the services)

The above implementation is generic enough to be applied to any service provider configurations. The following set of inputs was provided to the tool:

Table 4. Input from service providers to the tool

Sl.No	(From Provider)	Interface doc loc	Stage	Composite	QoS	Cost
1	1	url loc 1	1	Yes with 1	10	15
2	1		2	Yes with 1	10	15
3	1	url loc 2	3	0	15	17
4	2	url loc 3	2	Yes with 2	20	45
5	2		3	Yes with 2	20	45
6	2	url loc 4	3	0	10	25
7	3	url loc 5	1	Yes with 3	30	40
8	3		2	Yes with 3	30	40
9	3		3	Yes with 3	30	40
10	3	url loc 6	3	0	10	15
11	3	url loc 7	1	0	12	15
12	3	url loc 8	2	0	15	15
13	4	url loc 9	1	Yes with 4	35	45
14	4		2	Yes with 4	35	45
15	4		3	Yes with 4	35	45
16	4	url loc 10	3	Yes with 5	22	20
17	5		1	Yes with 5	22	20
18	5		2	Yes with 5	22	20

In Table 4 there are five service providers for a three stage business process. There are five composite services – four of them form composite from the same service provider and one of them spans two service providers. Two of the composites span 2 stages and the other three span all the three stages. For all the participating services (exposed or notional) the cost and quality attribute values remain the same (as it denotes the entire composite).

The output after the preprocessing stage is given in Table 5, showing the generated service identification numbers, interface doc identification numbers, input and output interface identification numbers (some of them are dummies as they are never exposed being in an intermediate position in a composite).

Table 5. Result of pre-processing

Service No.	(From provider)	Interface doc loc	Interface doc Id	Stage	I/P Intf. Id	O/P Intf. Id	Comp. Id	QoS	Cost
111	1	url loc 1	WSDL1121	1	100	200	1	10	15
211	1		WSDL1121	2	200	300	1	10	15
31	1	url loc 2	WSDL31	3	300	450	0	15	17
221	2	url loc 3	WSDL2232	2	175	300	2	20	45
321	2		WSDL2232	3	300	400	2	20	45
32	2	url loc 4	WSDL32	3	300	400	0	10	25
131	3	url loc 5	WSDL132333	1	150	250	3	30	40
231	3		WSDL132333	2	200	300	3	30	40
331	3		WSDL132333	3	350	450	3	30	40
33	3	url loc 6	WSDL33	3	300	400	0	10	15
13	3	url loc 7	WSDL13	1	125	175	0	12	15
23	3	url loc 8	WSDL23	2	200	300	0	15	15
141	4	url loc 9	WSDL142434	1	100	200	4	35	45
241	4		WSDL142434	2	200	300	4	35	45
341	4		WSDL142434	3	300	450	4	35	45
342	4	url loc 10	WSDL152534	3	300	450	5	22	20
151	5		WSDL152534	1	100	200	5	22	20
251	5		WSDL152534	2	200	300	5	22	20

It is important to note that identical input and output interface identification numbers indicate interface compatibility (except for the dummy interfaces identification numbers for interfaces internal to composites; these however pose no problem during the interface matching stage as services part of composites are not allowed to join with services outside the composites unless they form the end points of these composites). These interface identification numbers are generated after parsing of the WSDL files and evaluation of the interface description contents (identical service descriptions lead to same interface identification numbers – possibly leading to formation of communities). The interface identification numbers are generated to facilitate the internal implementation of the algorithm and bear no real significance to the final output.

The tool generates the following final output showing the categorization of the services into clusters and communities as well as the matching among the communities (and hence among the contained services):

Categorization of services into communities and clusters
```
cluster id = 1========================
community id = 100.001-----------------------------
service id = 111.............................
community id = 125.0-----------------------------
service id = 13.............................
community id = 450.001-----------------------------
service id = 131.............................
community id = 400.001-----------------------------
service id = 141.............................
community id = 500.001-----------------------------
service id = 151.............................
cluster id = 2========================
```

```
community id = 200.001-----------------------------
service id = 211..............................
community id = 350.001-----------------------------
service id = 221..............................
community id = 200.0----------------------------
service id = 23..............................
community id = 750.001-----------------------------
service id = 231..............................
community id = 800.001-----------------------------
service id = 241..............................
community id = 1000.001-----------------------------
service id = 251..............................
cluster id = 3=========================
community id = 300.0----------------------------
service id = 31..............................
service id = 32..............................
service id = 33..............................
community id = 600.001-----------------------------
service id = 321..............................
community id = 1050.001-----------------------------
service id = 331..............................
community id = 1200.001-----------------------------
service id = 341..............................
community id = 1200.002-----------------------------
service id = 342..............................
```

The matching among communities (services in these communities):
Format: communityId (serviceId,…) → (matching) → communityId(serviceId,…)

   200.001(211,) → 300.0(31, 32, 33,)
   400.001(141,)→ 800.001(241,)
   350.001(221,)→ 600.001(321,)
   100.001(111,)→ 200.001(211,)
   450.001(131,)→ 750.001(231,)
   200.0(23,)→ 300.0(31, 32, 33,)
   125.0(13,)→ 350.001(221,)
   750.001(231,)→ 1050.001(331,)
   500.001(151,)→ 1000.001(251,)
   1000.001(251,)→ 1200.002(342,)
   800.001(241,)→ 1200.001(341,)

From this list of community matches (and corresponding service matches) it is a straigtforward step to generate a matrix or graphical representation of service matches (and also using with the cost and quality attribute values stored in the respective Service objects). Again, it is important to note that the actual values of the clustereId, communityId and serviceId generated are of no real significance except for the fact that they enable the algorithm implementation as well as identification of the services, communities and clusters. The final list of service matching held in the Cluster and

Community objects are of interest. The result of the above matching is depicted in Fig. 3. Please note that service S23 does not have compatibility with any stage 1 service.

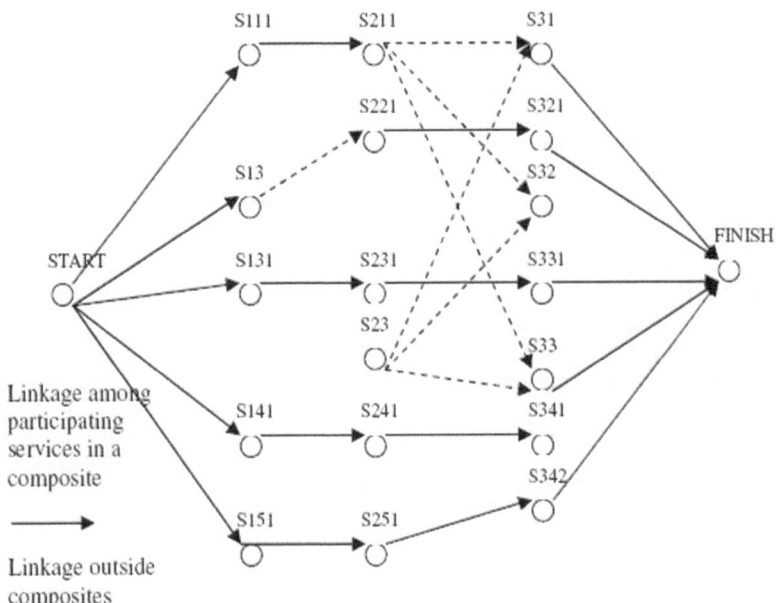

Fig. 3. Business process having three stages and five service providers has been demonstrated by the implementation. The services have been represented by the generated service ids and the matching among the different simple and composite services indicated by the arrows.

7 Conclusion

In this paper we developed an algorithm that takes as an input, constraints resulting out of special service provider configurations that could occur due to business and technical reasons, and generates output in the form of structured data ready for equivalent graph theoretic representation of the multiple service provider optimization problem. The graph theoretic representation thus derived could then be subjected to various optimization techniques as has been shown in other works cited in this paper.

References

1. New to SOA and Web services, http://www-128.ibm.com/developerworks/webservices/newto/#1
2. Lowe, J.W.: Pricing emerging web services, Geospatial solutions (January 2004)
3. Predicts 2007: SOA Advances, Gartner Research, ID No: G00144445 (November 17, 2006)

4. LaMonica, M.: Amazon servers, starting at 10 cents an hour (August 2006) http://news.zdnet.com/2100-9584_22-6109202.html#

5. StrikeIron adds a Dozen New Web Services to its Marketplace (August 2006) http://www.webservices.org/vendors/strikeiron_inc /strikeiron_adds_a_dozen_new_web_services_to_its_marketplace /(go)/Articles

6. Zeng, L., et al.: Quality Driven Web Services Composition, WWW2003, Budapest (May 20-24, 2003)

7. Hung, P.C., Li, H.: Web services Discovery Based on the Trade-off between Quality and Cost of Service: A Token-based Approach, ACM (2001)

8. Gao, A., Yang, D., Tang, T., Zhang, M.: Web Service Composition Using Integer Programming-based Models. In: ICEBE'05. Proceedings of the 2005 IEEE International Conference on e-Business Engineering, IEEE Computer Society Press, Los Alamitos (2005)

9. Gao, Y., Na, J., Zhang, B., Yang, L., Gong, Q.: Optimal Web Services Selection Using Dynamic Programming. In: ISCC'06. Proceedings of the 11th IEEE Symposium on Computers and Communications (2006)

10. Grundy, J., Hosking, J., Li, L., Liu, N.: Performance Engineering of Service Compositions. In: IW-SOSE'06, Shanghai (May 27-28, 2006)

Soya: A Programming Model and Runtime Environment for Component Composition Using SSDL

Patric Fornasier[1], Jim Webber[2], and Ian Gorton[3]

[1] Empirical Software Engineering, National ICT Australia and
School of Computer Science and Engineering, University of New South Wales
patricf@cse.unsw.edu.au
[2] ThoughtWorks
United Kingdom
jim@webber.name
[3] Pacific Northwest National Lab
WA 99352, USA
ian.gorton@pnl.gov

Abstract. The SOAP Service Description Language (SSDL) is a SOAP-centric language for describing Web Service contracts. SSDL focuses on message abstraction as the building block for creating service-oriented applications and provides an extensible range of protocol frameworks that can be used to describe and formally model component composition based on Web Service interactions. Given its novel approach, implementing support for SSDL contracts presents interesting challenges to middleware developers. At one end of the spectrum, programming abstractions that support message-oriented designs need to be created. At the other end, new functionality and semantics must be added to existing SOAP engines. In this paper we explain how component developers can create message-oriented Web Service interfaces with contemporary tool support (specifically the Windows Communication Foundation) using SSDL. We show how SSDL can be used as an alternative and powerful metadata language natively alongside existing tooling without imposing additional burdens on application developers. Moreover, we describe the design and architecture of the Soya middleware which supports SSDL-based development of Web Services on the WCF platform.

1 Introduction

Complex software systems can be constructed by composing many independently developed components using rules from an architectural framework. Service-oriented Architecture (SOA) [12] is the most recent design paradigm which guides software architects during the composition of component-based distributed software systems. In an SOA, independent components are called services. Services use messages to communicate and exchange structured information among each other while descriptions capture the form and patterns of

H.W. Schmidt et al. (Eds.): CBSE 2007, LNCS 4608, pp. 227–241, 2007.

these interactions. Together, services, messages and descriptions form the three main components of a basic SOA [5].

Web Services technology offers a suitable platform for building component-based service-oriented systems. However, simply using Web Services technologies will not automatically lead to a service-oriented system [25]. In particular, WSDL, one of the oldest Web Services specifications, is procedure call-centric and constrains Web Services practitioners from adopting a more message-oriented mindset.

The SOAP Service Description Language (SSDL) [19] is an XML-based language for describing message-oriented Web Services and can, in its crudest form, be a direct replacement for WSDL. SSDL provides an extensible mechanism, known as protocol frameworks, for capturing a service's messaging behavior into interaction protocols. These protocol frameworks are typically derived from formal modeling techniques, which allow model checkers to verify the correctness of a service (component) composition. Most importantly, the message-centric concepts underlying SSDL provide a natural fit with service-oriented design principles and promise to hold solutions for some of the problems which limit WSDL.

This paper introduces a programming model that uses metadata embedded in source code to describe SSDL contracts in a familiar, declarative manner. An implementation of this programming model called Soya is presented and further used to demonstrate how a runtime environment for SSDL-based Web Services can be implemented.

In section 2 we discuss the background and motivation of our research. Section 3 describes the notions and concepts of the SSDL language. We follow with a detailed explanation of Soya in section 4. Finally, we conclude the paper by providing an assessment of our current work and indicating future research directions.

2   Background and Motivation

2.1   Why SSDL?

Web Services have matured into a commoditized platform for building service-oriented systems and are having an enormous impact on interoperable distributed computing [23]. Using Web Services technology for creating distributed applications, however, does not mean that a component-based architecture will magically become service or message-oriented [25]. Specifically, WSDL's focus on operations as the primary abstraction for communication, for example, can encourage developers to use it as a traditional Interface Description Language (IDL) [14] and build systems that are architecturally similar to RPC-based systems. These solutions hence suffer from tight coupling at component and distribution boundaries.

Vendor products often encourage developers to use WSDL to generate service proxies for existing components (e.g. [22,10]) in order to shield the details involved in accessing remote services. While this seems reasonable at first, it eventually leads to brittle systems, because users of the service will not be aware of the inherently fundamental differences between local and remote invocations in terms of latency, memory space, concurrency and partial failure scenarios [31]. This is why calls across a network must be addressed by the programmer in ways fundamentally different to invocations on local components.

In its current (draft) version, the WSDL 2.0 core specification [29] is over a 100 pages long and comments on it have not been favorable, mainly complaining of its unnecessary weight and complexity [7]. Still, WSDL does not provide any support for describing service protocols, apart from the eight simple message exchange patterns that are defined in the WSDL adjuncts specification [30]. This means that given a WSDL contract, it is — except for the most trivial cases — generally not possible to determine if a certain sequence of service invocations will succeed or fail. To describe more complex interactions, additional specifications such as WS-BPEL [13] or WS-Choreography [26] have to be used in addition to WSDL. Unfortunately, this further increases the complexity of the Web Service description [21].

Even though the W3C's *Web Services Architecture* note [25] defines that a Web Service has "an interface described in a *machine-processable* format (specifically WSDL)"[1], it acknowledges that there might be some other semantics apart from the Web Services description (WSD) that are crucial for components to successfully interact with each other. The note further states that the information may not necessarily be "explicit, written or machine processable, but implicit, oral or human oriented"[2]. Clearly, it is desirable to have Web Service descriptions that are expressive enough to capture every aspect of the contract, therefore enabling full automation of the agreement on semantics and the subsequent component interactions.

SSDL offers solutions to some of the problems that WSDL currently exhibits. It presents a more lightweight approach to describing Web Services. By focusing on messages, SSDL encourages the creation of loosely-coupled service-oriented applications. Furthermore, SSDL supports developers working directly with messages as their fundamental abstraction and discourages them from thinking about exposing component interfaces directly as Web Services. Finally, providing mechanisms for capturing a service's messaging behavior can be leveraged in a number of ways by middleware. As a result, it can have positive effects on service development, binding and execution and thus considerably simplify the service lifecycle [3].

2.2   SSDL Tool Support

Unfortunately, almost no data exists that reports on experiences using SSDL as part of Web Services-based SOAs. There is only one set of published results from a project known to have used SSDL to model its services [4]. The lack of rich empirical data makes it hard to assess the capabilities and potential of SSDL as a service description language in a general sense.

---

[1] W3C, Web Services Architecture, 2004, section 1.4.

[2] W3C, Web Services Architecture, 2004, section 1.4.4.

One reason why SSDL has not been used more widely is the lack of tool support that aids developers in creating and consuming SSDL contracts. More importantly, no runtime environment exists for executing SSDL-based Web Services, thus preventing SSDL from being more than a specification on paper. Therefore, we have developed Soya, which is a programming model and runtime environment for creating and executing SSDL-based Web Services. Soya is intended to serve as a research vehicle and its use in future case studies will provide us with the empirical data we need to determine if the message-centric and formally verifiable SSDL approach has significant benefits compared to the incumbent approaches.

The implementation of Soya has presented a number of interesting challenges. At one end of the spectrum, we wanted to create straightforward programming abstractions that foster SSDL's underlying message-oriented practices. At the other end, we wanted to reuse contemporary SOAP-processing middleware and equip it with new functionality and semantics related to SSDL. The solutions we adopted to these issues, as well as the fundamentals of SSDL, are described in the following sections.

3   SSDL Language Features

The SOAP Service Description Language (SSDL) is an XML-based language for describing Web Services. It describes Web Services in a purely message-oriented way, focusing on messages as the building blocks for creating service-oriented applications. Hence fundamentally, SSDL provides the necessary mechanisms for describing the structure of SOAP messages. It further offers an extensible range of protocol frameworks that can be used to combine and relate messages into protocols. These protocols describe the messaging behavior of a Web Service and define how other services can interact with it. Additionally, some protocol frameworks may be formally verified using model checkers to ensure the absence of deadlocks or race conditions.

An SSDL contract can be separated into the following four major sections:

- **Schemas:** Defines the structure of SOAP message elements used by the service, normally using XML Schema [28];
- **Messages:** Declares the SOAP messages that a service supports, including body elements and header elements not inferred by an associated policy document;
- **Protocols:** Defines how messages relate to each other and the valid sequences in which they can be exchanged. Different protocol frameworks can be used, depending on the required level of formal verification and the number of parties involved in a protocol;
- **Endpoints:** Uses WS-Addressing [24] to define endpoints of Web Services that are known to support the given contract.

SSDL assumes SOAP (over arbitrary transport protocols) together with WS-Addressing as the only means of transferring messages between services. Consequently, defining bindings for different transport protocols is unnecessary and messages can be described in a more lightweight way compared to WSDL, which does not explicitly target SOAP. Likewise, adopting SOAP from the outset gives developers greater control over message structures, because it makes it possible to define SOAP header elements as part of the contract. Figure 1 illustrates how a message is defined in an SSDL contract.

```
<ssdl:messages targetNamespace="urn:my:messages" xmlns:s="urn:my:schema">
 <ssdl:message name="MsgA">
  <ssdl:header ref="s:MyHeaderX"
    mustUnderstand="true" />
  <ssdl:header ref="s:MyHeaderY"
    role=".../ultimateReceiver"/>
  <ssdl:body ref="s:MyBody" />
 </ssdl:message>
</ssdl:messages>
```

Fig. 1. A message defined as part of an SSDL contract. The **header** and **body** refer to XML schema elements.

Messages defined in this way can be combined and related into protocols that capture a service's messaging behavior. Making this information available to consumers promotes protocol-based integration [21] rather than interface-centric solutions. Currently, four protocol frameworks — MEP (Message Exchange Pattern) [18], CSP (Communicating Sequential Processes) [17], Rules [8] and SC (Sequencing Constraints) [32] — have been specified, but additional protocol frameworks can be created and plugged into SSDL, if needed. Figure 2 exemplifies how a service's messaging behavior can be captured using the SSDL Rules [8] framework, which constrains incoming and outgoing messages using preconditions. If desired, the same behavior could also be expressed using a different protocol framework, for example if multiparty choreography is required.

```
<ssdl:protocol xmlns:rls="urn:ssdl:rules:v1">
 <rls:rule>
  <ssdl:msgref ref="m:MsgB" direction="out"/>
  <rls:condition>
   <ssdl:msgref ref="m:MsgA" direction="in"/>
   <rls:not>
    <ssdl:msgref ref="m:MsgC" direction="out"/>
   </rls:not>
  </rls:condition>
 </rls:rule>
</ssdl:protocol>
```

Fig. 2. Messaging behavior specified using the SSDL rules protocol framework. The protocol defines that MsgB can only be sent after MsgA has been received and before MsgC has been sent.

4 Soya

Soya [6] is an open-source implementation of the SSDL specification [20]. It provides a programming model and runtime environment for creating and enacting SSDL contracts. Soya supports developers in building message-centric applications and offers mechanisms to define message structures and messaging behavior in a straightforward manner using metadata in order to express Web Service contracts within the host language environment for a component. Soya uses this component metadata to infer SSDL contracts that can then be exposed to other services. Most importantly, Soya enables users to execute SSDL-based Web Services. It ensures that incoming and outgoing service messages adhere to the messaging behavior defined in a deployed SSDL contract and dispatches the incoming messages to the the underlying component implementation.

The current prototype implementation of Soya is built on top of the Windows Communication Foundation (WCF) [11]. WCF is an extensible framework which can, amongst other styles, be used to build message-centric distributed applications.[3] This and the comprehensive set of XML APIs included in the .NET framework [9] were the main reasons why we chose WCF as the underlying communication system for Soya. Figure 3 highlights the relationship between Soya and WCF.

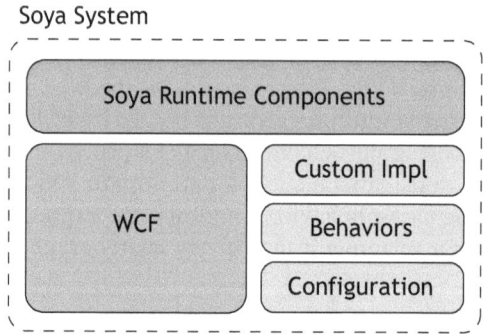

Fig. 3. Soya. Configuration files, injected behaviors and custom classes modify WCF's runtime behavior. The Soya runtime provides the SSDL specific functionality.

4.1 Defining SSDL Contracts Using C# Attributes

C# attributes are a mechanism for declaratively embedding metadata in C# component source code. This metadata adds additional information to the code that can be retrieved, processed and interpreted by other programs. In WCF's programming model, service and message contracts are typically defined in this

---

[3] Using WCF allows us to concentrate on implementing SSDL protocol support and delegate issues like session management, failure recovery, efficient processing of SOAP messages and so on to the underlying framework.

declarative manner [15]. Soya reuses this programming model and provides additional SSDL-specific attributes and functionality. On one side this allows developers to define the structure of messages supported by an SSDL contract. On the other side it describes how these messages relate to each other through the use of different protocol frameworks. This attribute-oriented approach makes it possible to specify contract data with very little code yet provides extensive control over the contract when warranted.

In Soya, we have adopted the attribute-oriented programming model for the following reasons:

- less code and hence less scope for error introduction;
- more easily maintainable due to single source location;
- seamless integration with WCF's programming model and provision of familiar idioms to existing C# programmers.

Defining Messages. Where possible, we reused existing WCF attributes to make the transition from WCF to Soya as smooth as possible. For concepts unique to SSDL, however, we had to introduce additional attributes (e.g. message names, message name-spaces, protocols ...). The following code shows how messages are defined in Soya using C# attributes:

```
[SsdlMessageContract] // Soya attribute
public class MsgA {
    [MessageHeader]      public string MyHeader;
    [MessageBodyMember]  public MyData MyBody;
}

[DataContract]  // WCF attribute
public class MyData {
    [DataMember] public int id;
    [DataMember] public string code;
}
```

Attributes can take additional property parameters that can be used to override default values and give developers more control over the message data. For example, to explicitly specify the qualified name of the SSDL message element in the code above, one would simply define values for the Name and Namespace properties as shown in the following code fragment:

```
[SsdlMessageContract(Name="...", Namespace="...")]
```

From the above examples, Soya infers the following XML Schema code, which is part of the SSDL contract:

```
<xs:element name="MyHeader" type="xs:string"/>
<xs:element name="MyBody" type="s:MyData"/>
<xs:complexType name="MyData">
```

```
<xs:sequence>
  <xs:element  name="id" type="xs:int"/>
  <xs:element  name="code" type="xs:string"/>
</xs:sequence>
</xs:complexType>
```

Additionally, Soya generates the following SSDL message element, which is likewise included in the SSDL contract description:

```
<ssdl:message name="MsgA">
  <ssdl:header ref="s:MyHeader"/>
  <ssdl:body ref="s:MyBody"/>
</ssdl:message>
```

As illustrated in the above examples, Soya reuses attributes defined by WCF wherever possible (e.g. MessageHeader, MessageBodyMember). Instead of generating WSDL, however, it uses the attribute metadata to create SSDL contracts.

Defining Messaging Behavior. Apart from defining messages supported by an SSDL contract, Soya's programming model may also be used to describe how these messages relate to each other. Soya has been designed to accommodate SSDL's extensible model and provides the necessary hooks to plug in new protocol frameworks. Of the four initial SSDL protocol frameworks, the MEP framework [18] is the simplest and least sophisticated. It does not demonstrate SSDL's full strength and has primarily been designed for capturing the Message Exchange Patterns defined by WSDL [30] so it can be used as a simple SOAP-centric language replacement for WSDL. The following lines show how simple MEP protocol interactions can be modeled using Soya's MEP attributes.

```
[Mep(Style=MepStyle.InOnly)]
public void Process(MsgA msg);

[Mep(Style=MepStyle.InOptionalOut, Out=typeof(MsgC),
 Fault=typeof(FaultX))]
public void Process(MsgB msg);
```

The attribute on the first method declaration defines an *in-only* MEP in which MsgA represents the incoming message. The second method declaration defines an *in-optional-out* MEP with MsgB representing the incoming message, MsgC being the outgoing message and FaultX standing for the optional fault message. From this code, Soya can generate the following SSDL protocol information which captures the messaging behavior in the SSDL contract:

```
<ssdl:protocol xmlns:mep="urn:ssdl:mep:v1">
  <mep:in-only>
    <ssdl:msgref ref="m:MsgA" direction="in"/>
  </mep:in-only>
```

```
<mep:in-optional-out>
  <ssdl:msgref ref="m:MsgB" direction="in"/>
  <ssdl:msgref ref="m:MsgC" direction="out"/>
  <ssdl:msgref ref="m:FaultX" direction="out"/>
</mep:in-optional-out>
</ssdl:protocol>
```

These examples show how Soya can use class information and attribute metadata to infer SSDL contracts. The examples also show how little additional code is necessary to create an entire SSDL contract including XML Schema definitions, protocol descriptions and method and fault declarations.

Exposing SSDL Contracts. The most fundamental purpose of a Web Service description is to capture the semantics that describe how two or more services can interact meaningfully, in a machine-processable format. It is thus crucial that this description is exposed, so interested parties can retrieve it and reason about the described service. This reasoning might range from simply checking a Web Service's compatibility to performing protocol-based integration of services [21]. The previous sections have suggested that Soya can infer SSDL from the service classes and attribute metadata. Soya builds an internal service model from this data. Using this model, Soya can generate an SSDL contract represented as XML information set [27]. The infoset can then be serialized into XML and published using, for example, HTTP or WS-Metadata Exchange [2].

4.2   Architecture and System Design

To better understand Soya, we distinguish between service deployment and service execution. First, we describe how a service implementation is turned into an executable instance and exposed to the network. Then, we illustrate what happens inside Soya when other services interact with a deployed service and how the Soya runtime enforces a service's SSDL contract.

Service Deployment. In Soya a service implementation typically consists of code representing the core application logic, metadata attributes describing the service's SSDL contract and configuration files specifying service endpoints, security settings and so on. A developer can deploy a service implementation by opening a `SoyaServiceHost` instance, which is a custom host implementation of WCF's `ServiceHostBase`. The following two lines show how a service (in this case `MyService`) is deployed:

```
host = new SoyaServiceHost(typeof(MyService));
host.Open();
```

Opening a `SoyaServiceHost` triggers the three following major activities, which are also graphically illustrated in Figure 4:

1. Reflect over service classes (i.e. service code and attribute metadata) and build an internal model representing the SSDL service contract from it;

2. Process application configuration files and add further artifacts, such as service endpoints or custom behaviors, to the internal model;
3. Create and configure WCF and Soya runtimes based on internal model.

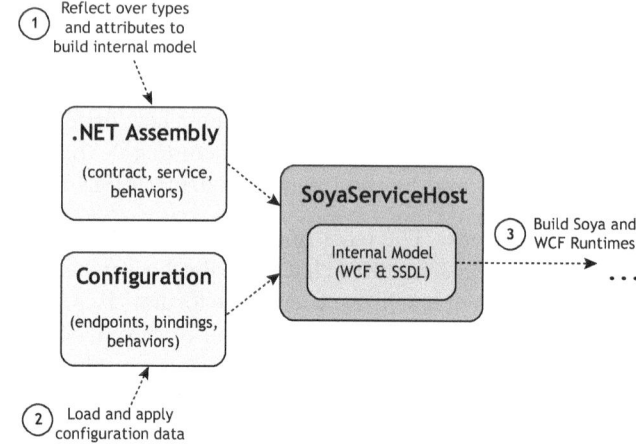

Fig. 4. Deployment of a service. The model is created from service type and attribute information as well as configuration data. Then, it is used to initialize the WCF and Soya runtimes.

Building the internal model constitutes most of the work the `SoyaServiceHost` performs after the `Open()` method is called. The internal model can be seen as an intermediary language between the service implementation and the SSDL contract description. It is used by the runtime as a blueprint for creating new stateful protocol instances and also to generate and expose SSDL metadata.

The `SoyaServiceHost` builds the internal model by reflecting over the service classes and applying configuration settings. It first of all identifies the SSDL protocol framework that has been used to model the service's messaging behavior and then uses protocol specific classes to process the class and attribute metadata. This includes inferring XML schemas, interaction protocols, and message descriptions and adding them to the model. Next, it processes the application's configuration files and adds further artifacts, such as service endpoints or custom behaviors, to the internal model. Finally, both the WCF and the Soya runtimes are created and configured. This includes injecting a message inspector into the WCF runtime that will later be used to intercept inbound and outbound messages. The message inspector, shown in Figure 5, bridges the two runtimes by passing intercepted messages from WCF to the Soya runtime. This terminates the service deployment and enables other services to start interacting with the deployed service through the specified endpoints.

Service Execution. When an incoming message is received from the network, it is first of all pushed through WCF's channel stack. The channel stack consists of different elements that deserialize, decode and decrypt the incoming bits into an untyped `Message` instance. Immediately after the message exits the channel stack, it is intercepted by a custom message inspector and passed to the Soya runtime for further processing.

Once a message is passed to the Soya runtime, the runtime firstly uses an `XsdValidator` to validate the structure of the message's elements. It compares the header and body elements with the SSDL contract that is represented by the service's internal model and tries to locate the message in the current contract. If the message validation or location fails, the message is rejected. Otherwise, the message is further processed by an `IProtocolValidator`. This validator checks if the incoming message is valid in terms of the messaging behavior defined in the service's contract (i.e. the protocol definition).

As opposed to the `XsdValidator`, which is stateless, the `IProtocolValidator` needs to maintain state between interactions, as validation is based on the state of a conversation in which the interacting services are at a given point in time. Internally, this validation is performed with a state machine. It is built from the protocol definition and the incoming and outgoing messages represent the state transitions. If the message causes the state machine to transit to an invalid state, the message is rejected. Otherwise, it is returned to the WCF runtime, where the untyped `Message` instance is mapped into a user-defined message instance. Finally, this user-defined message instance is dispatched to a local method of the service implementation. Figure 5 illustrates this mechanism and the same process (in reverse) applies to outgoing messages.

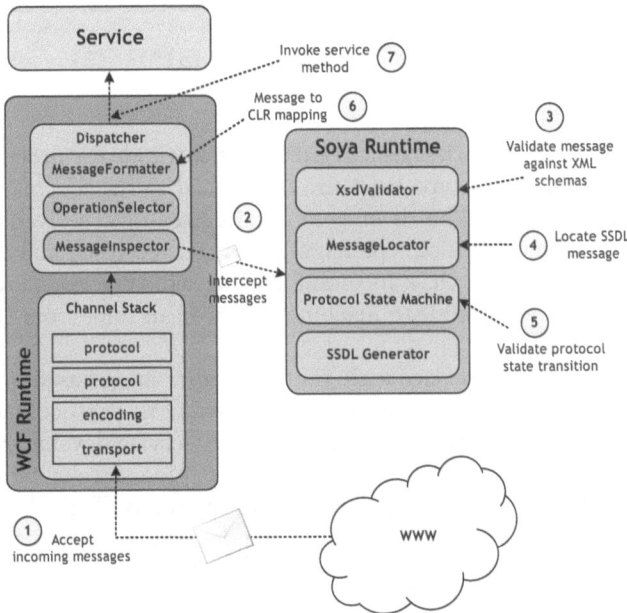

Fig. 5. Soya runtime architecture

4.3   Intelligent Message Dispatching

In SSDL the concept of *operations* or *service invocations* does not exist. Interactions between services are modeled purely as messages that are exchanged among services. Messages represent self-contained units of information and do not convey details of underlying APIs. SSDL expects that applications reason about the sequence of messages and derive appropriate actions from this. This concept has been described as the MEST (MESsage Transfer) architectural style [16].

Just like SOA, SSDL and MEST do not have operation abstractions, Soya does not have them either. Of course, since Soya is built using an object-oriented programming language, a local API method is ultimately invoked. This method, however, is not part of the service contract, but belongs to the service's internal implementation, thus enforces loose coupling. Soya inspects incoming messages and decides to which internal method the message should be dispatched. This decision is exclusively based on the messaging behavior defined in the service's contract and the state of the current conversation. Method names play no role in this decision-making process, meaning that given a different protocol state multiple arrivals of the same message type can result in a different dispatching behavior. This is illustrated in the following C# pseudo-code.

```
[Rule(Condition="!(MsgB == In)")]                    (1)
public void ProcessX(MsgA msg) {}


[Rule(Condition="MsgB == In")]                       (2)
public void ProcessY(MsgA msg) {}


[Rule(Condition="MsgA == In && !(MsgB == In)")] (3)
public void ProcessZ(MsgB msg) {}
```

The above pseudo-code defines three different methods for processing incoming messages. Messages of type `MsgA` are dispatched to the first method as long as no message of type `MsgB` has been received. `MsgB` can be received exactly once (after one or more messages of type `MsgA` have been received) and is dispatched to the third method. After that, incoming messages of type `MsgA` are dispatched to the second method. The state machine that we can infer from this is shown in Figure 6.

Each method contains service logic that does something based on the type of message and the current conversation state. If we had no protocol metadata, the first and second methods would be ambiguous. A service developer would need to write application code to determine the conversation state of the application, correlate messages and finally dispatch them to the correct logic. We understand that this imposes a significant burden on the developer. Therefore, Soya takes advantage of the protocol metadata and infers a state machine that defines the correct order of the exchanged messages. The state machine is used to decide to which methods messages need to be dispatched. Presenting the developer with this abstraction eliminates the confusion as what needs to be implemented.

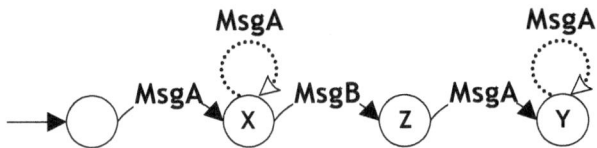

Fig. 6. State machine inferred from protocol metadata. X, Y and Z stand for the methods to which the message relating to the incoming transition will be dispatched.

5   Conclusion and Future Work

Web Service descriptions are machine-processable documents that capture the semantics that define how two services can interact meaningfully. Normally, Web Service descriptions are written in WSDL. In this paper we accept that there are significant drawbacks with WSDL for building service-oriented applications (e.g. focus on operations rather than messages, insufficient control over SOAP messages, high complexity, not expressive enough to capture sophisticated messaging behavior). The target for our empirical work instead uses an alternative Web Services description language called SSDL. Given the lack of empirical data on using SSDL as part of Web Services-based SOAs, we identified the need to further investigate and assess the capabilities of SSDL through empirical studies.

To that end we have developed Soya, a programming model and runtime environment for creating and executing SSDL-based Web Services. We have presented programming abstractions that not only allow developers to build SSDL services in a straightforward way but also encourage the creation of truly service-oriented applications without imposing unrealistic development burdens. Further, we have provided a detailed explanation of how we leveraged a contemporary SOAP engine by adding functionality and semantics related to SSDL, thus providing an advanced runtime environment for executing SSDL-based Web Services to the community.

The development of Soya has provided an extremely valuable insight into the creation, deployment and runtime enactment of SSDL contracts. In future investigations and case studies, we will use Soya as a research vehicle through which we can express our needs and experiences related to SSDL. Specifically, we will use Soya and SSDL to create a service-oriented system in the context of the Australian lending industry [1]. One one side, this will help us to validate the usability of Soya's programming model and the proper functioning of its runtime environment. On the other side, these experiments will provide us with the empirical data we need to determine, whether describing Web Services in SSDL has significant benefits compared to the incumbent approaches.

Acknowledgments

We would like to thank Liming Zhu, Savas Parastatidis and Pawel Kowalski for their constructive feedback and valuable support in creating this document.

National ICT Australia is funded through the Australian Government's Backing Australia's Ability initiative, in part through the Australian Research Council.

References

1. Lending Industry XML Initiative (LIXI). `http://www.lixi.org.au`
2. Ballinger, K., et al.: Web services metadata exchange, version 1.1 (2006)
3. Benatallah, B., Casati, F., Toumani, F.: Representing, analysing and managing web service protocols
4. de Mello, E.R., Parastatidis, S., Reinecke, P., Smith, C., van Moorsel, A., Webber, J.: Secure and provable service support for human-intensive real-estate processes. Technical report, University of Newcastle upon Tyne: Computing Science (2006)
5. Erl, T.: Service-Oriented Architecture (SOA): Concepts, Technology, and Design. Prentice Hall PTR, Englewood Cliffs (2005)
6. Fornasier, P.: Soya - SSDL engine. `http://soya.sourceforge.net`
7. Hinchcliffe, D.: Web service description languages: When there is nothing left to take away (2005) `http://hinchcliffe.org/archive/2005/05/10/215.aspx`
8. Kuo, D., Parastatidis, S., Webber, J.: Rules SSDL protocol framework. Technical Report CS-TR-902, School of Computing Science, University of Newcastle upon Tyne (2005)
9. Microsoft Corporation: .NET framework 3.0. `http://www.netfx3.com/`
10. Microsoft Corporation: Web services description language tool (wsdl.exe) `http://msdn2.microsoft.com/en-us/library/7h3ystb6.aspx`
11. Microsoft Corporation: Windows communication foundation (WCF) `http://wcf.netfx3.com/`
12. OASIS. Reference model for service oriented architecture v 1.0. (2006) `http://www.oasis-open.org/committees/soa-rm/`
13. OASIS. Web services business process execution language version 2.0. (2006) `http://docs.oasis-open.org/wsbpel/2.0/`
14. Object Management Group. IDL syntax and semantics chapter. `http://www.omg.org/cgi-bin/doc?formal/02-06-39`
15. Pallmann, D.: Programming INDIGO. Microsoft Press (2005)
16. Parastatidis, S.: The MEST architectural style (2004) `http://savas.parastatidis.name/2004/11/09/92ede84c-ca1f-41ab-8feb-8ba50d07e86f.aspx`
17. Parastatidis, S., Webber, J.: CSP SSDL protocol framework. Technical Report CS-TR-901, School of Computing Science, University of Newcastle upon Tyne (2005)
18. Parastatidis, S., Webber, J.: MEP SSDL protocol framework. Technical Report CS-TR-900, School of Computing Science, University of Newcastle upon Tyne (2005)
19. Parastatidis, S., Webber, J., Woodman, S., Kuo, D., Greenfield, P.: An introduction to the SOAP service description language. Technical Report CS-TR-898, School of Computing Science, University of Newcastle upon Tyne (2005)
20. Parastatidis, S., Webber, J., Woodman, S., Kuo, D., Greenfield, P.: SOAP service description language (SSDL). Technical Report CS-TR-899, School of Computing Science, University of Newcastle upon Tyne (2005)
21. Parastatidis, S., Woodman, S., Webber, J., Kuo, D., Greenfield, P.: Asynchronous messaging between web services using SSDL. Internet Computing, IEEE 10(1), 26–39 (2006)
22. The Apache Software Foundation. Axis2. `http://ws.apache.org/axis2/`

23. Vogels, W.: Web services are not distributed objects. IEEE Internet Computing 7(6), 59–66 (2003)
24. W3C. Web services addressing (2004)
    http://www.w3.org/Submission/ws-addressing/
25. W3C. Web services architecture (2004) http://www.w3.org/TR/ws-arch/
26. W3C. WS choreography model overview (2004) http://www.w3.org/TR/ws-chor-model/
27. W3C. XML information set (2nd edn.) (2004) http://www.w3.org/TR/xml-infoset/
28. W3C. XML schema (2004) http://www.w3.org/XML/Schema
29. W3C. Web services description language (WSDL) version 2.0 part 1: Core language (2006) http://www.w3.org/TR/wsdl20/
30. W3C. Web services description language (WSDL) version 2.0 part 2: Adjuncts (2006)http://www.w3.org/TR/wsdl20-adjuncts/
31. Waldo, J., Wyant, G., Wollrath, A., Kendall, S.: A note on distributed computing. Technical report, Sun Microsystems Laboratories, Mountain View, CA (1994)
32. Woodman, S., Parastatidis, S., Webber, J.: Sequencing constraints SSDL protocol framework. Technical Report CS-TR-903, School of Computing Science, University of Newcastle upon Tyne (2005)

Experience with Safe Dynamic Reconfigurations in Component-Based Embedded Systems

Juraj Polakovic[1,2], Sebastien Mazare[1], Jean-Bernard Stefani[2],
and Pierre-Charles David[3,*]

[1] FranceTelecom R&D, MAPS/AMS Lab, Grenoble, France
[2] SARDES Project, INRIA Rhône Alpes, Grenoble, France
[3] OBASCO Group, EMN/INRIA, Lina, Nantes, France

Abstract. Supporting dynamic reconfiguration is required even in highly constrained embedded systems, to allow software patches and updates, and to allow adaptations to changes in environmental and operating conditions without service interruption. Dynamic reconfiguration, however, is a complex and error prone process. In this paper we report our experience in implementing safe dynamic reconfigurations in embedded devices with limited resources. Our approach relies on a component-based framework for building reconfigurable operating systems, and the use of a domain specific language (DSL) for reconfiguration.

1 Introduction

Dynamic reconfiguration refers to the process of modifying a system's structure and behavior during its execution. Even in memory and energy constrained devices such as networked sensors or embedded appliances, dynamic reconfiguration is required to allow software patches and security updates, functional updates (e.g. introducing a new protocol), or the adaptation to new operating conditions, while ensuring service continuity. Dynamic reconfiguration, however, is a complex process, which can be very error-prone, as the reconfiguration programmer must maintain both the architectural and behavioral integrity of the system under modification. For example when replacing a module in a multi-threaded operating system, a quiescent state must be achieved, and the interface offered by the module must match what the rest of the system expects. (for a discussion of the intricacies of dynamic reconfiguration see e.g. [4, 29]).

Existing software infrastructures for embedded devices with limited resources such as e.g. TinyOS [19], Contiki [8], SOS [16], Mantis [3], FlexCup [23], either do not support dynamic reconfiguration (TinyOS), or provide low-level mechanisms for dynamic reconfiguration — typically dynamic linking of modules or components — that do not alleviate the issues involved in programming safe reconfigurations.

This paper reports our experiences with the implementation of a support for safe reconfigurations on embedded devices with limited resources. We rely on the THINK framework for the construction of component-based operating systems [11], that implements the FRACTAL reflective component model [5], to construct reconfigurable embedded software [25]. Safety of reconfigurations is achieved by a combination of

---

* This work has been done while the author was a post-doctoral fellow in France Telecom R&D.

H.W. Schmidt et al. (Eds.): CBSE 2007, LNCS 4608, pp. 242–257, 2007.
© Springer-Verlag Berlin Heidelberg 2007

architecture-based component replacement, and the use of a novel domain specific language (DSL), called FScript [6], that allows the succinct expression of modifications to a running architecture, and that supports various sanity checks on reconfiguration programs. This paper discusses our approach, and the associated support for the FScript language, with respect to goals of flexibility, efficiency, safety and simplicity of reconfigurations.

The remainder of this paper is structured as follows. In section 2 we describe our use case and discusses the challenges faced when designing and implementing a operating systems supporting safe reconfigurations. Section 3 details our approach for constructing reconfigurable operating system kernels and programming reconfigurations. The support for the FScript language is crucial, we show in section 4 the obtained implementation results. Section 5 discusses the lessons we learned and the future work. Follows a discussion of existing research and section 7 concludes the paper.

2   Use Case and Challenges

Use case: the Cognichip. Our objective is to allow reconfigurations on our target platform, called the Cognichip, based on the Atmel AVR ATmega128 8-bit micro-controller with $4kb$ data memory and $128kb$ code memory. We are currently experimenting approaches to construct mobile intelligent networked objects with cognitive radio [24] on top of this platform. At run-time, the Cognichip can be extended with different plugin devices, such as various sensors or device controllers enabling the Cognichip to act as a small intelligent information router. This feature requires to add additionnal drivers at run-time. Furthermore, informations from these devices are handled by applications installed either by the user or by a third-party, like the home internet provider, that also can be changed during the execution. With the THINK framework we already construct applicative operating systems tailored to this platform [15]. The operating system and the application are built as a unique THINK-based component-system. We want to enable dynamic reconfiguration of the system and application components, in order to support bugfixes, to reconfigure the underlying radio protocol components, and to add or remove device drivers. The addition of device drivers may require the reconfiguration of some low-level system components, for example adding a new brick in the protocol stack that requires a different timer implementation.

Challenges. Designing and implementing dynamic reconfiguration mechanisms in an embedded operating system is a challenging task. Issues related to reconfiguration mechanisms have an impact on the design of the system itself and must be considered early in the development phases. In order to replace a component in a system, the part of the system to be reconfigured (the *target*) must be clearly identified. Then, before the reconfiguration takes place, the reconfiguration target must reach a *stable state*. A common notion of stable state is that of *quiescent state*, i.e. a state in which no activity currently takes place in the target. When this quiescent state is detected, the state of the target must be captured and transferred to the new component, and the change of configuration can now take place. The change of configuration can imply changing some attributes, modifying the connections between modules, as well as altering the software architecture of the reconfiguration target. Before resuming the execution after the configuration change, the references to the old component must be redirected to the new one. As such, reconfiguration mechanisms in embedded operating systems raise new challenges beyond the operating system construction. We consider four main goals for a dynamic reconfiguration mechanism, already described by Hicks and Nettles [18], however adapted to embedded operating system construction and to the above use-case: (i) *Flexibility* Any part of the system should be reconfigurable, especially the system should not impose any non-reconfigurable core set of components. (ii) *Efficiency and Minimality* The reconfigurable operating system support for safe reconfigurations must respect performance constraints of the target platform. For embedded devices these limitations can vary from memory usage or CPU consumption, to power consumption or timing requirements of reconfigurations. (iii) *Safety* By *safety* of reconfigurations we mean that erroneous reconfigurations won't compromise the system consistency, i.e. the resulting architecture is valid. The reconfigurable system must also guarantee a behavior correctness during reconfigurations, e.g. that a module is not removed while accessed. (iv) *Simplicity* The reconfiguration process, including programming complex reconfigurations, must be simple for the reconfiguration programmer, in order to minimize the introduction of errors.

3   Foundations: FRACTAL, THINK and FSCRIPT

3.1   The FRACTAL Component Model

FRACTAL is a hierarchical and reflective component model intended to implement, deploy and manage a wide range of software systems including operating systems and middleware [5].

A FRACTAL component is both a design and a runtime entity that constitutes a unit of encapsulation, composition and configuration. Components provide *server interfaces* which are the access points to the services that they implement. They express their service requirements via *client interfaces*. FRACTAL distinguishes two kinds of components. *Primitive components* are implemented in a host programming language (e.g. C, Java) and can be seen as black boxes providing and requiring services through their interfaces. *Composite components* correspond to a composition of other components (called subcomponents), either primitives or composites. The existence of composite components makes the FRACTAL Component Model a hierarchical component model.

Components in the FRACTAL component model interact via client/server *bindings*. A binding constitutes a communication path between components and can implement arbitrary forms of communication (e.g asynchronous requests, synchronous requests and replies, multicasting and so forth). The simplest form of binding is a language reference (e.g. a method invocation).

A FRACTAL component logically comprises two different parts. The internal part, that we call *content* implements the functional interfaces of the component. The content is encapsulated by a *membrane* which can implement control over its behavior. In addition to the functional interfaces of a component, the *membrane* can provide an arbitrary set of control interfaces.

The presence of control interfaces makes FRACTAL a reflective component model where control interfaces provide the means to observe and manipulate the internal structure of a component. An important point is that the FRACTAL component model does not mandate a fixed and predefined meta-object protocol (i.e. a set of control interfaces). Instead, a programmer can define and implement his own set of control interfaces.

FRACTAL defines some standard control interfaces in order to manipulate a component's interfaces, its subcomponents, its client bindings, attributes, or its life-cycle (respectively called `ComponentIdentity`[1], `ContentController`, `Binding-Controller`, `LifeCycleController`).

FRACTAL components and FRACTAL component architectures can be described using an architecture description language (ADL). The FRACTAL ADL is a high-level declarative language in which programmers express software configurations in terms of interfaces, attributes, component compositions and bindings. Using the `membrane` construct, the programmer can specify which membrane to apply to a given component. An example of an ADL description is given in Figure 1.

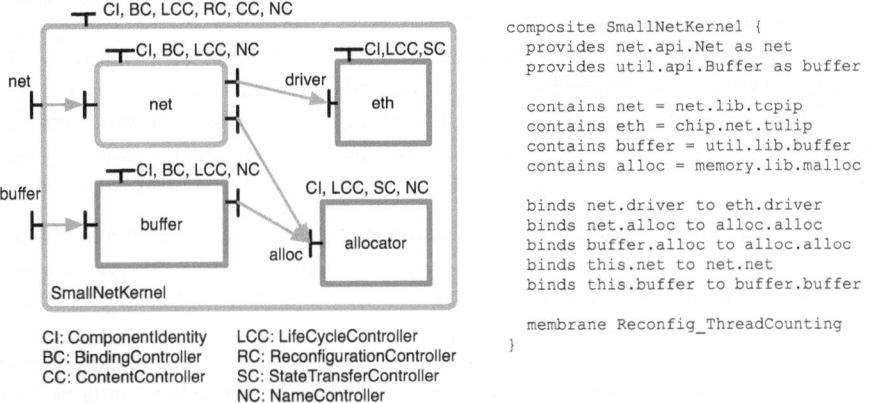

```
composite SmallNetKernel {
  provides net.api.Net as net
  provides util.api.Buffer as buffer

  contains net = net.lib.tcpip
  contains eth = chip.net.tulip
  contains buffer = util.lib.buffer
  contains alloc = memory.lib.malloc

  binds net.driver to eth.driver
  binds net.alloc to alloc.alloc
  binds buffer.alloc to alloc.alloc
  binds this.net to net.net
  binds this.buffer to buffer.buffer

  membrane Reconfig_ThreadCounting
}
```

CI: ComponentIdentity LCC: LifeCycleController
BC: BindingController RC: ReconfigurationController
CC: ContentController SC: StateTransferController
      NC: NameController

Fig. 1. A simplified view of a simple reconfigurable THINK-based kernel and its ADL description. The kernel provides a network interface and a buffer interface. The `eth` component implementing the network driver is architecture-dependent. The FRACTAL control interfaces are added to the components by the THINK ADL compiler based on the `membrane` keyword.

3.2 THINK

THINK is a general framework for building component-based systems and especially operating system kernels. The framework comprises a C implementation of the FRACTAL component model, an ADL with the associated ADL-to-C compiler, we call THINK ADL compiler, and a component library, called Kortex.

The initial version of THINK [11] was based on a flat component model. Our current version is now entirely based on the hierarchical FRACTAL component model. Thanks

---

[1] Called simply `Component` in the latest FRACTAL specification.

to the reflective capabilities of FRACTAL, a kernel architecture can be retrieved at run-time. If the kernel has a static architecture, i.e. it doesn't contain any component factories that could alter its architecture, the run-time kernel architecture is equivalent to the initial ADL description.

In a THINK-based OS everything is a component and with an adapted reconfiguration base mechanism, every component is reconfigurable. There is no predefined non-reconfigurable core, nor a core set of required components. In this way, we can build customized reconfigurable operating systems, including only the needed components. Such systems can range from small devices like networked sensors [15] to bigger devices, like handhelds, offering more functionality.

THINK-based OS are built using the THINK ADL compiler. This compiler translates the ADL code to ANSI C and compiles and links the generated code with component implementations (also written in C) using a standard C compiler and linker. The generated C code obeys to a binary format for components detailed in [11].

The THINK framework was lately enhanced with a number of base mechanisms for replacing safely a component without interrupting the service [25]. These mechanisms provide the detection of quiescent state, state transfer and reference redirection and are implemented as FRACTAL control interfaces.

The THINK framework provides several implementations for these interfaces. For a given component, the kernel developper chooses the appropriate set via the ADL membrane keyword and the THINK ADL compiler includes the appropriate interface implementations for reconfigurable components. Note this approach is extremely flexible and allows to specify different mechanisms at the scope of a single component.

- *Quiescent state* Quiescent state algorithm is provided via the component's ReconfigurationController interface implementation. In our previous work [25], we implemented two quiescent state algorithms for THINK-based kernels – *thread-counting* and *dynamic interceptors*.
- *State transfer* We have defined a StateTransferController interface that gives access to a component's internal state and allows us to build complex state transfers. It is up to the component programmer to implement this interface.
- *Reference redirection* Once a reconfiguration succeeded, client references are redirected using the standard BindingController interface of the client components.
- The actual architecture modifications are performed by the ContentController interface implementation that can add or remove components from a composite component.
- The LifeCycleController interface serves to initialize (start) or to stop a component, used to initialize a hardware driver or shutdown properly a device.

Consider the example of the SmallNetKernel shown in figure 1. The kernel developer writes the ADL description for the SmallNetKernel as shown in the figure below the graphical view of the kernel. Based on the membrane specification of this ADL description, the THINK ADL compiler will automatically generate FRACTAL control interface implementations for the SmallNetKernel component, concretely including the thread-counting quiescence algorithm. The graphical view shows the resulting set of control interfaces of the components.

3.3   The FScript DSL

The FRACTAL component model is defined in terms of APIs which make it possible both to *discover* the structure of a FRACTAL application and to *reconfigure* it at runtime. However, programming dynamic reconfigurations directly at this level make the code verbose, difficult to understand, and prevent analyzes to guarantee the behaviour before of the reconfigurations executing them, which can be essential for critical systems. FScript [6] is a Domain Specific Language [30] designed to overcome these limitations while retaining FRACTAL's advantages. FScript can be used to navigate intuitively inside a FRACTAL architecture and select parts of it, on which reconfigurations (either primitive FRACTAL operations or user-defined scripts) can then be applied. Here is a simple example of reconfiguration programmed in FScript which illustrates all of FScript constructs.

```
action auto-bind(c) = {
  // Selects the interfaces to connect
  clts := $c/interface::*[required(.)][not(bound(.))];
  foreach i in $clts do { // Search for candidates interfaces
    srvs := $c/sibling::*/interface::*[compatible($i, .)];
    if (not(empty($srvs))) { // Connect one of these candidates
      bind($i, one-of($srvs));
    }
  }
  return $c/interface::*[required(.)][not(bound(.))];
}
```

This defines a new reconfiguration action named `auto-bind`, which automatically connects a component's required interfaces by discovering the compatible server interfaces on sibling components. The body of the action consists in a sequence of simple statements (assignments, procedure calls and return) and control structures (iteration and conditionals).

As can be seen in this example, FScript uses a special notation to navigate inside the architecture and select elements from it. This notation, called FPath, is roughly inspired by XPath [31] and supports the same kinds of queries on FRACTAL architectures that XPath supports for XML documents. FPath expressions are used to navigate inside the architecture to select specific elements. The architecture is seen as a directed graph where nodes represent components, their interfaces, methods and attributes. Theses nodes are connected by labeled arcs representing the relationships between them: for example, a component node is connected to all its interfaces' nodes by arcs labeled `interface`. Each step of a path starts from an initial set of nodes and selects a new set by following one of these relationships. The resulting nodeset can then be filtered by name or by complex predicate expressions (including embedded path expressions).

As a concrete example, the second FPath expression in the above example (line 6) can be read as: "Starting from component `$c`, first select all its siblings (components which share at least one direct parent) in the architecture, whatever their name is (`/sibling::*`). Then, given these new components, select all their interfaces (`/interface::*`), but return only those for which the predicate in brackets holds. In this case, the predicate tests whether its parameter (denoted by a dot `.`) is compatible with the interface in the iteration variable `$i`." In short, this request will select all the interfaces owned by siblings of the parameter component which can be bound to $i (itself a required interface of $c which is not bound yet, see line 3).

FScript provides an extensible library of primitive functions and actions which gives the user access to all the features of the FRACTAL API. These primitives can be combined to create complex reconfiguration scripts using a voluntarily limited set of the control structures which, with the interdiction of recursive definitions, enable us to guarantee the termination of all reconfigurations: classical *conditionals* (if/then/else), *iteration* (foreach i in path do { body } on the result of an FPath expression (path), which always return a finite set of elements, and finally explicit and early *return* from an action (return). Compared to the use of the standard FRACTAL APIs in a general purpose language, FScript offers a number of advantages, which we discuss below.

Expressiveness gain. In THINK-based OS reconfigurations are performed in terms of operations allowed by the FRACTAL component model. The following sequence is necessary to replace the alloc component in the SmallNetKernel kernel shown in figure 1 (the new component is called new_alloc): (1)add the new component to the SmallNetKernel; (2) suspend the execution of the alloc component; (3) stop the alloc component (for example driver shutdown); (4) (retrieve state from the alloc component)[2]; (5) (inject state to the new_alloc component)[5]; (6) redirect the net component to use new_alloc; (7) redirect the buffer component to use new_alloc; (8) start the new_alloc component (for ex. initializations); (9) resume the execution in the SmallNetKernel component; (10) remove the unused alloc component. In FScript we would write the following reconfiguration code to achieve this reconfiguration:

```
k = $root/child::kernel              stop($o);
n := new('new_alloc');               unbind($k_alloc);
o := $root/child::alloc;             bind($k_alloc,
k_alloc :=                                $n/interface::alloc);
    $k/child::*/interface::alloc     start($n);
add($k, $n);                         resume($k);
suspend($k, $k/child::alloc);        remove($o);
```

The above shown FScript code shows the simplicity of our approach. In the shown code, the programmer expresses all needed operations to perform a dynamic reconfiguration. An equivalent C code is much harder to understand. For example, the bind operation corresponds to the bind method of the BindingController and accepts two parameters, the first FPath expression selects the alloc interface of the kernel component, the second FPath expression selects the alloc interface of the new interface. The equivalent C code is written in 10-20 lines of C code (considered without error handling that adds to the complexity and decrease readability of the C code). In the C code, we will find temporary variables to resolve real component locations and to obtain interface handles to finaly invoke the bind implementation.

Correctness checks. Correctness is obtained by simulation of the reconfiguration at compile-time and by generating error handling code, thus at run-time.

---

[2] For the sake of simplicity, we do not consider the state transfer in this prototype evaluation. State transfer mechanisms can be built using the StateTransferController.

At compile-time, the FScript compiler checks if the code is conforming to the target architecture. It verifies the conformance of interface types, the existence of components and the correct use of suspend/resume quiescent state operations. Performing these verifications at compile-time reduces the resulting size of the compiled reconfiguration code to be loaded by the target device in its constrained environment.

An explicit error-handling code can be written by the reconfiguration programmer in the FScript program, serving to perform additional architecture verifications at run-time. A checking code is automatically generated by the FScript compiler. It serves to make low-level C checks, as null pointers etc. preventing the possible crash of the system.

Easier evolutions in kernel architecture. FScript reconfiguration programs are easier to adapt and maintain over time. This is not the case of hand-written C code for reconfiguration. Consider the following scenario: the above described reconfiguration is commonly applied to change the allocator performances in some of the deployed embedded devices running a first generation of the SmallNetKernel, without the buffer interface. For some reasons the SmallNetKernel was updated and the new version provides a buffer implementation that uses the allocator component, as shown in figure 1. We need to change only one line in the FScript program to fit this scenario - the bind operation.

4   Implementation and Results

4.1   Implementing Support for FScript

We found that there were several possible strategies for implementing the FScript compiler, the central piece of our approach. We first discuss the implementation strategies and show our implementation together with the obtained results in the following section 4.2. The first general idea is to provide an interpreter in the native environment, embedded in the target operating system. All FScript programs are addressed to this interpreter and are interpreted and executed on the target platform.

The second strategy consists in compiling FScript programs on a remote host into a binary form, ready to be loaded and executed on the target platform. This approach alleviates the requirements on the reconfiguration support on the target platform. All necessary program verifications can be performed at compile time, resulting in a safe reconfiguration code. However, in such a distributed architecture, the FScript compiler, running on the reconfiguration host, has to know or retrieve the software architecture of the target OS and probably some additional meta-data. The retrieval of the software architecture is enabled with the use of the FRACTAL component model where component architecture representation is explicitly maintained at run-time.

There are several variations of this approach, shown in figure 2. The first variant (we call *systematic synchronization* in figure 2a), retrieves systematically the current configuration of the device's OS on each reconfiguration request. The variant shown in figure 2b, *no synchronization* makes assumption that the software architecture of the target subsystem to reconfigure evolves only through reconfigurations. For the sake of completeness, figure 2c, *reconfiguration via proxies*, shows an implementation of the

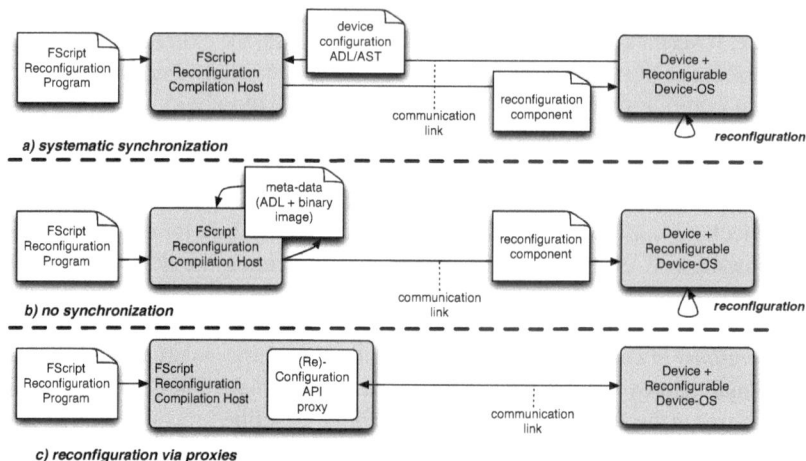

Fig. 2. Offline compiler: different implementations of synchronization between the FScript compiler and the target OS

synchronization using a proxy component system on the reconfiguration host having identical configuration as the target system and that forwards all reconfiguration actions to the former.

The choice of a solution for the FScript support implementation will depend on the hardware constraints of the target platform, criteria defined by the operating system or by the network provider the embedded system is connected to. We implemented an offline FScript compiler without synchronization and show the obtained implementation results in the next section.

4.2 An Offline FScript Compiler

For evaluation purpose we implemented an FScript compiler without synchronization (Figure 2b). In order to validate the minimality of our approach and evaluate the suitability for a platform like the above described Cognichip, we built a small prototype kernel on an 32-bit ARM-based handheld device. We are interested in evaluating the memory overhead of the run-time support for FScript and the amount of data transferred to the reconfigurable device.

Implementation of the FScript compiler. Our FScript compiler without synchronization works on the ADL description used to instantiate the target system, this is sufficient, as FScript semantics are defined exclusively in terms of FRACTAL architecture elements captured by the ADL. The FScript compiler generates the C implementation of a reconfiguration component.

Along with the new instances, the reconfiguration component is compiled as a relocatable THINK-based component with our THINK ADL compiler to produce an ELF[3] file ready to be sent to the target platform.

---

[3] The use of the ELF format is motivated by the availability of associated code and tools.

The target operating system provides a minimal run-time for executing reconfiguration components:

- *FScript helper functions* In order to minimize the transferred reconfiguration C code, some often used functions are provided by the run-time.
- *loader and linker* The linker functionalities are restrained to be capable of only loading the reconfiguration ELF file. It performs some symbol relocation and resolves references to the FScript helper functions, together with some standard functions (symbols), like `printf`.
- *introspection component* In the generated C code, the real component locations are not resolved. The resolution is done at run-time by the introspection component, using the introspection capabilities of FRACTAL architectures already available in the operating system.

Implementation results. Table 1 shows the sizes of the necessary components to build a run-time support for the binary reconfiguration code compiled from FScript. We separate the code size (`text` section) from the data size (`data` and `bss` section). On architecture like the AVR, the code is copied into the flash memory, whereas the data into the main memory. The data comprises C compiler allocated structures, like global variables, especially it doesn't give any information on stack or heap usage. As already stated, the linker has only minimal functionalities to satisfy the linking of the reconfiguration component.

Table 1. Sizes of the FScript run-time

	code size	data size
Introspection	2.7kb	100b
Loader and linker	4.9kb	300b
FScript helper	1.3kb	0b
Total run-time support	8.9kb	400b

Table 2. FScript offline compiler and a native interpreter (reconfiguration of the `alloc` comp.)

	compiler	interpreter
Transf. data type	ELF	FScript
Transf. data size	4.5kb	270b
FScript run-time	8.9kb/0.4kb	n.a.

In the table 3 we evaluated the size of the ELF file of the reconfiguration component. The functional content of the ELF file, i.e. reconfiguration code and new components, is about half of the file size. In the ELF header we find a symbol table, a string table and two relocation tables (code and data sections). The space occupied by the relocation tables are minimized due to the inlined nature of the THINK component structures we generated, the symbol and string tables occupy almost the rest of the header. The sizes of these table entries are directly related to the C symbol names (variables, functions etc.) and to the structure of the C code of the new components and of the generated C structures. The size is proportional to the amount of components in the file.

Table 2 summarizes the characteristics of the offline compilation approach and compares it to what we could expect from a native interpreter (we didn't implement). We are interested in comparing the amounts of data transferred to the reconfigurable device and the impact on the memory usage of the FScript support as it determines the suitability of the approach for constrained devices. The shown sizes are relative to the

Table 3. Details of the reconfiguration ELF file for the allocator reconfiguration example

Reconfiguration code	1.5kb
The new component (sbrk)	0.5kb
THINK component structures	0.2kb
Total content	**2.3kb**

ELF header	2kb
strings in the ELF tables	~ 1kb
Total size of the ELF-file	**4.3kb**

above described reconfiguration of the `alloc` component. We postpone the discussion of these results to the section 5.1.

The reconfigurable THINK-based kernel served for this evaluation occupies $109kb$ of code memory and $13kb$ of data memory. All kernel components are reconfigurable, the kernel contains an FScript support (helper functions, loader and linker) and a simple communication stack over the radio line. In the data sections (`data` and `bss`) we find static component data, buffers and component meta-data structures generated by the THINK ADL compiler (about $1kb$).

5   Discussion

5.1   Lessons Learned and Limitations

We found that our approach for providing safe reconfigurations in an operating system fulfills the goals of flexibility, safety and simplicity. However we didn't yet achieve the goals of efficiency and minimality, in order to build an FScript execution support on the Cognichip target platform.

Flexibility. Using the FRACTAL hierarchical component model allows reconfigurations to be properly scoped and to take place at different levels of granularity. Changing a single primitive component or a whole subsystem is done in the same way. Using this approach we were able to replace a single component, like the allocator, and the whole application.

Safety. The safety of our reconfigurations is achieved by using the FScript language. FScript programs are subject to compile time checks that help the reconfiguration programmer avoid non-trivial errors. The FScript compiler is responsible for analyzing if the reconfiguration performed results in a valid architecture and it also generates runtime error-handling code.

Simplicity. Our approach is simple thanks to the use of FRACTAL-based technologies at every stage of the reconfiguration process. We build reconfigurable operating systems, using a FRACTAL implementation, we program reconfigurations in a language based exclusively on elements of a FRACTAL architecture.

Efficiency and Minimality. The actual sizes of a reconfigurable kernel with an FScript support for an AVR platform may vary from those reported in the previous section (due to different code compactness and different data sizes). The above results show however a lack of the implemented approach – it requires extra memory usage on the target platform, inadapted for platforms like the Cognichip, with $4kb$ or $8kb$ main memory.

Indeed, the size of the ELF header is proportional to the number of components (due to the nature of the generate meta-data structures for THINK-based components), the overall size of the transferred file depends on the number of new components and the reconfiguration code is proportional to the complexity of reconfigurations. Thus, the processing of the received ELF file requires extra memory usage.

5.2 Perspectives

The above discussed prototype could be improved in several ways.

Optimize generated component structures. The ELF-header overhead is partially due to the structure of the C code generated by the THINK ADL compiler. For a component the compiler generates several cross-referenced global symbols. Each reference of such a symbol requires an entry in the relocation table found in the ELF header. We are currently experimenting the generation of inlined component structures revoking the necessity of cross-referenced symbols. This is a more general work on optimizations of component-based system architectures.

Loader. Our prototype uses a simple loader working on in-RAM copies of the ELF file. On architectures like the AVR, where the RAM size is limited, we plan to build a more efficient loader working with the flash memory as temporary storage.

External configuration representation and meta-data. The described implementation of the FScript interpreter works with an ADL representation of the device's configuration. The interpreter generates a code where real component locations are resolved at run-time. We envisage to include binary meta-data, as effective component locations, to the configuration representation gathered by the target device prior to reconfiguration. This would probably lead us to define an alternative binary format for the transmission of the reconfiguration component.

Offline pre-linking. We are currently working on a prototype implementation of the FScript compiler without the necessity of a run-time linker. All linking is done on the compilation host, linking locations are predetermined before the binary reconfiguration component is sent to the target. The memory usage of this prototype is thus minimal, this approach has severe limitations in flexibility.

FScript syntax evolution. Our actual FScript compiler checks the conformity of the usage of the suspend and resume operations for the quiescent state. This check is complex and we still found cases difficult to detect. Blocks in the FScript language would be useful to provide syntactically scoping rules to this quiescent state condition. The FScript compiler could then just insert the suspend and resume operations. A programmer would write:

Error handling. The reconfiguration code as it is generated by the FScript compiler contains little error handling assuming that all verifications were performed by the interpreter. We envisage to make this code more robust and evaluate the impact on its size. A C++ exception mechanism implementation appears to be a promising way to achieve a proper error handling.

6 Related Work

Dynamic reconfiguration has been heavily explored in research areas ranging from programming languages, down to middleware and operating system kernels. In the following, we restrict the analysis to reconfigurable operating systems. We organize our discussion around two research areas. We discuss first reconfigurable operating systems, and then operating systems for constrained embedded devices, like networked sensors.

Reconfigurable operating systems. General-purpose operating systems, such as Linux or Windows provide limited support for dynamic reconfiguration, typically limited to certain functionalities, like device drivers. It is possible to load and unload kernel modules, but for example replacement of a module while in use by the system is not possible. All such reconfigurations are performed manually and a verification mechanism, as implemented in this paper, is not available.

Component-based frameworks, such as OSkit [12] or eCos [9], provide a way to build customized and minimal kernels, based on compile-time selection of components to be included into the kernel. These systems also provide an architecture description language (ADL), such as Knit [27], to assist the assembly of the kernel. However, these systems have no support for dynamic reconfiguration.

Compared to monolithic operating systems, micro-kernels (e.g. L4 [22], or Pebble [13]) are a step further in providing reconfigurability - a user-level server is the unit of reconfiguration. However, a micro-kernel itself is not reconfigurable and if reconfigurability is implemented at the level of user-level servers, the system pays the price of the time-consuming IPC communication between these servers. An Exokernel approach [10] allows kernel developers to build systems on top of minimum hardware abstraction, however it is also up to the kernel developer to implement a reconfiguration support.

SPIN [2], provides a safe way to extend the kernel, by writing extensions as *spindles*. Compared to our approach, SPIN has several limitations. First, an underlying kernel core itself is not reconfigurable. Second, extensions are only limited to some predefined parts of the kernel. Third, the interactions between extensions and the kernel are expensive - an extension is a handler reacting to an event raised by a kernel module. And finally the safe extension mechanism requires a run-time compiler and verifier, which makes this approach unsuitable for constrained embedded devices.

In VINO [28], all reconfigurations are handled as transactions, largely using locking to synchronize the access to kernel modules. As such, transactions offer a basis for implementing a safe reconfiguration mechanism. The overhead of the transaction mechanism makes it inadapted to be used in embedded devices with limited resources. Reconfigurable operating systems including Synthetix [26], MMLite [17] or more recently K42 [1, 29] provide mechanisms for dynamic reconfiguration at a fine grain. Synthetix and MMLite use read-write locks to synchronize accesses to a reconfigurable component. K42 supports reconfiguration through a mechanism, which consists in introducing interceptors at run-time, resulting in no run-time overhead. Common to these systems is the fact that reconfigurations are still hand-written and as such do not alleviate the issues involved in programming safe reconfiguration.

Operating systems for networked sensors. TinyOS [19, 14], one of the first operating systems targeting networked sensors, is not reconfigurable, however, several different approaches exist on top of TinyOS in order to provide application reconfigurability. For instance XNP [20] allows to download and reinstall a new system image. XNP requires a reboot of the system and as such doesn't provide any service guarantee during the reconfiguration. Mantis [3] allows reconfiguration in the same manner.

FlexCup [23] is another mechanism built on top of TinyOS that provides a dynamic reconfiguration mechanism, allowing to reconfigure applications at the granularity of a TinyOS component. The mechanism relies on meta-data, generated during the compilation of the system, and a run-time linking mechanism based on these meta-data. However with FlexCup, TinyOS applications must be segmented into arbitrary binary components that can be reconfigured subsequently. Using the THINK approach for reconfigurations, all components found in a kernel are reconfigurable. Also, in a THINK-based operating systems, components are run-time entities and all necessary meta-data for retrieving and relinking a component are available through the use of the FRACTAL reflective component model.

Contiki [8, 7] is a reconfigurable modular operating system for networked sensors. A Contiki system uses a flat module architecture, a module being the unit of reconfiguration. Thus Contiki offers only a fixed granularity of reconfigurations, whereas in a THINK-based system, thanks to the hierarchy offered by the FRACTAL component model, reconfigurations can involve the whole application implemented by a complex component, or only its subpart implemented in some primitive component. Technically the approach shown in this paper is similar to Contiki, however, using a THINK-based OS with an explicit architecture representation, provides us with a support to verify the reconfigurations before execution. Contiki defines a non-reconfigurable core, in THINK-based OS, everything is a component, thus with an appropriate method, everything is reconfigurable. SOS [16] achieves reconfiguration using loadable modules and is similar to Contiki.

Maté [21] is a virtual machine (VM) built on top of TinyOS, Maté applications are written with a limited set of virtual machines instructions. Reconfigurations are performed as replacements of such applications running on top of the virtual machine. Compared to our approach, Maté achieves a different trade-off between the four goals of a safe dynamic reconfiguration mechanism. The granularity of reconfigurations in Maté is coarse (at the applications level), the core of the system, the virtual machine itself, can't be reconfigured. The byte-code interepretation in the VM guarantees the safety of reconfigurations. The radio communication in networked sensors being the most expensive resource, virtual machines provide energy-efficient update mechanisms, but VMs are more energy expensive during normal system execution. With respect to the energy efficiency we achieve a different trade-off with the THINK approach.

7 Conclusion

In this paper we discussed an approach for constructing safe reconfigurations of operating systems by using a reconfiguration DSL, called FScript. Based on a use-case for intelligent networked objects, we considered four goals for a mechanisms for safe reconfigurations – flexibility, efficiency and minimality, safety and simplicity. Our implementation of the FScript offline compiler for an ARM-based platform fulfills the above goals, however it reveals a prohibitive usage of the memory on the target platform, mainly due to the transfer format of the loadable code, that we will address in our future work by offline pre-linking the loadable code.

The THINK framework is freely available at `http://think.objectweb.org`.

References

[1] Baumann, A., Heiser, G., Appavoo, J., DaSilva, D., Krieger, O., Wisniewski, R.W., Kerr, J.: Providing dynamic update in an operating system. In: Proceedings of the 2005 USENIX Annual Technical Conference (April 2005)

[2] Bershad, B.N., Savage, S., Pardyak, P., Sirer, E.G., Fiuczynski, M.E., Becker, D., Chambers, C., Eggers, S.: Extensibility safety and performance in the SPIN operating system. In: Proceedings of the 15th ACM Symposium on Operating Systems Principles, ACM Press, New York (1995)

[3] Bhatti, S., Carlson, J., Dai, H., Deng, J., Rose, J., Sheth, A., Shucker, B., Gruenwald, C., Torgerson, A., Han, R.: MANTIS OS: An Embedded Multithreaded Operating System for Wireless Micro Sensor Platforms. MONET 10(4) (2005)

[4] Bloom, T., Day, M.: Reconfiguration and module replacement in Argus: Theory and Practice. IEE Software Engineering Journal 8(2) (1993)

[5] Bruneton, E., Coupaye, T., Leclercq, M., Quéma, V., Stefani, J.-B.: The Fractal Component Model and its Support in Java. Software - Practice and Experience 36(11-12) (2006)

[6] David, P.C., Ledoux, T.: Safe Dynamic Reconfigurations of Fractal Architectures with FScript. In: Thomas, D. (ed.) ECOOP 2006. LNCS, vol. 4067, Springer, Heidelberg (2006)

[7] Dunkels, A., Finne, N., Eriksson, J., Voigt, T.: Run-time dynamic linking for reprogramming wireless sensor networks. In: SenSys 2006. Proc. 4th ACM Conference on Embedded Networked Sensor Systems, ACM Press, New York (2006)

[8] Dunkels, A., Gronvall, B., Voigt, T.: Contiki - A Lightweight and Flexible Operating System for Tiny Networked Sensors. In: LCN'04. Proc. 29th Annual IEEE Int. Conf. on Local Computer Networks, IEEE Computer Society Press, Los Alamitos (2004)

[9] eCos. `http://sources.redhat.com/ecos`.

[10] Engler, D.R., Kaashoek, M.F., O'Toole Jr., J.: Exokernel: an operating system architecture for application-level resource management. In: Proceedings of the 15th ACM Symposium on Operating Systems Principles, ACM Press, New York (1995)

[11] Fassino, J.-P., Stefani, J.-B., Lawall, J., Muller, G.: Think: a software framework for component-based operating system kernels. In: Proceedings of the 2002 USENIX Annual Technical Conference (2002)

[12] Ford, B., Lepreau, J., Clawson, S., Van Maren, K., Robinson, B., Turner, J.: The Flux OS Toolkit: Reusable Components for OS Implementation. In: HotOS-VI. 6th Workshop on Hot Topics in Operating Systems (1997)

[13] Gabber, E., Small, C., Bruno, J., Brustoloni, J., Silberschatz, A.: The Pebble Component-Based Operating System. In: Proc. of the USENIX Annual Technical Conference (1999)

[14] Gay, D., Levis, P., von Behren, R., Welsh, M., Brewer, E., Culler, D.: The nesC language: A holistic approach to networked embedded systems. In: Proc. ACM PLDI, ACM Press, New York (2003)

[15] Germain, F., Ghozzi, M., Laval, J.-P., Jarboui, T., Marx, F.: The Cognichip: a flexible, lightweight spectrum monitor. In: COGnitive systems with Interactive Sensors (2006)

[16] Han, C.-C., Kumar, R., Shea, R., Kohler, E., Srivastava, M.: A dynamic operating system for sensor nodes. In: MobiSys. Proc. 3rd Int. Conf. on Mobile systems, applications, and services (2005)

[17] Helander, J., Forin, A.: MMLite: a highly componentized system architecture. In: Proc. 8th ACM SIGOPS workshop on Support for composing distributed applications, ACM Press, New York (1998)

[18] Hicks, M.W., Nettles, S.: Dynamic software updating. ACM Transactions on Programming Languages and Systems (TOPLAS) 27(6) (2005)

[19] Hill, J., Szewczyk, R., Woo, A., Hollar, S., Culler, D., Pister, K.: System architecture directions for networked sensors. In: Proc. 9th ASPLOS (2000)

[20] Jeong, J., Kim, S., Broad, A.: Network reprogramming. TinyOS documentation (2003) http://www.tinyos.net/tinyos-1.x/doc/ NetworkReprogramming. pdf

[21] Levis, P., Culler, D.: Maté: A tiny virtual machine for sensor networks. In: Proc. 10th AS-PLOS (2002)

[22] Liedtke, J.: On micro-kernel construction. In: Proceedings of the 15th ACM Symposium on Operating Systems Principles, December 1995, ACM Press, New York (1995)

[23] Marrón, P.J., Gauger, M., Lachenmann, A., Minder, D., Saukh, O., Rothermel, K.: FlexCup: A Flexible and Efficient Code Update Mechanism for Sensor Networks. In: Römer, K., Karl, H., Mattern, F. (eds.) EWSN 2006. LNCS, vol. 3868, Springer, Heidelberg (2006)

[24] Mitola, J.: Cognitive Radio: An Integrated Agent Architecture for Software Defined Radio. PhD thesis, Royal Institute of Technology (KTH) (2000)

[25] Polakovic, J., Ozcan, A.E., Stefani, J.-B.: Building reconfigurable component-based OS with THINK. In: 32nd Euromicro Conf. on Soft. Eng. and Advanced Applications (SEAA), CBSE Track (2006)

[26] Pu, C., Autrey, T., Black, A.P., Consel, C., Cowan, C., Inouye, J., Kethana, L., Walpole, J., Zhang, K.: Optimistic incremental specialization: Streamlining a commercial operating system. In: Proc. of the 15th ACM Symposium on Operating System Principles, ACM Press, New York (1995)

[27] Reid, A., Flatt, M., Stoller, L., Lepreau, J., Eide, E.: Knit: Component Composition for Systems Software. In: OSDI. Proceedings of the 4th USENIX Symposium on Operating Systems Design and Implementation (2000)

[28] Seltzer, M.I., Endo, Y., Small, C., Smith, K.A.: Dealing with disaster: Surviving misbehaved kernel extensions. In: OSDI. Proceedings of the 2nd USENIX Symposium on Operating Systems Design and Implementation (1996)

[29] Soules, C.A.N., Appavoo, J., Hui, K., Wisniewski, R.W., Da Silva, D., Ganger, G.R., Krieger, O., Stumm, M., Auslander, M., Ostrowski, M., Rosenburg, B., Xenidis, J.: System support for online reconfiguration. In: Proc. of the 2003 USENIX Annual Technical Conf. (2003)

[30] van Deursen, A., Klint, P., Visser, J.: Domain-specific languages: an annotated bibliography. SIGPLAN Notices 35(6) (2000)

[31] World Wide Web Consortium. XML path language (xpath) version 1.0. W3C Recommendation (November 1999) http://www.w3.org/TR/xpath

A Framework for Contract-Based Collaborative Verification and Validation of Web Services

Xiaoying Bai[1], Yongbo Wang[1], Guilan Dai[2],
Wei-Tek Tsai[3], and Yinong Chen[3]

[1] Department on Computer Science and Technology, Tsinghua University, China
`baixy@tsinghua.edu.cn`, `wang-yb04@mails.tsinghua.edu.cn`
[2] Research Institute of Information Technology, Tsinghua University, China
`daigl@tsinghua.edu.cn`
[3] Computer Science and Engineering Department, Arizona State University, USA
`{wtsai,yinong}@asu.edu`

Abstract. A key issue with Web Services (WS) is the verification and validation (V&V) of services to build trust between service providers and service users. This paper proposed a test-broker architecture so that all stakeholder within WS can contribute to improve the testing of the services. The test broker supports the submission, indexing, and querying of test artifacts such as test cases, defect reports and evaluations. It can also provide the services for the test generation, test coordination, and distributed testing services. The DCV&V (Decentralized, Collaborative, Verification and Validation) framework is proposed with a set of distributed and collaborated test brokers dedicated to different V&V tasks to enable scalable and flexible test collaborations. The paper explores the concept of design-by-contract and applies the principle to DCV&V. It identifies two categories of testing contracts including TSC (Testing Service Contracts) and TCC (Test Collaboration Contracts). It illustrates the application of TSC with contract-based test generation based on WS OWL-S specification. It elaborates TCC with the analysis of the test artifacts definitions.

Keywords: Web Services, Contract-Based, Verification and Validation.

1 Introduction

As a new computing paradigm, Service-Oriented Architecture (SOA) and its implementation Web Services (WS) are redefining the entire process of software development and new techniques are needed to support the new process. For example, new techniques are needed to ensure the trustworthiness of SOA and WS based software, as Bloomberg pointed out in 2002 that the success of WS depends on its capability to resolve the testing issues [6].

Standard-based dynamic collaboration is a key feature of WS systems. The generic WS architecture defines a loosely-coupled contract-based collaboration model among service providers, service brokers and service requesters for service publishing, discovery, and binding [21]. A service is an executable software

H.W. Schmidt et al. (Eds.): CBSE 2007, LNCS 4608, pp. 258–273, 2007.

component that resides on the service provider's server and remotely delivers results to the service requester or application. Service providers publish service descriptions and register it to a service directory such as a UDDI server. Service requesters look up the UDDI server, find the services satisfying their requirements, and bind to the service interfaces at run time. The cooperation among distributed partners is enabled by open standard specifications such as SOAP (Simple Object Access Protocol), WSDL (Web Service Description Language, UDDI (Universal Description, Discovery, and Integration), etc.

However, many issues exist in the dynamic collaboration model. One of the key issues is the verification and validation (V&V) of services to build trust between service providers and service requesters. With current SOA applications, the UDDI server serves as a service broker. But it only provides directory services for the service providers to publish services and for the service requesters to discover services. It is not accountable for the quality, including performance, dependability, and cost-effectiveness of the services. It will register any services as long as the identity of the service provider can be verified through the digital signature or other means.

WS V&V requires participation from all parties involved. Service brokers must ensure the quality of the services that they publish by performing independent testing. Service requesters test the services before purchase or use, based on their usage scenarios. CV&V (Collaborative Verification and Validation) was proposed to enable that different parties involved can share, exchange, and interoperate testing artifacts such as test scripts, failure and reliability reports, and ranking of test scripts, and services, etc. [17].

This paper proposes a decentralized CV&V (DCV&V) framework as an extension to our previous work on trustworthy UDDI [1] [19]. A test-broker architecture is introduced to the generic WS architecture. A test broker is a dedicated WS testing agent that is independent of UDDI capabilities and protocols. It provides the services for the publishing and discovering of test artifacts, and enables all the stakeholder in WS testing to flexibly communicate and cooperate. Test brokers that are distributed located can collaborate with each other that are dedicated to different CV&V tasks and focus on different problems.

Contracts are the basis for the mutual understanding among test collaborators. The paper identifies DCV&V contracts from two perspectives: TSC (Testing Service Contracts) and TCC (Test Collaboration Contracts). TSC is the communication between testing components and the SUT (service under test), including test generation and test exercising. The paper applies OWL-S service specification to illustrate contract-based test generation. Test cases are generated based on OWL-S process specification. The paper also discusses constraints-guided test generation. In addition to the data constraints and process pre-conditions supported by current WS specifications, the paper proposes intra-process constraints as a supplementary to process specifications. The constraints provide important information for negative test case generation.

TCC defines the way that testing components collaboratively design test cases, execute test plan, and evaluate test results.The paper identifies the key testing artifacts and their relationships in the TCC model and discusses how these artifacts can be exchanged among testing components.

The rest of the paper is organized as follows. Section 2 reviews related research, including WS CV&V and contract-based testing. Section 3 introduces the DCV&V architecture. Section 4 describes the definition of DCV&V contracts. Sections 5 discusses the contract-based test generation. Finally section 6 summarizes and concludes the paper.

2   Related Work

2.1   WS CV and V

WS V&V is gaining more and more attentions from research as well as industry [6][9][10][12][13] [15][16][20]. Most of the current studies have been focused on the formal verification of WS specifications. For examples, Shin proposed to use the automation-based model checker SPIN [15]; Howard et al. applied FSP (Finite State Process) notation [12]; and Srini and Sheila adopted DAML-S ontology to describe web service semantics and translated it into a Petri-net specification [16].

Tsai et al. proposed CV&V (collaborative verification and validation) and the WebStrar framework for testing services and service-based applications [18][17][19]. They analyzed the challenges of dynamic and just-in-time testing of SOA and proposed the CV&V model which is characterized by the collaboration and cooperation of all the parties involved in SOA to perform WS testing to ensure trustworthy computing. CV&V extends current WS architecture with testing capabilities.

In our previous work, the trustworthy service broker is proposed as an extension to UDDI server by adding just-in-time WS testing, evaluation, and ranking capacities [1][19]. A trustworthy UDDI maintains not only the service indexes, but also the service test repository. It can support test case submission from different parties, service testing before service registration and service checking out, service evaluation based on testing history results. The enhanced UDDI enforces quality control over the service lifecycle management.

This research is based on our previous work on CV&V [1][3][2][17]. Testing is dedicated to independent test brokers, which is independent on current UDDI capabilities and protocols. The test brokers provide testing services for all parties involved in WS. They collaborate with UDDI service brokers to enforce testing as a vital part to the service registration, discovery, and binding process. This paper introduces the design of the data structure, testing services, and collaboration contracts of the test brokers.

2.2   Contract-Based Testing

The concept of Design by Contract is widely used in object-oriented (OO) and component-based software development. A contract is a formal agreement between two cooperating components. In a client-server system, it specifies the interfaces provided by the server and the way for the client to access the operation. In OO and component-based appraoches, a contract is typically defined by assertions and associated concepts such as pre-conditions, post-conditions, and various constraints. The assertions are usually incorporated in the code and can be evaluated at runtime. A violation of the contract may indicate a bug.

The application of the design-by-contract concepts to software testing has been investigated. Most of current studies focus on test generation based on code assertions. Korat generated valid and non-isomorphic inputs and evaluate output correctness for Java programs based on JML assertions [5]. Karl Meinke viewed testing as a constraint solving or satisfiability problem and modeled the functional correctness of the systems using preconditions and post-conditions [14]. Briand showed that precisely defined contracts can considerably improve diagnosability (about 8 times) [7]. They also developed a classification of assertions and proposed a method of programming with assertions.

Contract-based WS testing has also been addressed. In WS, services exchange data and collaborate in a workflow via XML-based standard specifications. Hence, contracts in SOA have different representations beyond classical implementation-level. Heckel and Lohmann analyzed the three levels of WS contracts representation [13]: At the implementation-level using Boolean expressions of programming language, the XML-level of WS specifications, and the model-level to visualize contracts in graphs. They proposed graph transformation rules to visualize contracts which are also useful for simulation testing of the target services. Marcello Bruno et al. proposed that test cases can be used as the contract between service providers and service requesters [8].

This research identifies the DCV&V contracts at the specification level following the WS standard-based approach. The contracts are classified into two categories: one for the cooperation among testers and service participants (TSC), and the other for the cooperation among test participants (TCC). TSC enables automatic test generation based on WS specifications and test execution on the services under test. With TSC, it can incorporate testing into the generic SOA process. TCC allows the test participants to exchange testing data and knowledge including test plans, test cases, test scenarios, test results, defects, and reliability data.

The paper also discusses the unique problems of contract-based WS test generation based on OWL-S specification. In addition to the code-level assertions, it analyzes the constraints in WS specifications and proposed constraints at the intra-process level.

3   Decentralized CV and V Architecture

3.1   The Test Broker Architecture

The test broker enables the test collaboration among different parties participating WS testing. A test provider provides test knowledge such as test cases, executable test scripts, test results, defects, test rank, services rank, test/service evaluation models based on testing statistics, etc. A tester carries the published test cases and simulates testing on the target services. Both test providers and testers can be anyone including service providers, service users, or third party independent test participants. Particularly,

1. A test provider can be
   (a) the service provider who submits the service test specification together with the services;
   (b) the service requester who uses and evaluates the services for specific application domain; and
   (c) any independent tester who develops test cases based on the published service specifications.
2. A tester can be
   (a) the service provider who checks out the published test cases for testing its provided services;
   (b) the service requester who uses the test cases to validate the services to be selected;
   (c) the service broker who ensures that the service submitted is good enough for publication and registration;
   (d) an organization who issues quality certifications for services in specific domain; and
   (e) any independent testers who are interested in providing ranking and evaluation information for the public.

Figure 1 depicts the collaboration activities among different parties

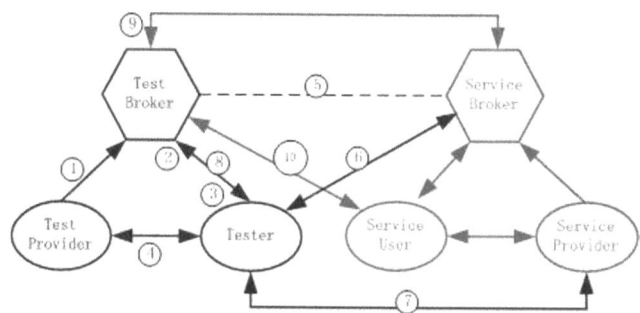

Fig. 1. The test broker architecture

1. A test provider submits test artifacts and publishes through the test broker.
2. A tester checks the test broker and searches for the test cases.
3. The tester gets the test case description, executable test scripts or linkage to the test services provided by the test provider.
4. In case the test cases can not be executed by the tester independently, the tester establishes the collaboration with the test provider.

5. The tester broker maintains the mapping between a test case and its target service under test.
6. The tester finds the services from service broker with the service reference associated with the test case.
7. The tester binds testing to the service located at the provider, tests the service and gets test results.
8. The tester submits the test results / bug reports to the test broker for further service evaluation.
9. The testing process can be integrated into the service publication process. The service broker can collaborate with the test broker for check-in / check-out testing so that only the services that satisfy the quality criteria can be published and returned to the users.
10. The testing process can also be integrated into the service discovery process. The service user can refer to the testing results and evaluation of services provided by the test broker as the basis for service selection.

3.2 Test Broker Data Structure and Services

Figure 2 shows the data structure of the test broker architecture. TestEntity represents the provider of the test cases. TestCase represents the published test cases which could be a specification or an executable script. The TestModel represents the technical interface of a test case. The TestBinding represents the binding from TestModel specification to the test provider. ServiceLinking specifies the corresponding tModel of the service under test.

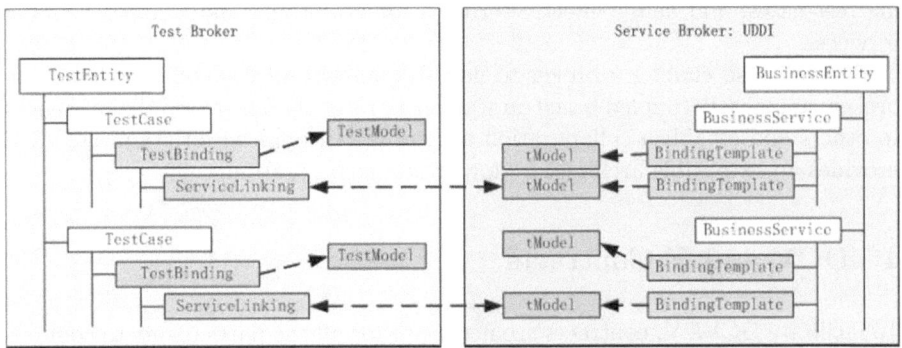

Fig. 2. The test broker data structure

The test broker maintains a test repository of test cases and test scripts, test results submission, defects report, and test/service evaluations. It supports the registration, publication, indexing and searching of test artifacts. It can also facilitate test generation and execution. Figure 3 shows the services a test broker provides.

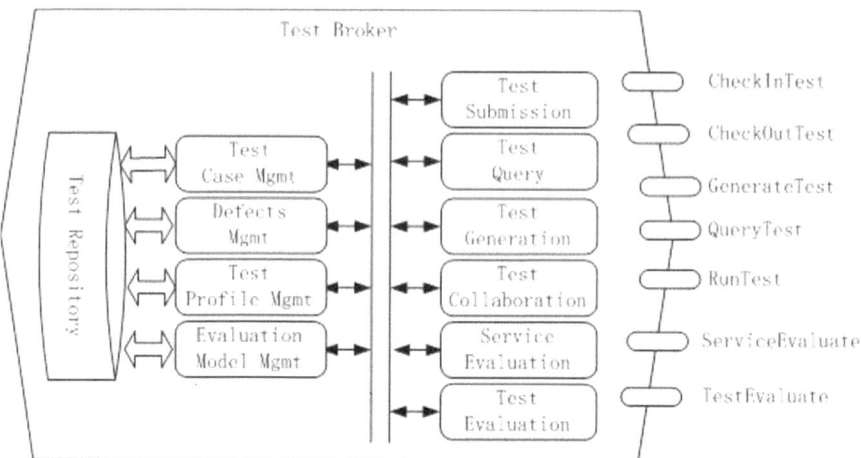

Fig. 3. The test broker services

3.3   Decentralized Test Brokers

There may exist multiple test brokers in the internet environment. A decentralized architecture (DCV&V) is established with a set of brokers dedicated to different V&V tasks to enable scalable and flexible collaborations among test participants. In DCV&V, a broker can be focused on a dedicated task for a small scale services. For example, a group can categorize test brokers into different domains. A test broker for banking services can accumulate sophisticated banking test cases, and define effective criteria for evaluating and ranking banking services.

DCV&V also enables a broker to flexibly join or quit the collaboration. The brokers are loosely coupled based on standard protocols. They keep the references to others and establish collaboration at runtime through negotiation. DCV&V provides an extensible architecture for testing collaboration.

4   DCV and V Contracts

To facilitate DCV&V, contracts are necessary for all the participants to communicate and cooperate in a mutually understood and agreed manner. Contracts are not only used among service providers and service requesters, but also among test participants. We classify the contracts into three categories based on the role of the contract.

1. TSC (Testing Service Contracts) defines the way test designer to get service specification for test case generation, test executors to exercise the test case on the service interface, and test evaluators to evaluate the services based on test results and defect reports.

2. TCC (Test Collaboration Contracts) defines the protocols for collaborative test design, execution and evaluation. DCV&V provides an open platform for WS testing in a democracy approach that anyone can participate in WS testing. Everyone can contribute from different aspects such as providing test cases, reporting defects, ranking service performance, etc.

The objective of the framework is to enable that

1. test providers can design the test case based on service specifications, and exchange test design with others;
2. testers can exercise the test cases on the target services and submit and publish the results for evaluation. Different test runs may be synchronized in a test plan;
3. different parties can exchange their data and knowledge of services and service testing, including service interface, service composition model, test cases, test plan, test results, defects and evaluation.

4.1   Testing Service Contract

4.2   Test Collaboration Contract

Test collaboration contracts can synchronize the behavior of test participants and facilitate the coordination of testing activities. Figure 4 identifies the key test artifacts abstracted in the collaboration contracts.

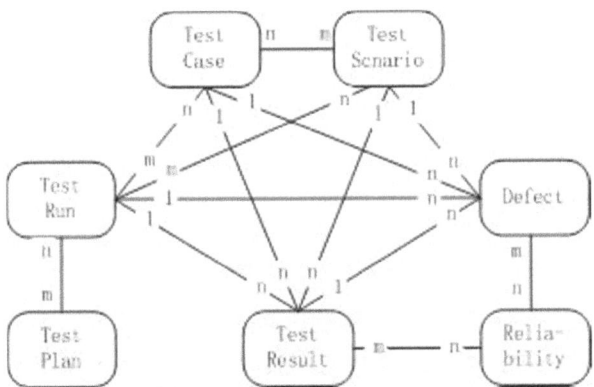

Fig. 4. The test collaboration contract

Test case is basis of collaboration contract. A test case specifies the pre-condition, post- condition, input data and actions, target services and operations. It is the basic unit for test execution.

Definition 1. *Test Case. TC :=< id, SUT, PreCond, PostCond, IN, OUT >, where*

1. *id is the unique identifier of the test case;*
2. *SUT :=< s_id, op_id > is the target service under test where s_id is the identifier of the service, and op_id is of the service operation;*
3. *PreCond := {assert} is a set of assertions to ensure the prerequisites of exercising the test case are satisfied;*
4. *PostCond = {assert} is a set of assertions to evaluate the correctness of execution results;*
5. *IN = {< name, value >} specifies the name and value of input parameters to the operation; and*
6. *OUT = {< name, value >} specifies the name and value of the outputs of the operation.*

Test cases can be organized into a structure for testing at a larger granularity. A test scenario is a composition of test cases. It defines a process over a set of test cases for validating system behavior with complex usage scenarios.

Definition 2. *Test Scenario. TS :=< id, < ctl, TC >>, where*

1. *id is the unique identifier of the test scenario;*
2. *ctl is the control of the execution order such as sequence, parallel, branch, etc.; and*
3. *TC = {tc} is the set of test cases composed in the test scenario.*

A test plan is an organization of test executions. It establishes the framework for a specific testing purpose by identifying the objective, focus, strategy, and evaluation criteria. A test plan organizes a set of test runs. Each test run represents an execution of a set of test cases or test scenarios. Each test case/scenario can be exercised in multiple test runs.

Definition 3. *Test Plan. TPlan :=< id, desc, {< TRun, Deploy >} >, where*

1. *id is the unique identifier of the test plan;*
2. *desc is the description of the test plan such as purpose and strategy;*
3. *TRun =< id, {tcs} > is the test run where id the run identifier and tcs is the test case/scenario exercised in the test run; and*
4. *Deploy =< host, load > defines the host computer to exercise the test run and the load for the testing.*

A test result records the pass/fail result of each test case/scenario in each test run. A failed test will be traced to its defect report. A defect records in details the phenomenon and the characteristics of a failed test. Reliability of the services under test is analyzed based on test results and defect reports.

Definition 4. *Test Result. TResult* $:=< id, run\_id, \{< tcs, pf, Defect >\} >$, *where*

1. *id is the unique identifies of a test result;*
2. *run_id is the reference to the test run;*
3. *tcs is reference to the test case/scenario in the test run;*
4. *pf is the pass/fail result record; and*
5. *Defect* $=< id, desc >$ *is a description of a defect if pf is failed.*

Following the of SOA standards, testing contracts can also be encoded in standard XML messages and exchanged among test participants.

5   Contract-Based Test Generation

The WS specification stack models service behavior and interoperation from various perspectives. WSDL describes the interface of individual services as a set of operations on messages. Process specifications such as BPEL (Business Process Execution Language) and WSFL (Web Services Flow Language) models service composition as a workflow, which defines the relationship and invocation order among services. Semantic specification like OWL-S introduces Ontology into service representation to improve the mutual comprehension of the operation semantics.

Based on the specifications, tests are generated at different levels, including the test data, test steps, test process for a test case and composite test cases. Test data are generated based on the analysis of XML schema data types of the interface specification. Test steps are generated based on the service operations. Test oracles are generated based on the output and post-condition specifications. Test processes are generated based on service process.

In this research, we use the OWL-S specification to illustrate the generation method.The ServiceModel of OWL-S is modeled as a workflow of processes, including atomic, simple and composite processes. The main process for composition of Web services is a composite process. Each composite process holds a Control Construct which is one of the following: Sequence, Split, Split-Join, Any-Order, Iterate, If-Then-Else, and Choice. An atomic process is a black-box which represents the service with IOPE (Input, Output, Precondition, Effect) features.

Based on the OWL-S specification, test cases are generated from two perspectives: test process generation based on the Petri-Net behavior analysis; and test data generation based on ontology reasoning.

5.1   The Example Hotel Booking System

In this section, we use an example of service-oriented "hotel booking" to illustrate the proposed approach. Suppose that a hotel provides a three-step booking service including:

1. GetAvailableRoom: to check the list of rooms available for reservation in a specified hotel.

2. SelectRoom: to select a room for reservation from the list of available rooms.
3. BookRoom: to submit the booking information of the selected room.

A customer first checks the rooms available in the hotel via GetAvailableRoom operation. He/She then selects a room with the preferred price or location by invocating SelectRoom operation. Lastly, he/she can book the selected room via BookRoom operation. Suppose GetAvailableRoom has an input as hotel_ ID and returns available_room_list, a list of rooms that are available. SelectRoom has an input as select_room_ID and returns the confirmed room ID. BookRoom has an input as book_room_ID.

Following gives the OWL-S specification of the example hotel-booking system.

```
<process:ControlConstructList rdf:ID="CCL_SelectRoom">
    <list:first rdf:resource="#Perform_SelectRoom"/>
    <list:rest>
        <process:ControlConstructList rdf:ID="CCL_BookRoom">
            <list:first red:resource="#Perform_BookRoom"/>
            <list:rest rdf:resource="http://www.daml.org/services/
            owl-s/1.1/generic/ObjectList.owl#nil"/>
        </process:ControlConstructList>
    </list:rest>
</process:ControlConstructList>
<process:ControlConstructList rdf:ID="CCL_BookRoom">
    <list:first rdf:resource="#Perform_GetAvailableRoom"/>
    <list:rest rdf:resource="#CCL_SelectRoom"/>
</process:ControlConstructList>
<process:CompositeProcess rdf:ID="CompositeProcess_BookRoom">
    <process:composedOf>
        <process:Sequence rdf:ID="Sequence_BookRoom">
            <process:components rdf:resource="#CCL_BookRoom"/>
        </process:Sequence>
    </process:composedOf>
</process:CompositeProcess>
```

5.2   Test Process Generation Based on Petri-Net

Test process is generated to cover various execution paths defined in an OWL-S composite process. We use the Petri-Net model to represent the OWL-S process and verify and validate the service process based on its Petri-Net model analysis.

Petri-Net is a graphical and mathematical model which provides a uniform environment for modeling and formal analysis. It can facilitate the description and study of the information processing systems that are characterized as being concurrent and distributed. Petri-Net model has a strong capability to model events and states in a distributed system and to capture sequential, concurrency and event-based control.

The processes organized by OWL-S control constructs are mapped to the Petri-Net by analyzing their execution semantics, the Perform actions, and the

IOPE of each Perform. A Perform is represented by a transition in the net. Its inputs and preconditions are mapped to the places holding tokens pointing to the transition that must be valid in order to enable the transition. The Perform output and effects are mapped to output arcs and places of the transition that will be triggered after the occurrence of the Perform transition.

Taking the hotel booking example, Figure 5 gives the corresponding Petri-Net model of its sequence construct. The three services GetAvailable Room, SelectRoom and BookRoom are mapped to three transitions T1, T2 and T3 respectively. Places P1, P2 and P3 respectively represent the partial states before activating the transitions.

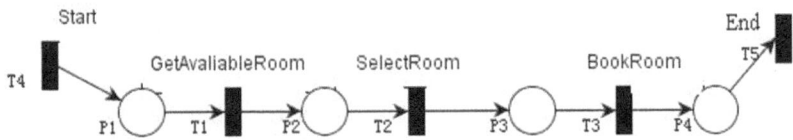

Fig. 5. The Petri-Net of the example

Based on the Petri-Net topology, test processes are generated by traversing the paths in the diagram. The key to test process generation is the control type analysis. Based on the operational semantics of the construct, sets of test cases are generated to cover branches and to manage the concurrency of various branches. For example, for splitting construct, test cases are generated to cover each branch in the split and enable the concurrent execution of multiple branches. While for choice construct, each branch will be covered by a test case separately. A set of test cases are designed to ensure each branch will be exercised at least once. For example, to test the hotel booking system, test cases are generated with three steps in the same sequence as the booking service: test_Get AvaliableRoom, test_Select Room, and test_Book Room. Following gives the algorithm for test process generation based on the Petri-net model.

```
Algorithm: WS test process generation
Input: The OWL-S Petri-Net
Output: Test cases for WS testing

GenTest (OWLPetriNet wpn)
    Get the transition trans from the Petri-Net;
    If (trans is the end of a Control Construct) return;
    If (trans is a Perform){
        Analyze precondition, postcondition;
        Analyze the input, output of WS;
        Generate test data for the Perform;
        Generate one test step;
        Fire transition;
    }
```

```
    else if (trans is the begin of a Control Construct) {
      Get the control type;
      Process the control type;
      Remove all nodes in the control construct;
    }
    Remove the transition from the Petri-Net;
end GenTest
```

5.3   Constraint-Guided Test Generation

Constraints are the restrictions on a data or process. They distinguish valid
from invalid inputs and operations. Hence constraints analysis is important for
generating negative, as well as positive, test cases. In current WS specifications,
constraints can be specified from three aspects:

1. WSDL defines operation data based on XML schema which defines constraints of the input data for each operation; and
2. OWL-S defines the pre- and post- conditions for each atomic process which
   specify the data dependencies among sub-processes within a composite
   service.
3. We define the process constraints to specify the intra-process restrictions in
   a composite service.

This section illustrates how the existing constraints can be applied to improve
test generation intelligence. In addition, this paper also introduces the intra-
process constraints specification as a complementary to OWL-S.

Data Constraints. In the XML standard, each simple type is associated with
a set of facets which characterize the particular aspects of a data type. Facets
are of two types: fundamental facets semantically abstract the data type, such as
equal, ordered, bounded, cardinality, and constraining; non-fundamental facets
are used to restrict the data values, such as length, pattern, enumeration, etc.

A data can be constrained from multiple facets. Restriction and value constraints on the data provide the basis for generating test data. When parsing
the WSDL file, the analyzer will extract the data, create instances of their corresponding data type, obtain and record the facet values with the data instances.

In this research, each facet is linked to a facet data generator. Test generator
coordinates the facets generators and composes the result data. For example,
suppose an input message "hotel_room_ID" of type "string" has following constraints: $\{length = "5", pattern = "[A - Z]\{2\}[0 - 9]\{3\}"\}$. That is, the "ho-
tel_ room_ID" is of 5 characters long with 2 choosing from A to Z and 3 from
0 to 9. The test generator then generates a set of sample data for testing as
below:

1. To generate valid data: patternGen() randomly select 2 characters from A,
   B, ,Z and 3 numbers in sequence.
2. To generate invalid data: patternGen() randomly select 2 characters outside
   A, B, ,Z and 3 number in sequence.

3. To generate invalid data: patternGen() randomly select m characters from A, B, ,Z and n number, where m+n=5 but not follow the pattern.
4. To generate invalid data: lenGen() randomly generates a string length n¡¿5, and patternGen() randomly generate n characters in sequence.

Suppose a data type is defined as $< t, \{fi, \{ti\}\} >$ where t is the type of the data, fi is a facet, and ti is a constraint value of facet fi for t. Following gives the algorithm for generating the data for the data.

Algorithm: Generate test data based on constraints

```
GenTestData (SDTSpec spec) {
    //Get data type t, and create an instance of t
    test_data = newTestData(t);
    // Get the generator for generating
    // facet generator of data type t;
    dt_gen = genFacetGen (t);
    For each fi do
        // Generate the facet generator
        f_gen = dt_gen.genFacet (fi);
        For each ti do
            // Generate the test data
            test_data.addValues (f_gen.genData (ti));
        End // for ti
    End // for fi
End GenTestData
```

OWL-S Preconditions. OWL-S supports pre-condition specification for each atomic process. A precondition is usually specified using Boolean expression. It identifies the restriction on the input data to the process in the context of the composite process. The methods for test generation based on Boolean expressions have been widely discusses.

An important aspect of test generation is to simulate abnormal inputs to test the system's robustness and exceptional handling capabilities. Based on the OWL-S precondition specification, it can effectively generate positive as well as negative test cases. Following is an example of precondition definition where the room id of to book must be the same as the selected room. Test cases generated from two aspects: book_room_ID equals select_room_ID and book_room_ID not equals select_ room_ID.

```
<process:inCondition>
    <expr:KIF-Condition>
        <expr:expressionBody>
            (= (?book_room_ID ?select_room_ID))
        </expr:expressionBody>
    </expr:KIF-Condition>
</process:inCondition>
```

Process Constraints. There also exist constraints among the sub- processes in a composite process such as the timing constraints. For example, after a customer submits the booking request, he needs to wait for 0.3-0.5 second for the database to update status of hotel rooms. If he checks the status before 0.3 second, he may not see the refresh of the database. However, a delay longer than 0.5 second is not durable for the customer.

Such intra-process constraints are also important testing points. In this research, we define the constraint specification as a supplementary to OWL-S and generate test cases based on the constraints.

Definition 5. *Process Constraints. A process constraint is defined as a five-tuple. $ProcCons :=< category, type, FV, PreProc, PostProc > Where,$*

1. *category is the classification of a constraint, such as timing constraint, dependency constraint;*
2. *type is the specific constraint type within a category such as delay, interval for timing constraint;*
3. *$FV := \{< faceti, valuei >\}$ defined the multiple facet values for the constraint. For example, the maximum and minimum value for a interval;*
4. *$PreProc := \{pi\}$ is the set of processes executed before the constraint; and*
5. *$PostProc := \{pi\}$ is the set of processes executed after the constraint.*

6   Conclusion and Future Work

The paper presents an on-going research on collaborative WS testing. Even though WS trustworthiness is gaining more and more attentions, WS testing is still a challenging topic due to the unique characteristics of WS. Traditional testing techniques are no longer valid to deal with dynamic collaboration and runtime composition. Our research aims at establishing a new testing approach to address the challenges. The paper reports our first attempts in this direction. The framework proposed in the paper is now under prototype implementation. More research, experiments, and implementation are necessary for our future work to evaluate and improve the proposed approach.

Acknowledgments. This research is supported National Science Foundation China (No. 60603035), National High Technology Program 863 (No. 2006AA 01Z157), Beijing Natural Science Foundation (No. 4072014), and IBM SUR project under the agreement (No. 20063000238).

References

1. Bai, X., Cao, Z., Chen, Y.: Design of a Trustworthy Service Broker and Dependence-Based Progressive Group Testing. The International Journal of High Performance Computing and Networking (to appear, 2007)
2. Bai, X., Dai, G., Xu, D., Tsai, W.T.: A Multi-Agent Based Framework for Collaborative Testing on Web Services. In: Proc. of WCCIA, pp. 205–210 (2006)

3. Bai, X., Dong, W., Tsai, W.T., Chen, Y.: WSDL-Based Automatic Test Case Generation for Web Services Testing. In: Proc. of IEEE SOSE05, pp. 207–212 (2005)
4. Bernhard, K.A.: Contract-Based Testing. In: Aichernig, B.K., Maibaum, T.S.E. (eds.) Formal Methods at the Crossroads. From Panacea to Foundational Support. LNCS, vol. 2757, pp. 34–48. Springer, Heidelberg (2003)
5. Boyapati, C., Khurshid, S., Marinov, D.: Korat: Automated Testing Based on Java Predicates. In: ACM SIGSOFT Software Engineering Notes, vol. 27(4), pp. 123–133. ACM Press, New York (2002)
6. Bloomberg, J.: Web Services Testing: Beyond SOAP, ZapThink LLC (2002) at http://www.zapthink.com
7. Briand, L.C., Labiche, Y., Sun, H.: Investigating the Use of Analysis Contracts to Support Fault Isolation in Object Oriented Code. In: Proceedings of the 2002 ACM SIGSOFT international symposium on Software testing and analysis, pp. 70–80. ACM Press, New York (2002)
8. Bruno, M., Canfora, G., et al.: Using Test Cases as Contract to Ensure Service Compliance across Releases. In: Benatallah, B., Casati, F., Traverso, P. (eds.) ICSOC 2005. LNCS, vol. 3826, pp. 87–100. Springer, Heidelberg (2005)
9. Canfora, G., Di Penta, M.: Testing Services and Service-Centric Systems: Challenges and Opportunities. IT Professional 8(2), 10–17 (2006)
10. Canfora, G.: User-Side Testing of Web Services, keynote address at CSMR (2005)
11. Ciupa, I., Leitner, A.: Automatic Testing Based on Design by Contract. In: Proceedings of Net.ObjectDays, pp. 545–557 (2005)
12. Foster, H., Uchitel, S., Magee, J., Kramer, J.: Model-based verification of web service compositions. In: Proc. ASE (2003)
13. Heckel, R., Lohmann, M.: Towards Contract-Based Testing of Web Services. Electronic Notes in Theoretical Computer Science, vol. 82(6) (2004)
14. Meinke, K.: Automated Black-Box Testing of Functional Correctness Using Function Approximation. In: ISSTA '04. Proceedings of the 2004 ACM SIGSOFT international symposium on Software testing and analysis, pp. 143–153. ACM Press, New York (2004)
15. Nakajima, S.: Model-checking verification for reliable web service. In: Proc.OOPSLA'02 Workshop on Web Services (2002)
16. Narayanan, S., Mcllraith, S.: Simulation, verification and automated composition of web services. In: Proc. WWW (2002)
17. Tsai, W.T., Paul, R., Yu, L., Saimi, A., Cao, Z.: Scenario-Based Web Service Testing with Distributed Agents. IEICE Transaction on Information and System E86-D(10), 2130–2144 (2003)
18. Tsai, W.T., Chen, Y., Paul, R., Liao, N., Huang, H.: Cooperative and Group Tesitng in Verification of Dynamic Composite Web Services. In: Proc. IEEE COMPSAC, pp. 1–4. IEEE Computer Society Press, Los Alamitos (2001)
19. Tsai, W.T., Paul, R., Cao, Z., Yu, L., Saimi, A., Xiao, B.: Verification of Web Services Using an Enhanced UDDI Server. In: Proc. of IEEE WORDS, pp. 131–138. IEEE Computer Society Press, Los Alamitos (2003)
20. Yi, X., Kochut, K.J.: A CP-nets-based Design and Verification Framework for Web Services Composition. In: Proceedings of the IEEE International Conference on Web Services, March 2004, pp. 756–760. IEEE Computer Society Press, Los Alamitos (2004)
21. Web Services Architecture[s], W3C Working Draft (November 14, 2002) http://www.w3.org/TR/ws-arch/
22. OWL-S, at: http://www.daml.org/services/owl-s
23. XML Schema Part 2: Datatypes (May 2001) http://www.w3.org/TR/xmlschema-2/

Towards Composing Software Components in Both Design and Deployment Phases

Kung-Kiu Lau, Ling Ling, and Perla Velasco Elizondo

School of Computer Science, The University of Manchester
Manchester M13 9PL, United Kingdom
{kung-kiu,lling,pvelasco}@cs.man.ac.uk

Abstract. In component-based software development, the design of components should be carried out separately from the deployment of components, in order to enable composition by independent third-parties. However, current component models are biased towards either the design phase or the deployment phase. In this paper, we argue that ideally component models should include both design and deployment phases, and it should be possible to compose components in both phases. We also demonstrate a preliminary implementation of composition in both phases in a component model we have defined.

1 Introduction

In component-based software development (CBD), components should be produced and used by independent parties. That is, component developers need not be the same people as component customers such as system developers. This implies that the *design* of components is carried out separately from the *deployment* of components.

In current component models [6,10], components are either objects or architecture units. These models tend to be heavily biased towards either the design phase or the deployment phase. In architecture-based models[6,10] like ADLs and UML2.0, components are design entities by definition, with or without corresponding binary components in the deployment phase. On the other hand, in object-based models[6,10] like COM, .NET, CCM and Fractal, components are objects that are executable binaries, and are therefore more deployment phase entities than design phase entities.

In this paper, we argue that ideally component models should include both design and deployment phases, in order that CBD can meet its objective of building systems from pre-existing components with maximum reuse and minimum time-to-market. In particular, it should be possible to compose components in both design and deployment phases, in an idealised life cycle for components.

We motivate and define the idealised life cycle, based on commonly accepted desiderata for CBD. We discuss composition in each phase, and demonstrate a preliminary implementation of composition in both phases in a component model we have defined.

2 An Idealised Component Life Cycle

The life cycle of components [4] consists of three stages: (i) the *design phase*, when components are designed, defined and constructed in source code, and possibly

H.W. Schmidt et al. (Eds.): CBSE 2007, LNCS 4608, pp. 274–282, 2007.

compiled into binaries; (ii) the *deployment phase*, when binaries of components are deployed into the execution environment; and (iii) the *run-time* phase, when component binaries are instantiated and executed in the running system. Ideally, composition should be possible in both the design and the deployment phase while the system is being constructed. Composition means component reuse, and therefore composition in both phases will maximise it. It also means design flexibility in the sense that the deployed components, in particular composite components, can be designed, by composition in either phase.

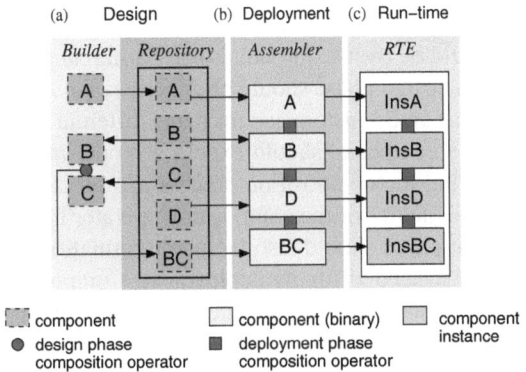

Fig. 1. An idealised component life cycle

Accordingly, we have defined an idealised component life cycle [11,10], and the kind of composition meaningful in its phases (Fig. 1). The idealised life is based on the following commonly accepted desiderata of CBD [2,5,14,12].Firstly, components should be pre-existing reusable software units, which developers can reuse for different applications. This necessitates the use of a repository in the design phase. Secondly, components should be produced and used by independent parties, i.e. component developers and system developers. This is important for ensuring that components are truly reusable by third parties and requires the use of proper tools that can interact with a repository, in the design and deployment phases. Thirdly, it should be possible to copy and instantiate components, so that their reuse can be maximised, both in terms of code reuse and in terms of components' scope of deployment. Thus, components should be distinguished from their instances, and therefore differentiate the design and deployment phases from the run-time phase. Fourthly, components should be composable into composite components which in turn can be composed with (composite) components into larger composites (or subsystems), and so on. This requires that composites can be deposited in and retrieved from a repository.

Design Phase. In the design phase, components have to be constructed, catalogued and stored in a *repository* in such a way that they can be retrieved later, as and when needed. Components in the repository are in *source code*, or they may have been compiled into *binary*.

Components here should be composed into well-defined *composites* using suitable *composition operators*, ideally supported by a composition theory. It should be also possible to store composites in, and retrieve them from the repository, and use them for further composition, like any components.

A *builder* tool can be used to (i) construct new components, and then deposit them in the repository, e.g. A in Fig. 1 (a); (ii) retrieve components from the repository, compose them and deposit them back in the repository, e.g. in Fig. 1 (a), B and C are composed into a composite BC that is deposited in the repository.

To promote its reuse, components in design phase should be *templates* that provide services. They should be normally identified and designed by *domain experts* as basic building blocks for the domain in question. They should be generic, rather than system-specific so that they should be (re)used to build many different applications. Similarly, composition operators in design phase should be generic *composition schemes* to coordinate components which can be customised for many different systems.

To support its reuse, a composite should expose a proper *interface*. This interface should be generated during the composition process and its content should be determined according to the semantics of the composition operator involved.

Components in design phase should also include information of the *environmental dependencies* or *resources* needed for its deployment. Composition in design phase should generate such information for composites. For instance, deployment contracts [8] could be used to specify this kind of information.

Deployment Phase. Ideally, composition in deployment phase should follow on from, and thus exploit composition in design phase. That is, as far as possible, the composites here should be built directly from the (composite) components created in design phase.

In the deployment phase, components have to be retrieved from the repository, and if necessary compiled to *binary* code and then composed. The result of deployment phase composition is a whole *system* in binary code, and so this is the end result of system design and implementation. The completed system should be then *ready for execution*.

As in design phase, composition should be carried out via *composition operators*. However, here they should be able to specify detailed coordination between components as required by the specific application.

An *assembler* tool can be used to retrieve components from a repository, compile them into binary code, and then assemble them into a system. For example, in Fig. 1 (b), binaries of A, B, D and BC are retrieved and composed into a system.

Composite components in the deployment phase should have *interfaces* that allow them to be instantiated and executed at run-time. These interfaces should be generated during the composition process.

Composition in deployment phase should be supported by suitable *deployment tools*, for example, for checking component compatibility with one another and with the execution environment, a tool for checking deployment contracts would be useful. Also with such tools, it should be possible to deploy a composite in many different systems, possibly with different execution environments.

Run-time Phase. In the run-time phase the constructed system is *instantiated* and *executed* in the run-time environment, e.g. A, B, D and BC in Fig. 1 (c). Although there is no further composition in this phase, it may be desirable to adapt component instances or composition operators so as to dynamically re-configure the executable system. We do not discuss this here, since our focus is on composition.

3   Towards Composition in Both Design and Deployment Phases

We have done some preliminary work to realise composition in both design and deployment phases. Our work is based on a component model we have defined [7].

In our component model, there are two basic entities: (i) *computation units* and (ii) *connectors*.[1] A computation unit performs only computation (by providing a set of methods) and does not invoke any computation outside itself. There are two kinds of connectors: (i) *invocation* connector, which is used to invoke a computation unit; and (ii) *composition* connector, which composes components.

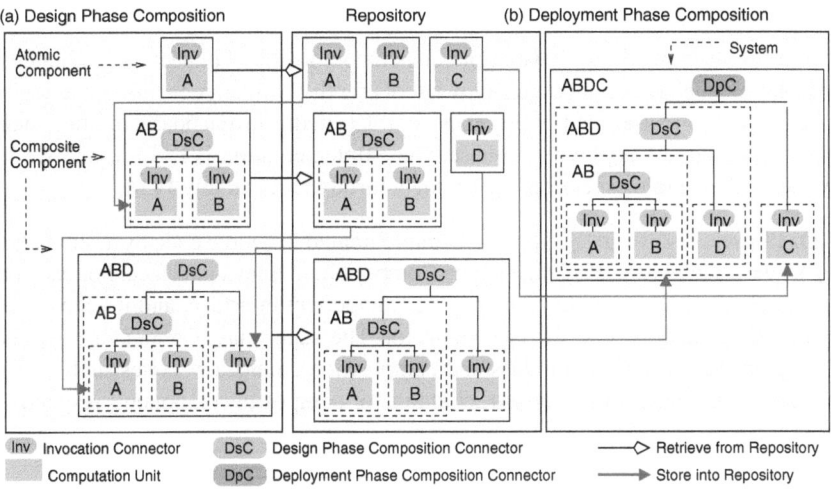

Fig. 2. (a) Design phase and (b) deployment phase composition in our component model

Components are defined in terms of computation units and connectors. There are two kinds of components: (i) an *atomic* component, which consists of a computation unit with an *invocation* connector (e.g. A in Fig. 2 (a)); and (ii) a *composite* component, which consists of a set of components (atomic or composite) composed by a composition connector (e.g. AB and ABD in Fig. 2 (a)).

In [9], we have introduced a basic set of composition connectors which encapsulate the three standard control structures: *sequencing*, *branching* and *looping*.

Composition connectors are defined by a *type hierarchy*, so that they allow hierarchical component composition. Every (composite) component has one top-level connector, which is either an *invocation* connector (for an atomic component) or a composition

---

[1] They are exogenous connectors [9].

connector (for a composite component). This connector represents the only access point to the component, and also its *interface* for further composition.

The semantics of components and composition operators in our component model is such that composition can take place in both the design and deployment phase. Fig. 2 illustrates this, in a direct comparison to the idealised life cycle.

In the design phase (Fig. 2 (a)), the composite AB is built from atomics A and B by the *design phase composition connector*, and in turn it can be further composed with atomic D by having its top-level connector connected by another composition connector, to build up the composite ABD which is deposited back into the repository.

In the deployment phase (Fig. 2 (b)), the composite ABD is retrieved form the repository and composed via a *deployment phase composition connector* with component D to yield system ABDC. If required, further composition can be done. At the end of the composition process, the final system should be ready to execute in the target execution environment.

3.1   Preliminary Implementation

In our preliminary work, we have implemented composition connectors in both design and deployment phases, but not full-blown tools for the builder, repository or assembler. Neither have we incorporated deployment contracts in the design phase, or implemented deployment tools for deployment phase. Our implementation is in Java, and we have also assumed a simple execution environment throughout, namely JVM.

Design Phase. A software component is implemented in source code by a set of classes (Fig. 3) in design phase. We define a type Component in a Java interface. For each component, there is a class that implements the Component interface, and it keeps a reference to a Connector type as the top connector. The super class Connector is extended by The *Invocation* connector class and composition connector classes such as *Pipe*, *Sequencer* which are used to construct atomic or composite components respectively.

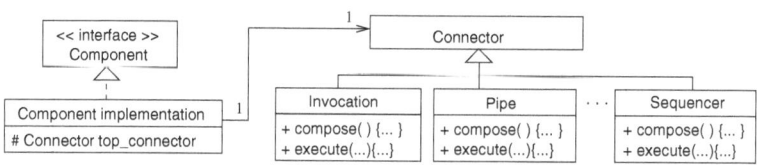

Fig. 3. Overall structure of a set of classes for constructing components

A builder tool in design phase is used to construct components. For an atomic component, the computation unit is a Java class that implements the services and does not call services outside itself. The builder tool specifies the computation unit name in the source code of *Invocation* connector (`compose` method), and generates an atomic component class which refers to the *Invocation*. For a composite component, it is constructed by builder tool by specifying the top level connectors of the constituent components in the source code of the composition connector. Because according to the hierarchical composition, the connection point for the sub component is always its top level connector. The generated composite component class file refers to the top composition connector, which again serves as the connection point when this composite component is connected by a higher level connector, so as to create a bigger composite component.

Component interface specifies all the services provided by the component and desired data for instantiation. An atomic component interface is given by the component developer and presented in an XML format. The interface of a composite is generated by the composition connector automatically in terms of the interfaces of the constituents and the composition scheme.

The way to invoke a component is calling the top level connector (`execute` method) with the method name and parameters. Internally it calls the lower level connector recursively until it reaches a computation unit. One point worth noting is the components in this phase are templates, therefore their behaviour is not fixed with specific set of calling methods at this stage.

Currently, the component repository is a java file directory. In the next step, repository needs to be fully interacted with the builder tool and both of them need to be enhanced to support (atomic or composite) component deposit after construction automatically and multiple copies of component retrieval. Besides, deployment contracts specification needs to be integrated when the builder tool automates the construction of components.

Deployment phase. For deployment composition we have a set of classes which integrate our *composition framework* (Fig.4 (a)). Deployment phase connectors are implemented as a set of classes with the superclass **DPConnector**. Each subclass defines a *constructor* to instantiate it, and overrides the `execute` method to implement its corresponding logic. A class **System** defines a valid composition in this phase. According to our model, the class **System** holds a reference to deployment phase connector, which represents the interface and the only access point to it.

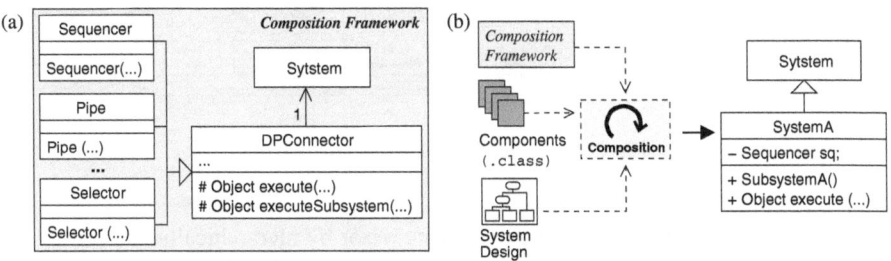

Fig. 4. (a) Our deployment phase composition framework and (b) its use to compose a System

To build a system, during the composition process we (re)use the binaries of the components generated in the design phase, our composition framework, as well as the design of the composition for the desired system (Fig.4 (b)). The result of the composition process is new class that extends **System** and declares a constructor containing the code for setting up the composition, and a `execute` for calling its top-level connector's to allow the system's execution, e.g. `sq.execute(...)` when a *Sequencer* connector `sq` is the top level connector of the SystemA shown in Fig.4 (b).

Making a system a new class allows to generate a binary that can be packaged as a named, versioned, shippable and deployable unit. The final system is meant to be deployed within a execution environment and eventually be executed on it.

In the current implementation, systems' interfaces are generated as a XML file containing very basic information such as the mechanisms to instantiate and execute it, but it can be extended to include more detailed information for its proper deployment.

A system instantiated via its constructor and executed by calling its `execute` method. The `execute` method contains a call to `executeSubsystem` method defined in the DP-Connector superclass for each one of the components and/or subsystems it connects. In the `executeSubsystem`, the hierarchical execution of each connected element is carried out until reach the *Invocation* connectors of atomic components, where reflection techniques are used to dynamically execute the required operation in their computation units.

An Example. Consider a Drink Vending Machine System which serves different kinds of drinks, i.e. coffee, juice and tea. Besides the traditional paying mechanism, it accepts coinless dispensing of drinks to holders of drink cards. The architecture for this system is shown in Fig.5 and it includes the atomic components: ProductManager and ReceipeManager –which deal with the drinks' prices and recipes; CoinBox, CardReader –which deal with paying for the drinks; and a set of Dispensers –which deal with the pouring of ingredients during the drink making.[2]

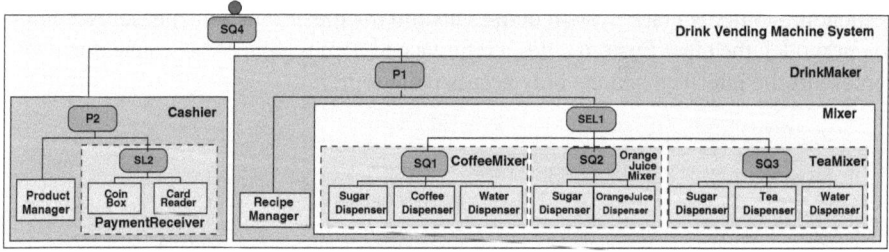

Fig. 5. Drink Vending Machine architecture

In the design phase, we build the composite Mixer by hierarchically composing the dispenser components as depicted in Fig.5. The composite Mixer can deal with the making of different drinks according to the top-level *Selector* condition's provided value, e.g. *product name* = "*coffee*". Due to the Mixer encapsulates functionality suitable for similar applications in the same domain, constructing it in the design phase and putting it in the repository facilitates its further reuse.

---

[2] Each one of these components is created at design phase by connecting a *Invocation* connector to the Java class representing the corresponding computation unit.

The Mixer can be compiled into a `.class` file, and reused at deployment-phase to create the final system by firstly composing it with the RecipeManager, and then with the Cashier subsystem –which has been composed from the CoinBox, CardReader and ProductManager atomic components.

The interface of the final system exposes the way it can be instantiated and executed. For buying a drink the *product name, type of payment, amount* or *card number* are required.

4 Discussion and Conclusion

The advantages of composition in both phases composition are not present in current component models. In most of these models, composition is carried out in the design phase only (e.g. architecture description languages (ADLs), UML 2.0, PECOS, Pin, Fractal, EJB, COM, CCM, Koala, SOFA and KobrA), leaving the deployment phase with the only task of implementing what is defined in design phase [10]. In JavaBeans and POJO [13], composition is carried out in the deployment phase only.

Our approach also allows design flexibility. Developers can choose either to build up composite components in design phase for reuse purpose, or assemble components with application specific configuration in the deployment phase. However, there is a balance between design and deployment phase composition. The former is carried out by the component builder guided by domain knowledge for constructing reusable building blocks; the latter is carried out by the system developer targeting particular applications with environmental settings.

As future work, we intend to implement builder, repository and assembler tools to automate the composition in both phases, as well as deployment tools. In addition, we will investigate reference semantics where a constituent component is used by different composite components, and the issue of further composition and deployment of the component in such a scenario. We will also consider adaptation and re-configuration at run-time, as in approaches such as Hadas [1] and Gravity [3].

References

1. Ben-Shaul, I., Holder, O., Lavva, B.: Dynamic adaptation and deployment of distributed components in hadas. IEEE Trans. Softw. Eng. 27(9), 769–787 (2001)
2. Broy, M., Deimel, A., Henn, J., Koskimies, K., Plasil, F., Pomberger, G., Pree, W., Stal, M., Szyperski, C.: What characterizes a (software) component? Software - Concepts and Tools 19(1), 49–56 (1998)
3. Cervantes, H., Hall, R.S.: Autonomous adaptation to dynamic availability using a service-oriented component model. In: Proc. ICSE04, pp. 614–623. IEEE Computer Society Press, Los Alamitos (2004)
4. Christiansson, B., Jakobsson, L., Crnkovic, I.: CBD process. In: Crnkovic, I., Larsson, M. (eds.) Building Reliable Component-Based Software Systems, pp. 89–113. Artech House (2002)
5. Heineman, G.T., Councill, W.T.: Component-based software engineering: putting the pieces together. Addison-Wesley, Reading (2001)

6. Lau, K.-K.: Software component models. In: Proc. ICSE '06, pp. 1081–1082. ACM Press, New York (2006)

7. Lau, K.-K., Ornaghi, M., Wang, Z.: A software component model and its preliminary formalisation. In: de Boer, F.S., Bonsangue, M.M., Graf, S., de Roever, W.-P. (eds.) FMCO 2005. LNCS, vol. 4111, pp. 1–21. Springer, Heidelberg (2006)

8. Lau, K.-K., Ukis, V.: Defining and checking deployment contracts for software components. In: Gorton, I., Heineman, G.T., Crnkovic, I., Schmidt, H.W., Stafford, J.A., Szyperski, C.A., Wallnau, K. (eds.) CBSE 2006. LNCS, vol. 4063, pp. 1–16. Springer, Heidelberg (2006)

9. Lau, K.-K., Velasco Elizondo, P., Wang, Z.: Exogenous connectors for software components. In: Heineman, G.T., Crnković, I., Schmidt, H.W., Stafford, J.A., Szyperski, C.A., Wallnau, K. (eds.) CBSE 2005. LNCS, vol. 3489, pp. 90–106. Springer, Heidelberg (2005)

10. Lau, K.-K., Wang, Z.: A survey of software component models. 2nd edn., Pre-print CSPP-38, School of Computer Science, The University of Manchester (May 2006) http://www.cs.man.ac.uk/cspreprints/PrePrints/cspp38.pdf

11. Lau, K.-K., Wang, Z.: A taxonomy of software component models. In: Crnkovic, I., Larsson, M. (eds.) Proc. of 31st Euromicro Conference, pp. 88–95. IEEE Computer Society Press, Los Alamitos (2005)

12. Meyer, B.: The grand challenge of trusted components. In: Proc. ICSE03, pp. 660–667. IEEE Computer Society Press, Los Alamitos (2003)

13. Richardson, C.: POJOs in Action: Developing Enterprise Applications with Lightweight Frameworks. Manning Publications Co., Greenwich, CT (2006)

14. Szyperski, C., Gruntz, D., Murer, S.: Component Software: Beyond Object-Oriented Programming, 2nd edn. Addison-Wesley, Reading (2002)

Author Index

Lecture Notes in Computer Science

For information about Vols. 1–4510

please contact your bookseller or Springer

Vol. 4562: D. Harris (Ed.), Engineering Psychology and Cognitive Ergonomics. XXIII, 879 pages. 2007. (Sublibrary LNAI).

Vol. 4561: V.G. Duffy (Ed.), Digital Human Modeling. XXIII, 1068 pages. 2007.

Vol. 4560: N. Aykin (Ed.), Usability and Internationalization, Part II. XVIII, 576 pages. 2007.

Vol. 4559: N. Aykin (Ed.), Usability and Internationalization, Part I. XVIII, 661 pages. 2007.

Vol. 4558: M.J. Smith, G. Salvendy (Eds.), Human Interface and the Management of Information, Part II. XXIII, 1162 pages. 2007.

Vol. 4557: M.J. Smith, G. Salvendy (Eds.), Human Interface and the Management of Information, Part I. XXII, 1030 pages. 2007.

Vol. 4553: J.A. Jacko (Ed.), Human-Computer Interaction, Part IV. XXIV, 1225 pages. 2007.

Vol. 4552: J.A. Jacko (Ed.), Human-Computer Interaction, Part III. XXI, 1038 pages. 2007.

Vol. 4551: J.A. Jacko (Ed.), Human-Computer Interaction, Part II. XXIII, 1253 pages. 2007.

Vol. 4550: J.A. Jacko (Ed.), Human-Computer Interaction, Part I. XXIII, 1240 pages. 2007.

Vol. 4549: J. Aspnes, C. Scheideler, A. Arora, S. Madden (Eds.), Distributed Computing in Sensor Systems. XIII, 417 pages. 2007.

Vol. 4548: N. Olivetti (Ed.), Automated Reasoning with Analytic Tableaux and Related Methods. X, 245 pages. 2007. (Sublibrary LNAI).

Vol. 4547: C. Carlet, B. Sunar (Eds.), Arithmetic of Finite Fields. XI, 355 pages. 2007.

Vol. 4546: J. Kleijn, A. Yakovlev (Eds.), Petri Nets and Other Models of Concurrency – ICATPN 2007. XI, 515 pages. 2007.

Vol. 4545: H. Anai, K. Horimoto, T. Kutsia (Eds.), Algebraic Biology. XIII, 379 pages. 2007.

Vol. 4544: S. Cohen-Boulakia, V. Tannen (Eds.), Data Integration in the Life Sciences. XI, 282 pages. 2007. (Sublibrary LNBI).

Vol. 4543: A.K. Bandara, M. Burgess (Eds.), Inter-Domain Management. XII, 237 pages. 2007.

Vol. 4542: P. Sawyer, B. Paech, P. Heymans (Eds.), Requirements Engineering: Foundation for Software Quality. IX, 384 pages. 2007.

Vol. 4541: T. Okadome, T. Yamazaki, M. Makhtari (Eds.), Pervasive Computing for Quality of Life Enhancement. IX, 248 pages. 2007.

Vol. 4539: N.H. Bshouty, C. Gentile (Eds.), Learning Theory. XII, 634 pages. 2007. (Sublibrary LNAI).

Vol. 4538: F. Escolano, M. Vento (Eds.), Graph-Based Representations in Pattern Recognition. XII, 416 pages. 2007.

Vol. 4537: K.C.-C. Chang, W. Wang, L. Chen, C.A. Ellis, C.-H. Hsu, A.C. Tsoi, H. Wang (Eds.), Advances in Web and Network Technologies, and Information Management. XXIII, 707 pages. 2007.

Vol. 4536: G. Concas, E. Damiani, M. Scotto, G. Succi (Eds.), Agile Processes in Software Engineering and Extreme Programming. XV, 276 pages. 2007.

Vol. 4534: I. Tomkos, F. Neri, J. Solé Pareta, X. Masip Bruin, S. Sánchez Lopez (Eds.), Optical Network Design and Modeling. XI, 460 pages. 2007.

Vol. 4533: F. Baader (Ed.), Term Rewriting and Applications. XII, 419 pages. 2007.

Vol. 4531: J. Indulska, K. Raymond (Eds.), Distributed Applications and Interoperable Systems. XI, 337 pages. 2007.

Vol. 4530: D.H. Akehurst, R. Vogel, R.F. Paige (Eds.), Model Driven Architecture- Foundations and Applications. X, 219 pages. 2007.

Vol. 4529: P. Melin, O. Castillo, L.T. Aguilar, J. Kacprzyk, W. Pedrycz (Eds.), Foundations of Fuzzy Logic and Soft Computing. XIX, 830 pages. 2007. (Sublibrary LNAI).

Vol. 4528: J. Mira, J.R. Álvarez (Eds.), Nature Inspired Problem-Solving Methods in Knowledge Engineering, Part II. XXII, 650 pages. 2007.

Vol. 4527: J. Mira, J.R. Álvarez (Eds.), Bio-inspired Modeling of Cognitive Tasks, Part I. XXII, 630 pages. 2007.

Vol. 4526: M. Malek, M. Reitenspieß, A. van Moorsel (Eds.), Service Availability. X, 155 pages. 2007.

Vol. 4525: C. Demetrescu (Ed.), Experimental Algorithms. XIII, 448 pages. 2007.

Vol. 4524: M. Marchiori, J.Z. Pan, C.d.S. Marie (Eds.), Web Reasoning and Rule Systems. XI, 382 pages. 2007.

Vol. 4523: Y.-H. Lee, H.-N. Kim, J. Kim, Y. Park, L.T. Yang, S.W. Kim (Eds.), Embedded Software and Systems. XIX, 829 pages. 2007.

Vol. 4522: B.K. Ersbøll, K.S. Pedersen (Eds.), Image Analysis. XVIII, 989 pages. 2007.

Vol. 4521: J. Katz, M. Yung (Eds.), Applied Cryptography and Network Security. XIII, 498 pages. 2007.

Vol. 4519: E. Franconi, M. Kifer, W. May (Eds.), The Semantic Web: Research and Applications. XVIII, 830 pages. 2007.

Vol. 4517: F. Boavida, E. Monteiro, S. Mascolo, Y. Koucheryavy (Eds.), Wired/Wireless Internet Communications. XIV, 382 pages. 2007.

Vol. 4516: L. Mason, T. Drwiega, J. Yan (Eds.), Managing Traffic Performance in Converged Networks. XXIII, 1191 pages. 2007.

Vol. 4515: M. Naor (Ed.), Advances in Cryptology - EUROCRYPT 2007. XIII, 591 pages. 2007.

Vol. 4514: S.N. Artemov, A. Nerode (Eds.), Logical Foundations of Computer Science. XI, 513 pages. 2007.

Vol. 4513: M. Fischetti, D.P. Williamson (Eds.), Integer Programming and Combinatorial Optimization. IX, 500 pages. 2007.

Vol. 4511: C. Conati, K. McCoy, G. Paliouras (Eds.), User Modeling 2007. XVI, 487 pages. 2007. (Sublibrary LNAI).